DOMINICAN REPUBLIC

ANA CHAVIER CAAMAÑO

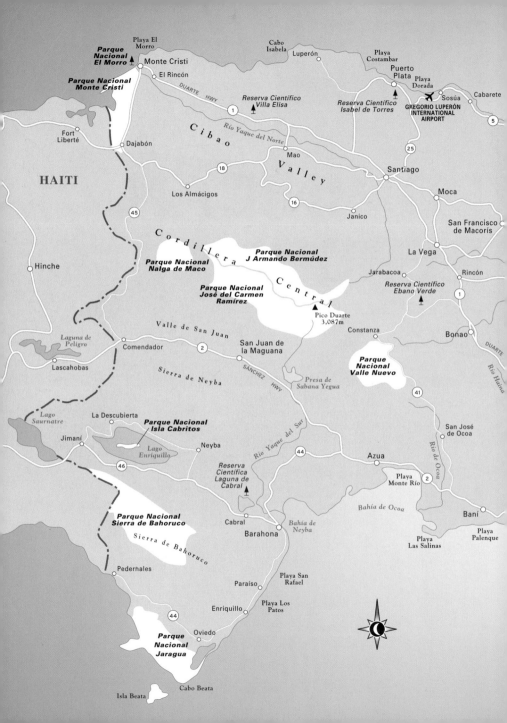

SANTUARIO DE BALLENAS JOROBADAS
★ DEL BANCO DE LA PLATA

DOMINICAN REPUBLIC

ATLANTIC OCEAN

Playa Grande

Río San Juan

Parque Nacional Cabo Frances Viejo

Playa El Bretón

Playa Diamante

Bahía Escocesa

Playa Boza De Bojolo

Nagua

Las Terrenas

Samaná Peninsula

Las Galeras

Playa Rincón

Cabo Samaná

5

Río Yuna

Sánchez

Santa Barbara de Samaná

Bahía de Samaná

Contuí

Parque Nacional Los Haitises

Sabana de la Mar

Reserva Científica Lagunas Redonda y Limón

Miches

El Cedro

Cordillera Oriental

Santo Domingo

Coastal Plain

Monte Plata

103

107

Hato Mayor

El Macao

Río Ozama

Bayaguana

Río Magua

Río Soco

El Seíbo

El Macao

Bávaro

Playa Cabeza de Toro

1

Santo Domingo

4

MELLA HWY

4

San Pedro de Macorís

3

La Romana

Higüey

Punta Cana

Playa Punta Cana

Parque Nacional Submarino La Caleta

Boca Chica

LAS AMÉRICAS HWY

LAS AMÉRICAS INTERNATIONAL AIRPORT

Playa Boca Chica

Playa Juan Dolio

Isla Catalina

Playa Bayahibe

Boca de Yuma

Playa Juanillo

San Cristóbal

Playa La Caleta

Playa Dominicus

Parque Nacional de Este

Isla Saona

Caribbean Sea

0   20 mi

0   20 km

© AVALON TRAVEL PUBLISHING, INC.

DISCOVER THE DOMINICAN REPUBLIC

My memories of yearly visits to the Dominican

Republic are dominated by my senses: the smell of the ocean while running through the shallow waters of Boca Chica when I was a little girl; the feel of the rough terrain while traveling through La Península de Samaná as a teen in a hot, stuffy van, over-crowded with relatives; the taste of afternoon espressos served in the backyard of our house as an adult; and the impossible-to-ignore sound of merengue transcending the decades.

On my last visit I arrived at a busy airport on the northern coast and hailed a cab to the Puerto Plata bus station. The humidity poured over me like syrup and I bought a slushy, cold Presidente beer to remedy the thick heat of the late Caribbean afternoon while waiting for the bus. I was on my way to the capital city of Santo Domingo on the southern coast of the island, and my family was waiting. The bus finally left a few hours later, weaving through the small streets

catching a ride to Bahía de las Aguilas

to the bigger *carretera* (highway) that carried us outside of town. The Atlantic Ocean disappeared behind the mountains, and scads of children on their way home from school were at the roadside waving to the bus passengers, while men on *motoconchos* (mopeds) honked at one another and tried to overtake the bus. As we made our way through the countryside the smells of open fires and fried plantain seeped into the windows of our bus, and I thought, this is the Dominican Republic that most tourists don't get to see – the life away from the luxurious resort complexes.

While it is an over-used sentiment, it can't go unnoticed that the Dominican Republic truly is a country of synchronized contrasts. It is a country of great antiquity and promising modernity but one deeply rooted in tradition and cultural pride. It is a land where mangrove-lined coasts, lizard-inhabited deserts, coconut grove beaches, and mountainous peaks coexist. The Atlantic Ocean on the northern coast and the Caribbean Sea on the southern coast rock and sway as if dancing to the beat of a romantic *bachata*. Peaks and dales continue the curvaceous trend inland until the sultry heat and thick brine of the ocean air give way to the cool mountain breezes of the

humpback whale in the Bahía de Samaná

Cordillera Central – the mountain range home to the Caribbean's tallest peak, Pico Duarte. Perilously carved roads on the edge of the Cordillera Central crest with breathtaking vistas of tropical forests and plush river valleys. Speeding drivers, on their way down these passes, swiftly outrun mule-drawn carts loaded with sugarcane, tobacco, and vegetables. The abundant interior blooms with produce: Fertile valleys rife with rivers, farms, and plantations coexist with the southwest's salty and crocodile-pervaded Lago Enriquillo, which dips to more than 40 meters below sea level and is the lowest point in the Caribbean. Tropical rainforests collide with cactus-dotted deserts. And in the bustling capital city of Santo Domingo, 16th-century architecture sits alongside trendy bars and restaurants on the narrow cobblestone streets of Ciudad Colonial.

The Dominican Republic was the fountainhead for the New World and has given the western hemisphere many "firsts." The first Catholic mass was said on the northern shore; the first paved road, the first hospital, and first university were all built in Santo Domingo. These creations were the fulfillment of Columbus's dreams to set up a flourishing Spanish colony. But along with these

Taíno cave drawings

impressive beginnings, the modern-day Dominican Republic owns a tragic history with the subsequent genocide of the Taíno people, troubled Haitian/Dominican relations, and a brutal 20th-century dictatorship.

Columbus's legacy is present in Santo Domingo's Ciudad Colonial with well-preserved 16th-century cathedrals, forts, and cobbled walkways rich with Gothic architectural touches. Elsewhere, Caribbean gingerbread and a variety of Victorian styles still exist, especially in the refurbished homes around the Parque Central of Puerto Plata on the northern Costa Ámbar. In the sprawling cities of Santo Domingo and Santiago, antiquity gives way to modernity with stylish shopping malls and chic accommodations. But transcending time are the rural single-story clapboard homes built in the same manner for generations and often painted in cheerful colors that seem to exist only in the Caribbean sunlight.

Although there is an obvious gap between the desperately poor and the opulently wealthy here, most Dominicans are in the pursuit of enjoying life to its fullest. On any given day or night, a party or gathering is happening. Many visitors to the Dominican Republic are

Carnaval mask in La Vega

© ANA CHAVIER CAAMAÑO

struck by this infectious way of life and take the sentiment back to their homes like a souvenir in their suitcase.

Most tourists flock to the country for its famous white-sand beaches and swaying palms, which teeter on the cliché of a post-card metaphor, but the Dominican Republic has other alluring attributes. It is home to the world-renowned windsurfing capital of Cabarete, white-water rafting on the Río Yaque del Norte, and diving among some of the Caribbean's best-preserved reefs. The raucous Merengue Festival in Santo Domingo offers dancing and people-watching opportunities, and whale-watching in the Bahía de Samaná is the main draw in winter months. In the underbelly of the island you can explore Taíno history in various *cuevas* (caves), such as Cueva de las Maravillas, where you'll see some of the best examples of Taíno art in the Caribbean. And the adventurous traveler has an abundance of opportunities, such as paragliding over the mountain ranges in Jarabacoa or canyoning down amazing waterfalls in Damajagua. Regardless of which region you choose, or what you seek, the Dominican Republic's recreational grab bag makes it a dynamic destination that offers something for every kind of traveler.

Fuerte San Felipe, Puerto Plata

Contents

MAP CONTENTS

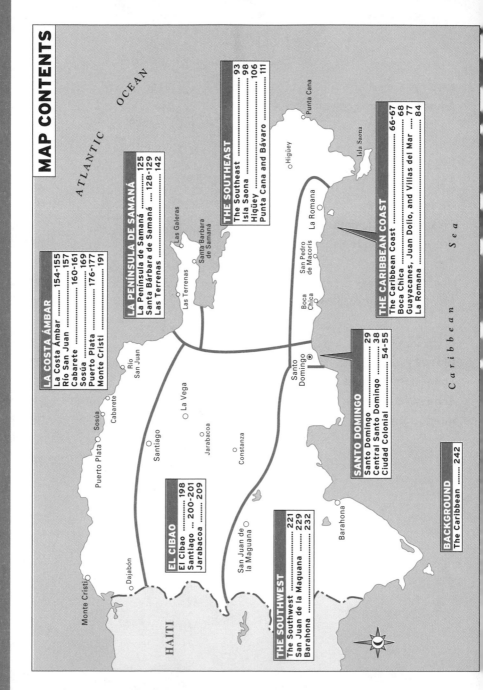

ATLANTIC OCEAN

Caribbean Sea

HAITI

Monte Cristi
Dajabón
Puerto Plata
Sosúa
Cabarete
Santiago
La Vega
Jarabacoa
Constanza
Río San Juan
Las Galeras
Las Terrenas
Santa Bárbara de Samaná
Santo Domingo
Boca Chica
San Pedro de Macorís
La Romana
Isla Saona
Higüey
Punta Cana
San Juan de la Maguana
Barahona

The Lay of the Land

SANTO DOMINGO

Known as one of the Caribbean's most cosmopolitan cities, Santo Domingo offers fine international dining, merengue-bumping dance clubs, cultural events with world-renowned acts, and top-notch accommodations. Rich with historical sights and restored colonial buildings, the central area of **Ciudad Colonial** (Colonial City) is the bread and butter of Santo Domingo's tourism industry. The oldest cathedral of the New World, **Catedral Primada de América,** and a climb to the top of the **Fortaleza Ozama** for a 360-degree view of the city should not be missed. Outside the Ciudad Colonial, visit the peaceful **Jardín Botánico Nacional** (National Botanical Garden) for a nice respite from the bustling city.

THE CARIBBEAN COAST

Running east from Santo Domingo to La Romana, this coastal area is perfect for a low-key beach vacation. The towns of Boca Chica, Guayacanes, Juan Dolio, Vilas del Mar, and San Pedro de Macorís all offer old-world charm, beautiful beaches, and grand golf courses. Enjoy some of the best diving in the protected waters and shipwrecks of **Parque Nacional Submarino La Caleta;** wade in the shallow water of **Playa Boca Chica;** watch a rowdy baseball game at Sammy Sosa's old stomping grounds in **San Pedro de Macorís;** and marvel at the Taíno art at **Cueva de las Maravillas.** Also along this coastline is **Casa de Campo,** one of the most famous resorts in the entire Caribbean, popular for its world-class golf courses and the nearby **Altos de Chavón** artists' village.

THE SOUTHEAST

The southeast region—including the popular **Bávaro and Punta Cana** area—offers an affordable Caribbean vacation with gorgeous beaches, choice snorkeling, exceptional golf courses, and luxurious but bargain accommodations. Ecotourism is enjoying a steady rise in this region, which is home to two large national parks: arid **Parque Nacional del Este** and the mangrove-lined and cave-rich **Parque Nacional Los Haitises.** Just offshore, the most popular day trip of the region is to the powdery white-sand beaches of **Isla Saona,** with a stop at **La Piscina Natural,** a starfish-inhabited sandbar.

LA PENÍNSULA DE SAMANÁ

This small sliver of land has become the Dominican Elysian fields of expats and independent travelers. The major communities—**Las Terrenas, Las Galeras,** and **Samaná**—have an individualistic feel and shun the "cookie cutter" vibe typical of other regions. **Humpback whales** are the main draw to this region during winter months, when thousands of them come to the Bahía de Samaná to breed and give birth. In the warm waters of the bay and reachable by catamaran is **Cayo Levantado,** an island with a great beach. A more ecostyle expedition is a horseback ride to **Salto El Limón,** where a 52-meter-high waterfall is the payoff after a long trip. At the tip of the peninsula and reachable only by boat is remote **Playa Rincón,** one of the top five most beautiful beaches in the Caribbean.

LA COSTA ÁMBAR

Stretching from the lowland lagoon in Río San Juan to the high cliffs and salt flats of Monte Cristi, the Amber Coast's undulating topography is famous for the all-inclusive resort trend of the centrally located **Puerto Plata** and **Playa Dorada** area. Recently, though, **Playa Grande,** the windsurfing mecca of **Cabarete,** and the wonderful diving conditions of **Sosúa** have shifted tourists' attention eastward. West of Puerto Plata is tiny **Luperón,** whose pretty beaches are the gateway to the less tourist-trodden northwest section. **Parque Nacional Monte Cristi,** in the remote northwestern corner of the country, is home to the picturesque **El Morro** rock and the diving purist's dream site at the well-preserved reefs of **Los Cayos de los Siete Hermanos.**

EL CIBAO

The central region of the country, including the Cordillera Central and the Valle del Cibao, is experiencing an explosion in ecotravel and adventure tourism. Its year-round springtime climate and national parks and scientific reserves home to endemic flora and fauna attract nature lovers and Dominican city folk looking to enjoy time off from the humid heat of the capital. And the challenging multi-day trek up **Pico Duarte**—the highest point in the Caribbean—continues to attract more people to the area each year. Outdoor activities abound, including parasailing, white-water rafting, and canyoning in **Jarabacoa** and **Constanza.** Amid all this natural beauty is the nation's second largest city, **Santiago,** a vibrant metropolis and home to **Centro León,** one of the best museums in the country.

THE SOUTHWEST

Offering a diverse range of landscapes—desert terrain, white-pebbled beaches, verdant valleys, freshwater lagoons, saltwater lakes—this region is a perfect choice for visitors seeking a unique experience. Along **Highway 44,** on the southern coast of the **Península de Pedernales,** you'll encounter gorgeous coastline vistas. At the largest park in the nation, **Parque Nacional Jaragua,** flamingo nesting grounds are just a boat ride away on the shores of **Laguna de Oviedo.** North of the park, the terrain turns to desert surrounding the salty **Lago Enriquillo**—the lowest point in all of the Caribbean—where crocodiles and iguanas lounge about. And from the small village of Las Cuevas, you can access **Bahía de Las Águilas,** the most pristine beach in the country, reachable only by boat.

Planning Your Trip

Since the Dominican Republic is a small area—almost 49,000 square kilometers (or slightly more than twice the size of New Hampshire)—a lot of ground can be covered in a short amount of time. Traveling from the Caribbean Sea on the southern coast to the Atlantic Ocean on the northern coast takes about four hours by car. In three weeks a majority of the locations outlined in this guide could be explored. Your approach is completely up to you.

If a beach vacation with just you, your book, and a swimsuit screams paradise, then perhaps the all-inclusive resort vacation is for you. This is the easiest vacation since all you have to do is look for the best deal and enjoy the ambience. You won't even need to carry cash at an all-inclusive resort. These complexes are tailor-made for those who want to escape from their daily grind and just relax without having to worry about any logistics. The southeast and Costa Ámbar regions are the best for this type of vacation. Most people spend about a week at an all-inclusive, while some spend only a few days.

Independent travelers will most likely prefer to stay clear of the all-inclusive resort and explore the region of El Cibao. A week and a half can be filled with exploration and adventure sporting here while making sure to give your body a day's rest in between daring pursuits. Freedom wanderers with less time available might enjoy La Península de Samaná. This arm of land extending off the northeastern edge of the country offers a lot in a condensed area. Plenty of action can be packed into a short trip (a few days), but to get the real languid feel that the peninsula is famous for, plan on spending a week.

All main roads lead to Santo Domingo. It is the perfect spot for home base for a city-lover or those who want to do lots of excursions. If you make Santo Domingo your base you could easily travel the entire countryside and come back to "civilization" in between jaunts.

When you have decided what the goal of your vacation is—relaxation or adventure, city shopping or historical tour—planning will be a little bit easier. How much time do you have? Five days would be a perfect amount of time for an all-inclusive in Punta Cana, but not enough time to add a weekend in the city into your stay. Perhaps the most difficult thing about planning your trip to the Dominican Republic is trying to fit everything into a short amount of time. You may have to commit yourself to one region or two activities depending on time limitations.

WHEN TO GO

Most of the Dominican Republic enjoys balmy weather with average temperatures of 28–31°C (82–88°F) throughout the year. Of course, that doesn't take into account the humidity, which can make it feel as hot as the sun's surface. The exception to this climate is in the central mountains, especially in Jarabacoa, where temperatures can sink to near freezing at night.

The heaviest tourist season is December–February, so everything will generally be more crowded and more expensive during these months. In La Península de Samaná the tourist season starts in December and tapers off in March when the humpback whales are mating and giving birth in the waters of the Bahía de Samaná. Another great reason to visit during this time is the opportunity to take part in the pre-Lenten festival Carnaval, which is celebrated every weekend in February throughout the entire country and is one of the oldest traditional festivals the country.

Another popular time to visit is during Semana Santa (Holy Week), which is celebrated the week before Easter Sunday. Dominicans usually take their vacations during this time as well, making it difficult to book last-minute hotel rooms along the coasts and in the mountains. Take heed, though; Semana Santa is traditionally a pretty wild vacation time (like spring break), so many beaches are closed to swimming and other water activities because of the high incidence of drunken accidents. However, Semana Santa is an especially great time to go to Santo Domingo; the city becomes a different animal entirely because a vast majority of the locals have left town for vacation. If you want to experience the city without all the hectic ferocity that it normally has, Semana Santa is perfect timing.

While it may be tempting to take advantage of cheap airfare in the summer months (and indeed many do during July and August), the tradeoffs are mosquitoes, hurricanes (in August and September), and extreme humidity. But the pluses are shorter lines and less-crowded resorts. The rainy season runs from May to October and sometimes through December in the northern half of the country. November, while a gamble rain-wise, would be a good time to visit, right before the tourist onslaught arrives.

WHAT TO TAKE

The Dominican climate is mostly warm, so lightweight options like linen trousers, skirts, and shirts are a good choice. Pieces of clothing that can be layered are suitable since it can get chilly at night. There is always the chance of rain, particularly in the mountains and on the Península de Samaná, so a lightweight rain jacket is a good thing to have.

If you're going to the coastal regions during the cooler months (December–February) you may need to bring a sweater or blazer and even jeans because ocean breezes can pick up at night. In the interior (especially the Cordillera Central) temperatures can dip to almost freezing at night, so warm clothing is highly recommended. Don't count on mountain hideaways having heat. Although some do, electricity can be rather iffy, so bring warm pajamas.

The diversity of the landscape and wide range of activities mean several types of footwear are a good idea: sandals for the beaches, sneakers or boots for walking and hiking, and dress shoes for nighttime entertainment. Consider taking water shoes for wallowing in the surf if you are nervous about cutting your feet or stepping on an unsuspecting sea critter.

Dominicans always look their best when socializing, especially in the cities. Jeans and T-shirts are too casual for evening wear. In fact, many discos and restaurants have strict dress codes. At night men can don slacks and a nice shirt, but many women really pull out all the stops with high heels, skirts, dresses, or nice pants and a blouse. Sightseeing during the day calls for light clothing but not shorts or tank tops and never beach wear. While tank tops are fine for walking around outside, definitely take a shirt to slip on before you enter establishments. Many historical sites and churches have strict rules about what is appropriate attire. For instance, going into the cathedral in the Ciudad Colonial wearing short shorts, flip-flops, and a midriff tank top is considered very disrespectful. Dominicans take pride in their appearance and will expect the same from you. Sloppiness is seen as a lack of manners.

Explore the Dominican Republic

THE 21-DAY BEST OF THE DOMINICAN REPUBLIC

If you can swing it, three weeks in the Dominican Republic would give you sufficient time to dive into each of the various regions. With such biodiversity in one country, you may be surprised to discover just how wide the spectrum of activities ranges. This itinerary is for someone who is active and excited to dig into the nature and culture of the Dominican Republic. It is meant only as a "highlights to hit" itinerary. If you're traveling along and happen to fall in love with the surf scene in Cabarete, for instance, simply stop and keep surfing.

DAY 1

Arrive at Aeropuerto Internacional Las Américas in Santo Domingo and settle into your hotel in the Ciudad Colonial. If you arrive during the day, set out on foot to explore the colonial sights and orient yourself. For dinner go to one of the restaurants on the **Plaza de la Hispanidad.**

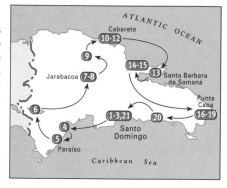

DAY 2

Spend the day exploring the Ciudad Colonial and all of its sights, including the New World's first street, **Calle de las Damas,** and ruins of the first hospital, **Ruinas de Hospital San Nicolás de Barí.** Leave time for the oldest cathedral in the western hemisphere, the **Catedral Primada de América,** and the **Museo de las Casas Reales.** Have dinner along the water at **Adrian Tropical** for a wonderful view of the stars and the surf while enjoying typical Dominican favorites like *mofongo* (mashed plantains). Afterward, stroll along the Malecón to the **Renaissance Jaragua Hotel** to dance the night away in its hot club, **Jubilee.**

DAY 3

In Santo Domingo's **Plaza de la Cultura,** the Taíno artifact exhibit at the **Museo del Hombre Dominicano** is a first-rate way to learn about the pre-Columbian history of the nation. Catch a taxi to the peaceful **Jardín Botánico Nacional** to learn about the biodiversity of the Dominican Republic. Grab dinner in the Ciudad Colonial and save all your energy for dancing at **Guácara Taína,** located in the belly of an enormous cave. Make sure your rental-car reservations are in place for your drive to Barahona the next day.

DAY 4

On your way to **Barahona,** in the arid region southwest of Santo Domingo on the Península de Pedernales, detour to see the **Reserva Antropológica El Pomier** north of San Cristóbal and marvel at hundreds of ancient Taíno drawings. Check into the **Hotel Costa Larimar** before heading out to dinner and dancing at **Los Robles.**

DAY 5

Get up very early for a day of beautiful scenery and a visit to a deserted beach. Drive to Las Cuevas, a small community of fishermen who can also give you a boat ride to your ultimate destination, one of the last completely unspoiled and most remote beaches in the country, **Bahía de las Águilas.** If time permits, on your way back stop for a dip in the freshwater lagoons *(balnearios)* of San Rafael or Los Patos.

DAY 6

Take Highway 46 toward Lago Enriquillo, making a quick stop at the **Polo Magnético** to witness first-hand the quirky phenomenon of your car rolling mysteriously uphill. Continue your drive around the Lago Enriquillo loop, stopping at the **Parque Nacional Isla Cabritos** to see crocodiles, flamingos, and iguanas lounging by the saltwater lake. Head back to Barahona by night and enjoy a more casual dinner at the locally popular **Restaurante and Pizzería D'Lina.**

DAY 7

Return to Santo Domingo to return the rental car and catch a bus to the cooler mountainous village of **Jarabacoa.** Visit the waterfalls and swimming holes of the **Saltos de Jimenoa** and **Salto de Baiguate.** Stay at the **Rancho Baiguate** and make reservations with its excursion team to try an adventure sport such as canyoning or rafting on the **Río Yaque del Norte.** Rest up for your next day of adventure.

DAY 8

While canyoning is indeed a thrilling and mind-boggling adventure, don't forget to enjoy the scenery as you navigate down waterfalls and across streams. Later go for pizza in Jarabacoa's **Pizza de Calidad,** off the main drag in a quieter section of town.

DAY 9

Catch an early bus north along Highway 5 and stop in Santiago to visit the **Centro León** cigar factory and art museum in the morning. Eat lunch in Puerto Plata at **Aquaceros Bar & Grill,** right along the Malecón, and then take a taxi to **Fuerte San Felipe** and the **Museo del Ámbar Dominicano** before heading to the snorkeler's favorite haunt, Sosúa (about 25 kilometers east of Puerto Plata) via bus or *guagua.*

DAY 10

Dive or snorkel off the coast of Sosúa with a reputable outfitter like **Fat Cat Diving.** Have dinner at Sosúa's romantic **La Puntilla de Piergiorgio** for Italian food with an out-of-this-world view of the Atlantic.

DAY 11

Early in the morning take off to the surfer-filled hot spot of **Cabarete** and settle in to your hotel. Explore the one main drag running parallel to the beach and then head over to **Playa Cabarete** and sign up with a windsurfing outfitter, like **Vela,** to teach you the ropes or rent you equipment. Cabarete's lively yet casual nightlife revolves around the bars along Playa Cabarete.

DAY 12

Head over to **Kite Beach** to try out kitesurfing. **Kite Club** has lessons available, and you can join the club for weeks at a time. It's also a super-cool place to just chill by the surf and watch an international cast of surfers.

DAY 13

Continue farther east toward the town of **Samaná** on the skinny arm of La Península de Samaná. If it's **whale season** (January–March) take a tour with **Victoria Marine** to see the humpbacks in the bay with an afternoon stop on **Cayo Levantado,** where lunch is served on the beach and a catamaran ride back to shore is included. If it's not whale season, take a horse-riding trek to see **Salto El Limón,** a waterfall that ends in a spectacular pool.

DAYS 14–15

Head to **Las Galeras** along Highway 5, the sleepiest of towns on the peninsula, and hire a boat captain to take you to the exquisitely undeveloped and natural **Playa Rincón**. Or, if a day of relaxing on a beach plus a night of dancing sounds more your speed, head over to **Las Terrenas** instead. While the beach isn't pristine like Playa Rincón, this town has a more lively feel and more nightlife to choose from. For dinner and dancing, head over to the **Pueblo de Los Pescadores.**

DAYS 16–19

Return to Samaná and take the ferry across the Bahía de Samaná to Sabana de la Mar, then catch a bus to **Punta Cana** and check in to an all-inclusive resort like **Bahía Príncipe Clubs and Resorts** and begin the pampering portion of your trip. Spend your days at the pool, the beach, or getting a massage. At night, this resort offers many options like dancing, cabaret-style shows, and karaoke.

DAY 20

Rent a car in Punta Cana and take your time getting back to Santo Domingo. Don't miss the **Altos de Chavón** artists' village, a fantastic place to stop for lunch and watch artists at work, and perhaps buy a one-of-a-kind piece of jewelry or art. At 15 kilometers east of San Pedro de Macorís stop and see the **Cueva de las Maravillas,** with more than 500 Taíno pictographs on the cave walls.

DAY 21

Back in Santo Domingo, spend part of the day shopping along Calle El Conde for last-minute gifts and souvenirs, like rum, cigars, and art. Try **Mercado Modelo** for any jewelry and tourist gifts. Have lunch at **Bar & Restaurant Anacaona** before you leave for the airport.

THE TAÍNO HISTORY TOUR

Before Columbus, the indigenous Taíno people were a well-organized and peaceful society living on the island. Upon "discovery," their entire population was wiped out, but their influence on Dominican culture was not lost. Their history has come together like a puzzle put together from artifacts recovered at sites, cave drawings, and leftover cultural practices. The Taíno influence can still be heard in remnants of language that have been adopted into regular Spanish, and Dominicans still make a type of bread that has existed since Taíno days. A visitor could easily spend a week exploring just Taíno sites with some traditional beach fun along the way. This itinerary is designed for travel with a rental car and can easily be tailored to fit your personal financial and scheduling needs.

DAY 1

Fly into Punta Cana airport and rent a car. Drive to the burgeoning tourist destination of **Bayahibe** and check into one of the area's best all-inclusive resorts, the **Iberostar Hacienda Dominicus.** This resort maintains a beautiful beach strip for its guests to enjoy, and you can enjoy dinner within the hotel at one of its five restaurants and later learn how to merengue at the disco.

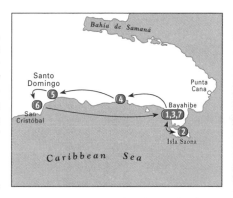

DAY 2

At the tour package desk next to the lobby in the hotel, reserve a ride aboard a catamaran out to beautiful Isla Saona. Once on Isla Saona, walk to the **Cueva Cotubanamá**, a cave where Taíno families hid out from the Spanish. Spend the day at the beach soaking in the paradise they once lived in. Buffet lunch is served on the beach for all-inclusive guests. This can also be arranged through independent boat captains at the Bayahibe point.

DAY 3

Just south of Bayahibe is **Dominicus Americanus,** where the entrance to the **Parque Nacional del Este** is located. Here, check out **La Cueva de Berna** and **Cueva del Puente,** caves with some easy and not-so-easy to spot Taíno drawings. Guides can be hired at the entrance to the park. Make

sure to take a bottle of water on the journey into the park; it is a hot and arid place. This is a close day trip and you don't have to check out of your Bayahibe resort.

DAY 4

On your way to Santo Domingo, stop and take a guided tour at the **Cueva de las Maravillas,** where you'll see some of the best examples of Taíno art in the Caribbean. Pictograms have been pristinely preserved and look as if they were drawn in recent years.

DAY 5

While in Santo Domingo, check out the fantastic collection of Taíno artifacts at the **Museo del Hombre Dominicano** at the Plaza de la Cultura. At the front desk ask for a guide or some literature in your language. This is a wonderful mid-journey education on Taíno culture and rituals. Stroll through the **Ciudad Colonial** and visit some of the museums. An important piece of the native Taíno's story is the period of Spanish colonialism.

DAY 6

Take a day trip just north of San Cristóbal to the **Reserva Antropológica El Pomier,** the most significant collection of rock art found in the Caribbean. These finds are from not only the Taíno but the Igneri and Carib tribes as well, and are about 2,000 years old. Take a lunch break at **Fela's Place** before you head back to Santo Domingo.

DAY 7

Get up early to return to Bayahibe to spend your last day soaking up the sun on **Playa Bayahibe** before your departure the next day. No trip to the Caribbean would be complete without a seafood dinner. **Restaurante La Punta** always offers the freshest of catches.

THE BEACH LOVER'S GUIDE TO PARADISE

You: a bevy of swimsuits, sarongs, sunglasses, and trashy novels. The Dominican Republic: a plethora of dreamy beaches waiting for you to write your name in the sand. This is a winning combination for the ultimate two-week sun and sand experience—a beach lover's tour to some of the best beaches in the country. This itinerary takes you to both all-inclusive resorts where they manicure their beaches and to wild, remote hideaway coves. Beaches in three different regions are covered here, but if you only have a week, then this itinerary can easily be tailored to just visit one or two of the regions.

DAYS 1-2

Arrive at the Punta Cana airport. Check into the **Bahía Principe Clubs and Resorts,** where you can begin your trip by soaking in the tranquil vibe. On the grounds of this resort is **Pueblo Principe,** a mock village where there are gift shops, live music at night, a lively disco, and a casino. For a fantastic seafood lunch, make reservations through your hotel for the **Capitán Cook** restaurant in El Cortecito. The restaurant will send a water taxi to fetch you and take you to its seaside digs.

DAY 3

Make your way north with a brief stopover on **Playa Limón,** popular with excursion tours because of its exquisitely beautiful coconut groves. Continue onward until the commuter town of Sabana de la Mar, where you'll catch a ferry to the **Península de Samaná,** home to some of the country's most beautiful beaches.

DAYS 4-5

If you stay at **Occidental Gran Bahía** in the town of Samaná, you can schedule a whale-watching tour (provided it's whale-watching season – December-March) with **Victoria Marine** with a side trip to Cayo Levantado for the afternoon. At night, stroll along the **Malecón** until you find a restaurant that suits your tastes. Hire a unique-to-Samaná multi-person *motoconcho* to take you back to the hotel.

DAYS 6-7

Take a taxi or bus up Highway 5 to **Las Galeras** and one of the most famous Dominican beaches, Playa Rincón. Reachable only by boat, this stunning three-beach sandy stretch is backed by a thick forest of palms. You can find boat captains at **Playa Las Galeras** in town willing to take you to the other secluded beaches on the tip of the peninsula, including **Playa Frontón** and **Playa Madama**. Another good daytime activity offered by **Enzo's Rancho** is horseback riding through the countryside culminating in a picnic lunch on the beach.

DAY 8

To get off of the peninsula, take a *guagua* back to Samaná and grab a bus to Río San Juan. Try snorkeling at **Laguna Gri-Gri** or check out the thick band of golden sand with a rough surf on **Playa Grande**. Also close by is **Playa Caletón,** a much more quaint and cozy experience. Here, the best place to stay is at **Occidental Alegro Playa Grande.**

DAYS 9-10

Head west to Cabarete by *guagua,* where you'll be in the company of water-sport junkies. Kiteboarding, surfing, and windsurfing lessons are big business here. **Vela,** right on **Playa Cabarete** in town, is a well-known outfitter for sailboarders. Even if you're not interested in a water sport, beaches like **Bozo Beach, Kite Beach,** and **Playa Encuentro** are great places to watch those who are. Lively nighttime entertainment can be found at **Las Brisas,** where you can dance with the locals and tourists alike.

DAYS 11-12

Just west of Cabarete, a short *guagua* ride away, spend the night and dine in Sosúa's affordable **Hotel Waterfront.** The next day hang out on **Playa Alicia,** which offers a less frequented and more serene beach experience than Sosúa Beach. Go snorkeling in the **Bahía de Samaná,** a cheap and fun activity.

DAYS 13-14

Get up early and catch a taxi to the first all-inclusive resort ever built in Playa Dorada: **Jack Tar Village.** Spend your last days being pampered one last time. The Jack Tar is known for having some of the best cuisine in the Playa Dorada complex. Before heading to the Aeropuerto Gregorio Luperón for your departure, take a taxi into **Puerto Plata** and go to the **Museo del Ámbar Dominicano** and learn about the ancient resin found in the Dominican Republic.

THE 8-DAY NATURE LOVER'S TREK

The Dominican Republic has an astonishingly diverse ecosystem on two-thirds of the island of Hispaniola. Today, 25 percent of this area is protected and includes nine scientific reserves and sanctuaries and 16 national parks (three of which are submarine), covering over 12,000 square kilometers. If you don't have enough time to explore all of the country's mountainous highlands, pine savannas, mangroves, coastlines, sand dunes, rivers, and lagoons, following this itinerary will take you to the most diverse areas for a week of nature-loving fun.

DAY 1

Fly into Santo Domingo and rent a four-wheel-drive vehicle; head 201 kilometers southwest to the coastal town of **Barahona.** Check into the independently owned budget-friendly **Hotel María Montez.** Enjoy some fresh seafood at **Brisas del Caribe** right on Barahona's Malecón and some dancing at hot spot **Los Robles.**

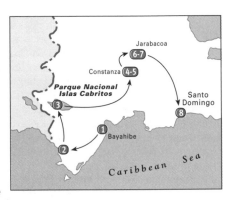

DAY 2

Get an early start and drive along the very picturesque coastal Highway 44 to **Parque Nacional Jaragua,** the largest national park in the country, and hire a boat guide at the gate who'll take you to **Laguna de Oviedo.** There you can view the 130 bird species that live in the park (including flamingos), iguanas, and a cave that has Taíno drawings. Continue on to **Las Cuevas** village and hire a boat captain to take you to one of the last virgin beaches in the country, **Bahía de las Águilas.** The locals in Las Cuevas offer fresh seafood lunches prepared on the beachfront. Head back to your hotel in Barahona for the night.

DAY 3

Take the arid and very hot **Lago Enriquillo Loop Road** to get to **Parque Nacional Isla Cabritos.** Stroll through the gardens at the entrance gate and mingle with the numerous ricord and rhinoceros iguanas. Purchase a tour that will take you to **Lago Enriquillo** to see American crocodiles and flamingos hang out by the mouth of the **Río de la Des-** cubierta. Bring along your bathing suit for a dip in the park's sulfur *balneario* back at the entrance park at the end of your tour. After your respite in the park, continue the loop and head for the Taíno rock carvings at **Las Caritas.** After circling the lake on the Loop Road, stop for lunch in **Neyba.** Head back to Barahona for your last night in the southwestern region.

DAY 4

From Barahona, travel to **Constanza,** in a beautiful circular valley surrounded by mountains 1,200 meters above sea level. Stay at **Alto Cerro** and enjoy the ranch's horseback-riding tour through the countryside. Dine at **Lorenzo's,** famous for its *chivo guisado* (goat stew) and other typical Dominican fare.

DAY 5

Take a day trip to hike in the **Parque Nacional Valle Nuevo** (20 kilometers south of Constanza), where bird-watching reigns supreme. Afterward make the bumpy ride to a three-tiered waterfall, **Salto de Aguas Blancas,** and take a dip in its serene pool surrounded by the protected forest. If you still have energy you can take a drive to the **Reserva Científica Ebano Verde,** created to protect the 621 plant species, amphibians, reptiles, and small mammal species (such as solenodons and bats), and 59 species of birds. Enjoy a six-kilometer hike here along a trail where trees are marked with information about their species. Back in Constanza, have a plate of *la bandera dominicana* (chicken, beans, rice, and fried plantains) at **Aguas Blancas.**

DAY 6

Drive north to **Jarabacoa,** the gateway village to the central mountains and the national parks **Armando Bermúdez** and **José del Carmen Ramírez.** Stay at the **Gran Jimenoa** hotel, right on the bank of the Río de Jimenoa, and take short hikes to the waterfalls of **Jimenoa** and **Baiguate,** where you can dip into the pools.

DAY 7

Paraglide with **Fly Vacher** (of Jarabacoa) and see the virgin Dominican waterfalls, rivers, and mountains from the air. Afterward, stay grounded with a jeep tour of the countryside with **Rancho Baiguate.** Wind down at night with a real Dominican-cuisine meal at **Restaurante El Rancho.**

DAY 8

Have breakfast next to the rushing **Río de Jimenoa** in the **Piedras del Río** restaurant of the Gran Jimenoa hotel. Drive to Santo Domingo for your departure at Las Américas airport.

ADVENTURE SPORTS

The topographical landscape of the Dominican Republic is an extensive and intricate one—deserts, mountains, mangroves, forests, rainforests, rivers, waterfalls; short of an iceberg or two, the country's just about got it all covered. Because of this varied topography, the DR has bloomed into a full-force adventure tourism destination.

CANYONING AND CASCADING

Canyoning uses equipment such as harnesses, helmets, ropes, and other climbing and rappelling tools to navigate up, down, across, under, and through waterfalls. Cascading is very similar to canyoning, but cascading does not use equipment other than the occasional rope and tends to cover shorter distances. Canyoning is more intensive and requires a greater level of physical fitness. **Damajagua,** a half hour outside Puerto Plata, is one of the best places to enjoy this sport.

HIKING

For serious hikers, the 47-kilometer climb to **Pico Duarte,** along the Cordillera Central in the **Parque Nacional Armando Bermúdez,** is the ultimate trek. At over 3,087 meters, Duarte is the highest peak in the Caribbean, and it will take at least two days to ascend. Your reward is an amazing vista of the Cibao Valley. Shorter options would be to hike to the waterfalls of **Saltos de Jimenoa** and **Salto Baiguate** by Jarabacoa or in the high hills of **Constanza. La Península de Samaná** is also a wonderful place to trek.

MOUNTAIN BIKING

Adventure companies like **Iguana Mama** of **Cabarete** offer single-day mountain-bike tours as well as two-week-long bike trips; many incorporate other adventure activities. A favorite fat-tire ride is in the lush mountains of **Jarabacoa**. For a road-bike excursion, the **Lago Enriquillo Loop Road** has a good surface and not a lot of traffic.

PARAGLIDING

Sail through the sky with breathtaking views of the mountain ranges in **Jarabacoa,** hands down the best place to brave the skies with eagle-eye views of the Cibao Valley, waterfalls, and rivers. **Fly Vacher** offers paragliding lessons and excursions.

QUAD RIDING OR ATVING

Four-wheel all-terrain vehicles can navigate terrain that is difficult to access with regular vehicles, such as tropical forest paths and mountain areas like the **Cordillera Septentrional** and **Cordillera Central.**

RIVER RAFTING

Río Yaque del Norte stretches over 290 kilometers in the Cordillera Central. The river reaches an impressive altitude of 2,580 meters, making it an exhilarating, raucous river-rafting route. The most respected outfitter in Jarabacoa is **Rancho Baiguate.**

ROCK CLIMBING

On the Península de Samaná, **Playa Frontón** is a popular area for climbing, with rocky cliffs overhanging a perfect sandy beach. Hire a boat from Playa Las Galeras or hike an hour to get there. The **Parque Mirador del Sur,** in Santo Domingo, has some free climb sites, but it can be quite crowded on the weekends.

WATER SPORTS

With its miles of coral reefs, diversity of underwater life and environment, and excellent visibility and temperature conditions, the Dominican Republic is one of the best places in the Caribbean for **scuba diving.** In the north, **Sosúa** is particularly popular for both beginning and advanced divers. Maximum depths of key diving sites range 8.5-36 meters. The southern shores – around **Bayahibe** and **Pedernales** – boast a vast sea of pristine coral reefs for the more adventurous diver. To get started, you must get certified. Classes are offered just about everywhere along the coast.

Good old-fashioned **surfing** remains the front runner of adventure sporting. **Playa Encuentro,** near Cabarete, is the ideal surfing spot. Wintertime offers up the best conditions with consistent swells December–April. Although the swells vary the rest of the year, the water temperature (around 26°C, 79°F) makes for a good ride most any time. **Playa Preciosa,** by Río San Juan, has a good ride too, but the waters are a bit more dangerous (strong undertows).

Cabarete has the best beaches for **windsurfing** and **kiteboarding.** Wind conditions shift throughout the day – from light in the morning to heavier later in the day – allowing adventurers of all levels to find their niche. From mid-December to April consistent winds average 13-17 knots (24-32 kph, 15-20 mph). Wind speed picks up some June–September and can reach 13-22 knots (24-41 kph, 15-25 mph). During May and between October and December, the winds are less consistent.

Kiteboarding, sometimes called kitesurfing, is a combination of surfing, paragliding, windsurfing, wakeboarding, and kite flying. It is fairly easy to learn once you figure out how to control the kite and get the hang of a few board maneuvers. There are quite a few kiteboarding schools in Cabarete, most on **Kite Beach.**

SANTO DOMINGO

Those who have never visited Santo Domingo sometimes believe the capital city to be a third-world town with nothing culturally significant to offer, but this perception could not be further from the truth. This progressive cosmopolitan city offers a unique cultural experience for a variety of travelers: Couples will find romance in the quiet of the 500-year-old orchid- and bougainvillea-filled courtyards, singles will enjoy an unbeatable nightlife (with the best gay and lesbian scene in the country), museum-lovers will be satiated by the archaeological and arts and crafts exhibits, and the history buffs will find much to explore in the various colonial landmarks.

This frenetic metropolis is abuzz with the constant din of traffic and a wax and wane of action throughout the day. Activity rises with the morning sun: *Colmados* (small stores) sell their wares to the accompaniment of merengue soundtracks blaring from their radios, animated haggling takes place in marketplaces, businesspeople pile into *públicos* heading for work, and vendors roam residential neighborhoods shouting out their daily produce offerings in sing-song voices. When the sun hits its hottest temperature, the frenzy of the day reaches its liveliest, and the streets are choked beyond capacity with diesel trucks, *motoconchos,* and honking cars. Then around noon, the city suddenly, as if on cue, quiets down for an extended lunch hour. Many Dominicans retreat into the shade of their homes for a big meal, perhaps a nap and a cold shower to battle the heat, and regroup for the afternoon when it's once again business as usual.

© ANA CHAVIER CAAMAÑO

HIGHLIGHTS

◖ **Ciudad Colonial:** Stroll the same cobbled walkways and historical haunts where the Spanish plotted their conquests and pirates ravaged the city. Dine or even sleep in their former homes (page 31).

◖ **Parque Colón:** Flanked by the oldest cathedral in the western hemisphere, colonial architecture, and pubs offering refreshing antidotes to the hot sun, Parque Colón is a perfect spot for relaxing after sightseeing (page 32).

◖ **Fortaleza Ozama:** Climb your way to the top of a 16th-century fort that was the first line of defense against pirate invaders; peer over the edge to the Río Ozama (page 32).

◖ **Catedral Primada de América:** Sit under the great arching ceiling of the oldest cathedral of the New World. Sir Francis Drake and his men captured and occupied it during their month-long siege of the city (page 35).

◖ **Faro a Colón:** Study the exhibits at this controversial lighthouse and visit the country's homage to Christopher Columbus, where his remains are rumored to be at rest (page 39).

◖ **Jardín Botánico Nacional:** Take an afternoon for a leisurely and quiet stroll through the plush and serene National Botanical Garden and learn about the biodiversity of the Dominican Republic (page 40).

LOOK FOR ◖ TO FIND RECOMMENDED SIGHTS, ACTIVITIES, DINING, AND LODGING.

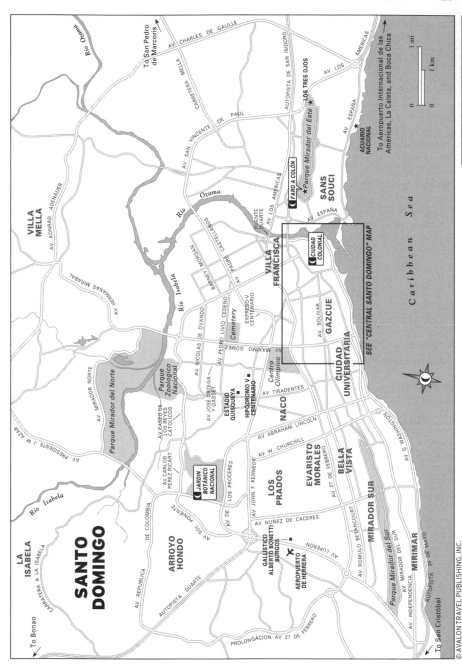

SANTO DOMINGO

To San Pedro de Marcoris

AV CHARLES DE GAULLE

AUTOPISTA DE SAN ISIDORO

AV LOS TRES OJOS

AMERICAS

To Aeropuerto Internacional de las Américas, La Caleta, and Boca Chica

0   1 mi

0   1 km

CARRETERA MELLA

AV SAN VINCENTE DE PAUL

Río Ozama

ACUARIO NACIONAL

Parque Mirador del Este

AV ESPAÑA

VILLA MELLA

AV KONRAD ADENAUER

Río Isabela

Río Ozama

PUENTE DUARTE

AV LOS AMERICAS

FARO A COLÓN

SANS SOUCI

AV ESPAÑA

Caribbean Sea

AV HERMANAS MIRABAL

BARNEY MORGAN

AV PADRE CASTELLANOS

VILLA FRANCISCA

CIUDAD COLONIAL

EXPRESO V CENTENARIO

AV NICOLAS DE OVANDO

AV PEDRO LIVIO CEDEÑO

Cemetery

AV BOLIVAR

GAZCUE

AV MAXIMO GOMEZ

SEE "CENTRAL SANTO DOMINGO" MAP

Parque Mirador del Norte

Parque Zoologico Nacional

AV PASEO DE LOS REYES CATOLICOS

AV JOSE ORTEGA Y GASSET

Centro Olímpico

CIUDAD UNIVERSITARIA

AV MIRADOR NORTE

ESTADIO QUISQUEYA

HIPODROMO V CENTENARIO

AV TIRADENTES

NACO

AV PRESIDENTE J M AZAR

AV ABRAHAM LINCOLN

AV W CHURCHILL

EVARISTO MORALES

BELLA VISTA

AV G WASHINGTON

AV CARLOS PEREZ RICART

JARDIN BOTANICO NACIONAL

AV DE LOS PROCERES

AV JOHN F KENNEDY

LOS PRADOS

AV 27 DE FEBRERO

Río Isabela

LA ISABELA

AV REPUBLICA DE COLOMBIA

AV SOL PONIENTE

AV NUÑEZ DE CACERES

AV ROMULO BETANCOURT

MIRADOR SUR

ARROYO HONDO

GALLISTICO ALBERTO BONETTI BURGOS

AEROPUERTO DE HERRERA

AV LUPERON

AV MIRADOR DEL SUR

Parque Mirador del Sur

MIRIMAR

SANTO DOMINGO

CARRETERA A LA ISABELA

AUTOPISTA DUARTE

AV INDEPENDENCIA

AV 30 DE MAYO

To Bonao

To San Cristóbal

PROLONGACION AV 27 DE FEBRERO

AUTOPISTA 30 DE MAYO

Caribbean Sea

Although still busy, afternoons in Santo Domingo are much more relaxed than the mornings. Calle El Conde is still alive with shoppers and traffic picks up again, but the traditional espresso break around 4 P.M. allows worker bees to begin to wind down before the end of their work day, and around 6 P.M. most employees head home for dinner.

At nightfall, Santo Domingo's nightlife scene takes center stage and is sure to satisfy almost every need. You can dance in trendy clubs until dawn, eat in countless restaurants serving culinary favorites from around the world, or romance Lady Luck at the casinos along the Malecón. If you time your visit right, you can experience one of the exciting festivals that the city hosts: Carnaval, the merengue festival, or the Latin music festival, all of which go on until the wee hours of the morning.

A city of firsts, Santo Domingo boasts the first hospital, paved street, and university of the New World, in addition to the oldest surviving cathedral and European fortress. Founded by Christopher Columbus's brother, Bartolomé, this city has survived the centuries; many buildings still stand and have been maintained or renovated within the Ciudad Colonial. Today, portions of the original walls of the city can still be seen, but greater Santo Domingo continues to expand in physical size and in population, which is nearing 2.5 million people.

History and modernity coexist here: Many hotels, restaurants, and bars in the Ciudad Colonial are restored from their original 16th-century buildings and homes and still offer the modern comforts that tourists have come to expect. The tourism industry has recognized the uniqueness of the Ciudad Colonial and has begun stringent efforts to maintain its historical significance along with supplying visitors with modern amenities.

All major roads lead to Santo Domingo, which makes it a good choice for a base for your vacation, especially if you love city life and all it has to offer but need the beach or the mountains peppered into your visit. Transportation options are plentiful, and traveling to many beautiful destinations in the country can be done in a morning from Santo Domingo.

PLANNING YOUR TIME

Santo Domingo is a vibrant city with a lot to offer. Tourists can touch the same fortress walls where Columbus, Cortés, and Ponce de León once leaned. History buffs will need more than a day to soak it all in and may want to hire a guide in order to fully appreciate the significance of all the sights. Others can probably cover the **Ciudad Colonial** in a day with a self-guided tour, making sure to hit a museum or two and save some time for shopping on El Conde.

For certain, the major tourism draw for Santo Domingo is the Ciudad Colonial, particularly the **Fortaleza Ozama** and **Catedral Primada de América,** but other sights are worth visiting as well, like the **Jardín Botánico Nacional** and the **Faro a Colón.**

HISTORY

Santo Domingo was recently named a UNESCO World Cultural Heritage Site. Its history is both glorious and sad. While it has so many bragging rights as the City of Firsts, those firsts came at a very high price during different periods of time in this city's many centuries of existence. Many lives were lost (Taíno mostly) to pave the way for the city to be built and prosper.

Santo Domingo is the result of many failed attempts at settlement. Columbus couldn't catch a break. His first settlement at La Navidad was annihilated, and the same happened to his second try at La Isabela. His third settlement, Nueva Isabela, on the eastern bank of the Río Ozama, although thriving, was eventually leveled by a hurricane. Finally, with the help of his governor, he founded Santo Domingo de Guzmán (the city's official name), an 11-block area on the western bank of the Río Ozama. And it began to thrive. At the same time, the brutalization of the Taíno natives raged on with forced labor.

Santo Domingo began to weaken, and

pirates were catching wind of its vulnerability. In 1586, Sir Francis Drake, the English buccaneer, came to town and seized it for a month until he finally got the Spanish to pay him a ransom to get it back. He wasn't the last to try to take Santo Domingo, either. William Penn of England tried, and former slave François Dominique Toussaint L'Ouverture of Haiti succeeded until February 27, 1844, when Juan Pablo Duarte finally won independence for the Dominican Republic. All of this happened in the Ciudad Colonial.

Sights

Most historical sites in Santo Domingo are within the Ciudad Colonial (Colonial City). Churches, homes, the first European fortress in the western hemisphere, and other colonial-era buildings are all within walking distance of one another, although you could always flag down a horse-drawn carriage if you need a break from walking.

In the greater Santo Domingo area there are many other sights worth visiting, such as the expansive Jardín Botánico (Botanical Garden), the Faro a Colón (Lighthouse of Columbus), where the remains of the explorer are said to be laid to rest, and the Plaza de la Cultura's Museo del Hombre Dominicano (Museum of the Dominican Man), which features an impressive display of Taíno artifacts.

Guided Tours

To get an *official* guide, go to the Parque Colón and look to the ones sitting near the cathedral or in the shade of the trees around the park. The key tip-off that they are official is the outfit—khaki pants and light blue dress shirt—and they have licenses (sometimes hanging around their necks) with the official state tourism logo on it. Ask to see it. These walking tours cost US$20–30 and last about 2.5 hours. The guides will take you to the major sites of the Ciudad Colonial. Always be sure to agree on the price before going with the guide. Some are notorious for trying to make an extra buck by the time the tour is over.

Another alternative is to join a large group for a tour. Major agencies include **Prieto Tours** (Av. Francia 125, tel. 809/685-0102, www.prieto-tours.com), **Omni Tours** (Ro-berto Pastoria 204, tel. 809/565-6591, www.omnitours.com.do), and **Metro Tours** (Av. 27 de Febrero, tel. 809/544-4580, www.metrotours.com.do).

◖ CIUDAD COLONIAL

Along the western bank of the Río Ozama, where its waters meet the Caribbean Sea, lie 11 square blocks that make up the fountainhead of colonialism. Fortresses still stand guard over the harbor where Columbus's men finally docked their armada back in 1498.

Today the district offers tourists a walk back into history to when the conquistadors ambled along to the clinking of their armor and the gold in their pouches. Sixteenth-century architecture cohabits with the speeding mopeds of the new millennium. The smell of luscious Dominican cuisine curls through the air around the vendors and through the windows of museums.

With some buildings dating back to the early 1500s, efforts have been made to maintain the historical integrity or, in some cases, reincarnate them into hotels, pubs, cafés, and restaurants. But one thing is certain; you will find many authentic "firsts" here. Since it is the first European city in the New World, Santo Domingo boasts the first university, hospital, cathedral, and palace, to name a few.

Amid the historical surroundings is some of the best shopping in the city, on **Calle El Conde** and throughout the Ciudad Colonial. From cigar shops, small bookstores, and music stores to art, jewelry, and designer clothing, the Ciudad Colonial satisfies the interests and purchasing urges of even the hardest to please travelers.

After a long day of discovering the diversions available in the old city, finding a cozy spot amid the narrow cobblestone streets to relax and enjoy the lull that sets in with dusk is not a hard task to accomplish. Romantic courtyard restaurants and pubs offer the respite you'll need before setting out later in the evening should you decide to take advantage of the area's livelier nighttime entertainment choices. Once again, the Ciudad Colonial comes through for everyone. Karaoke singers, club-goers, and jazz enthusiasts have no worries; you will be satisfied.

The Ciudad Colonial of Santo Domingo is the most glorious of the "must-sees" in the capital and should not be missed.

(Parque Colón

This park (Calle El Conde and Arzobispo Meriño) is a good place to start your tour of the New World's first city. It is a central meeting point for locals and tourists alike. It stands in front of the first cathedral in the hemisphere, has a statue of Christopher Columbus, and is abuzz with activity. Pigeons flit about, as do gadget hawkers, tour guides, and shoeshine boys. This is by far the best spot for people-watching, and the sidewalk cafés are always full with people taking full advantage of the vantage point.

(Fortaleza Ozama

Fortaleza Ozama (Calle de las Damas, tel. 809/686-0222, 9 A.M.–6:30 P.M. Mon.–Sat., 9 A.M.–4 P.M. Sun., US$0.50) was built in 1502 and underwent many changes and alterations for the next two centuries. From its prime position on a steep hill overlooking the mouth of the Ozama River, the Spanish launched conquests to Jamaica, Cuba, South America, and Mexico. It served as the first line of defense against attackers with its huge cannons, some of which are still aiming ominously at the waters below. Until the 1970s it served many functions, including as a military post and a prison, until it was opened to the public.

© ANA CHAVIER CAAMAÑO

Plaza Colón

Inside the walls of the fort, the looming Torre del Homenaje (Tower of Homage), evoking classic Spanish castle design, is the oldest portion of the fort and has walls two meters thick. A climb to the top, up the narrow stairwells, is rewarded with a 360-degree view of the city. Also on-site is El Polvorín (The Powder House), which acted as the artillery and ammunition house. Standing in the middle of the walled yard is a bronze statue of Gonzalo Fernandez de Oviedo, a famous historical chronicler who was put in charge of the fort; he lived and died there. His room was on the second floor of the fort and was turned into a prison cell after his death.

Optional and informative tours are offered by the guards at the front gate of the fort for about US$4 per person and given in Spanish, English, and French.

Calle de las Damas

In front of the Fortaleza Ozama and running north to the Plaza de la Hispanidad is **Calle de las Damas** (Street of the Ladies), the oldest paved street in the New World. It was constructed in 1502 for the wife of Diego Columbus so that she and her lady friends could go for afternoon strolls without mussing their dresses. **Plaza de María de Toledo** is a connecting passageway between Calle de las Damas and Calle Isabel La Católica, and was named for Diego Columbus's wife.

Along the Calle de las Damas is the *reloj del sol* (sundial) that was built for the royalty who lived in the Museo de las Casas Reales, which is directly in front of it. It's perfectly positioned so that a mere glance from the royal windows would reveal the time of day.

Panteón Nacional

Built in 1747 as a Jesuit church, the Panteón Nacional (Calle de las Damas and Mercedes, 9 A.M.–5 P.M. Tues.–Sun., free) served mostly as a warehouse and a theater until 1958, when Rafael Trujillo had it converted into a shrine for the country's most illustrious people. No doubt, he had selfish forethought of a memorial to himself, an idea that never materialized.

Spanish dictator Francisco Franco donated the central chandelier. Today, some of the country's most influential people and political figures are honored here and entombed behind marble walls. The building is constructed entirely of massive limestone blocks with a neoclassical facade. Shorts, tank tops, and sneakers are discouraged.

Plaza de la Hispanidad

Much larger than Plaza Colón, the Plaza de la Hispanidad is another good spot for people-watching. Located in front of the Alcázar de Colón, this very sunny plaza's northwestern side is lined with buildings that were built in the 16th century and now have restaurants and bars in them. These establishments put their tables out on the sidewalk, making it a wonderful place to lounge with a beer at sunset, but it can be very hot during the day as there is virtually no shade.

Just down the hill, in back of the Alcázar de Colón, is the **Puerto de San Diego.** It was built in 1571 and was the original main gate to the city. Some remnants can still be seen of the original wall that was erected to protect Santo Domingo from attackers rising from the river.

Monasterio de San Francisco

Sitting now in ruins is the Monasterio de San Francisco (Calle Hostos and Calle Emiliano Tejere), built in the early part of the 1500s for the first order of the Franciscan friars to come to the island. While it once was a glorious structure, originally with three connecting chapels, it underwent some disastrous events. First it was looted and then torched by Sir Francis Drake when he seized the city in 1586. It was restored but suffered earthquakes in 1673 and 1751; both times it was rebuilt. Its grisliest usage was when it served as an insane asylum from 1881 to the early 1930s (when a hurricane finally blew through). The chains used to hold the "patients" can still be seen. It was never restored. Now performances are staged amid the dramatically well-lit rubble in one of the oldest neighborhoods in Santo Domingo.

Ruinas del Hospital San Nicolás de Barí

A few blocks south of the Monasterio de San Francisco are the Ruinas del Hospital San Nicolás de Barí (Calle Hostos). They are the ruins of the first hospital built in the New World. The order to build came in 1503 by Governor Nicolás de Ovando. The design is in the classic form of a Latin cross, and it fared better than the monastery despite enduring the same catastrophes. Then in 1911 it suffered dire damage at the hands of a hurricane, forcing it to be felled as it was deemed a hazard to pedestrians.

Parque de Independencia

At the end of Calle El Conde, the Parque de Independencia (Independence Park) is the juncture of old and new Santo Domingo. It marks historical events and commemorates the long battle for independence. At the entrance to the Parque de Independencia is the **Puerto del Conde,** named for the Conde (Count) de Peñalba, who led the resistance to the Brit-

ish invasion in 1655. This is also the site of a march for independence that occurred in 1844 to overthrow the occupying forces from Haiti, thereby securing their independent republic and raising the Dominican flag for the first time. The **Altar de la Patria** is the resting place of three of the Dominican Republic's most celebrated figures: Juan Pablo Duarte, Francisco del Rosario Sánchez, and Ramón Matías Mella.

Puerta de la Misericordia

The Gate of Mercy (Arzobispo Portes, near Palo Hincado) was erected as the western door to the city and is part of the original walls. It got its name because of the way some of the less fortunate locals would flock to it for protection during hurricanes and earthquakes. This is also where the first shot was fired on February 27, 1844, in the struggle for independence from neighboring Haiti.

Casa de Francia

The former home of Hernán Cortés, the

honoring the founding fathers of the Dominican Republic at the Parque de Independencia

© ANA CHAVIER CAAMAÑO

Casa de Francia (Las Damas 42) is purportedly where he organized his brutal plans for conquering the Aztec nations of what is now modern Mexico. It served as a residence for nearly three centuries until it went through a series of government-owned incarnations and now houses the French Cultural Alliance and French Embassy. Although visitors cannot venture into the building (except for the lobby), walking past you cannot help but admire the facade. It is made of stone and is thought to be from the same designer as the Casa del Cordón.

Casa del Cordón

The House of the Cord (Calle Isabel La Católica at Emiliano Tejera, 8:15 A.M.–4 P.M. daily) is the first European residence in the western hemisphere; it belonged to Diego Colón before he built the Alcázar de Colón. It is named for the stonework on the facade of the house of a sash and cord. It is also the alleged spot where Drake went to a forced line-up of the women of Santo Domingo; he then collected all of their fine jewelry. The house is now home to the Banco Popular.

Hostal Nicolás de Ovando

Perhaps one of the most charming homes of colonial Santo Domingo, the Hostal Nicolás de Ovando (Las Damas at General Luperón) was built in 1509 and the home of Governor Nicolás de Ovando, who is responsible for choosing the site on which Santo Domingo was built (after it had been destroyed by a hurricane in its original location). Christopher Columbus was often a guest of this home and you can be too. It is now a luxurious Sofitel hotel (see *Accommodations*).

【 Catedral Primada de América

The Catedral Primada de América (Calle Arzobispo Meriño, Parque Colón, 9 A.M.–4 P.M. daily, free) had its first stone placed by Diego Columbus himself in 1514. Construction went on until 1540 with many different architects adding to the combination of Gothic, Roman, and baroque styles. Unfortunately, it's hard to

© ANA CHAVIER CAAMAÑO

Catedral Primada de América is the oldest cathedral in the New World.

know exactly what it used to look like inside because when Sir Francis Drake came to town with his greedy band of pirates, they set up camp inside the cathedral and took everything, including what was nailed down, with them when they left. Dominicans are very proud of the fact that this cathedral is widely considered the first cathedral of the New World. Whether that is the historical truth or not is a source of contention that most Dominicans wave off with a patriotic flick of the wrist. Check out the great arching ceilings, sculptures, paintings, and 14 chapels inside. Make sure you're not wearing shorts or a tank top.

Iglesia de Nuestra Señora de las Mercedes

The Iglesia de Nuestra Señora de las Mercedes (Church of Our Lady of Mercy, Las Mercedes at José Reyes, free) is one of the most historical in all of Santo Domingo and one of the most frustrating to get in to see since its hours are notoriously irregular. It was built in the 1530s and was, of course, sacked by Sir Francis Drake. It was reconstructed afterward but it suffered hurricanes and earthquakes as well. Perhaps the most alluring aspect of the church (aside from the fact that it's still standing) is its elaborately carved mahogany altar and pulpit with a demon serpent. Note the cloister adjacent to the church; it is in its original condition.

Iglesia Santa Bárbara

Built in 1574, the Iglesia Santa Bárbara (Calle Isabel La Católica, free) was constructed in honor of the patron saint of the military, so it's a little bit church and a little bit fortress. The baroque structure is an amalgamation of pieces due to, yet again, the sacking that Drake gave it. The rebuilt church was put together like jammed puzzle pieces with three arches, two of which are windowless. Still, these additions are probably what kept it from toppling during some hefty hurricanes through the ages.

Just behind the church is the **Fuerte de Santa Bárbara** (Juan Parra at Av. Mella), which was erected in 1570 as a security defense for the city but was to no avail when Drake blew through town. He easily captured it in 1586, and the rubble goes to show how quickly it went down.

Iglesia y Convento de los Dominicos

Just south of El Conde is the **Dominican Church and Convent** (Av. Duarte at Padre Billini, free). It was built in 1510 and is the first convent of the Dominican order in the Americas. The outside of the building is an imposing structure, built of stone and brick with Spanish tile accents. Above the great wooden doors is a vine-like ornamentation leading up to the signature central round window at the top of the facade. Pope Paul III visited in 1538, granting the title of university after being impressed by the theology and teachings of the church. Hence, it became the first university of the New World. It was here that Father Bartolomé de las Casas did much of his famous writing about the Spanish atrocities committed against the Taíno people. Once inside the rosary chapel, don't forget to look up. The unique ceiling depicts classical gods and astrological figures on a zodiac wheel.

Capilla de Nuestra Señora de los Remedios

The chapel (Calle de las Damas at Las Mercedes) was built in the 1500s in classic Gothic style, intended as a private chapel and mausoleum for the prominent families of Santo Domingo, like the Ovando family. This tiny church is unmistakable as you walk along Calle de las Damas, with its brick facade and three arched belfries. It was rebuilt in 1884 after being shut down for a short period because it was pronounced unsafe. Today, masses are held there.

Museo de las Casas Reales

Constructed in the 16th century in Renaissance style, the Museum of the Royal Houses (Calle de las Damas, tel. 809/682-4202, 9 A.M.–5 P.M. daily, US$1) was the Palace of the Governor and the Audiencia Real (Royal Court), which was a panel of judges created to check the power of the governor. The museum has an excellent re-creation of the colonial era using real colonial-period objects, including treasures recovered from sunken Spanish galleons, gilded furniture, art, and replicas of the *Niña,* the *Pinta,* and the *Santa María.* Each room has been re-created according to its original decor and usage. Taíno artifacts are on display as well. If you only have time for one museum, make this one it.

Museo Alcázar de Colón

Museo Alcázar de Colón (Plaza de la Hispanidad, 9 A.M.–5 P.M. Tues.–Sun., US$1.75) was a house that was originally used by Diego Columbus, Christopher's son, and his wife, María de Toledo. When they left the house in the early 1500s, they left it to friends who took good care of it for nearly 100 years. After that, it became a prison and a warehouse even until it was abandoned and actually became the city dump at one point. It is unbelievable when you walk through it today that at one point only a couple of walls were left standing. The restoration took three turns from 1957 to 1992, and the building that stands today is a successful attempt at historical accuracy. It is filled with items that were said to have once belonged to Columbus and his family.

Larimar Museum

On the ground floor of this museum (Calle Isabel La Católica 54, tel. 809/689-6605, www.larimarmuseum.com, 9 A.M.–6 P.M. daily, free) is a shop with a wonderful selection of good quality larimar and amber jewelry with a very friendly and helpful staff. Remember; all prices are negotiable. The museum is upstairs, and if you ask, one of the staff members can give you a guided tour for free; they are very knowledgeable. There are encased examples of the rare pectolite mined only in the Dominican Republic. Exhibits explain everything from the mining procedure to how the jewelry is made. Signage is in Spanish and English.

Museo Mundo de Ámbar

In the Amber World Museum (Calle Arzobispo Meriño 452 and Restauración, tel. 809/682-3309, www.amberworldmuseum.com, 9 A.M.–6 P.M., US$2) you'll see impressive examples of the ancient resin for which the Dominican Republic is famous. Along with an explanation of the formation of amber, which often trapped insects, leaves, and even some lizards, there is a beautiful display of some examples of such findings. You can watch an audiovisual tutorial on the mining process and on how amber jewelry is made. Signage is in English, German, and Spanish.

Quinta Dominica

This very small museum (Padre Billini at 19 de Marzo, 9:30 A.M.–6 P.M. Mon.–Sat., 9 A.M.–2 P.M. Sun., free) doesn't have a permanent collection but has an impressive array of ever-changing exhibits. Colonial art is the main focus but not always what is on the menu. Past exhibits have included modern metal sculptures and religious mosaic art. The building is a renovated colonial home with a very pretty garden courtyard perfect for a rest from the bustle of the street. Signage is in Spanish only, and there is rarely literature available, but it doesn't impede the enjoyment of the art.

Museo de la Atarazana

This museum (Calle Vincente Celestino Duarte, tel. 809/682-5834, 9 A.M.–6 P.M. Thurs.–Tues., US$1) is filled with sunken treasures recovered from Spanish galleons that went down in the waters off the coast of the Dominican Republic, particularly the *Concepción,* which went down in the Bahía de Samaná. Coins, crucifixes, spoons, swords, plates, and silver bars, among other things, have all been found and are on display here. Signs are in Spanish and English.

CENTRAL SANTO DOMINGO
Plaza de la Cultura

At the Plaza de la Cultura (Calle Pedro Henríquez Ureña) there are three museums, the national theater, and the national library.

Museo del Hombre Dominicano (Museum of the Dominican Man, tel. 809/687-3622,

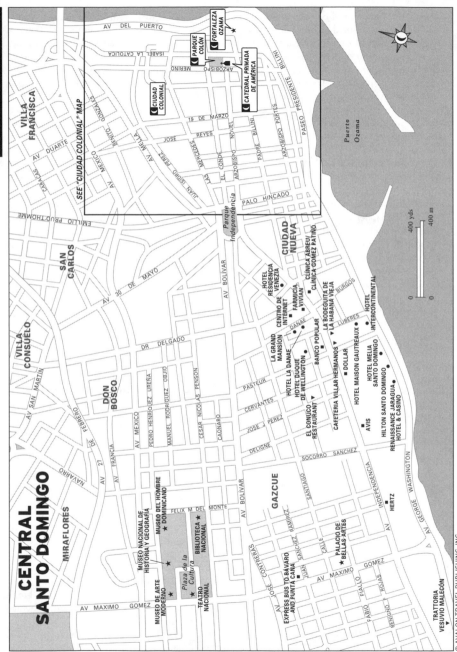

CENTRAL
SANTO DOMINGO

© AVALON TRAVEL PUBLISHING, INC.

10 A.M.–5 P.M. Tues.–Sun., US$0.75) has an impressive collection of Taíno artifacts, including tools, pottery, and other items from their daily lives. There is a section devoted to the Carnaval traditions of the Dominican Republic, one for the African influence on Dominican culture, an exhibit on the effects slavery had on the history of the island, and an example of a typical rural Dominican domicile. Unfortunately, signage is all in Spanish. Make sure to ask for the English-speaking guides available at the front desk. Staff won't offer them up freely; you have to request the service. Many things were unmarked, so a guide would be very helpful. Tips are appreciated. There is a small café on the fourth floor, and elevators make this an accessible museum.

The **Museo de Arte Moderno** (tel. 809/685-2154, 10 A.M.–5 P.M. Tues.–Sun., US$0.30). Located right next to the Museum of the Dominican Man, this multi-level museum is an exciting step into the modern world after all that history. Paintings and sculptures by well-known and emerging Dominican artists are on display in a wonderful setting. As you enter, you're on the second level, which contains temporary exhibits, as does the bottom floor. The levels above contain the permanent exhibits. Save a good amount of time to wander and ponder.

The **Museo Nacional de Historia y Geografía** (tel. 809/686-6668, 10 A.M.–5 P.M. Tues.–Sun., US$0.20) is conveniently organized in chronological order according to time periods and includes exhibits on Haitian/Dominican relations as well as the Trujillo years, with many of his personal effects (it is a little creepy). This is not the best of the museums in the bunch, but it's worth a stop if you're in the area.

Palacio Nacional

The National Palace (Av. México at Av. 30 de Marzo, tel. 809/687-3191) is open to tours only by appointment and isn't a light visit. If you're granted a tour, dress your best. No shorts or flip-flops. Dominicans dress well for business appointments and expect you to do the same.

This huge palace covers an entire block and is constructed of roseate marble from Samaná by Italian neoclassical design. It was inaugurated in 1947 and is ornately decorated inside with gilt mirrors, mirrors inlaid with gold, and mahogany furniture. The most impressive area is the Room of Caryatids; 44 sculptures of draped women rise like columns, reminiscent of Versailles.

Palacio de Bellas Artes

The Palace of Fine Arts (Av. Máximo Gómez, tel. 809/687-9131) is an impressively large theater that holds special performance events including the symphony, dance productions, and exhibits. Events are quite sporadic, so look in the local papers, consult with the concierge at your hotel, or call for a schedule.

PARQUE MIRADOR DEL ESTE
◖ Faro a Colón

Located in the Parque Mirador del Este (Eastern Lookout Park), the Lighthouse of Columbus (tel. 809/592-1492, 9 A.M.–5 P.M. Tues.–Sun.) costs a lot of money, was built in controversy, and houses controversy within as well. On the eastern bank of the Río Ozama, this gigantic structure stands 10 stories high and is in the shape of a cross. When there is sufficient power (almost never) or on special occasions, the high-powered lights along the top shine into the night, forming a white cross in the sky. With one flick of a switch, the *faro* can cause a blackout throughout Santo Domingo and has become a rather tired joke among the locals.

However, inside the structure is what is truly interesting. In the midsection of the cross is a tomb, guarded by soldiers in all-white uniforms, containing what is thought by many to be Columbus's remains. This is a controversial topic, as Spain and Italy both claim to have his remains elsewhere. Throughout the rest of the long structure are various displays of the indigenous people from many different nations—an ironic juxtaposition with the highly glorified and proudly displayed remains of Columbus.

Los Tres Ojos

The Three Eyes (Parque Mirador del Este, 9 A.M.–5 P.M. daily, US$1.75) has been a tourist draw for a very long time. Many tour groups stop here. Inside are caverns containing limestone sinkholes. A very steep staircase leads down to the underground caverns. Inside it is not a claustrophobia-inducing cave, but rather very tall and wide open. While it is called "The Three Eyes" there are actually four pools (sinkholes) with stalactites all around. The pools are filled with very clear and frigid water. In the deepest pool the "Dominican Tarzan" will do a demonstration, climbing to a high point and jumping off into the depths, for a tip of course. You can cross the third pool for an additional US$0.35 to the fourth hidden "eye." It is quite a tourist trap, but a rather pretty one at that.

Acuario Nacional

Just south of the Parque Mirador del Este is the National Aquarium (Av. España, 9:30 A.M.–5:30 P.M. Tues.–Sun., US$1), which is best saved if you have kids to entertain. There is a tank with a Plexiglas underwater walkway where kids love to see the rays, turtles, and huge fish "fly" above them. Also on-site is a shark tank and turtle-breeding project. Kids have fun; adults may find it unimpressive.

NORTHERN SANTO DOMINGO

☖ Jardín Botánico Nacional

The National Botanical Garden (Av. República de Columbia, 9 A.M.–6 P.M. daily, US$1.25) is a lush and expansive display of many different kinds of plants—aquatics, orchids, bromeliads, a bamboo garden, many kinds of trees, and even a Japanese garden. This botanical garden is well taken care of, and there is a trolley (US$1.25) that you can catch every 30 minutes. It drives you around and you hear explanations of the different areas in many languages. It is wonderful to enjoy the shady grounds and serenity, which you can't find in many places in the very frenetic Santo Domingo.

While there, visit the **Ecological Museum** (9 A.M.–4 P.M. daily, US$0.35), which has encased displays of the many ecosystems of the Dominican Republic, including the deserts, mangroves, mountains, and beaches. This portion is air-conditioned. Children enjoy this park, especially the trolley (it looks like a little train) and the wide open spaces for running.

Parque Zoológico Nacional

The National Zoological Park (Av. los Reyes Católicos, 9 A.M.–6 P.M. Tues.–Sun., US$1) is your opportunity to to see the rare solenodon, if you missed seeing it in the wild. There is a rather impressive array of endemic and exotic animals. Watch the aquatic birds in their simulated lake, or the crocodiles in a makeshift pond. Visitors without herpetophobia will enjoy the snake exhibit. There is even a barless tiger enclosure that makes animal lovers breathe a little easier. But many of the other animals are not so lucky and are in less-than-optimal cages. Taking a taxi (make sure to arrange for the return trip with the driver) is best as the zoo is in a remote corner of the city.

SOUTHWEST SANTO DOMINGO

Parque Mirador del Sur

The Southern Lookout Park (Av. Mirador del Sur) is popular with the yuppies of Santo Domingo. You'll find food vendors, shaded paths, and broad avenues, which are closed to traffic for three hours in the early morning and after dinner so that joggers, rollerbladers, and bicyclists can have free reign. The park has a wealth of limestone caves, some of which have been turned into restaurants and bars.

Entertainment and Events

NIGHTLIFE

Santo Domingo boasts a great nightlife scene, from casinos to pubs and karaoke bars to dance clubs. Most dance clubs stay open until early in the morning (anywhere from 3 A.M. to 6 A.M.) and feature Latin music mixed in with American and European club-style dance music. Women traveling solo or with other women should know that it is not uncommon to be asked to dance by a man you don't know. If you do not wish to dance with him simply say *"no gracias."* Even though Dominican men are very persistent and might not take your first answer, simply repeating it politely will probably work. Still, it is best for women to keep track of each other (as in any city). Many establishments have a dress code that doesn't allow you to wear jeans, T-shirts, or tennis shoes. If you don't abide by these dress codes, you run the risk of being turned away at the door.

The Ciudad Colonial in particular has a plethora of nighttime entertainment options worth visiting. Independently owned bars and restaurants are tucked into the centuries-old buildings all along the cobbled streets. It is a major part of the charm that massive corporations have been held at bay this long. But they are encroaching. One popular café has opened its worldwide chain doors directly across from the oldest cathedral in the hemisphere, making history and hard-rocking corporations strange bedfellows.

It is a relatively safe area to walk around in the evening, provided you do not walk alone and stay on the well-lighted streets. Take a taxi

MUSIC AND DANCE – DOMINICAN STYLE

MERENGUE

As the national music and dance of the Dominican Republic, the merengue has a colorful history. Actually, the dance has several histories, depending on whom you talk to. One story about the development of the merengue claims the dance was the result of a sympathetic group of partying villagers who, out of sympathy for a war hero who had just returned home with a limp, danced as though they too had been wounded. Another story says that the dance was based upon the foot-dragging movement that resulted from slaves whose feet were chained together as they cut sugarcane in the fields. Another theory asserts that merengue's roots can be found in the African and French minuet. The idea is that slaves who observed the ballroom dances of their masters adapted their own version set to the music of drumbeats. Where their masters' dances were on the stiff side, however, the slaves developed their movements to have a more upbeat rhythm. And yet one more possibility is that merengue was spawned from a type of Cuban music called *upa upa*.

Today, merengue has several variants, including the more formal ballroom merengue and the contemporary club merengue, which incorporates the hips more in its movements. Famous merengue musicians include Sergio Vargas and Fernandito Villalona.

BACHATA

Bachata, another popular music and dance in the Dominican Republic, originated in the more rural areas of the country. It is a guitar-based music derived from the bolero. *Bachata* tends to be a bit on the more dramatic side, dealing with lost love, lost hope, and betrayal, all in a fog of heavy drinking and sex – with a touch of humor and/or romance. In general, the music is almost a kind of blues of the Caribbean. Juan Luis Guerra is a Dominican musician famous for *bachata*, as well as for merengue, and for combining the two genres.

late at night, though (whether alone or with others). Taxi rates go up (not much) around midnight, but it's worth your safety; haggling for a price is harder at night.

Dance Clubs

The hotel bars along the Malecón have some of the hottest dance clubs in the city. Besides tourists, they are also frequented by a lot of the wealthy youth of Santo Domingo. Most clubs have a US$5–10 cover charge depending on whether it's live music or a DJ.

Of the hotel bars, **Jubilee** (Hotel Jaragua, Av. George Washington 367, tel. 809/221-2222, 9 P.M.–3 A.M. Tues.–Sat.) is the hottest and the swankiest. This is popular not only with tourists, but with many wealthy Dominicans dressed in their best "clubbing gear" and spending a lot on fancy drinks.

Guácara Taína (Av. Mirador del Sur, tel. 809/533-0671, 9 P.M.–3 A.M.) is a very unique experience and was quite popular, although now it is more frequented by tourists and tour groups. It is in the belly of a massive cave—so massive that it can hold 2,000 people and has multiple dance floors. You should definitely take a taxi here. Dance the salsa and merengue amidst stalactites and stalagmites.

Loft Lounge and Dance Club (Tiradentes 44, Naco, tel. 809/732-4016, www.loft.com.do) has various events like live merengue, salsa, jazz, and pop music, which are all listed on its website. Casual but nice dress is required.

Montecristo Café (Calle José Amador Soler and Abraham Lincoln, tel. 809/542-5000, 6 P.M.–5 A.M.) is a very popular spot. Named after the fictional Count of Monte Cristo, this English-style pub re-creates the story of this character through its decoration. There are different activities like video nights, wine-tastings, raffles, and of course, dancing to rock, merengue, and salsa. Appetizers are available.

Jet Set (Independencia 2253, tel. 809/535-4145, 10 P.M.–late) is a semi-casual place to hear good salsa and merengue. Sometimes the music is live. The dance floor fills after midnight.

Bars and Pubs

Atarazana 9 (Ciudad Colonial, Atarazana 9, tel. 809/877-6258, 9 P.M.–3 A.M., free) is just off Plaza de la Hispanidad in a safe area for tourist bar-hopping. Enjoy live music in this very historic building. The drinks are great.

Abacus (Ciudad Colonial, Hostos 350 and Luperón, tel. 809/333-7272) is a good place for a stylish cocktail with your friends. The lounge has couches and soft lighting with DJ music.

Parada 77 (Ciudad Colonial, Calle Isabel La Católica 225, tel. 809/221-7880, 9 P.M.–3 A.M. Mon.–Fri., 9 P.M.–"infinity" Sat.–Sun.) is not a typical tourist bar at all, and it's not for everyone. This small bar is at the far end of Isabela La Católica and is a budget option for the younger art crowd. It got its name from being bus stop (*parada*) number 77, so they never changed it. Not fancy in the least, it is almost completely devoid of furniture save for the bar stools and a few tables and chairs; management says this "encourages dancing." The only pictures allowed on the walls are of revolutionary thinkers (like Charlie Chaplin, Che Guevara, and Bob Marley), and the rest is decorated with the graffiti, poetry, and artwork of patrons from all over the world clear up to the ceiling. Just ask for a pen from the very friendly bartender and leave your mark—I did. An eclectic variety of mostly alternative and world music is played, as well as merengue and salsa on occasion. The young-adult crowd is gay-friendly. There is an empty leg cast hanging on the wall that the manager said had "a long story" that would "go untold." It's that kind of odd Dominican humor that appeals. Coming here is a way to experience a different but very real part of Santo Domingo that tourists rarely see.

In stark contrast to Parada 77 (and at the opposite end of the same street), **K-ramba** (Ciudad Colonial, Calle Isabel La Católica 1, tel. 809/688-3587, 10 A.M.–3 A.M. Mon.–Sat.) is a very popular tourist bar owned by an Austrian expat. There is indoor and outdoor seating and rock music is played. Many tourists feel safe going here late at night.

Le Cellier Bar a Vin wine bar (Malecón,

Calle Numero Dos and Malecón, tel. 809/689-8640, 6 P.M.–late, closed Sun.) is a half block off of the Malecón in what could be a great place. It is decorated like a real wine cellar with dusty bottles and an uneven floor. It serves appetizers, desserts, and empanadas. Tuesday and Thursday are "romance nights," and on Thursday women drink house wine for free 6–10 P.M. There's live music Monday and Wednesday. If it weren't for the horribly inattentive staff, this would be a real gem. However, it is a great location for ducking out of the heat and car exhaust fumes after walking along the Malecón for a while. Here's hoping they get their act together.

Walking past **Proud Mary** (Ciudad Colonial, Av. Duarte 55, tel. 809/689-6611, 8 P.M.–late, closed Mon.) you'll notice one thing right off the bat. There is no Latin beat pumping from inside. That might make some keep walking, but to many it's a magnetic pull. Maria, Spanish expat and owner of this 40-person-capacity bar, is indeed proud to say that she plays blues, jazz, and soft rock and that you will *never* hear Latin music coming from her stereo. Maria made the bar herself; literally every piece of decor was hand-crafted by her or a family member, and she enjoys talking to the expats and foreigners that hang out here (she has a few languages under her belt). It is a dimly lighted, wonderfully welcoming place with bar stools, some tall tables made of old cable spools, and a small couch area in the back. The music is uncommon in this merengue-or-die town, and played loud enough to enjoy but low enough to meet new friends. The full bar has good prices. Dress is casual.

8 Puertas (Ciudad Colonial, Calle José Reyes) caters to the young, hipster alternative crowd. From the street it appears modern, highly designed, and hip. There isn't a lot of furniture, but it does have a very sleek bar with bartenders working fast to keep up with the crowd jamming to the alternative American tunes. It gets harder to order a drink the later it gets because so many people have shown up to join in with the cool kids. It's gay-friendly.

Gay and Lesbian Nightlife

Santo Domingo is a very metropolitan city. Entertainment options for the increasingly open gay community are becoming more stable. In past years, gay establishments would have the life span of a bumblebee, but now, with an ever-growing out gay community, establishments are able to set up camp and stay (for longer anyway). Santo Domingo celebrated its first gay pride parade, with nearly 600 participants, in 2001.

If you'd like to have a nice cocktail in a comfortable environment and then have a change of scenery to do some dancing well into the night, head to **Punto** and **Arena** (Ciudad Colonial, Las Mercedes 313, www.grupoarena.com). Punto (free) is a lounge on the first floor of a beautifully renovated mansion, and although the owners covered an originally open-air courtyard, they did not hurt the overall design. It is utterly charming. Iron tables and chairs are collected in the courtyard, which is filled with plants and romantically lit. There is a pool table in an alcove and a full bar with a friendly staff. After your drinks and conversation at Punto, head upstairs to Arena, by far the best place for dancing in the gay and lesbian scene of Santo Domingo (midnight–late, US$5.50). Here you'll find a huge dance floor with one of the best DJs around spinning everything from techno to house, salsa, merengue, hip-hop, and funk. It caters to both men and women and is straight-friendly. Casual dress is acceptable (that means no shorts). After the party is over, you'll find taxis lined up outside.

Jay Dee's bar (Ciudad Colonial, José Reyes 10, tel. 809/333-5905, midnight–4 A.M. Wed.–Sun., closed Mon. and Tues., US$3.50), owned by an American expat, is popular with locals and tourists alike. Not as upscale and trendy as Arena, it has been in operation for nearly 10 years, a very long time in Santo Domingo gay bar years. Friday and Saturday nights the small dance floor can get very crowded (and really hot). The music is American pop, club, and Latin. Sometimes there are drag and dancer shows on the weekends. The cover cost gets you a free *cuba libre* (rum and Coke) or Presidente (beer).

CARNAVAL AND ITS MASKS

Carnaval, generally observed throughout the Dominican Republic during the month of February (though for some areas, March), is steeped in tradition and historical significance. This Catholic-based, pre-Lenten festival was brought to the island by the Spanish and throughout the centuries has blended with the customs of Taíno and African cultures. It has become a celebration of life in a country whose people have such a rich cultural and diverse heritage. Different regions tend to have their own customs and rituals pertaining to the occasion, but all exhibit a wealth of spirit and creativity, with local folklore coming alive in the form of masks and the characters adopted by those who don them.

La Vega is one of the most popular places to experience Carnaval, which it has been practicing for over 500 years. The celebration occurs every weekend during the month of February, culminating on the last Sunday of the month. Preparations – particularly the planning and crafting of costumes – begin months in advance. Registered groups of at least 10-15 people team up to create a theme for themselves and carry on together in the streets. La Vega's signature character is the *diablo cojuelo* (mischevious devil). Generally, the masks tend to be on the more grotesque side, with horns and elaborate facial features. People wearing these demon-esque masks run through the crowds walloping folks with inflated pig or cow bladders and whips. Other sub-events – like music and food and dancing – are often scheduled throughout the month, but the costumes and raucous, prankish behavior of the people sporting them truly make Carnaval a spectacular celebration.

Santiago is also host to a very popular Carnaval, one of the more traditional celebrations.

Parades and mask-making competitions often get things started. Masks here tend to display a more animal-like theme, with two styles in particular: From the La Joya sector, masks sport horns aplenty, while the Los Pepines masks have a more duck-like appearance. The traditional *lechon* (pig) character originated in Santiago.

In Santiago, as well as in La Vega, the celebrations occur on two levels, the public and the private. While the street festivals with their dance troupes and parades are the main attractions, private businesses and clubs often conduct their own parties as well.

Most masks are derived from the theme of *el diablo* (the devil) but are known by different names and vary in depiction in different regions. The *diablo cojuelo* is the lame devil, named so because, having fallen when he was banished to earth, he walks with a limp. Those who wear the mask of this character must hobble about the streets. *Cachuas,* in **Cabral,** are horned devils. In **Monte Cristi,** the theme of *civiles* and *toros* presides, where the *toros* run about chasing down the *civiles*. In Santo Domingo and other areas men dressed as large-breasted women flirt with the crowds, who yell at them, *"Roba la gallina!"* which means, "Steal the hen!"

The largest and most spectacular Carnaval is celebrated in **Santo Domingo.** People from all over the country – and the world – commence to memorialize the day the Dominican Republic won its independence from Haiti. Costumes and celebrators of all regional backgrounds come together in the capital, where devils, duck-faced monsters, *toros,* transvestites, and horn-headed creatures run amok in the joyful spirit of their country.

The Sports Bar (Ciudad Colonial, Palo Hincado 114, tel. 809/333-5622, www.thesportsbar.blogspot.com, 8 P.M.–2 A.M., Wed.–Sun.) is a neighborhood pool hall owned by an American expat. Here, the drinks are cheap, the atmosphere is good, and the people (lots of locals) are friendly.

CASINOS

Most of the hotels along and near the Malecón have casinos in them. Casinos in the Dominican Republic are generally much smaller and have fewer games than the ones you find in the posh hotels of North America. Some major ones in Santo Domingo are the **Hotel InterContinental** (Av. George Washington 218, tel. 809/221-0000, www.intercontinental.com/santodomingo), **El Napolitano** (Av. George Washington 101, tel. 809/687-1131), and **Hotel Santo Domingo Casino** (Av. Independencia, tel. 809/221-1511).

They are generally open 4 P.M.–4 A.M. You can play with Dominican pesos or U.S. dollars (preferred). The odds are generally similar to Las Vegas odds, meaning profits kept by the casinos and winnings that walk away with the gamblers are similar in Santo Domingo. Just like in Vegas, you'll find blackjack, craps, and slot machines. You'll find video poker, too, but often it is a Caribbean version of the kind you find in Vegas. Texas Hold 'em and Seven Card Stud are missing from the poker atmosphere and are replaced by a Caribbean version. Stay clear of Keno and Super Keno—the odds are horrendous. While tipping the dealer may feel like a custom to you, it is not expected here as casinos have their dealers pool their tips to be evenly distributed among the other dealers (if at all). If you have questions, feel free to ask; most dealers speak English.

THEATER AND CINEMA

In the **Teatro Nacional** (National Theater, Plaza de la Cultura, tel. 809/682-7255, US$2–15) you can see performances for an amazingly affordable price. Ballet, symphony, drama, and opera performances are all held here. The ticket office is open 9:30 A.M.–12:30 P.M. and 3:30–6:30 P.M. For show information and times, call the box office, check the weekend edition of the newspaper, or ask the concierge at your hotel.

If sitting in a dark theater on your Caribbean vacation appeals, then **Cinemacentro Dominicano** (Av. George Washington, tel. 809/688-8710) and **Hollywood Diamond Cinemas** (Av. Abraham Lincoln, Diamond Mall, tel. 809/683-1189) both show Hollywood new releases as well as releases from around the world. It could be a good rainy-day option.

FESTIVALS

Carnaval is celebrated throughout the country during the month of February, having its swan song on the last weekend of February or first weekend in March in Santo Domingo. Representatives come from all the other towns with their town-specific costumes to take part in a long parade and street party. The Malecón (Av. George Washington) is closed to traffic; stages, booths, and vendors set up camp for entertainment, and the party doesn't stop until well into the morning. Elaborately decorated floats and expertly designed costumes that won contests in their respective towns all come to be seen in the festivities. The scene along the waterfront explodes with color and jubilation.

Every June the **Latin Music Festival** (tel. 809/487-3802, www.festivalpresidente.com) attracts top-name Latin entertainers and wows crowds for three days of salsa, *bachata,* merengue, *reggaeton,* Latin rock, and jazz. These greats perform for massive crowds at the Olympic Stadium. Big names like Fernando Villalona, Marc Anthony, Sergio Vargas, Jennifer Lopez, and Frank Reyes have performed.

The **Merengue Festival** of Santo Domingo is the largest one of its kind in the whole country, held for two weeks every year at the end of July and beginning of August. Events highlighting the country's signature music take place all over the city but center on the Malecón. The festival starts with a parade of dancers and musicians along the Malecón and includes food, drink, and arts.

Shopping

Santo Domingo is a great place for all your shopping needs. If you're staying in the Ciudad Colonial, you will most likely find those must-haves in the shops on Calle El Conde or while you're walking around in the Ciudad Colonial. If you're willing to hunt for particular items or are looking for something specific, you can check out the shopping malls, flea markets, and high-end boutiques outside the Ciudad Colonial. Perishable items to buy in the Dominican Republic are Dominican rum, cigars, and coffee. If you're looking for longer-lasting mementos, Dominican-made larimar jewelry, amber, and original Dominican art are great choices.

ARTS AND CRAFTS

Most of the paintings that are pushed in your face around all the tourist areas of the Dominican Republic are bright, colorful depictions of rural life duplicated ad nauseam; these are actually Haitian paintings, not of good quality. Most of the crafts available are the heavily duplicated faceless peasant woman dolls and anything made of shells. For the real Dominican deal, you'll need to search harder for the galleries and stores that carry the fine arts and crafts by established and emerging artists.

The Swiss Mine (Ciudad Colonial, Calle El Conde 101, tel. 809/221-1897, 9 A.M.–6 P.M. Mon.–Sat., 9:30 A.M.–3:30 P.M. Sun.) has a good collection of paintings in the back, in addition to the jewelry in the front of the store. Some are Dominican and quite good. If you're looking for guidance in what to buy, ask the Swiss owner for help. She has a good knowledge of what she's selling, many opinions, and advice on the topic.

One-of-a-kind bags and purses are made at **Macuto Bolsos y Accesorios** (Ciudad Colonial, Calle Arzobispo Meriño 258, tel. 809/685-2215, 9 A.M.–6 P.M. daily) right in the back room and are brought out to the front to be sold, even as you shop. Bringing them out one by one is the designer himself,

Caonabo Sanchez. Caonabo uses delightful materials and fabrics in his designs, which are simple and functional. From the petite wrist bag to the large beach tote, the bag you purchase will not have an exact match anywhere in the world. The prices are great, but ask about the sales rack anyway.

What is a Tennessee expat doing in the Dominican Republic? Selling unique art, that's what. **Plaza Toledo Bettye's Galeria** (Ciudad Colonial, Calle Isabel La Católica 163, tel. 809/688-7649, 9 A.M.–6 P.M., closed Tues.) has colorful paintings (the good kind) donning the walls as well as jewelry and home furnishings like mirrors and interesting knickknacks.

Galería de Arte María del Carmen (Ciudad Colonial, Arzobispo Meriño 207, tel. 809/682-7609, 9 A.M.–7 P.M. daily) has been in operation for decades and has a good selection of original paintings. The staff is friendly, helpful, and very knowledgeable about the art pieces and the artists themselves.

BOOKS AND MAPS

Librería Pichardo (Ciudad Colonial, José Reyes at El Conde, 8 A.M.–7 P.M. Mon.–Fri., 8 A.M.–6 P.M. Sat.) has been around a long time. Located half a block off of El Conde, it looks like just a newsstand from the front, but if you go inside, you'll find stacks and stacks of mostly Spanish-language books.

If you're looking for foreign-language dictionaries and maps, **Editorial Duarte** (Ciudad Colonial, Arzobispo Meriño at Mercedes, tel. 809/689-4832, 8 A.M.–7 P.M. Mon.–Fri., 8 A.M.–6 P.M. Sat.) is a good stop to make. It has a good selection of novels in Spanish as well.

Mapas Gaar (Ciudad Colonial, Espaillat at El Conde, tel. 809/688-8004, www.mapas-gaar.com.do, 8:30 A.M.–5:30 P.M. daily) is the best map maker in the Dominican Republic. Its store and offices are on the third floor of an office building just off of Calle El Conde. It has a good selection of regional, city, and road maps.

© ANA CHAVIER CAAMAÑO

Test your bargaining skills at Mercado Modelo.

CLOTHING AND ACCESSORIES

All along El Conde, you'll find various shoe, clothing, and accessory shops—even some great fabric stores. The prices for fabric are very good. Should you want to explore the rest of the city's shopping, the options are endless. But there are a couple of malls and stores worth highlighting. **Plaza Central** (Av. 27 de Febrero and Av. Winston Churchill) has a great variety of services and stores including clothing, music, jewelry, nail salons, and a food court.

For leather goods handmade in the Dominican Republic, head to **Fiori** on the second floor of Plaza Central (tel. 809/567-1298, 9:30 A.M.–7:30 P.M. Mon.–Sat.), which sells women's and men's bags, wallets, belts, and briefcases, all designed in and made from real Dominican leather.

Joyería Gift Shop (Plaza Central, tel. 809/872-0090) has all the typical gift shop items—jewelry, T-shirts, paintings, lacquered frames—but the prices are a bit lower. These are not rock-bottom prices on amber and lari-

mar, but they are better than in the Ciudad Colonial. (To get the same deals that stores give to locals, you have to shop outside the Ciudad Colonial entirely.) This shop is worth a visit if you're coming to the mall, but don't make a special trip. In 2005, the owner was "in the process" of opening a sister store on Calle Isabela La Católica in the Ciudad Colonial. How that will affect prices remains to be seen.

Dominican-owned **Multi Centro La Sirena** (Calle Winston Churchill between Ángel S Cabral and Gustavo Mejía Ricart, tel. 809/682-3107, 8 A.M.–10 P.M. Mon.–Sat., 9 A.M.–8 P.M. Sun.) is a multipurpose department store with everything you will need at great prices. It's an especially good option if you are visiting for an extended amount of time. Inside are household objects, clothing, personal hygiene items and other necessities, and a full-scale grocery store.

Ladies with a severe passion for shoes will have a ball in Santo Domingo. If there is one thing the women in Dominican culture know, it's how to build an outfit from the shoes up. You'll find a lot of shoe stores with great prices on El Conde, but if you're looking for something special and are willing to spend a little more time and money, go to **D'Bertha Shoes** (Calle Mercedes Laura Aguiar 6, tel. 809/482-0914, www.dberthashoes.com). Yes, it is a special taxi ride, but those who love shoes understand the lengths one will go to for the perfect pair of strappy sandals. And chances are you'll find them here. This is a local favorite that has a fantastic selection of styles (high heels and comfort shoes), bags, and belts. The best part? Directly adjacent is the special clearance room filled with shoes at very low prices. The staff is very helpful once they've realized you're a serious shoe-aholic.

JEWELRY

Flor Ámbar Gift Shop (Calle de las Damas 44, tel. 809/687-3793, 9 A.M.–6 P.M.) has a good selection of amber and larimar jewelry as well as other types. Other gift options include paintings, framed butterflies, coral, and fossils. Maps are for sale by the register.

Even if you don't end up buying a piece of larimar jewelry, visiting the **Larimar Museum** (Calle Isabel La Católica, tel. 809/689-6605, www.larimarmuseum.com, 9 A.M.–6 P.M.) will be worth your time. The store, located on the ground floor, has a wonderful selection of good quality pieces, and there's a very educational larimar museum upstairs. The very friendly staff members speak multiple languages and are very knowledgeable. The store also sells a lot of amber pieces.

Be mindful of purchasing jewelry and accessories made from tortoiseshell or coral. Certain species of turtles and coral (especially red coral) are endangered.

MARKETS

Get your haggling hat on! Whether you're just going to dig around, or actually want to purchase something, the **Mercado Modelo** (Av. Mella between Tomás de la Concha and Del Monte y Tejada, 9 A.M.–5 P.M.) is a feast for your eyes and an overload of your senses. Located north of the Ciudad Colonial in a two-story building, this is a true litmus test of your bargaining skills. Wood carvings, Haitian paintings, music, cigars, and jewelry galore are only a small fraction of what you'll find at this market. Definitely dress down to come here, otherwise you'll be a target for high prices. The neighborhood isn't good after sunset.

The **Pulga de Antigüedades** (Ciudad Colonial, Plaza de María de Toledo, Calle General Luperón, 9 A.M.–4 P.M. Sun.) is a great flea market where prices are marked a lot higher with the expectation that you'll haggle.

CIGARS

Despite the preconception that Cubans are not to be competed with, many cigar aficionados would argue that Dominican cigars are the best in the world. Whatever the official word, they are readily available, and choosing some to take home can be a fun task. A full box can run up to US$120, but definitely shop around first.

Boutique del Fumador (Ciudad Colonial, El Conde 109, tel. 809/685-6425, 9 A.M.–7 P.M. Mon.–Sat., 10 A.M.–3:30 P.M. Sun.) is a factory outlet for Caoba cigars located right on the Plaza Colón; you can watch the cigars being rolled.

To simply purchase cigars, **Taíno Cigars Shop** (Ciudad Colonial, Calle Isabel La Católica 52, tel. 809/221-5684, 9 A.M.–5 P.M.) offers fair prices on many cigar brands and accessories.

MUSIC

You will most definitely see men roaming the streets with stacks of merengue, *bachata,* and salsa CDs for purchase. These are pirated copies. To be on the safe side, head to El Conde, where you will find good, reputable music shops (and the CDs will actually have music on them!). **Musicalia Outlet** (Ciudad Colonial, El Conde, tel. 809/221-8445, 9 A.M.–12:30 P.M. and 2–5 P.M. Mon.–Sat.) has a good selection of many different genres.

Sports and Recreation

Baseball is not just the national sport, it's the national obsession. The country is famous for producing some of the world's best players. Many Dominicans follow the Dominican teams religiously from the end of October through January and in the off-season turn their attentions to the U.S. season. Many "hometown" boys who spent their lives playing stickball in the streets go on to hone their skills playing for the Dominican teams and then, with any luck, get snatched up by the Major Leagues from the United States, so watching American baseball can give a great sense of national pride. If you are in town during the baseball season, it would be a shame to miss such a huge piece of Dominican culture and identity; see a game at the **Estadio Quisqueya** (Av. Tiradentes at San Cristóbal, tel. 809/540-5772, US$1.50–15). Vendors sell snacks and drinks with agility and breakneck speed. Experiencing a game in this stadium is a quick way to get to know complete strangers. Excited hugs often are exchanged with whomever is nearest when a good play is made. It is a great example of how happy and passionate Dominicans are in general. There are six teams in the Dominican Republic and two call Santo Domingo home base—the Tigres del Licey (Tigers of Licey) and Leones de Escogido (Lions of the Chosen One). The rivalry between the two is similar to the New York Yankees and Boston Red Sox. You can usually get tickets just by showing up before the game. Game times are 5 P.M. Sunday and 8 P.M. Tuesday, Wednesday, Friday, and Saturday.

Horse racing takes place in the **Hipódromo V Centenario** (Km 14.5 on the Autopista de las Américas, tel. 809/687-6060, free) which is halfway to Las Américas airport. Races start at 3 P.M. Tuesday, Thursday, and Saturday.

If you thought baseball was at the crux of Dominican culture then you've never seen **cockfighting.** It's been around longer and is taken very seriously. Admittedly, it is not for everyone. A cockfight can be over in the flap of a wing, or it can be a bloody battle lasting up to 15 minutes. The **Coliseo Gallístico Alberto Bonetti Burgos** (Av. Luperón, near the Herrera airport, tel. 809/565-3844, US$8–19) has matches held on Wednesday and Friday at 6:30 P.M. and Saturday at 3 P.M. This is the nicest *gallera* in the country, big and air-conditioned. Fighting cocks are treasured birds. Their owners have pampered them their entire lives, fed them with the best grains, and exercised them daily. The cocks are carried in the crook of the owner's arm like a crown being taken to a king, almost as if what is about to happen is all incredibly civilized. But fights are often to the death.

Accommodations

CIUDAD COLONIAL

Most visitors to Santo Domingo prefer to stay in the Ciudad Colonial because many of the accommodations here are filled with charm and beauty. The enchanting courtyards and well-restored rooms within the converted colonial buildings brim with history and a romantic ambience that is impossible to resist. The typical Spanish brick archways and wrought-iron balconies decorated with flowers overlook cobblestone streets. There is the added bonus of being within walking distance of a majority of the city's historical sites, shopping along Calle El Conde, world-class dining options, and fun nightlife.

Under US$50

Hotel Aída (Espaillat 254, tel. 809/685-7692, fax 809/221-9393, US$27 d with fan only) has a convenient location near El Conde and is family run. Unfortunately, the rooms have no windows. Some sleep three, and all rooms have private hot-water bathrooms. Given its low price and central location, it is popular and often full.

Hotel Freeman (Isabela La Católica, tel. 809/689-3961, US$30 d) has rather plain rooms, but they are clean. All have two queen-size beds and a private bathroom. The best thing this hotel has going for it is its location, just a half a block from Parque Colón.

US$50-100

The charming **Antiguo Hotel Europa** (Arzobispo Meriño at Emiliano Tejera, tel. 809/285-0005, US$75 d), built at the turn of the 20th century, has since been remodeled and has beautiful wrought-iron balconies. Most of the modern, standard rooms have a balcony (but make sure to request it), and all have a queen-size bed and tile floors. The Europa is a couple of blocks away from Plaza de la Hispanidad. Continental breakfast included in the rate. Its Terraza Restaurant and Bar has Dominican cuisine and is on the roof, offering fantastic views of the ruins of the San Francisco monastery and the Ciudad Colonial. There is also a lobby bar.

El Beaterío Guest House (Av. Duarte 8, tel. 809/687-8657, elbeaterio@netscape.net, US$70 d with a/c) is in a good location if you want to walk around the city. It was originally a 16th-century abbey, renovated to what is now an 11-room hotel. A stone-floored courtyard with wrought-iron balconies, terracotta rooftops, and tiled stairways make this an impressive sight. The rooms are small but comfortable. Breakfast is included in the rate.

Hotel Conde de Peñalba (El Conde at Arzobispo Meriño, tel. 809/688-7121, www.condepenalba.com, US$75 with windows) has probably the best location in the whole Ciudad Colonial, right in front of the Parque Colón. Try to get a room that has a balcony overlooking the park. The restaurant on the first floor is a very popular spot for guests and nonguests alike. The rooms are comfortable and the bathrooms are quite small.

The 96-room **Hotel Mercure Comercial** (El Conde and Hostos, tel. 809/688-5500, www.accorhotels.com, US$94 d) was renovated in 2000. All rooms have phones, TVs, fridges, and nice bathrooms. Tax, service, and breakfast are included in the rate. This is a favorite for business travelers; it has Internet service. Located right on the busy El Conde, the restaurant out front offers fantastic people-watching.

US$100 and Up

◖ Sofitel Nicolás de Ovando (Calle de las Damas, tel. 809/685-9955, www.sofitel.com, US$238–354 d) is easily the most luxurious hotel in the city, located in the renovated home of the first governor of the New World, Nicolás de Ovando. It is said that Christopher Columbus was once his guest here. The hotel has 107 elegant rooms and suites with stone walls and high dark wood ceilings. All rooms have marble bathrooms, TV, air-conditioning, safe boxes, phones, and Internet hookups. The pool overlooks the Río Ozama, and there is a well-equipped gym and a library. Buffet breakfast is included in the rate.

(Sofitel Francés (Las Mercedes at Arzobispo Meriño, tel. 809/685-9331, www.accorhotels.com, US$170 d), a restored colonial mansion, is the sister-hotel to the Sofitel Nicolás de Ovando. Rooms have high ceilings, very comfortable beds, and dark wood furnishings. They surround the beautiful courtyard that holds the comfortable tables and chairs of the restaurant, which serves wonderful food. Breakfast is included in the rate.

A boutique hotel, **(Hodelpa Caribe Colonial** (Isabela La Católica 159, tel. 809/688-7799, www.hodelpa.com, US$100 d) has 54 rooms and is centrally located in the Ciudad Colonial with many restaurants, bars, and shops right outside the front door. Rooms are in art deco style and are very clean and comfortable. All have air-conditioning, TV, and fridge. There's a bar, restaurant, and Internet services on-site.

MALECÓN

Hotels along the Malecón are more modern. They are mostly high-rise buildings and the antithesis to the old-world charm of the Ciudad Colonial and Gazcue neighborhoods. Even though some do offer phenomenal views of the Caribbean Sea (provided you get a room with a view), the ocean is not accessible in this area. These hotels do put you right in the thick of the hotel nightclubbing and casino scene. If that is your main focus, you're best off to stay here. However, it's a long walk to the Ciudad Colonial (or a short taxi ride).

US$100 and Up

At the **Hotel Centenario Intercontinental** (Av. George Washington 218, tel. 809/221-0000, www.intercontinental.com/santodomingo, US$210 d), the simple elegance of the lobby is just a hint of what is to come. The rooms, although somewhat small, are very comfortable and tastefully decorated, with cable TV and pay-per-view plus a minibar.

Tennis courts and a swimming pool with a Jacuzzi are on-site.

Although it is not the best hotel on the strip, **Renaissance Jaragua Hotel & Casino** (Av. George Washington 367, tel. 809/221-2222, www.renaissancehotels.com, US$150) is a massive one and you can't miss it. It's like being on the strip in Vegas. This hotel is known for its large casino and one of the most popular nightclubs, Jubilee (see *Nightlife*). It is best to upgrade to a deluxe or suite; they are in better condition, as the standard rooms are, well, sub-standard.

The rooms in **Hotel Melia Santo Domingo** (Av. George Washington 365, tel. 809/221-6666, www.solmelia.com, US$140 d) are comfortable and nicely appointed, though not unique. There are two good restaurants (one with lunch and dinner buffets and one that is a grill). The pool on the second-floor terrace is a nice escape from the busy world outside the hotel. The hotel offers a casino, health spa, tennis courts, and a disco. Service is good.

The 228-room, 21-floor **(Hilton Santo Domingo** (Av. George Wash-ington 500, tel. 809/685-0202, www.hiltoncaribbean.com/santodomingo, US$120 d) was brand-new in 2005 and spotlessly polished and impressive. It boasts the city's largest casino, and the rooms almost all have a stunning ocean view from floor to ceiling windows. Duvets cover the stylishly decorated and very comfortable beds. Amenities include Internet hookup, electronic safety boxes, cable TV, and minibars. The pool is on the seventh floor and has a bar next to it. This is a full-service hotel.

GAZCUE

The historic neighborhood of Gazcue is a residential area just west of Parque Independencia. It was the neighborhood of Santo Domingo's upper class, and some of the buildings date back to the 1930s. The streets are shaded in a beautiful full canopy of trees. Today, restaurants have moved into the area as well as some fashionable cafés. Gazcue is a possible alternative to the Ciudad Colonial because it has more budget options. You'll get more for your money if you're willing to walk to the Ciudad Colonial or take a very short taxi ride for your sightseeing.

Under US$50

Hotel Maison Gautreaux (Félix Mariano Lluberes 8, tel. 809/412-7837, fax 809/412-7840, www.maisongautreaux.net, US$32 d) is only one block off of the Malecón, but what a difference a block makes in price. All rooms have air-conditioning, hot-water bathrooms, cable TV, safe boxes, and hairdryers. The rooms are clean, simple, and nicely appointed. There is a restaurant on-site.

At **Hotel La Danae** (Calle Danae 18, tel. 809/238-5609, US$28–35) rooms have air-conditioning, minifridges, and cable TV, and there's a kitchen that guests can use. There is a price difference in the rooms depending on whether you're in the front or the back (old or new, respectively). The rooms are very simple but they are clean.

At **La Grand Mansíon** (Calle Danae 26, tel. 809/682-2033, US$23), try to get one of the rooms with windows; the ones that don't have windows can feel cramped. Better yet, ask for the one with its own terrace. This hotel is good value for the money.

US$50-100

At **Hotel Duque de Wellington** (Av. Independencia 304, tel. 809/682-4525, www.hotelduque.com, US$60–70), it's kind of like you went home to visit family. The decor feels that way, quaint and like Grandma had a hand in it. Rooms have air-conditioning, TV, phones, fans, and security boxes and are clean and comfortable. There is an on-site restaurant, Pasta & Algo Mas, which offers Italian food, and a travel agency. Room service is available. It's on a rather busy street. This is a gay-friendly hotel.

The rooms at **Hotel Residencia Venezia** (Av. Independencia 45, tel. 809/682-5108, www.residence-venezia.com, US$60 d) are clean and have hot-water bathrooms and a kitchenette. Despite a rather cramped feeling, the rooms are quite comfortable. If you can swing a suite (US$67), you'll have more space, including a balcony.

Food

Santo Domingo has an impressive array of historical sites, accommodation choices, and things to keep you busy. It is perhaps no surprise, then, that the city has a bewildering array of restaurant choices as well. It is an epicure's paradise with choices from classics like Italian favorites, pub food, and French cuisine to seafood, Caribbean fusion, and sushi. If you're searching for a restaurant serving local cuisine, check the menu (typically posted outside of the front door or in the window of the establishment) for the words *comida criolla* and for dishes like *mofongo* (a plantain dish), *arroz con pollo* (rice and chicken), or any kind of meat served *guisado* (in a stew-like sauce).

CIUDAD COLONIAL
Cafés and Pubs
La Cafetera Colonial (El Conde 253, tel. 809/682-7114, 7:30 A.M.–10 P.M., US$2–5) has been around for decades, and locals say it has barely changed at all. Men who have been going to this café/diner for 25 years or more are still content to while away their afternoons perched on the stools at the counter talking about the old days. Sandwiches, fresh juices, and breakfasts are good, but the espresso and the pineapple cake will likely never be equaled elsewhere on the planet. This is a top pick for its sentimental presence on El Conde.

The restaurant of **Restaurant & Hotel Conde de Peñalba** (El Conde at Arzobispo

© ANA CHAVIER CAAMAÑO

street vendors selling *agua de coco* (coconut water) in the Ciudad Colonial

Meriño, tel. 809/688-7121, www.condepenalba.com, US$2–15) is in the best people-watching position, right across from Parque Colón. Sandwiches, omelets, and a good variety of international choices are on the menu, in addition to a good international beer selection. Try the Gallego sandwich for US$5. Just a few storefronts down is **Bar & Restaurant Anacaona** (Calle El Conde 101 and Calle Isabel La Católica, tel. 809/682-8253). Anacaona has a relaxing atmosphere under a huge tree for shade on a hot day. The fish in coconut sauce is a wonderful choice. Service is good, beer is cold, and the bathrooms are clean. These two restaurants are like "dueling banjos" for hungry tourists. They have perfect locations and similar prices.

Comida Criolla

The charming **Meson de D'Bari** (Hostos and Salomé Ureña, tel. 809/687-4091, noon–midnight, US$6–14) has been fashioned from what was once a private colonial home. Dominican art hangs on the walls and is for sale,

making it like dining in an art gallery. The *cangrejos guisados* (crab stew) and *filet a la criolla* (filet of beef) are signature dishes. Many more Dominican-style seafood and steak entrées are on the menu. The bar is quite a popular spot for nighttime entertainment as well with live music on the weekends.

Café de las Flores (El Conde between Sánchez and José Reyes, tel. 809/689-1898, 9 A.M.–10 P.M. daily, US$4–10) has tables right on the walkway of El Conde; this is great for people-watching. The food is relatively cheap. Choices include breakfast sandwiches, *asopao* (soup), *mofongo*, meat, paella, and other typical Dominican dishes. The bright murals on the walls and the ceiling fans make it look achingly like a tourist trap; granted, there are better restaurants, but this location is tops for a quick lunch while shopping Calle El Conde.

International

Meson La Quintana (Calle La Atarazana 13, tel. 809/687-2646, 12:30 P.M.–1 A.M. Mon.–Sun., US$4–18), a Spanish restaurant, is appropriately located across from the Alcázar de Colón. Tapas are the specialty, served in a typical Spanish decor. Outdoor seating is available at night.

Italian-owned **Ristorante da Franco** (Calle Salomé Ureña 59, tel. 809/689-3447, lunch at noon for parties with reservations only, 8 P.M.–late for dinner, US$8–20) is an Italian restaurant in a renovated colonial house. The fine dining experience is inside on the second floor or on the rooftop, which is half covered over and is a peaceful way to end a very busy day of sightseeing. The view isn't spectacular, but the stars are enough to make you enjoy your meal slowly—it's a romantic restaurant. During the week it is very quiet, a rare experience in Santo Domingo. Sunday is barbecue and jazz night. The mushroom risotto is a wonderful choice. There are many seafood, pasta, and meat dishes.

Eclectic is the perfect word to describe **(Coco's Restaurant** (Padre Billini 53, tel. 809/687-9624, US$10–30). This treasure of a restaurant has a menu with British and Thai influences; the decor has touches of British pub and Spanish colonial—it is in a 370-year-old renovated private home complete with romantic courtyard. The owners, Christopher Gwillym and Colin Hercok, are very welcoming and talented restaurateurs, and it shows with their local and tourist following. Coco's has been in business since 1992. The chef stylishly changes the menu daily, but typical dishes include homemade pâté, sweet stuffed pear, lamb rack with mint gravy, beef casserole, and Tudor honey pork with apple and rosemary. Occasional curry nights require reservations.

(Restaurant Caffe Bellini (Calle Arzobispo Meriño 155 and Padre Billini, tel. 809/686-3387, noon–3 P.M. and 7 P.M.–2 A.M., US$13–35) is in a house that was built in 1524. It has been renovated into a stylish and sleek restaurant serving Italian dishes that have attracted such celebrities as Shakira, Andy Garcia, and Isabela Rosellini (three times!). You will be well fed here, with good-sized portions of fantastic food. Specialties include spaghetti with king crab (not on the menu; you must ask

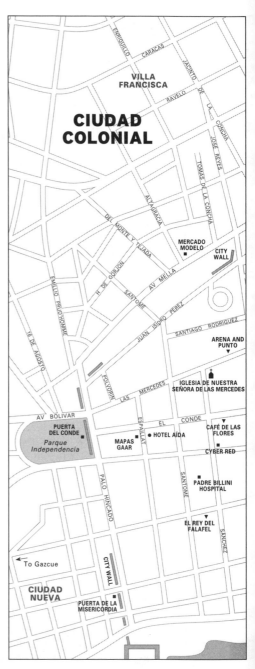

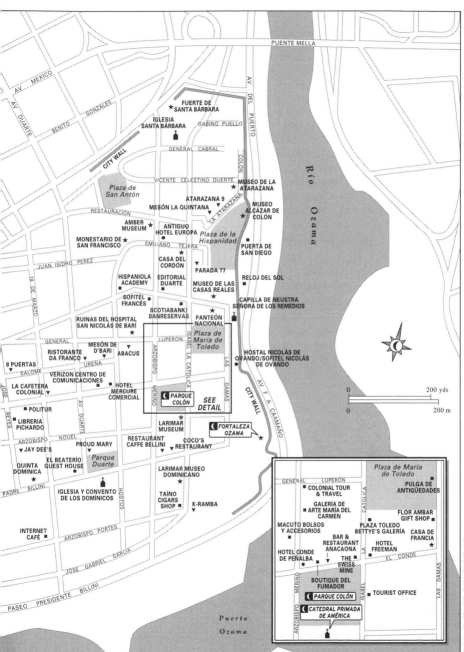

PUENTE MELLA

AV. MEXICO
AV. DUARTE
BENITO
GONZALES
CITY WALL

FUERTE DE
★ SANTA BÁRBARA
IGLESIA
SANTA BÁRBARA   GABINO PUELLO

GENERAL CABRAL

AV. DEL PUERTO
COLÓN

Río Ozama

VICENTE CELESTINO DUERTE   MUSEO DE LA
Plaza de   ★ ATARAZANA
San Antón   ATARAZANA 9
RESTAURACIÓN   MESÓN LA QUINTANA ▼   MUSEO
                    LA ATARAZANA   ALCÁZAR DE
AMBER ★   ANTIGUO   ★ COLÓN
MUSEUM   HOTEL EUROPA Plaza de la
MONESTARIO DE ★   Hispanidad
SAN FRANCISCO   EMILIANO TEJERA   ■ PUERTA DE
               CASA DEL   SAN DIEGO
JUAN ISIDRO PEREZ   CORDÓN
19 DE MARZO   HISPANIOLA EDITORIAL ▼ PARADA 77
                ACADEMY   DUARTE   MUSEO DE LAS   RELOJ DEL SOL
                ■   ■   CASAS REALES
                SOFITEL ●   ★
                FRANCÉS   SCOTIABANK/   CAPILLA DE NEUSTRA
RUINAS DEL HOSPITAL   BANRESERVAS SEÑORA DE LOS REMEDIOS
SAN NICOLÁS DE BARÍ ■   SCOTIABANK/ PANTEÓN
GENERAL   ● BANRESERVAS NACIONAL
MESÓN DE   LUPERÓN Plaza de
RISTORANTE   D'BARI ▼   María de
DA FRANCO ▼   ABACUS   Toledo
8 PUERTAS   UREÑA   ISABEL LA CATÓLICA   HOSTAL NICOLÁS DE
SALOMÉ   VERIZON CENTRO DE   OVANDO/SOFITEL NICOLÁS
LA CAFETERA   COMUNICACIONES   DE OVANDO
COLONIAL ▼   ■   HOTEL   ARZOBISPO   AV. F. A. CAAMAÑO
POLITUR   MERCURE   MERIÑO   CITY WALL
LIBRERIA   COMERCIAL   (PARQUE   LAS DAMAS
PICHARDO   ★ COLÓN   SEE
ARZOBISPO   NOUEL   DETAIL
JAY DEE'S   PROUD MARY   Parque   LARIMAR ★
EL BEATERÍO   Duarte   MUSEUM   (FORTALEZA
QUINTA   GUEST HOUSE   RESTAURANT   COCO'S   OZAMA ★
DOMINICA   ●   CAFFE BELLINI ▼   RESTAURANT
★   LARIMAR MUSEO
PADRE   BILLINI   IGLESIA Y CONVENTO   DOMINICANO
INTERNET   DE LOS DOMÍNICOS   ★
CAFÉ ■   TAÍNO
         ARZOBISPO PORTES   CIGARS   K-RAMBA
                SHOP ▼
JOSE GABRIEL GARCIA
PASEO   PRESIDENTE   BILLINI
Puerto
Ozama

N
0   200 yds
0   200 m

Detail inset:

Plaza de María
de Toledo
GENERAL   LUPERÓN   PULGA DE
COLONIAL TOUR ■   ANTIGÜEDADES ■
& TRAVEL
GALERÍA DE   FLOR AMBAR
■ ARTE MARÍA DEL   GIFT SHOP ■
CARMEN
MACUTO BOLSOS   PLAZA TOLEDO   CASA DE
Y ACCESORIOS   BETTYE'S GALERÍA   FRANCIA
■   BAR &   ★
         RESTAURANT   HOTEL
HOTEL CONDE   ANACAONA   FREEMAN
DE PEÑALBA ■   ● EL CONDE
         THE ■
         SWISS
         MINE
BOUTIQUE DEL
FUMADOR
(PARQUE COLÓN   ■ TOURIST OFFICE
(CATEDRAL PRIMADA
DE AMÉRICA

CATÓLICA   ISABEL   MERIÑO   ARZOBISPO   LAS DAMAS

for it); steak filet on the grill with white cream sauce, porcini mushrooms, and green peppers; and lobster shrimp cognac prepared with portobello mushrooms and fresh tomatoes.

Middle Eastern

El Rey del Falafel (Padre Billini and Sanchez, tel. 809/688-9714, US$4–8) has Middle Eastern food for something different. Here in this tiny restaurant, enjoy falafel sandwiches, shawarma, hummus, and the like. Next door is a more spacious (but not by much) bar that has Arabic music and jazz on Thursday and Sunday. It is a very mixed crowd (all ages are present, as well as families, and it's popular with 30-somethings).

Seafood

Pescadería Comedor Mora (Calle Profesor Gómez and Summerwells, open 24 hours), a budget seafood option, has a large open-air dining area with ceiling fans, but you order at a counter deli-style. It's rather a chaotic place; you just have to jump in and make yourself known—Dominicans don't really form orderly lines, not here anyway. Parking is available across the street. Options include *cangrejo guisado* (crab in sauce), fish in coconut sauce, *ensalada de pulpo* (octopus salad), fried seafood, paella, yucca, rice dishes, shrimp, and beer.

GAZCUE

El Conuco Restaurant (Gazcue, Calle Casimiro del Moya 152, tel. 809/686-0129, US$5–12) is unbelievably touristy, but the food is very good and the entertainment makes it a favorite for tourists. Through its corny veneer, its success is deserved because it serves very authentic and tasty Dominican fare like *la bandera dominicana* by buffet or more exotic items like cow's-foot stew à la carte. The highlight of your visit (aside from the food) is when the entertainment dances the merengue and *bachata* with one performer dancing on top of a bottle.

Cafeteria Villar Hermanos (Av. Independencia at Pasteur, tel. 809/682-1433, 8 A.M.–

10 P.M., US$2–9) is a very popular place known mostly for its fantastic sandwiches, which are made on fresh bread in the traditional Dominican way, pressed flat with a hot iron. There are different kinds of meats to choose from and even some vegetarian ones. Some big ones can feed more than one person. This is a very economical way to eat.

La Bodeguita de la Habana Vieja (Av. Independencia 302, tel. 809/476-7626, noon–midnight, US$7–12) is a popular spot with the locals for its easy-going atmosphere and great food. The atmosphere is mixed. You won't want to wear shorts here (there are white tablecloths), but there is a TV playing, adding to its casual feel. There are a number of international dishes on the menu, but Cuban is the specialty, with favorites like *ropa vieja* (shredded beef served in a sauce).

MALECÓN

At **Adrian Tropical** (Av. George Washington, tel. 809/221-1764, US$11–20) the view alone is worth splurging on a meal like this. There are three Adrian Tropicals in town; make sure this is the one you go to. It is on the Malecón, built onto the cliffside over the water of the Caribbean Sea. The specialty is *mofongo* (the *camaronfongo* is the best), but other options are good as well, like the *pescado Boca Chica,* which is a big fried fish. Make sure to get a table on the patio, although there is indoor seating as well.

Trattoria Vesuvio Malecón (Av. George Washington 521, tel. 809/221-1954, for pizza delivery tel. 809/221-3000, US$12–17) is a fixture in Santo Domingo, widely regarded as one of the top Italian restaurants since 1954. There are two Vesuvios and they are right next to one another. The Trattoria is the more casual (sleek and modern interior) of the two (Vesuvios on the Malecón is right next door). The specialty is gourmet pizza, but their art does not stop there: seafood, calzones, beef, veal, pasta, hamburgers, quesadillas, the list goes on. Vesuvios on the Malecón is well known for its seafood and is much more formal.

EAT LIKE A DOMINICAN

Want to try some local cuisine when you're in the Dominican Republic but don't know what to order while at the restaurant? Here are some key words to help make deciphering the menu a lot easier.

aguacate – avocado

asopao – a thick soup made with rice and seafood or meat; very delicious and usually made for special occasions

arroz – rice

ayuma – gem squash

bacalao – codfish

bandera dominicana – typical Dominican lunch of rice, beans, plantains, and meat

batata – sweet potato

casabe – cassava bread, thick tortilla made with dried yucca

chicharrones – fried pork rind

chivo – goat

cocido – meaty stew

concón – the crunchy rice that sticks at the bottom of the pan (If you are a guest in someone's house, they will offer you the *concón* first because you are the guest. It is considered the best part.)

fría – cold (If you see a sign that says *fría fría,* that means there is very cold beer for sale!)

frito – fried

garbanzos – chickpeas

guandules – pigeon peas

guanábana – soursop

guisado/guisada – stewed (e.g., *pollo guisado* or chicken stew)

guineo – banana

guayaba – guava

habas – faba beans

habichuelas negras – black beans

habichuelas blancas – white beans

habichuelas rojas – red kidney beans

habichuelas pintas – pinto beans

lambí – conch

lechosa – papaya

lentejas – lentils

limoncillo – Spanish lemon

locrio – a combination of rice, meat (or seafood), and vegetables

longaniza – spicy pork sausage

mangú – mashed plantains (This is a very typical Dominican breakfast food, served with onions; it often has eggs or sausage on the side.)

maní – peanuts (These are also known as *cacahuate* and *cacahuete,* and are often sold between the cars at stoplights in Santo Domingo.)

mariscos – seafood

mofongo – plantains mashed with a mortar and pestle (not to be confused with *mondongo*)

mondongo – tripe (Feeling gutsy? Try this atypically typical dish.)

moro – dish made with rice and beans or pigeon peas

papa – potato (Not to be confused with the other *papa* – the Pope. It's all about context.)

picadera – appetizers or buffet

picante – spicy hot (Dominican cuisine is known to be more flavorful than spicy.)

pica pollo – breaded fried chicken

pincho – brochette/kebab

plátano – plantain

Presidente – leading brand of beer sold in the Dominican Republic

puerco en puya – spit-roasted pork

rabo encendido – literally, "tail on fire" (It is an oxtail soup.)

rés guisada – beef stew

salsa – sauce (unless you're in a disco – then someone is asking you to dance)

salsa de tomate – tomato paste

sancocho – a stew made with up to seven types of meat (This is a traditional and cherished Dominican culinary treasure. It is often served at special occasions or after a late night of partying. It's very good served with rice, avocado, and a *fría fría.*)

tayota – chayote

yuca – cassava, root of the yucca plant

CENTRAL SANTO DOMINGO

La Taberna del Pescador (Av. Winston Churchill 10 and Av. Gustavo Mejía Ricart, Plaza Robledo, Evaristo Morales, tel. 809/540-9361, www.latabernadelpescador.com, noon–3 P.M. and 7 P.M.–midnight, US$10–25), another locals' favorite seafood joint, across from La Sirena Shopping Center and behind Burger King, is decorated with the typical sea gear (nets and fake fish) amid dark wood features, a live crab and shrimp aquarium, and a bar with a red-tiled roof. The pleasant atmosphere is enhanced by the Mediterranean flavors of the dishes. Try the *filet of dorado a la Milanesa;* the grilled lobster, shrimp, and calamari plate; or be decadent with the lobster ravioli in cream sauce. There are good meat choices for those in your party who don't want seafood.

Peperoni (Plaza Universitaria La Julia, Av. Sarasota 23, tel. 809/508-1330, www.peperoni.com.do, noon–3 P.M. and 7 P.M.–1 A.M.) is a trendy and popular spot with chic decor that serves international cuisine of all types. Try the sushi roll Dominican-style with tuna, avocado, and *plátano maduro* (ripe plantain); pasta; sandwiches; burgers; or polenta-crusted sea bass. The eclectic menu deserves to be explored.

Il Capo (Calle Sarasota, tel. 809/534-6252, noon–midnight, US$4–15) Italian restaurant is in the commercial center near the Embajador Hotel. It has a casual, family atmosphere and good food. Bruschetta, ravioli, seafood, and meat dishes are on the menu, but the best choice is the excellent pizza, which can be delivered as well. If you're in the area and are looking for a nice casual dinner, this is a perfectly acceptable choice.

Meson Cienfuegos (Calle Sarasota, tel. 809/532-1765, noon–midnight, US$10–25) is in the same commercial center as Il Capo. This Spanish restaurant serves traditional tapas and entrées amid a Spanish wine cellar decor with a very nice wine list. Try the paella for US$17 for two people.

NORTHERN SANTO DOMINGO

Restaurante Sully (Av. Charles Summer and Calle Las Caobas, Ensanche Carmelita, Los Prados, tel. 809/562-3389, 2–3:30 P.M. and 7 P.M.–midnight, US$3–7) is a casual restaurant specializing in seafood. Dishes range from Spanish paella to seafood stew. It has a large list of international and domestic drinks and fine wines. This is a very popular restaurant with the locals. You'll definitely need a taxi, and securing a ride back is best.

SOUTHWEST SANTO DOMINGO

Eating at **El Meson de la Cava** (Av. Mirador Sur 1, tel. 809/533-2818, noon–1 A.M., US$10–20) is dining like you've probably never done before, inside the belly of a massive cave. This is a formal restaurant with waiters in tuxedos, stalactites, and white tablecloths. Elegance and good food make for a dining experience but it's not particularly fantastic cuisine. International choices include many fish dishes (like shrimp in a white wine sauce), veal cutlets, and lamb chops. Reservations are required.

Information and Services

Tourist Office

The most convenient Oficina de Turismo (Isabela la Católica 103, tel. 809/686-3858, 9 A.M.–3 P.M. Mon.–Fri.) is across from Parque Colón. You'll find many brochures and maps. The staff is helpful and speaks Spanish, English, and French.

Health and Emergency Services

Clínica Abreu and the adjacent **Clínica Gómez Patiño** (Av. Independencia at Burgos, tel. 809/688-4411, open 24 hours) are highly recommended as the best places in the city for foreigners needing medical care. Lots of different languages are spoken, and doctors have been medically trained in the United States.

Padre Billini Hospital (Av. Sánchez between Arzobispo Nouel and Padre Billini, tel. 809/221-8272, open 24 hours) is closest to the Ciudad Colonial. The wait is long, but you'll get a free consultation.

Farmacia San Judas Tadeo (Independencia 57 at Bernardo Pichardo, tel. 809/685-8165) is open 24 hours and will deliver to the Ciudad Colonial and Gazcue. **Farmacia Vivian** (Independencia at Delgado, tel. 809/221-2000) will give you the same service.

The **Politur** (El Conde at José Reyes, tel. 809/689-6464, open 24 hours) can help you in most emergency situations, and most officers speak different languages. Dialing 911 will give you the regular police.

Money

For money in the Ciudad Colonial, you'll find ScotiaBank (tel. 809/689-5151) and BanReservas (tel. 809/960-2108), both located on Calle Isabel La Católica where it intersects with Las Mercedes. Both are open 8:30 A.M.–5 P.M. and have ATMs. It is best to get your cash during the day when there are a lot of people around.

In Gazcue, go to **Banco Popular** (Av. Independencia at Pasteur, tel. 809/685-3000, 9 A.M.–8 P.M. Mon.–Sat., and 9 A.M.–1 P.M. Sun.); it has an ATM, but since it is inside Farmacia Carmina, it is not available after hours.

Communications

Verizon Centro de Comunicaciones (El Conde 202, tel. 809/221-4249, fax 809/221-4167, 8 A.M.–9:30 P.M.) offers international calling services.

For Internet services in the Ciudad Colonial, go to **Internet Café** (José Reyes at Arzobispo Portes, 10:30 A.M.–10 P.M. Mon.–Sat., noon–10 P.M. Sun.) or **Cyber Red** (Sánchez 201, tel. 809/685-9267, 9 A.M.–9 P.M.), which is just off of El Conde. You can also make international calls at this location.

For Internet service in Gazcue, go to **Centro de Internet** (Av. Independencia 201, tel. 809/238-5149, 8:30 A.M.–9 P.M. Mon.–Sat., 8:30 A.M.–3 P.M. Sun.). It has decent service and offers international calling as well at very low rates (to the U.S. for US$0.17 per minute and to Europe for US$0.25).

Travel Agencies

If you should need additional plans within the Dominican Republic or help with travel changes, these are some reputable resources.

At well-established **Colonial Tour & Travel** (Arzobispo Meriño 209, tel. 809/688-5285, www.colonialtours.com, 8:30 A.M.–1 P.M. and 2:30–5:30 P.M. Mon.–Fri., 8:30 A.M.–noon Sat.), English, French, and Italian are spoken.

Giada Tours & Travel (Av. Independencia 304, tel. 809/686-6994, 8:30 A.M.–6 P.M. Mon.–Fri., 9 A.M.–2 P.M. Sat.) can arrange for international and domestic travel as well as city tours. It's in the Hotel Duque de Wellington.

Library

Biblioteca Nacional (Plaza de la Cultura, Av. Máximo Gómez, between Av. México and Bolívar) has a good collection and is a good place to take a time out for a good read.

Spanish Lessons

If your goal is to have an immersion vacation and you need to learn some language skills to get that going, here are some options for Spanish language schools.

Hispaniola Academy (Hostos at Mercedes, tel. 809/688-9192, www.hispaniola.org) is in the Ciudad Colonial and offers a variety of packages. A week-long intensive course is the quickest. There are also accommodation options with a family or in a hotel. The academy also has Dominican culture classes like cooking and dance.

Instituto Intercultural del Caribe (Aristides Fiallo Cabral 456, tel. 809/685-5826, www.edase.com) offers packages ranging in intensity and length and accommodation choices. This school operates on the intercultural exchange philosophy; there are opportunities to mix and mingle with language students from the Dominican Republic and instructors often take the learning outside of the classroom to apply it in the real world.

Newspapers

To check out the local news or happenings in the city, pick up a newspaper. *Listín Diario* (www.listin.com.do) has the widest circulation. It and *El Caribe* (www.elcaribe.com .do), *Hoy* (www.hoy.com.do), and *Diario Libre* (www.diariolibre.com.do) are circulated in the morning.

Getting There

BY AIR

Santo Domingo is served by the **Aeropuerto Internacional Las Américas** (tel. 809/549-0328), which is 22 kilometers east of the metropolitan area.

Major carriers are: **Air Canada** (Av. Gustavo Mejía Ricart 54, tel. 809/541-2929), **Air Europa** (Av. Winston Churchill 459, tel. 809/683-8020), **Air France** (Av. Máximo Gómez 15, tel. 809/686-8432), **American Airlines** (El Conde, tel. 809/542-5151, airport tel. 809/549-0043), **Continental Airlines** (airport tel. 809/549-0757), **Iberia** (Av. Lope de Vega, tel. 809/686-9191, airport tel. 809/549-0205), **Lufthansa** (Av. George Washington, tel. 809/689-9625), **US Airways** (Av. Gustavo Mejía Ricart 54, tel. 809/540-0505, airport tel. 809/549-0165).

BY FERRY

Only one connection exists: to and from Mayagüez, Puerto Rico, three times a week, run by **Ferries del Caribe** (tel. 809/688-4400, Mayagüez tel. 787/832-4400, www.ferriesdelcaribe.com, in Spanish). The ticket office and boarding port in Santo Domingo are at Avenida del Puerto, which is across from the Fortaleza Ozama. It is a 12-hour journey to Puerto Rico that you can do in an airplane-type seat (US$182), or in a private cabin with a window (US$295). From Santo Domingo, scheduled trips depart on Sunday, Tuesday, and Thursday at 8 P.M. and arrive in Mayagüez the next morning. From Mayagüez, ferries depart Monday, Wednesday, and Friday at 8 P.M. and arrive in Santo Domingo the next morning.

BY BUS

Caribe Tours (Av. 27 de Febrero at Av. Leopoldo Navarro, tel. 809/221-4422, www.caribetours.com.do, in Spanish) offers the most departure times and covers a wider area of the country than the **Metro** (Calle Francisco Prats Ramírez, tel. 809/566-7126) bus company does. But both offer satisfactory service with big comfortable buses.

Most destinations in the Dominican Republic are within a four-hour ride. Ticket prices can fluctuate with the ever-changing economy but are usually quite low (under US$8). It is best to call or ask for a brochure and schedule at the station.

The express bus to **Bávaro/Punta Cana** (Juan Sánchez Ruiz at Máximo Gómez, US$3.75) is a direct service departing at

7 A.M., 10 A.M., 2 P.M., and 4 P.M. daily for a four-hour trip.

At **Parque Enriquillo** in the Ciudad Colonial, you can catch second-class bus options for **Baní, Boca Chica, Higüey, Juan Dolio, La Romana, Puerto Plata, San Cristóbal, San Pedro de Macorís, Santiago**, and **Sosúa**. These buses are not direct and make many stops in between. Expect prices for these to be under US$6.

BY CAR

Renting a car is easy at the airport. Many major companies have booths after you clear customs. Some companies are: **Avis** (airport tel. 809/549-0468; Av. Independencia at Socorro Sánchez, tel. 809/685-5095), **Budget** (airport tel. 809/549-0351; Av. John F. Kennedy at Av. Lope de Vega, tel. 809/566-6666), **Dollar** (airport tel. 809/549-0738; Av. Independencia 366, tel. 809/221-7368), **Hertz** (airport tel. 809/549-0454, Av. José Ma Heredia 1, tel. 809/221-5333). Shopping around on the Internet is always best for seasonal deals and special promotions.

Getting Around

TAXIS

A taxi from Las Américas airport is around US$25–30 and takes about a half an hour. When you exit the airport, there will, most likely, be dozens of taxi scouts looking for passengers for the taxi drivers they represent. Do not let them take your bags or even walk you in the direction of a taxi until you've agreed on a price. This is the hook and you will be expected to tip them. If you disagree on the price, chances are there will be another scout or driver that will outbid them. There is always room for haggling, but agree on the price before you let them help you with the bags or get in the car.

Santo Domingo is a very big city. If you plan to explore outside of the Ciudad Colonial, taxis are cheap and there are many of them. The taxis don't go by the meter system; it is usually just a quoted rate (around US$3). It is incredibly inexpensive, but you can haggle the price if you wish. Although it is not standard practice for the taxi drivers to just drive and wait for someone to flag them down, it isn't uncommon. More likely, though, they hang out at designated spots like along Parque Colón and Parque Duarte in the Ciudad Colonial.

Another way to get a cab is by calling, or having someone call for you. You tell them where you are and where you are going, and they let you know what car to look for and how long it will be. Not all taxis have air-conditioning, so if you want one that does, mention it; it may cost you a bit more. Agree on the price before you get in (with or without air-conditioning).

Taking a taxi at night is the best way to stay safe. Keep in mind that prices go up around midnight and haggling gets more difficult.

Techni Taxi (tel. 809/567-2010) has quick service, as do **Super Taxi** (tel. 809/536-7014) and **Apolo Taxi** (tel. 809/537-7771).

PUBLIC TRANSPORTATION

This is a very cheap option. You can get from one end of the city to the other for around US$0.25. Look for a sign that says *parada* (stop); they are found on major roads. In the Ciudad Colonial, you can find one at Parque Independencia where it meets Avenida Bolivar and Avenida Independencia.

Públicos are rough-looking cars and minivans that run the same major thoroughfares that buses do, but they stop anywhere you flag them down. Technically, they're supposed to have the word *público* on the license plate, but many don't, and even the ones who do want quicker results than waiting for you to be able to read the plates. Often, it comes down to the driver honking and waving at you to see if you want a ride. If you point like you'd like them to curb the car, they will. It costs about US$0.35, and sometimes the drivers will jam-pack their cars. If you're not comfortable with this, don't take a *público*. Beware: Although this is a safe means of transportation, pick-pocketing is common, especially when the seats are jammed full.

Motoconchos are the mopeds that buzz around and hang around parks. You can ride on the back of one of these, though you might feel like the drivers are maniacal demons. Don't expect a helmet to be offered up but do expect a lot of weaving between tight traffic jams and scary turns. Agree on a price before hopping on, if you dare.

THE CARIBBEAN COAST

East of Santo Domingo lie the city-dweller's quick-getaway towns—Boca Chica, Guayacanes, Juan Dolio, Vilas del Mar, San Pedro de Macorís, and La Romana—a slow-paced region complete with comfortable accommodation choices, local charm, beautiful beaches, and splendid golf courses. Here, old-world pastoral meets present-day tourism where the verdant, waving fields of sugarcane stand beside new golf courses and the turquoise waters of the Caribbean beaches are enjoyed without the super-heavy tourist traffic of other regions. This precarious balance between country life and international tourism makes this region an increasingly popular destination.

Historically devoted to the production of sugar and cattle raising, the Caribbean coast's popularity had not been on a consistent upswing until recently. While plantations and ranches still exist, the ever-expanding tourism industry is stretching its long arms to grapple plantation owners for their fertile inland acreage and the seaside locals for their white-sand properties along the Caribbean beachfront. Easy accessibility has aided in the growth of tourism in this region as well. Both Las Américas international airport and the airport at La Romana serve the resorts here, and their proximity to Santo Domingo makes these towns easy day-trip options for those using the capital as home base.

Whether you are fleeing the heat of the city or arriving directly by airplane, you are sure to find a leisurely escape from your regular routine here. Spend your days in the shallow, warm waters of Boca Chica, the all-inclusive

THE CARIBBEAN COAST

HIGHLIGHTS

◖ Playa Boca Chica: Protected by a coral reef that results in warm, shallow waters, the greatest water depth at this beach is about 1.2 meters, making Playa Boca Chica safe for children. It is sometimes called the Dominican Republic's biggest swimming pool. It is a good day-at-the-beach destination since it is only a 15-minute drive from Santo Domingo (page 68).

◖ Parque Nacional Submarino La Caleta: This is one of the smallest national parks in the country, but it is also one of the most popular. The massive coral reef and submerged shipwreck, *The Hickory*, provide divers a wonderful arena for viewing sea life (page 76).

◖ Tetelo Vargas Stadium: San Pedro de Macorís is known to diehard baseball fans as the baseball city or "land of the shortstops." In a country whose national passion is baseball, this is mecca. In this stadium, many Major League heroes, including Sammy Sosa, began their careers. Home to the local baseball team, Las Estrellas Orientales (The Eastern Stars), the large stadium becomes a major attraction between October and February for the nation's baseball season (page 81).

◖ Cueva de las Maravillas: The beauty of this island runs deep. The award-winning Cave of Wonders is like a Taíno art gallery containing hundreds of rupestrian paintings, along with an impressive array of stalactites, stalagmites, and columns. Elevators and smooth walkways make it very wheelchair-accessible (page 82).

◖ Altos de Chavón: This replica of a 16th-century Italian village is also home to a school of art and design. Shop in the many stores for original student art, souvenirs, and jewelry. Enjoy a show in the 7,000-seat amphitheater or dine in one of the many alluring restaurants (page 85).

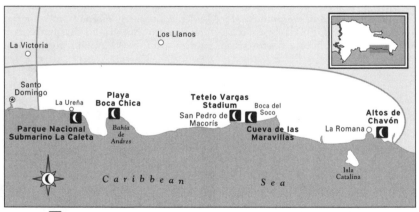

LOOK FOR ◖ TO FIND RECOMMENDED SIGHTS, ACTIVITIES, DINING, AND LODGING.

resorts of Juan Dolio, the picture-postcard beaches of Guayacanes, or on the internationally recognized Teeth of the Dog golf course at the Casa de Campo resort. At night cheer on the baseball players in the world-famous Tetelo Vargas Stadium in San Pedro de Macorís or enjoy one of the many casinos in the all-inclusive resorts.

Sea lovers will find some of the best sites on the island for diving and snorkeling. This coast is famous for its coral reefs just offshore and two shipwrecks where the clear, calm waters provide a perfect stage for viewing various creatures in their natural habitats. Land lovers can explore the limestone caves that litter the coastline and feature Taíno drawings.

PLANNING YOUR TIME

The Caribbean coast is a manageable area situated perfectly for lots of excursions within the region or to neighboring areas. The areas best suited for home base are Boca Chica (because of its lagoon-like waters and proximity to Santo Domingo), Guayacanes and Juan Dolio (because of their beaches and numerous resorts), and La Romana (because of its luxurious and world-famous Casa de Campo resort and the tourist destination of Altos de Chavón).

All the towns listed in this chapter are, more or less, between Las Américas and La Romana airports, making arrivals and departures a breeze and keeping travel time within the area down to less than a couple of hours by car. In addition, Santo Domingo is within a convenient distance for a weekend of shopping, clubbing, cultural events, and sightseeing. No matter what you are calling home base, excursions can be arranged to the Santo Domingo or other sites by your hotel.

Should you dare to drive on the highway (it can be a truly hair-raising experience), Highway 3 is well marked and is the spine from which these towns and sights emerge, making navigation uncomplicated.

Just 22 kilometers outside of Santo Domingo is **Parque Nacional Submarino La Caleta,** where you can spend your time diving and exploring the coral reefs and the shipwreck

of the *Hickory*. About 15 minutes farther east by car is Boca Chica, where the waters are shallow, warm, and clear like bathwater. Partying is a way of life in Boca Chica, but folks here also enjoy the long lazy days of basking in the sun and eating fried fish. It's a perfect afternoon getaway if you're staying in Santo Domingo or if a beach vacation with a little bit of city mixed in is for you.

Within a half an hour from Boca Chica, you will be in the areas of Guayacanes, Juan Dolio, and Villas del Mar. Guayacanes was an old fishing village that has a lovely beach where the locals tend to hang on Sundays, and Juan Dolio and Villas del Mar are really a long strip of hotels and resorts. Picking a resort along here boils down to what you want your vacation to be like. If you require a lot of lying around on the beach time, then choose wisely, because getting to anything outside of what is offered in your hotel will require a small effort of travel and ingenuity on your part. If you want a little of both, be sure to pick a resort that offers lots of excursions. Many of them do.

San Pedro de Macorís is best left for the months of October through January when it is baseball season in the Dominican Republic. Games are mostly at night. Other than the stadium, tourism isn't developed in this town, unfortunately, but you will pass through to get to **Cueva de las Maravillas,** one of the best sights that this coast has to offer. Many of the resorts in this area offer excursions to the cave at an extra cost, and you will not be sorry you took the time away from sunbathing to go deep underground and see cave paintings that look as though they were drawn yesterday. About three hours are needed for a visit to the cave since a one-hour tour is given and travel time from either Juan Dolio or La Romana hotels can be around a half hour.

For many, La Romana is just a passageway to **Altos de Chavón.** However, a stop for lunch or a morning cup of coffee with a croissant at **Trigo de Oro** is suggested before you head off to the biggest tourist attraction of the southern coast. This little town offers some interesting sights as well, like the cigar factory tour at **La Romana Cigars**.

Once you've reached Altos de Chavón, prepare to spend a few hours there. Buy some orig-inal art from the artists attending the school of design housed there. Again, resorts all over the country offer excursions to this sight, so ask at the desk of your hotel.

Boca Chica

A little farther east down Highway 3 from Paruqe Nacional La Caleta, and only a five-minute drive east of Las Américas international airport, sits the former fishing village of Boca Chica. This was the hot spot for the rich in Trujillo's days. The wealthy from Santo Domingo would come to their Hamptons-esque getaways, wearing their best and using their posh seaside villas for their elaborate parties.

In the early 1950s, the first major hotel was opened due to the popularity of travel to this area, but by the 1970s, Boca Chica's reputation with tourists waned because of the development of tourism on the north coast.

However, the lagoon-like waters of the Bahía de Andrés could not be ignored for long, and international (mostly European) travelers started to return by the 1990s.

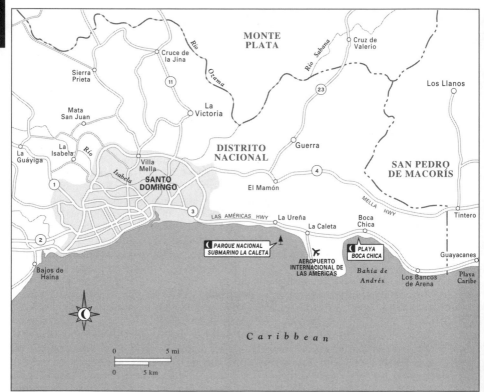

This financial flux has kept Boca Chica in constant economic doubt, and its reputation has been dragged through the mud by the severe prostitution and tourist scamming that evolved due to those hard times. Although these illicit activities are on a downward trend, they still exist and are being monitored by the local Politur (national tourism police) office. Nevertheless, a strange dichotomy exists between the larger hotel chains catering to families and some (but not all) of the small and cheaper hotels catering to the single male travelers looking for the debauchery side of Boca Chica. Many of the small hotels are doing their part in trying to clean up the act of Boca Chica.

Aside from this reputation, Boca Chica has benefited from the north and southeast

coasts' infestation of all-inclusive resorts. Tourists who desired a less gentrified vacation destination and wanted to roam less-traveler-populated areas began to flock to Boca Chica and its smaller hotels once again, bringing their currency with them. Granted, big corporation hotel chains are following, but part of that road-less-traveled spirit still exists.

Boca Chica has a wide variety of restaurants, shops, and bars, many of which are owned by expats who couldn't end their vacations, left their homelands, and decided to open their own businesses. Most of these are along the street parallel to the beach, which gets closed to traffic at night to make way for a more laid-back but festive environment. Midweek visits are best if you want more

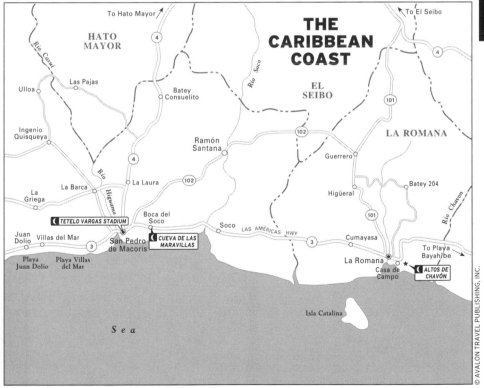

tranquility, as this little town is a busy and lively place on the weekends.

SIGHTS

With very few sights in the area, scuba diving, water sports, sunbathing, and fishing are some of the main activities available in Boca Chica. Most of these recreational items center in and around the balmy waters of Playa Boca Chica.

◖ Playa Boca Chica

Once you've spent a moment with your feet in the fine, powdery, white sand and waded in the clear blue waters of Playa Boca Chica, it is not hard to understand why this beach is the town's main attraction. A coral reef at the mouth of the Bahía de Andrés (which

you can wade out to) makes it impossible for big breakers and big fish to get through, resulting in calm water that is safe for children.

Playa Boca Chica is about five kilometers long and on the far east side sits the **Coral Hamaca by Hilton Resort.** Farther along is the **Don Juan Beach Resort** and its dive center, Treasure Divers; **Hotel Zapata** is toward the far western end. Between these locations are multiple restaurants and bars.

Beachgoers can rent the tables and chairs spread all across the beach, for a price. But haggling is a must and settling on a price before sitting down is essential. The same goes for ordering food and drinks to be brought to you by those offering service. It is easy to get taken for a ride if you don't agree on price before-

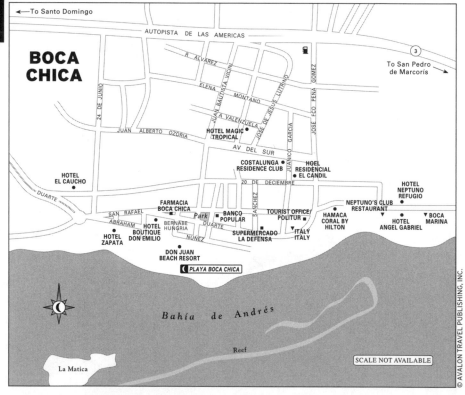

hand. After the price is negotiated, sit back, relax, and enjoy!

During low tide, it is possible to walk out to the islands of **La Matica** and **Los Pinos** (which used to be called La Piedra, "The Rock," before Australian pines were planted on it), just offshore, to do some bird-watching. The depth of the water averages only about 1.2 meters (in some spots it is only ankle deep), making it a pleasant journey either by foot or by shallow boat, which can be rented at the beach. La Matica (The Little Shrub) is more a mangrove than an island and a favorite spot for herons. Los Pinos (The Pines) has more hard ground to climb onto, and the mosquitoes can be aggressive. Reaching Los Pinos is a bit more difficult than getting to La Matica. Wear water shoes if you go walking.

During the weekdays mostly locals selling their wares and tourists enjoying the water and sun frequent the beach. Sunday at Playa Boca Chica is much more crowded— Dominicans from the city and surrounding areas come to the beach to cool off.

Some of the larger all-inclusive hotels have built walls surrounding the beach space in front of their hotels in an effort to block the locals from entering. By Dominican law, this is illegal, but the law is not enforced and it is a common practice of big resort chains. Often they have armed guards to keep their guests quarantined from the rest of the beachgoers/locals. Anyone without the hotel's bracelet on will be stopped from entering. Sure, peddlers are kept at bay, but should you be a guest at one of these resorts, venturing beyond the resort walls to mingle with the Dominicans on their rightful beach means you can get your hair braided and have fried fish, *chicharrones* (fried pork skins), and *yaniqueques* (johnny-cakes) brought to you from the *freidurías* (frying establishments). At Playa Boca Chica you can also do your shopping for trinkets, souvenirs, and jewelry as you lie in the sun thanks to the wandering peddlers. These vendors and hawkers can be aggressive, but a stern yet polite "*no gracias*" should do the trick when you've had enough.

ENTERTAINMENT AND EVENTS

Boca Chica is a beach town and not known for high cultural entertainment, but the bigger hotels tend to offer a wide variety of water sports and activities for daytime fun and have their own shows in the evenings. The **Hamaca Coral by Hilton** has a casino open to the public and one of the most formal discos in the area. Here you can find either live music or great salsa and merengue beats for a younger crowd. Those who are not guests of the hotel must pay a cover charge for the disco.

Keep in mind that while Boca Chica has one of the safest beaches for children to swim in and many family-friendly hotels, it also has a long-standing sex tourism scene. The sex industry has sustained Boca Chica's bad reputation, and prostitution is big business here. After sundown, the atmosphere shifts from lazy beach town to a more debased one and blatant offers for prostitution are not unheard of.

Many of the Boca Chica hotels (both all-inclusives and some smaller ones) that are trying to eradicate the smudge on their town's reputation have instituted a policy that anyone who isn't a guest of the hotel but wants to enter must purchase a pass. This cuts down on a lot of the prostitution because many of the sex-seeking travelers do not want this kind of bother and extra expense and, therefore, stay elsewhere.

The **Merengue Festival** (for information contact the tourism office in Santo Domingo, tel. 809/221-4660, fax 809/682-3806, www.dominicana.com.do) is held in the third week of July. A spillover of the same festival that takes place along Malecón in Santo Domingo, this street festival is a lively expression of the merengue music and dance particular to the Dominican Republic. Dancing, exhibitions, food, drink, and games all take place along the main street, Calle Duarte.

SHOPPING

Boca Chica is not a choice place to do your shopping. Since the capital is so close, a day (or even an afternoon) in the Ciudad Colonial would

THE HISTORY OF SUGAR

Although sugar adds sweetness to our lives, its history is one of bitterness and slavery.

When the Moors invaded Europe in the 7th century, they brought their technology of sugar production with them. But it wasn't until the crusades in the 11th century that Europeans learned of the spice, as they reclaimed their land and grabbed the sugar plantations away from the Arabs.

On Columbus's second voyage to the New World, he brought with him some sugarcane to plant in the hope that he could start an industry on the island. The climate was perfect for it and it soon thrived. The first sugarcane mill began working in about 1516 in the Dominican Republic.

Columbus "recruited" the Taíno people to work the fields, as it was too arduous for his own men. But as the Taíno started dying off because of disease and abuse, the Spanish soon turned to Africa for more workers. That was when the sugar industry became married to African slavery and forever influenced the Caribbean and eventually the Americas. The slave trade began.

By the end of the 1800s, slavery was officially outlawed. But with the boom of the sugar industry in the late 19th century came an increasing economic need for more workers willing to do the back-breaking work of cutting cane. The African slaves were replaced by thousands of Haitian immigrants who came to earn money. A 1920 census estimated that 28,000 Haitians were working in the cane fields. When the sugar refineries began shutting down a few years later and production waned, dictator Rafael Trujillo tersely requested that the immigrants leave the Dominican Republic; when they didn't, he slaughtered them.

Today there are over 500,000 Haitians working in the agricultural *bateys* (small towns located near sugar cane fields where Haitians live and work), and they are brutally exploited. Often they are rounded up and deported (during 2000, the average was 10,000 per month). Many are beaten, robbed, or killed. These crimes have been called modern-day slavery by human-rights' advocates.

Despite the obvious bitter stains on the history of sugar's journey to the Dominican Republic, the industry has benefited the country as well. For years, the Dominican Republic was economically dependent on sugar, with most of the production in the southeast region. In 2004, some 5.3 million metric tons of sugarcane were produced.

Today tourism has surpassed sugar in economic importance, but sugar remains one of the country's most important exports.

© ANA CHAVIER CAAMANO

give you the best opportunity for perusing a better variety of keepsakes, and you'll also find far better prices. Still, there are a few shops and stalls peppering the town along **Calle Duarte,** which runs directly parallel to the beach for about five or six blocks. Here you can find rum, cigars, artwork (but it is the typical Haitian kind and not authentic Dominican artwork), clothes, and crafts. The prices in these shops are very high compared to Santo Domingo. However, if you just stay on the beach, the shopping vendors will come to you (barrage you is more like it) with briefcases filled with jewelry, women ready to braid your hair, massages, and various local arts and crafts. Keep in mind that these vendors have hiked the prices way up expecting that there will be a healthy amount of haggling.

SPORTS AND RECREATION
Golf
The nearest golf course to Boca Chica is the 9-hole **San Andrés Caribe Golf Club** (Km 27 Las Américas Hwy., tel. 809/545-1278), open 8 A.M.–6:30 P.M. The cost is US$17, and a caddy will cost you US$6 more. This par-36 course, which opened in 1993, is a good beginner's course and a great afternoon activity. Lessons are offered for US$10/hour. Club and cart fees are extra. Don't expect a lot from this course if you're a serious golfer.

Diving and Snorkeling
Many of the all-inclusive hotels offer their guests beginning diving lessons in their pools and ocean dive excursions. PADI certification courses are often available. Look for offers for dives to the nearby *Hickory* and *El Limón* shipwrecks at **Parque Nacional Submarino La Caleta** and **Islas Catalina and Saona.** These islands can be reached from Boca Chica but are more accessible from the town of **Bayahibe** (see the *Southeast* chapter).

The Don Juan Beach Resort is home to **Treasure Divers** (Calle Abraham Núñez 4, tel. 809/523-5320, fax 809/523-4819, www.treasuredivers.de/eng/). Located directly on the beach, it offers many diving

and snorkeling excursions to beautiful reefs and the striking shipwrecks in the area, as well as combination packages including night dives. A unique venture is the thrilling cave diving at **La Sirena,** a freshwater cave filled with stalactites and stalagmites, limestone formations, and air spaces to dive up into. The water is crystal clear and warm. Certification courses are offered at Treasure Divers' dive school. All excursions are priced separately. Multiday packages start at US$209 per person. English, Spanish, and German are spoken.

The Don Juan Beach Resort also has public rentals of other sports gear and equipment, such as paddleboats (US$8), Jet Skis (US$22), and catamaran tours (US$23).

ACCOMMODATIONS
Under US$50
Boca Chica is filled with small, low-budget options. The **Hotel Angel Gabriel** (Calle Duarte 27, tel. 809/523-9299, www.hotelangelgabriel .com, US$50 d) has been in operation since November 2004 offering clean rooms, free breakfast, a pool, and proximity to the beach. If you're interested in something roomier, a two-bedroom suite with a kitchenette will cost you US$85. Another great low-budget option is the **Hotel Neptuno Refugio** (Calle Duarte, tel. 809/523-9934, fax 809/523-9863, www .dominicana.de/neptuno.htm, US$45 d). This quiet five-story hotel is across from Neptuno's Club Restaurant on the far eastern end of Boca Chica. If you have questions about the town, owner Rita Reyes is very knowledgeable. She has flyers and information in the office but speaks only Spanish. Small apartments are also available, and prices vary according to your view (US$50 for interior garden, US$55 for park, and US$60 for an ocean view). All rooms are equipped with cable TV, air-conditioning, permanent lights, hot water, a minibar, and security box, and there's daily cleaning service. The apartments are similar but with kitchenettes and private balconies. Discounts are given to those who stay longer than a week.

The **Hotel Magic Tropical** (Calle Duarte, tel. 809/523-4254, fax 809/523-5439,

THE CARIBBEAN COAST

www.magic-tropical.com, US$20–60 s/d) is nothing fancy, but its rates are a steal. It has 20 rooms and apartments, a pool, garden, bar, small restaurant that serves buffet breakfast (which is included in the room price). All apartments have cable TV, air-conditioning or fan, a bathroom with a shower, terrace, kitchenettes, and Internet access. Languages spoken are English, Spanish, German, Italian, Romanian, and French.

While Boca Chica is not a gay and lesbian destination, there are a few gay-friendly hotels in town. Two are a short walk from the beach (then again, everything in Boca Chica is a short walk from the beach) and in more residential neighborhoods. The **Hotel Residencial El Candil** (Calle Juanico Garcia #2 at 20 de Diciembre, tel. 809/523-4252, fax 809/523-4232, www.comdata.nl/hotel-boca-chica-candil, US$30/room, US$35/studio, US$50–80/apartments, all based on double occupancy in high season) is the slightly cheaper of the two and has more security (all outside guests must leave identification at the front desk). Prices include taxes and airport transfer from Las Américas airport when staying a minimum of four nights. The apartments have air-conditioning, refrigerators, cable TV, equipped kitchenettes, hot water, safes, and telephones. This colonial-style, 24-room hotel is 150 meters from the beach and has a swimming pool and bar.

Another gay-friendly option is the **Costalunga Residence Club** (Av. del Sur 3, tel. 809/523-6883, www.costalunga.net, US$40–80 d). This hotel is a good value for the money. The Costalunga has a restaurant and pool; it's a five-minute walk to beach (or you can rent a motorbike from the hotel). It is a bit more relaxed on the security rules than El Candil, despite being in a residential area. Apartments have air-conditioning, kitchenettes, bathrooms, cable TV, and safes.

Hotel El Caucho (Calle Diciembre 5, tel. 809/523-5102, www.elcaucho.com, US$20–60 s/d), only a two-minute walk from beach, was renovated in 2003 and now has bright, clean rooms with balconies and air-conditioning.

There are two restaurants (one Dominican and one Italian) on the premises. This gay-friendly hotel is very laid-back and has a pool that is cleaned daily. The bar area doubles as a cybercafe open to the public. Spanish, English, Italian, and French are spoken here. You can arrange for city and airport transportation to and from the hotel. Although this hotel can be cheery, it has developed a reputation for being quite relaxed on its rules about letting hotel customers bring in outside guests. If you do not want to be in this type of atmosphere, stay elsewhere.

US$50-100

Midrange hotels are more difficult to find in Boca Chica than budget or pricey ones. One of the best options is **Hotel Zapata** (Calle Abraham Núñez 27, tel. 809/523-4777, fax 809/523-5534, www.hotelzapata.com, US$60–65 s/d, US$85 apartments) because it is one of only a few hotels located directly on Playa Boca Chica and is the most affordable of all of them. In this family-owned, 22-room hotel, you can enjoy a standard room complete with air-conditioning and cable TV. Some of the rooms have balconies. Two-bedroom apartments that fit up to four people are also available. The restaurant on-site cooks up both Creole and international favorites.

The **Hotel Boutique Don Emilio** (Calle Duarte 74, tel. www.bocachicaplaya.com /donemilio.htm, US$75 d, including breakfast), built in 1997, has an à la carte restaurant and a bar. All the rooms have air-conditioning, TV, and a refrigerator. Free parking and rent-a-car/taxi service can be arranged at the front desk.

US$100 and Up

The **Hamaca Coral by Hilton** (Calle Duarte 26 and Avenida Caracol, tel. 809/523-4611 or 877/GO-HILTON, 877/464-4586 for reservations from the United States, fax 809/523-6767, www.coralbyhilton.com, US$302 d high season) is the all-inclusive grande dame of the beach. If you're looking for a worry-free Boca Chica vacation, this is it. It was the first hotel in town and is still considered by many the best. The Hamaca is the most posh, the biggest, and has the biggest portion of Playa Boca Chica blocked off for its own guests (even though it is illegal to do so), thereby keeping the beach peddlers off the property. It offers oodles of activities, including water sports, tours and excursions, three tennis courts, spa services, and a fitness center for hotel guests. You will never go hungry with the multiple restaurants on-site. The casino and disco are some of the most popular nightlife spots in town. Outside guests have to pay a cover for entry into the disco, but the casino is free to the public. Prices do vary, so it is best to check the website for frequent deals.

The **Don Juan Beach Resort** (Calle Abraham Núñez, tel. 809/523-4511, U.S. tel. 800/820-1631, fax 809/688-5271, www.caei.com/djbr, US$135 s high season) is slightly more affordable then the Hamaca Coral. This all-inclusive alternative to the Hamaca has three restaurants, four bars, and an ice cream parlor on site. For nighttime entertainment, there is also a small disco, but the main draw to this resort is its connection to **Treasure Divers** scuba school, where you can get certified and go on great diving excursions. This resort's beach isn't as sealed off from the locals as the Hamaca's is, so some vendors may approach you on the beach. Children under 2 years old staying with two paying adults can stay free, and children 2–12 years old receive 50 percent off the per-person rate if they are staying in same room with two paying adults. Some wheelchair-accessible accommodations are available.

FOOD

Since Boca Chica was once a small fishing village, the seafood here is fresh and plentiful. Both Dominicans and foreigners own many of the restaurants here, so international choices such as Italian, Creole, American, and Swiss cuisine can be found. The most adventurous way to find food is to stroll down the beach or Calle Duarte and browse the many small restaurants and *freidurías* (stands where fish

and other things are fried) until you find one that is appealing to you. The local dishes like *lambí criolla* (conch in a Creole-style sauce), *yaniqueques* (a type of fried bread), and the daily fried fish with fresh lime squeezed over it are delectable choices for lunch. They are fast, fresh, and traditional Dominican dishes. When buying food from the vendors or at the beachside restaurants, make sure the prices are solid before ordering or you could find yourself with an astronomical bill. It is an unfortunate but common scam to hike the bill up for the tourist who doesn't know the exchange rate beforehand.

Should you need provisions for your room or have a kitchen in your room and want to cook on your own, there is a supermarket called **Supermercado La Defensa** (Calle Duarte 24, tel. 809/523-4321) next to the Baninter bank.

If getting away from the beach crowd for a bit sounds appealing, then the **Down Town Restaurant** (Calle Mella 9, tel. 809/523-4433, US$3–14) is for you. Located in a residential neighborhood, this open-air, thatched-roof, wheelchair-accessible restaurant serves seafood dishes like octopus in a vinaigrette sauce, chicken, rice dishes (try the *lambí* with rice for US$6.50), sandwiches, and pizza.

However, if hanging where it's happening is more attractive to you, then there is a string of restaurants to choose from along Calle Duarte. One is **Italy Italy** (Calle Duarte 101, in the Plaza Turística, tel. 809/523-4001, morgantithomas@yahoo.com, 8:30A.M.–1 A.M., US$14–17), which has a casual atmosphere and specializes in, you guessed it, Italian food.

◀ **Boca Marina** (Calle Duarte 12A, tel. 809/523-6702 or 809/688-6810 reservations, fax 809/523-6750, bocamarina@hotmail.com/, 11 A.M.–midnight, US$9–24) is definitely a hot spot that requires reservations during peak season. The 130-option menu features seafood. Located in the tourist zone of Boca Chica and directly *on* the water, this restaurant allows you to appreciate the natural beauty of Boca Chica while dining amid the

© ANA CHAVIER CAAMAÑO

Buy *yaniqueque* (fried bread) at the *fritura* (fried food) stands in Boca Chica.

seashell decor. The food is prepared fresh with a distinctively Mediterranean influence. If you can swing it, try the grilled lobster for about US$24 per pound. One of the most popular dishes is shrimp in Thai sauce. During the day, Boca Marina poses as a beach club where people can swim, sunbathe, order food and drinks, and rack up a hefty-but-worth-it bill. It's a "be seen in the scene" place. Boca Marina is good for families as well since it has a special kids' swimming area and a special children's menu. At night the atmosphere is soaked in romance, and if you're fortunate enough to be in Boca Chica for a full moon, Boca Marina is a must for a late dinner. Secure and free parking is available.

Similar to Boca Marina but more affordable is **Neptuno's Club Restaurant** (Calle Duarte 12, tel. 809/523-4703, fax 809/523-4251, www.hotelviewarea.com/neptunosclub, 9 A.M.–10:30 P.M. Tues.–Sun., US$10–40). Specialties are seafood, including popular dishes like mahi mahi ceviche and Spanish tapas to get your appetite going. Guests arrive by land and sea, anchoring boats just a bit clear of the shallow swimming space and walking in the water to get a table on the deck. This is a wonderful spot to spend your afternoon with the kids swimming and enjoying great and affordable food. Neptuno's boasts that it uses only organic food (such as the vegetables that are grown by local nuns and sweetwater shrimp free of chemicals) and never uses a microwave. There's a full bar, service for large groups, secure parking, and wheelchair-accessibility.

INFORMATION AND SERVICES

It wasn't until recently that the national tourism office took notice that there was a distinct need for a branch in Boca Chica. The **Oficina de Turismo** (Calle Duarte and Caracol, 2nd floor, tel. 809/523-5106, fax 809/523-4444) is in the same building as the **Politur** (tourist police) office (tel. 809/523-5102). But if you have an emergency, dial 911, or for the regular police department call 809/523-4778.

For money transfer and exchange, there are a number of different locations, but a couple of trusted ones are **Western Union** (Calle Duarte 65, tel. 809/523-4625, 8 A.M.–5 P.M. Mon.–Sat.) and the **Banco Popular** (Calle Duarte 43, tel. 809/523-4300).

Making a long-distance call can always be done through your hotel, but this is the most expensive option you have, and you (most likely) have to let the front desk know that you want to do so. Even though it's not as convenient as picking up your phone in your room, the most cost-effective way of making long-distance phone calls is to buy a pre-paid long-distance calling card. These are sold at any *colmado* or grocery store. Gift shops sometimes have them also. These calling cards can be used on any public phone.

Although using the **post office** (Calle Duarte, 8 A.M.–5 P.M. Mon.–Fri., 9 A.M.–noon Sat.) isn't recommended (service is completely unreliable), it is located across from the Parque Central.

Health and Medical Care

Medical care is limited throughout the country and Boca Chica is no different. If you have a medical concern, most of the all-inclusive hotels have a medical center or a doctor on staff. The **Farmacia Boca Chica** (Calle Duarte #17, tel. 809/523-4708, 8:30 A.M.–9 P.M. Mon.–Sat., 8:30 A.M.–7 P.M. Sun.) is centrally located and you can find most things you'll need. Of course, it is always best to bring any medication you take and anticipate needing in your carry-on baggage.

Internet

Hotel El Caucho (Calle Diciembre 5, tel. 809/523-5102, www.elcaucho.com, open 24 hours), a two-minute walk from beach, has a cybercafé that is open to public for a fee and is free for hotel guests. This is a very good option for communication with the folks back home if nothing is urgent, especially in lieu of postcards, since the postal service is abysmal.

GETTING THERE
From Santo Domingo

If you're visiting for the day from Santo Domingo and you have chosen to drive, take Highway 3 east; there is a toll of RD$15. You will pass the exit for Las Américas international airport. Your trip will be about 31 kilometers (30 minutes). Should you leave the chaos to the local drivers' more-than-capable hands, a taxi should run you about US$25. You can also catch a Boca Chica express bus from the northern side of Parque Independencia. The bus runs until 9 P.M. and will cost you about US$2.50. Your other option to get to Boca Chica is to flag down a *guagua* (US$1) from Parque Enriquillo or Parque Independencia heading east. Just remember that the *guaguas* stop running after dark.

From the Airports
Aeropuerto Internacional Las Américas (tel. 809/549-0450) is accessible by many major international airlines. If you haven't arranged for pickup with your hotel prior to your arrival, you can hire a taxi for about US$15. Boca Chica is about a 10-minute ride east of the airport. As you exit customs and baggage claim, you will be faced with a throng of taxi drivers, all trying to offer you a ride. Don't let them take your bag until you've secured a price for the ride. From **Aeropuerto Internacional La Romana** (tel. 809/556-5565) you will have a 1.75-hour ride west, which which will cost you about US$80.

GETTING AROUND
Walking is the easiest and best solution to getting around within Boca Chica. However, if you want to experience the motorcycle taxis called *motoconchos,* you can find them all over town. The young men who drive these scooters are found standing next to them or whizzing around honking at the tourists to see who needs a ride. Negotiate a cheap price before getting on one. Beware: These men drive erratically, the streets are filled with potholes, and the cars don't always see them, so a ride can be quite risky.

WEST OF BOCA CHICA
◖ Parque Nacional Submarino La Caleta

This is among the smallest of the national parks, but it's also one of the most popular. While it has a stretch of shoreline, the big attraction here is the underwater preserve. Parque Nacional Submarino La Caleta is just 20 kilometers east of Santo Domingo and has a large coral reef, Taíno caves, and two shipwrecks in its underwater portion. The park was created in 1984 when the former treasure-hunting ship, the *Hickory,* was intentionally foundered to draw more divers to the area. This 44-meter-long ship, which sits about 18 meters below the surface of the water, was originally used to scour the Bahía de Samaná for treasures from the Spanish galleons that sank there in the 1700s. It is now home to many sea creatures and sits in the warm, calm waters of the Caribbean Sea, making it an ideal spot for the diving newbie as well as for the experienced diver to explore. The **El**

Limón tugboat, which was scuttled in 1998, is also a showplace for fish like trumpetfish, blue tangs, and squirrelfish, and other sea creatures. Visibility is excellent.

Although the shipwrecks hog a lot of the publicity for the attraction to this park, don't forget to flipper over to the shallow coral gardens to navigate the spur-and-groove formations and take in the impressive varieties of hard and soft corals and fish.

La Caleta, as it is popularly known, is easily reached from a number of beach resorts and dive centers in Boca Chica. Best known is **Treasure Divers,** on the beach at the Don Juan Beach Resort (see *Sports and Recreation*), where travel and diving packages are offered for every skill level.

Unfortunately, damage to the coral reefs is a constant threat due to illegal fishing (sometimes chemicals such as bleach are used to fish!), artisanal fishing, and hurricanes. Nevertheless, La Caleta remains a highly regarded dive site.

Guayacanes, Juan Dolio, and Villas del Mar

If the Boca Chica is too busy for your relaxing holiday, then head a few kilometers east to Guayacanes, Juan Dolio, and Villas del Mar. These three small beach communities are considerably less touristy than Boca Chica and are smack-dab in the middle of the eastern Caribbean coastal region, making both the capital and La Romana good day-trip destinations.

Solitude is the number one reason that visitors return to these beach towns. This area is for the quiet vacationer who doesn't need too many choices but maybe wants to get in some golf, beach time, and even a little dancing and good food without the long lines of the more popular beach areas of Punta Cana and Bávaro. There are all-inclusives here, but they aren't as heavily marketed as the ones in Punta Cana and Bávaro.

BEACHES
Playa Caribe is in the small fishing community of Guayacanes. While this is a quieter destination than Boca Chica, it still is a rather popular beach when the weekend rolls around. Although most tourism has been funneled into the Puerto Plata and Punta Cana areas, in the last couple of decades hotels and resorts in this area have slowly begun sprouting up.

Playas Juan Dolio and Villas del Mar make up a stretch of beach that was developed, over decades, into a five-kilometer-long sprawling string of seaside hotels and resorts. Since there isn't much in the close vicinity of these towns, selection of your hotel becomes a more weighty decision. Unless you invest in some excursions at extra cost, you should think of your vacation to Guayacanes, Juan

Dolio, and Villas del Mar in an "all I'm gonna do is lie on the beach" kind of way.

The water is rougher here than that of the placid Playa Boca Chica, and the beach does attract the usual souvenir hawkers. While the beaches here are nice, they aren't as picturesque as others in the nation. Mainly, the advantage of this beach rests in its proximity (a one-hour ride) to the capital. It's a good place to get both tranquil beach time and lively city in one vacation.

ENTERTAINMENT

This area just isn't the place where the "partying kind" goes to vacation. Most of the entertainment is in the all-inclusive hotels. Some of the resorts will let outsiders into their discos for a cover charge or into their casinos for free.

Outside of the hotels, you can visit some of the restaurants in the area and mingle with the other travelers and vacationing Dominicans.

There are two bars: **El Batey Disco** (Calle Central 84) and **Chocolate Bar** (Calle Central 127), near the Decameron Hotel in Juan Dolio. The first is a late-night dance spot playing mostly merengue. The latter is more of a hangout where you can belly up to the bar, order an ice-cold Presidente beer, and perhaps take your turn at the pool table. Both are open late (until they feel like closing).

One more diversion is gambling. The casino at the **Coral Costa Caribe Beach Hotel** (Calle San Pedro de Macorís, Juan Dolio, tel. 809/562-6725, 8 P.M.–4 A.M.) is an elegant, American-style casino with live music.

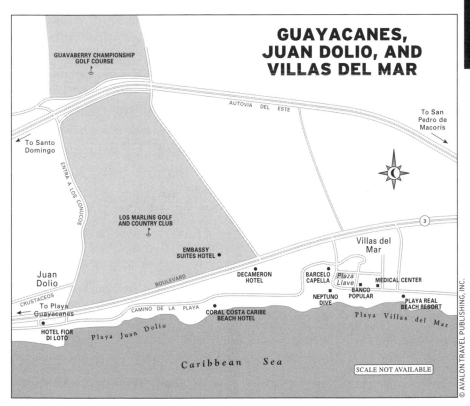

GUAYACANES, JUAN DOLIO, AND VILLAS DEL MAR

GUAVABERRY CHAMPIONSHIP GOLF COURSE

AUTOVIA DEL ESTE

To San Pedro de Macorís

To Santo Domingo

ENTRA A LOS CONUCOS

LOS MARLINS GOLF AND COUNTRY CLUB

3

Villas del Mar

EMBASSY SUITES HOTEL

Juan Dolio

BOULEVARD

DECAMERON HOTEL

BARCELO CAPELLA

Plaza Llave

MEDICAL CENTER

CRUSTACEOS

To Playa Guayacanes

CAMINO DE LA PLAYA

NEPTUNO DIVE

BANCO POPULAR

PLAYA REAL BEACH RESORT

CORAL COSTA CARIBE BEACH HOTEL

Playa Villas del Mar

HOTEL FIOR DI LOTO

Playa Juan Dolio

Caribbean Sea

SCALE NOT AVAILABLE

SPORTS AND RECREATION

Golf

Los Marlins Golf and Country Club (Las Américas Hwy., Juan Dolio, tel. 809/526-3315, fax 809/526-1130, sankrom@metrocountryclub.com, greens fees US$55, US$6 for caddy), designed by architect Charles Ankrom, is an 18-hole, par-72 course of 6,396 yards. This is a popular course for Dominican golfers and businesspeople looking to unwind from their busy schedules. Opened in 1995, it has a clubhouse, pro shop, restaurant, bar, putting green, and driving range. Packages are available through the area's all-inclusive hotels. Greens fees do not include a cart.

The **Guavaberry Championship Golf Course** (Km 55, Nuevo Autovia del Este, Juan Dolio, tel. 809/333-4653, fax 809/333-3030, www.guavaberrygolf.com, greens fees US$99) is superior in beauty, amenities, and price. It has 7,156 yards and was designed by the South African–born professional golfer Gary Player. This course is a par-72, 18-hole course with rolling hills, wide fairways, and several sets of trees to challenge you. The amenities include a gourmet restaurant, pro shop, piano bar, meeting rooms, pool, and terraces. Reservations are recommended. Special packages can be arranged through the all-inclusive resorts or via the website for Guavaberry.

Diving and Snorkeling

Many dive sites are accessible from this area. The coral reefs offshore create a wonderful viewing spot for different types of coral and fish. If you have an underwater camera, take it! Most of these excursions can be booked with the resorts or through independent dive centers such as **Neptuno Dive** (on the Juan Dolio beach next to the Barceló Capella resort, tel. 809/526-2005, fax 809/526-2538, www.neptunodive.com, US$36 for one dive), which is one of the best. Everyone, from beginners to those seeking instructor development courses, is welcome to take one of the many classes. If you want to brave the ocean after nightfall you'll need to pay an additional US$20. Excursions such as a day dive to **Isla Catalina,** which includes the bus and boat ride out to the island, lunch, and drinks will cost US$75, or try cave diving at **Cueva Taína** for US$65 (for an additional fee, you can take a horseback ride around the cave site). Paying in advance over the Internet will save you 20 percent. Prices listed here do not include the 16 percent tax.

ACCOMMODATIONS

Under US$50

Unique **Hotel Fior di Loto** (Calle Central 517, Juan Dolio, tel. 809/526-1146, fax 809/526-3332, hotelfiordiloto@hotmail.com or hotelfiordiloto@yahoo.com, US$20–40 d depending on the season) is by far the best value in the area. It is gay-friendly and has been the little darling of Juan Dolio since the early 1990s. With its noticeably Indian flare, it caters to the traveler seeking solace. You can take yoga classes, meditate, get a massage, or take in a dance class. The rooms are very simple but cozy; some have cooking facilities. Laundry service is available and there is a generator, plus a big deck for private sunbathing. The restaurant serves local, Indian, and vegetarian choices. Transportation is close by and staff can help you arrange some should you need it, even from Las Américas airport. Banks and shopping are near and the beach is 50 meters away.

US$50-100

Playa Esmeralda Beach Resort (Guayacanes, tel. 809/526-3434, fax 809/526-1744, www.hotel-playaesmeralda.com, playa.esmeralda@verizon.net.do, US$72 d). This small, 44-room hotel is popular with German tourists. The rooms are comfortable with air-conditioning, ceiling fans, and terraces. There is a pool, a bar, and a restaurant serving Dominican and Italian dishes. Diving lessons are available in the pool, and the front desk can help with excursion offers. Even though the offer of free drinks 10 A.M.–11 P.M. sounds like party central, this is a rather quiet hotel, like much of Guayacanes, so if you're looking for a fiesta, it isn't for you.

Embassy Suites Hotel at Los Marlins

Grand Resort (Juan Dolio, tel. 809/688-9999, fax 809/526-1130, www.embassysuites.com, US$109 d) is a true golfer's hotel—greens fees to the Los Marlins golf course are included in your price, and although this hotel is not on the beach, it is overlooking the tropical golf course. All 126 rooms are two-room suites. This hotel is perfectly suited for the business traveler (complete with secretarial service, including translations) and is a good place for families since kids under 18 staying with an adult stay free! There are three restaurants and three bars. Every morning you can enjoy a complimentary breakfast, and complimentary cocktails are served nightly 5:30–7:30 P.M. Amenities include two pools (one with a swim-up bar), a Jacuzzi, a children's area, a pro shop, spa, fitness center, and beauty salon. Car rental on-site and to-and-from airport shuttles (available on request) make transportation a breeze. All rooms have private balconies, high-speed Internet access, wet bars, cable TV, air-conditioning, and safety deposit boxes.

US$100 and Up

Costa Caribe Coral by Hilton (Juan Dolio, tel. 809/526-2244, fax 809/526-3141, www .coralbyhilton.com, starting at US$320 d). This big all-inclusive is near both Los Marlins and Guavaberry golf courses and has the best casino in the area. The 534-room resort is simply gigantic, filled with stuff to do for every type of visitor but mostly popular with the traveler who wants mostly to hang in the resort. There is guaranteed food 24 hours a day here, so gorge away. It's what vacations are for! There are six bars, nightly live entertainment, a disco that attracts people from other resorts as well, three pools, a kids' club, tennis, basketball, beach volleyball, minigolf, and various water sports, and you can get your PADI scuba certification. It's like a small town.

Barceló Capella (Juan Dolio, tel. 809/526-1080, capella.dh@barcelohotels.com.do, www.barcelo.com, US$160 d). This resort, with its Victorian-esque architecture, is a complete vacation package on its own. Again, this is a venue where many vacationers enjoy themselves without ever leaving the grounds. It boasts a great location, right on the beach, but bring some shoes; there is a great deal of coral, which makes it great for snorkeling but murder on your feet. As with most large all-inclusive resorts, the grounds are impeccably kept lush gardens, and the rooms are spacious and have all the regular amenities like minifridges, hair dryers, and irons. There is a disco, two pools, and a spa. It is a popular destination for honeymooners, who book special suites containing a Jacuzzi and king-size bed, as well as for families, whose children will be well occupied by the many child-specific activities available.

All-inclusive **Playa Real Beach Resort** (Juan Dolio, tel. 809/526-1114, fax 809/526-1397, www.amhsamarina.com, from US$140 d) has 391 rooms and is right on the beach. A staggering six restaurants serve Italian, Mexican, and seafood, and snacks can be found 24 hours a day. So you don't get bored there are four bars, a disco, two pools, water sports, bicycles for exploration of Juan Dolio, day and night entertainment, a spa, and horseback riding (to name a dizzying few activities). It is a popular hotel with locals and tourists alike and is considered one of the more affordable all-inclusives in the area.

FOOD

If you are staying at an all-inclusive hotel, the food there will be plentiful and somewhat varied. However, should you want to get out for a bit and treat yourself to a gourmet meal, **Deli Swiss** (Calle Central 338, Guayacanes, tel. 809/526-1226) serves up some expensive but fresh and fantastic seafood. The prices vary dramatically as everything is cooked according to what is fresh. Suffice it to say that this won't be cheap, but it will be fantastic. The wine list is one of the best in the country. If you're not a wine connoisseur, let the waitstaff choose for you. Enjoy classical music while dining on the oceanfront terrace as garlic and the smell of the sea intermingle.

⬤ Aura Beach House (Juan Dolio, tel. 809/526-2319, 11 A.M.–1 A.M., US$10–27) is the newest and trendiest attraction for both jet-set tourists and upscale Dominicans coming from the city, so make reservations. Situated directly on the beach, this place is gorgeous, very tastefully decorated in white with natural woods and shells. This is more of a beach club by day, where you can sun yourself on chaise lounges in the sand, lunch at interspersed tables, or even contemplate life out on comfortable loungers in the shallow waters offshore, where the servers wade out to you with your drinks and food. It's a place to spend the day in luxury on the beach. Swim a little, eat a lot, and spend a bunch. At night, aglow with candlelight, it transforms into a romantic must. Specialties include ceviche, salads, sushi, sashimi, seafood, pasta, crepes, and desserts. It's definitely a place to see and be seen yet relax at the same time.

Hotel Fior de Loto (Calle Central 517, Juan Dolio, tel. 809/526-1146, fax 809/526-3332, hotelfiordiloto@hotmail.com or hotelfiordiloto@yahoo.com, 6–9 P.M. daily, US$5–7) offers a much more down-to-earth dining experience, and it is open to the public. If the "lifestyles of the rich and famous" at Aura Beach House don't suit you, Hotel Fior de Loto's restaurant might. It serves Italian, Dominican, and Indian cuisine and homemade desserts. And here's the greatest shock—it has vegetarian dishes as well—very hard to find in this highly carnivorous country.

INFORMATION AND SERVICES

Unfortunately, there isn't much in terms of services in Juan Dolio, Guayacanes, or Villas del Mar, not even a tourism office. Despite the growing number of tourists, the towns have yet to offer the wider variety of services that you can find in Boca Chica. Your best

bet is to ask at your hotel (most have someone who will speak English) for anything you might need.

Plaza Llave (Juan Dolio) is across from the Barceló Capella and has gift shops, Internet access, money exchange, and a beauty shop. A few blocks down the main street is a **medical center** (tel. 809/526-1070).

If you desperately need to send something via mail, ask at your hotel's front desk. Do not send anything of any value through the postal service in the Dominican Republic.

GETTING THERE

A taxi ride from Las Américas international airport takes you along Highway 3 and past Boca Chica. It will cost about US$30, and the ride to the Guayacanes/Juan Dolio area is about 30 minutes. From Santo Domingo, catch a bus from Parque Independencia (around US$2) and in about an hour you will arrive in the area.

Of course if you are in a neighboring town, all you have to do is go out to Highway 3, stand on the side of the road with traffic going in the direction you want to travel, and flag down a *guagua.* Before you get in, confirm the price (which is never very much, just be sure to have small bills), hop in, and enjoy traveling the way the locals do.

GETTING AROUND

There is no need for motorized anything in Guayacanes and Juan Dolio. There is so little traffic within town. *Motoconchos* are an option and they are all over the island. Just agree on a price before you get on. Many hotels have bikes to loan you or know where you can get one. Just ask at the front desk. Hotels can get you taxis, too, and they usually have rates posted or quickly available.

San Pedro de Macorís

At the junction where the Río Higuamo empties into the Caribbean Sea sits San Pedro de Macorís, a town that came to life as a major player in the production of sugar in the latter part of the 19th century. Many people from the Leeward and Windward Islands migrated or were "imported" to work here in the sugarcane fields. These people and their descendants are known today as *cocolos*. When they arrived they brought their distinctively African-influenced culture and traditions, with which they have added color and festivity to the town of San Pedro. This is most evident while enjoying the dances, music, and costumes of the **Cocolos Festival** (see *Events*).

By the time World War II came around, causing a worldwide sugar shortage and driving up the cost, San Pedro de Macorís began to bulge with rich plantation owners and the town seemed to be on the right track to permanent prosperity. It was the "star" of the Caribbean, rife with money and cultural standing. But as the sugar prices dropped and people lost their jobs, San Pedro's economy slumped and the city began to deteriorate. People began leaving their homes in the desperate hope of finding jobs elsewhere. Since then it has never truly regained its former glory.

San Pedro de Macorís is also known for another resource that they seem determined to never stop producing—baseball players. Almost every Major League team has at least one Dominican on its roster. Some of the most famous players (Sammy Sosa, Pedro Guerrero, Pedro Gonzalez, and George Bell) have come from this town. It has become the main attraction here, especially since there is not much more to see or do within the city limits. Fans of the game who visit the area during the **baseball season** (Oct.–Jan.) should be sure to catch a game. In the off-season of American baseball, you can often find some of today's brightest big league baseball stars coming home to play for their former teams.

While at the stadium, you can purchase a bottle of rum to enjoy during the game. This land of sugarcane and baseball is also home to the distilleries of Brugal and Barceló, rum companies that produce millions of liters a year of what is arguably some of the best rum in the world.

Aside from sugar, rum, and baseball, in 1972 San Pedro gained a free trade zone, where native and foreign companies set up camp to manufacture their goods (such as textiles, shoes, electronic parts, etc.), offering jobs (albeit low-paying ones lacking many workers' rights) to the residents of San Pedro. In exchange, these companies are offered certain tax and customs incentives.

SIGHTS

Tetelo Vargas Stadium

Home to **Las Estrellas Orientales** baseball team and some of the most elite players in the country, the Tetelo Vargas Stadium (Av. Circunvalación) is the most well-known building in town. Boys who used to play stickball in the *campo,* with their makeshift milk-carton gloves, are now the graceful, competitive, and hungry-for-success Eastern Stars, as their name translates. Baseball season in the Dominican Republic is October–January. If you don't speak Spanish, ask at your hotel for tickets to a game and a taxi to take you. However, if you do speak Spanish, show up at the box office nice and early on the day of the game; you can get a ticket for about US$20 for front-row seats or about US$2 for bleacher seats. Games are usually at night.

Catedral San Pedro Apóstol

This cathedral (Calle Charro near Av. Independencia, open daily 8 A.M.–8 P.M.) is not a major landmark, but it has a beauty all its own and has had a tumultuous struggle to stay standing. The church was constructed in 1850. In 1865, the church was leveled by a hurricane and later reconstructed. As if that weren't enough, it was devastated by fire in 1886. It was then that the present temple was erected. In 1996 it was elevated to a cathedral. In 2000, a five-year remodeling phase was set into motion. But as of 2005, no real progress had been made. The parishioners remain infuriated about this delay, and have demanded that the government finally pay attention to the stained glass, marble floors, and carved wood, which could very well be ruined forever if ignored any longer.

(Cueva de las Maravillas

Located 15 kilometers east of San Pedro de Macorís at Boca del Soco on the San Pedro de Macorís–La Romana Highway, the Cave of Wonders (tel. 809/696-1797, www.cuevadelasmaravillas.com, 9 A.M.–6 P.M. Tues.–Sun., adults US$2, children under 12 US$1) is most certainly a highlight of the Caribbean coastal region and should not be overlooked when you're in the area. Discovered in 1926, this cave has been the subject of many scientific studies because in its 840 meters, over 500 pictographs, petroglyphs, and engravings have been preserved as if drawn yesterday. It truly has the richest sample of rock art in the Antilles and also an impressive array of stalactites, stalagmites, and columns. The government took a great deal of care to make the cave accessible to visitors, and in 2003, the cave's team of architects won the Gold prize in the International Landscape Architecture Bienal Award. It has a 240-meter footpath and is equipped with museum-quality lighting. Ramps and elevators make it wheelchair-accessible. Also on-site is a museum, a shop, a place to buy snacks, and restrooms. You will receive a one-hour tour from a knowledgeable

SPEAKING OF TAÍNO

Even though the Taíno people were nearly extinguished by Christopher Columbus and his men, their language has not completely disappeared. Over time, portions of it have appeared in the Spanish-speaking part of the Caribbean. More than 800 words are still used. Most of these words are for objects (for instance, *chichí* for baby), geographical places (like the city of Higüey), personal names, and flora and fauna. Often, the words are so widely used that they are mistaken for having Spanish origins, or the two languages can be interchangeable, as in the case of the Spanish *poquito* and the Taíno *chinchín*, both meaning "a little bit."

Just as the Taíno contributed to today's Dominican speech, so have some words found their way into regular English usage. The following are some examples:

hamaca – hammock
huracán – hurricane
barbacoa – barbecue
canoa – canoe
casabe – cassava
guayaba – guava
iguana – iguana

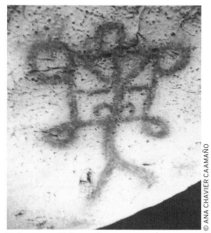

Taíno rupestrian art

© ANA CHAVIER CAAMAÑO

maíz – maize
maraca – maraca
sabana – savanna
tabaco – tobacco
caníbal – cannibal

guide. No photos are allowed unless arranged beforehand.

EVENTS

The **Cocolos Festival,** held on June 29, is also the feast of St. Peter and St. Paul and is a perfect time to view the customs and traditions of the *cocolos* immigrants, the sugarcane field workers for the industry in the late part of the 19th century. Their African heritage is preserved through the vibrant, multicolored, mirrored costumes worn by the *guloyas* (dancers), who roam around the city streets performing the traditional dance to furious drumbeats—as the rum flows, of course.

ACCOMMODATIONS

Since San Pedro isn't a popular destination for tourists, there are few hotels and only one good one in the town itself. Many people who visit San Pedro do so on a day trip or just overnight to go to a baseball game. The **Howard Johnson Hotel Macorix** (Av. Gaston Fernando Deligne, tel. 809/529-2100, fax 809/529-9239, www.hojo.com, US$65–125 d), built in 1969, is showing its age a little but has 170 clean rooms, a pool, tennis court, restaurant, disco, business center, concierge service, and room service. The rooms are satisfactorily equipped with air-conditioning, a fridge, cable TV, and a balcony. Check-in is at 3 P.M.

FOOD

Near the Catedral San Pedro Apóstal and on the waterfront, **Robby Mar** (Av. Francisco Dominguez Charro 35, tel. 809/529-4926, open 10 A.M.–midnight, US$10–20) is the best restaurant in town; it has outdoor and indoor seating. The restaurant serves seafood, meats, salads, pastas, and other choices. The crab and lobster are fresh and sold by weight (without the shell)—try them grilled or with a garlic sauce. The owner, Tony, speaks English well and can help with any suggestions.

The Howard Johnson hotel is home to the **Bar Restaurant Apolo** (Av. Independencia 53, tel. 809/529-3749, 11 A.M.–11 P.M.), which serves Chinese food that is far from remarkable in a casual environment.

INFORMATION AND SERVICES

Despite the fact that San Pedro de Macorís is not a major tourist destination, an **Oficina de Turismo** (tel. 809/529-3967, fax 809/246-3206) serves the area.

The Howard Johnson has an ATM and money exchange service for guests, and the concierge can help you find anything you require. Outside the hotel try **Banco Popular** (Calle 27 de Febrero 7, tel. 809/529-0313) or **Banco Progreso** (Av. Independencia 48, tel. 809/529-6933). For money transfers go to **Agente de Cambio Vimenca** (Calle Alejo Martinez 13, tel. 809/529-0012, 8 A.M.– 10 P.M. Mon.–Sat., 8 A.M.–6 P.M. Sun.; it can do **Western Union** transactions.

To make a long-distance call, go to the **Tricom** office (Av. Independencia 75, tel. 809/476-0688). Just down the block is **Farmacia Andreita** (Av. Independencia 55, tel. 809/529-2529) for any pharmaceutical needs.

GETTING THERE

From Santo Domingo and Las Américas international airport San Pedro de Macorís is a little over an hour's drive east along Highway 3.

If you're staying in the Juan Dolio resort area, catching a *guagua* or taxi will cost around US$1 or US$10 each way, respectively. Flag one down that is traveling in the right direction. Ask the driver to let you off as near to your destination as possible.

GETTING AROUND

San Pedro de Macorís is a congested town filled with trucks going to the industrial areas, sugarcane fields, and distilleries and has heavy clogs along the poorly marked streets and highways that run through. This leaves the traffic in a chaotic battle. Hire a taxi for your transportation rather than braving the back of a *motoconcho*.

THE CARIBBEAN COAST

La Romana

Just like San Pedro de Macorís, La Romana was a sugar town. The town began to prosper in the 1960s when an American company, Gulf + Western Industries, became the owner of a sugar mill and began to invest heavily in other industries like cattle and cement. The company cleaned La Romana up and in the mid-1970s built the now world-famous **Casa de Campo** resort about 1.6 kilometers east of the town. Many wealthy and famous people, such as Bill Clinton, Julio Iglesias, and Mi-chael Jackson, come to spend their money at this luxurious resort while golfing on the world-class courses, buying or renting the lavish villas, or getting married in a whirlwind Dominican "quickie" wedding. In turn, the town was eventually able to afford a new state-of-the-art airport and bring in even more tourists than before.

La Romana is, to this day, a quaint little town with surprisingly little to offer tourists, but since it is geographically close to Casa de Campo it reaps the benefits of the foreign currency the resort brings to the region. If it weren't for the development of Casa de Campo and its adjacent tourist attraction, **Altos de Chavón**, this little town would still be a sleepy little seaside village.

SIGHTS
Isla Catalina

Isla Catalina is the second largest island off the southeastern coast of the Dominican Republic. Named "Toeya" by the Taíno, it was renamed in honor of Saint Catalina by Columbus. Its beaches are powdery white and its waters are shallow and warm. There is an entry fee of US$1 as it is protected government land. The island itself is uninhabited, but the coral reef just offshore is populated by many sea creatures, which makes for a good afternoon of diving or snorkeling. Although it is located just off the coast of La Romana, it is mainly accessed through dive excursion companies and resorts in Boca Chica, Juan Dolio, and the surrounding areas. Tours typically charge US$30–70 (including lunch).

This island is used by many cruise ships as a stopping point for their patrons to stretch their sea legs and get in a day of snorkeling and hiking. The highest elevation is seven meters above sea level. There is no fresh water, only mildly salty water from which the animals drink, so take some water with you. Be sure to take your binoculars to view some exotic birds, wild monkeys (yes, monkeys), and

LA ROMANA

HOTEL FRANO
JOAQUIN SUAREZ
PEDRO ABREU
PADRE
CALLE B
CALLE A
CALLE PRIMERA
CALLE A GARCIA
JULIO A
SANTA ROSA
LLUBERES
GARCIA   DICKSON
DOLORES TEJADA
TENIENTE AMADO GARCIA GUERRERO
GASTON FERNANDEZ DELIGNE
TIBURCIO MILAN LOPEZ
ESPAILLAT
ENRIQUILLO
HECTOR RENE GIL
G. LUPERON
SCOTIABANK
JUAN DE UTRERA
D'ACOIRIS EMPANADAS
FARMACIA DINORAH
EUGENIO N MIRANDA
DUARTE
HECTOR P QUESADA
Cemetery
VARIEDADES GIFT SHOP
30 DE MAYO
HERIBERTO PAYAN
AVENIDA
LIBERTAD
FRANCISCO DEL CASTILLO MARQUEZ
DR TEOFILO
CREALES
FERRY
TRINITARIA
BUS STOP
BANINTER
IGLESIA DE SANTA ROSA DE LIMA
SANTA ROSA
PEDRO A LLUBERES
SHISH KABOB
TEOFILO HERNANDEZ
JUMBO SUPERMARKET/ VERIZON
Parque Central
Río Dulce
RESTAURACION
FRANCISCO RICHIEZ
POST OFFICE
CYBERNET CAFÉ
TRIGO DE ORO
CORALES RESTAURANT CAFÉ AND BAR
ALTAGRACIA
SANTA ROSA
To Higüey

SCALE NOT AVAILABLE

Caribbean Sea

rattlesnakes. These animals were all left here after a failed attempt at making Isla Catalina a zoo. The mosquitoes are relentless, so make sure to have some repellent.

Beaches
La Romana has three beautiful beaches: **El Caletón, La Minita,** and **La Caleta.** La Caleta is closest to the city and is the most visited during the summer. La Minita is walled into the Casa de Campo protective watch. It is a small but nice beach inaccessible to outsiders. To hang with the locals at the beach, visit El Caletón.

La Romana Cigar Factory
Located in a warehouse neighborhood one block off of Calle Padre Abreu, this small cigar factory (Calle Tiburcio Milan Lopez 31, mid-mornings are best as hours tend to fluctuate) is a worthwhile stop whether you're a smoker or not as it is an interesting look into one of the Dominican Republic's most notable crafts and exports. About 60 employees roll cigars here (it's not a big operation), and you can see all the different types of tobacco, the processes, and the techniques that go into this art. After-ward, with a more complete knowledge of the craft, you can choose from a wall of different blends and qualities. Almost any taxi or *moto-concho* driver will know where this factory is. Save about an hour for this tour. If you don't speak Spanish go with a guide just in case no one there can translate that day.

🄲 Altos de Chavón
The most visited tourist spot in the southeast is undoubtedly Altos de Chavón (Casa de Campo, tel. 809/523-8011, fax 809/523-8312). High above the Río Chavón sits this beautifully crafted mock 16th-century Mediterranean village. In the 1970s it was built to give guests of Casa de Campo and other tourists something to do, and it is now also home to an art school affiliated with the Parsons School of Design in New York.

Cobbled passages, plazas constructed of black river pebbles and sun-drenched coral,

Iglesia de Santa Rosa de Lima on the Parque Central in La Romana

azalea-dripping stone archways, and wooden shutters on terracotta-roofed buildings create a time-warp sensation as you weave your way from café to boutique, shopping for original student artwork, jewelry, or souvenirs.

Attractions include top-notch restaurants, the Church of St. Stanislaus, and a 5,000-seat open-air amphitheater where concerts are regularly held. The Altos de Chavón **Regional Museum of Archaeology** (tel. 809/523-8554) houses more than 3,000 artifacts that document the island's pre-Columbian heritage from the pre-ceramic era to the Taíno people. In the three art galleries (call 809/523-8470 for more information), you can stroll amid the show-cased art of Dominican and international established and emerging artists.

Any amount of time spent at Altos de Chavón is a treat. Even though it seems a bit odd to have built a replica of a 16th-century Mediterranean village in the Caribbean and greatly removed from modern Dominican life, it is a rich addition to your island getaway vacation.

THE CARIBBEAN COAST

THE CARIBBEAN COAST

© ANA CHAVIER CAAMAÑO

Stroll the romantic cobbled paths of Altos de Chavón.

ENTERTAINMENT

Most travelers who come to La Romana do so for the afternoon or just pass through, so the nightlife is almost completely limited to Casa de Campo and the other all-inclusive resorts such as the **Santana Beach Resort** (tel. 809/412-1010, fax 809/412-1818, www.santanabeach.com), where you can buy a night pass that entitles you to dinner, drinks, and entrance into the discos. There are more nightlife options available in nearby Bayahibe (see the *Southeast* chapter).

Dinner at one of the many restaurants at Altos de Chavón is a romantic option that can be followed with dancing at the disco.

SHOPPING

Variedades Gift Shop (Pedro A. Lluberes and Altagracia 54, tel. 809/556-2785) sells crafts and jewelry made of semiprecious larimar, amber, and coral as well as cigars, paintings, and other art. If you haggle you can get very fair prices for the art.

Yina Bambu Shop (Carretera Romana, Km 4.5, tel. 809/550-8322, 7:30 A.M.–7 P.M.) has been around for a long time selling tourist keepsakes and Dominican crafts as well as Haitian paintings, CDs of Dominican music, and those crazy-big preserved spiders! It sells larimar and amber jewelry as well. But if you're looking for original art, go to Altos de Chavón instead; you'll pay a fatter bill, but you'll have a one-of-a-kind piece.

Altos de Chavón's **La Tienda** (Casa de Campo, tel. 809/523-3333, ext. 5398) is the perfect place to go for original art. Since it is the home of a school of design, many of the students artworks and crafts are actually for sale. Handmade purses, clothing, paintings, and jewelry are a few of the choices. Other shops are filled with things like Dominican souvenirs and fine linen.

SPORTS AND RECREATION
Fishing

Casa de Campo (tel. 809/523-3333, fax 809/523-8547) offers deep-sea and freshwater-river fishing trips from its private marina.

The main catch in the sea is marlin and you have the option of half-day (US$592) or full-day (US$790) charters. These prices are per boat and include fishing rods, bait, boat captain and mate, sodas, and bottled water.

In the river, championship snooker are waiting to be hooked. The river is a good excursion for photographers, too. The very scenic Río Chavón was the backdrop for the films *Apocalypse Now* and *Rambo*. A three-hour tour (including boat, guide, bait, tackle, and refreshments) will cost US$46 per person with a four-person limit per boat.

Golf

People travel from all over the world to golf on the Pete Dye–designed **Teeth of the Dog** course (Casa de Campo, tel. 809/523-8115, fax 809/523-8800, golf@ccampo.com.do, 7:30 A.M.–5 P.M., greens fees US$150–205 depending on the season, caddies US$15). This 18-hole, par-72 course opened in 1971 and quickly shot up to the number one course in the Caribbean. It is currently ranked number 34 in the world by *Golf* magazine. Seven of the holes are along the ocean, and the terrain is challenging to even the best professionals around the globe. Reservations are *highly recommended* as space can sometimes be booked as far out as 12 months.

Another golf course in the Casa de Campo complex is **The Links** (tel. 809/523-8115, fax 809/523-8800, golf@ccampo.com.do, greens fees including cart are US$147). It is more inland and opened in 1975. With its undulating hills, the layout resembles traditional British and Scottish courses, featuring small greens and several lagoons. Most golfers attest that it is equally as challenging as the Teeth of the Dog course. It too is an 18-hole, par-72 course. You can reserve a time 24 hours in advance.

Yet another option for golf at Casa de Campo, **Dye Fore** (tel. 809/523-8115, fax 809/523-8800, golf@ccampo.com.do, greens fees US$150–205 depending on the season) is the newest of the resort's courses. It hugs the village of Altos de Chavón. Designed by Pete Dye as well, this spectacularly beautiful 18-hole golf course has breathtaking views of the village, the Rio Chavón, and the Caribbean Sea. If you stray from the fairway, however, you will be punished in this terrain. This is a challenging course.

Snorkeling

Isla Catalina is the closest spot to snorkel off the coast of La Romana. **Casa de Campo** (tel. 809/523-3333, US$37 per person) is best equipped for snorkeling excursions. The cost includes the charter of the boat but not the rental of fins and a mask, which is US$5 per hour. If you are on the all-inclusive plan at the resort, the gear fee is waived.

Isla Catalina can also be reached from the Bayahibe resorts and excursion companies outlined in the *Southeast* chapter.

Tennis

Casa de Campo's tennis center, **La Terraza** (tel. 809/523-3333, 7 A.M.–9 P.M., US$20 per hour during the day and US$25 at night) has been called the "Wimbledon of the Caribbean" by *Travel + Leisure* magazine. The center begins its day at dawn sweeping the courts and marking the lines on the 13 Har–Tru clay courts. At night 10 of the courts are equipped with lights. This is a luxury tennis club complete with ball boys, instructors, teaching pros, a pro shop, and a spectator's deck. Lessons are available at extra cost.

ACCOMMODATIONS

This region doesn't have many options outside of Casa de Campo, which is certainly the big kahuna of the Caribbean Coast. There are a few small hotels in town, used mainly by traveling businesspeople or tourists just passing through town.

Under US$50

The 41-room **Hotel Frano** (Calle Padre Abreu 9, tel. 809/550-4744, US$30) is a good value for the money. Rooms are comfortable with a private bathroom, air-conditioning, TV, and hot water. A restaurant on-site serves excellent Dominican food. You can experience the town of La Romana itself, but you'll have to travel to see the beach. If you stay here and pay in pesos, they will not charge you tax.

Dejavue (Calle 1ra. Reparto Torres, tel. 809/556-2949, fax 809/556-8061, ventas@dejavuehotel.com, www.facilconexion.net/work/dejavue/ or www.dejavuehotel.com, US$45 d) is one of the nicer small hotels in La Romana. It has a bar and restaurant serving tasty Dominican food and great drinks, a pool, and rooms with TV, hot water, and air-conditioning.

US$50-100

Santana Beach Resort & Casino (Carretera San Pedro de Macorís, tel. 809/412-1010, fax 809/412-1818, h.santana@mail.cotursa-hotels.com, www.santanabeach.com, US$85 d) offers an all-inclusive resort experience for a lot less money than Casa de Campo. It has six restaurants, five bars (one of which is a swim-up bar in the gigantic pool), children's activities with a separate pool, nonmotorized water sports, a fitness center, a casino that has free entrance and drinks, tennis, and nightly entertainment. Amenities include a medical center, optional excursions, and the Dominican Village, which has a beauty shop and a mini-market. A standard room is called a junior suite and has two queen-size beds, air-conditioning and ceiling fan, cable TV, a stocked minibar, private terrace or balcony, full bathroom with shower and tub, and a safety box (at extra cost).

US$100 and Up

C Casa de Campo (tel. 800/877-3643 or 809/523-3333, fax 809/523-8548, www.casadecampo.com.do, US$353 per night and up in high season) is the crown jewel of La Romana without a doubt. Some argue that it is the best resort not only in the Dominican Republic, but in the entire Caribbean. After all, celebrities vacation here. Bill Clinton plays golf here. Michael Jackson married Lisa Marie Presley here. Julio Iglesias owns a villa here. Yes, it is the resort that appeals to the rich and famous, and it shows. The food is good, the reputation is better, and the amenities are the best of the best. It is more like a town than a resort. The property is huge—it has its own beach, marina, equestrian stables, shooting gallery, tennis courts, world-class golf courses, many restaurants and bars, spa, even a full-size grocery store. It's clean, walled off, and security is tight. All-inclusive packages include unlimited drinks, no menu restrictions, unlimited horseback riding, tennis, and nonmotorized water sports at Minitas Beach, and one round of 25 shots of skeet/trap shooting.

FOOD
Casa de Campo

Casa de Campo's **Marina & Yacht Club,** which is actually a residential area designed to look like Portofino, Italy, is the resort's new swanky US$100 million dollar project. Around the Plaza Portofino are many nice restaurants, international boutiques, galleries, jewelers, and even impromptu entertainment. The restaurants that are particularly notable are **Peperoni Café** (tel. 809/523-2228, noon–1 A.M.), which serves international cuisine including sushi; **Cafe Bellini Restaurant** (tel. 809/523-2348, 11 A.M.–midnight), which serves fantastic Italian food; and **Chinois** (tel. 809/523-2388, noon–4 P.M. and 6:30–11:30 P.M., which has Cantonese-style lunch and dinner (a little over-rated, but still better than most all-inclusive restaurants). Part of the charm of the restaurants in this area is their atmosphere. The Marina & Yacht Club is quite alluring as you sit back and watch the easy bobbing of the luxurious yachts. Reservations are recommended for all three restaurants.

In the main area of Casa de Campo, restaurants include **Lago Grill** (tel. 809/523-3333, 7–11 A.M. and noon–3 P.M. Mon.–Sat., 6:30–11 A.M. and noon–4 P.M. Sun., US$6–14, breakfast buffet US$16) and **El Pescador** (tel. 809/523-3333, noon–4 P.M. and 7–11 P.M. daily, US$10–30). The first is a breakfast and lunch buffet with ample terraced space offering a view of the Teeth of the Dog golf course. The breakfast specialties are omelets prepared to your personal liking and a fresh-squeezed juice bar. El Pescador, an à la carte restaurant for lunch and dinner, is cozy and on the oceanfront. The atmosphere is casual but the service is fantastic. Order grilled meats,

© CASA DE CAMPO, LA ROMANA, DOMINICAN REPUBLIC

THE CARIBBEAN COAST

Casa de Campo's marina in La Romana

seafood (the best in the area), catch of the day, salads, hamburgers, and oven-baked pizzas. It also offers a children's menu. Reservations are recommended.

Altos de Chavón

Dine amid the romantic scenery of the artists' village. **La Piazetta** (tel. 809/523-3333, 6–11 P.M.) is an à la carte Italian restaurant befitting its surroundings, complete with serenading musicians. There's a delicious antipasto bar, homemade pastas, seafood in varied sauces, meat, and poultry. And no Italian restaurant would be complete without succulent desserts and rich coffees. A children's menu is available. Don't forget to check out the humidor with cigars. Reservations are required.

Mexican restaurant **El Sombrero** (tel. 809/523-3333, 6–11 P.M., US$11–17) has an open terrace with typical Mexican decorations (mariachis too). The menu offers spicy Mexican fare (try the fish in garlic sauce), a "welcome" tequila, and tasty margaritas made of tropical fruits. Reservations are required.

La Romana Town

Corales Restaurant Café and Bar (Calle Eugenio A. Miranda 57, tel. 809/556-9444, 8 A.M.–noon, US$2–20) is Dominican-owned with a charming ambience indoors or in the romantic courtyard. Dress casual but nice. The varied menu includes sandwiches, empanadas, seafood, pasta, and meat. Try the special seafood soup and enjoy a cocktail from the full bar.

A true gem of a place, **Trigo de Oro** (Calle Eugenio A. Miranda, tel. 809/550-5650, US$2–10) is a wonderful French-owned café in a converted historical home. The chefs make all their own pastries. It is set apart from the street by a fence with lush greenery, making an inviting, shady courtyard and veranda where you can have a quiet cup of coffee and conversation. There's a full bar with wine and beer as well. Coffee and desserts are a specialty. Although it seems posh, the prices are cheap. The chocolate croissants are to die for.

D'Acoiris Empanadas (Calle Eugenio A. Miranda and Trinitaría, next to the Parque

Central), great for an inexpensive and quick meal, has juice, sandwiches, and empanadas. **Delicias Mariscas** (Av. Libertad, tel. 809/556-2832) has some excellent seafood for the most reasonable prices around.

Got a hankering for something other than the usual Dominican or Italian choices? Try **Shish Kabob** (Calle Francisco del Castillo Marquez 32, tel. 809/556-2737, 9:30 A.M.–midnight, US$5–30) for some Middle Eastern food. Grilled kabobs, kabob pizza, and *dolmades* (stuffed grape leaves) are on the menu, along with a ton of other tasty choices like baba ghanoush.

Tucked back into a very commercial area, on Calle Juan de Utrera, you will find **La Romana Market Place.** This is where the locals shop for fresh produce, housewares, and all kinds of everyday things.

INFORMATION AND SERVICES

Fortunately, La Romana has an **Oficina de Turismo** (Teniente Amado García, tel. 809/550-6922, 8 A.M.–2 P.M. Mon.–Fri.).

For exchanging currency, there is a **Baninter** (Calle Trinitaría 59, tel. 809/556-5151, 8:30 A.M.–5 P.M. Mon.–Fri.). It has an ATM. Another bank is **ScotiaBank** (Calle Trinitaría, 8:30 A.M.–4:30 P.M. Mon.–Fri., 9 A.M.–1 P.M. Sat.).

Jumbo Supermarket (Av. Libertad) has all the things you might need. It's more of a super center, selling food along with providing such services as a bank, American Air office, Verizon, Western Union, and Nestlé Ice Cream.

Long-distance calls can be made at **Codetel** (Calle Trinitaría 51, tel. 809/220-4403, 8 A.M.–6 P.M. Mon.–Fri., 9 A.M.–1 P.M. Sat.). In addition to the **Verizon** office in the Jumbo Supermarket, there is another on Calle Trinitaría, which is open 8 A.M.–10 P.M. daily. Another option is **Tricom** (Calle Hector Rene Gil, tel. 809/520-5707).

The post office (Calle Francisco del Castillo Marquéz, tel. 809/556-2265) is two blocks north of the Parque Central.

High-speed Internet access is alive at **Cybernet Café** (Calle Eugenio A. Miranda by the Parque Central, tel. 809/813-5514, cybernetcafe2000@hotmail.com, 8:30 A.M.–9 P.M. daily), across from ScotiaBank.

Farmacia Dinorah II is on the side of Parque Central (tel. 809/556-2225).

GETTING THERE

From Las Américas international airport you will have an 80-minute drive along Highway 3. As you enter La Romana from the east, Highway 3 turns into Avenida Padre Abreu in La Romana's city limits. Take a right onto Santa Rosa. This street will take you to the Parque Central, where you will find the bus stations and the **Iglesia de Santa Rosa de Lima** directly across from the park. You will also be in the general area for many of the communication centers, banks, cafés, and restaurants.

To take a bus from Santo Domingo, catch the one on the southeast corner of Parque Enriquillo that says it is going to Higüey. This bus stops at the station across from Parque Central in La Romana. It costs about US$5.

From La Romana airport it is easiest to hail a taxi into town. It will cost very little and take only 10 minutes.

GETTING AROUND

La Romana is just small enough that renting a car is a little ridiculous unless you're planning on going on many excursions alone. To hire a taxi or a *motoconcho,* walk to the top of the Parque Central right in front of the church; they wait there. It will cost less than US$4 to go anywhere in town by *motoconcho* and US$7 for the taxi within the city. Don't forget to haggle and secure a price before agreeing to the arrangement.

Dead set on car rental? La Romana airport has a branch of **Budget** (tel. 809/813-9111, www.budget.com, 9 A.M.–5 P.M. Mon.–Fri., 10:30 A.M.–2:30 P.M. Sat.). Another option is **Honda Rent a Car** (Calle Santa Rosa 84, tel. 809/556-3835, 8 A.M.–6 P.M. Mon.–Fri., 8 A.M.–4 P.M. Sat. and Sun.).

THE SOUTHEAST

Opulent tourism and bucolic Dominican life strangely coexist in the southeast region of the Dominican Republic. It is still not uncommon to see a motorcade of tour buses slowing down on the highway behind an oxen-driven cartload of sugarcane. It wasn't until the latter part of the 20th century that tourism really took off in this section of the republic, and the one-time rookie region quickly became the nation's leading economic powerhouse, overthrowing the incumbent Puerto Plata on the north coast as the favorite destination for travelers looking for paradise. The agricultural, livestock, and sugarcane industries that once ruled the area have had to bow down to the powerful allure of the pristine beaches, which have become the livelihood of the area and the country. But along with the mushrooming all-inclusive resorts along the southeastern coastline and Costa del Coco, the job opportunities for Dominicans have increased as well.

The southeast region's main tourism areas—including Bayahibe along the Caribbean coast and La Costa del Coco of the Atlantic side—deliver what many visitors expect from a Caribbean vacation: exquisite beaches, first-class snorkeling, catamaran rides, phenomenal golf courses, and luxurious accommodations. Their all-inclusive resorts are famous for being the best bargains in the Caribbean, and indeed, a good portion of the southeastern coastline is lined with these mega-complexes, boasting the largest number of hotel rooms in the country.

In addition to all of the tourist development, the southeast is home to two of the nation's larger national parks, Parque Nacional del Este

© ANA CHAVIER CAAMAÑO

HIGHLIGHTS

◖ Bayahibe and Dominicus Beaches: The plush white sand, tall coconut trees, and turquoise waters of these beaches are drawing tourists in ever-increasing numbers. Yet, the towns of Bayahibe and Dominicus Americanus remain laid-back and quiet (page 97).

◖ Isla Saona: This island is part of the Parque Nacional del Este and is the most popular day trip taken by tourists vacationing in the southeast or Costa del Coco regions. After a boat trip through the crystalline waters where the Caribbean Sea meets the Atlantic Ocean, visitors can enjoy the powdery white-sand beaches of this picture postcard of an island (page 97).

◖ La Piscina Natural: It doesn't seem right, but you can sit in the middle of the Caribbean Sea. La Piscina is a starfish-inhabited sandbar off the southwestern coast of the Parque Nacional del Este's peninsula. It's a hit with excursion boats taking visitors

to Isla Saona. Although it can get quite congested with tourists, it is worth a short visit to bathe in the ultra-tranquil clear and balmy water (page 98).

◖ Parque Nacional del Este: This arid national park occupies almost the entire southeastern peninsula. It holds evidence of Taíno life; ruins, cave drawings, and burial sites have recently been discovered. This park is also home to some 539 species of flora, 144 types of birds, and the endangered bottle-nosed dolphins and manatees frolicking offshore (page 99).

◖ Parque Nacional Los Haitises: This is a treat for the ecocurious traveler. You enter the park by boat through the semi-spooky, mangrove-studded coastline. More than 750 species of plants, 110 species of birds, bats, and even the endangered manatee are at home in the extensive cave systems and lagoons throughout the park (page 122).

LOOK FOR ◖ TO FIND RECOMMENDED SIGHTS, ACTIVITIES, DINING, AND LODGING.

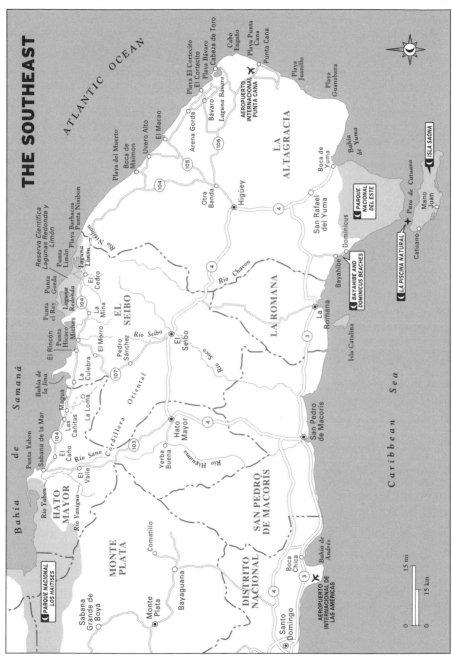

THE SOUTHEAST

ATLANTIC OCEAN

Bahía de Samaná

PARQUE NACIONAL LOS HAITISES

Sabana Grande de Boyá

MONTE PLATA

Monte Plata

Bayaguana

Comatillo

HATO MAYOR

Río Yabon

Punta Yabon

Sabana de la Mar

El Caño

Las Cañitas

Río Sano

El Valle

Río Yanigua

Magua

La Loma

Bahía de la Jina

El Rincón

Punta Hicaco

Miches

El Morro

El Cedro

La Mina

EL SEIBO

Río Seibo

Pedro Sánchez

Cordillera Oriental

La Culebra

Yerba Buena

Hato Mayor

Río Higuamo

DISTRITO NACIONAL

Santo Domingo

AEROPUERTO INTERNACIONAL DE LAS AMÉRICAS

Boca Chica

Bahía de Andrés

SAN PEDRO DE MACORÍS

San Pedro de Macorís

Río Soco

El Seibo

Reserva Científica Lagunas Redonda y Limón

Playa Barbacoa

Punta Nisibón

Playa del Muerto

Boca de Maimón

Punta Limón

Laguna Limón

Laguna Redonda

Punta el Rey

Punta Gorda

Río Nisibón

Uvero Alto

El Macao

Arena Gorda

Playa El Cortecito

El Cortecito

Playa Bávaro

Cabeza de Toro

Cabo Engaño

Playa Punta Cana

Punta Cana

Playa Juanillo

Playa Guamabana

Bávaro

Laguna Bávaro

AEROPUERTO INTERNACIONAL PUNTA CANA

LA ALTAGRACIA

Otra Banda

Higüey

Boca de Yuma

Bahía de Yuma

San Rafael del Yuma

Dominicus

PARQUE NACIONAL DEL ESTE

Bayahibe

BAYAHIBE AND DOMINICUS BEACHES

LA PISCINA NATURAL

Paso de Catuano

Mano Juan

ISLA SAONA

Catuano

LA ROMANA

La Romana

Río Chavón

Isla Catalina

Caribbean Sea

San Rafael del Yuma

ATLANTIC OCEAN

105

106

104

107

103

104

4

3

© AVALON TRAVEL PUBLISHING, INC.

0 15 mi

0 15 km

and Parque Nacional Los Haitises, and eco-tourism is enjoying a steady rise in popularity. Visitors can hike miles of unspoiled beaches and forests, paddle boats through mangroves in search of manatees, keep their eyes open for endemic and rare land animals (such as the rat-like solenodon), and take bird-watching excursions. The Parque Nacional del Este, found where the waters of the Atlantic Ocean meet the Caribbean Sea, is an intensely hot and dry expanse, and the vastly different Los Haitises (as it is commonly referred to) is a mangrove-lined tropical forest with a plush interior. Limestone caves dot both of these parks, protecting the ancient Taíno drawings found within many of them. A day of exploration to these caves is a trip back to a time when the Spanish conquistadors and native inhabitants of the islands were making their first impressions on each other, some of which is documented on the walls within.

The Dominican Republic's Ministry of Tourism is profoundly proud of the development of the tourism industry in this area, and it focuses much of its marketing attention on the maintenance and future of the area. Lately that has included the protection and development of ecofriendly tour options. Those looking for posh accommodations and isolation within the luxurious bubbles of all-inclusives will be perfectly satisfied with their choice to travel to the southeast. While there are indeed

THE MYSTERIES OF LA ALETA

In 1997, scientists were wandering around in the Parque Nacional del Este and stumbled upon a subterranean chamber more than 30 meters deep and filled with water. Diving in temperatures of roughly 24°C (74°F), the scientists encountered three layers of water, two clear and one middle sulfuric layer. Below this sulfur layer, many Taíno artifacts were found on a mound, perfectly preserved because of the lack of ambient light (thanks to the sulfur layer) and because of a lack of oxygen in the environment. Wooden artifacts, *higüeros* (gourds), baskets, war clubs, bowls, hatchet handles, and ceramic vessels were found. It is possible that looters made off with highly decorated items. Carbon dating of what the scientists were able to hold on to dated the artifacts to A.D. 1035-1420. Because of the level of preservation, the Manantial de La Aleta (Spring of the Fin) is one of the most important archaeological sites in the Caribbean.

But what were these things doing that far underground? Analysis of the items indicates that the well at La Aleta was ceremonial. Some of the decorated pottery may have held offerings of food, and some had images of bats on them. The Taínos considered bats sacred. A very rare *dujo*, which is a wooden stool made solely for a Taíno chief to sit on during ceremo-nies, was also found. It is quite literally a "seat of power." Another artifact was a wooden vomiting spatula, which was an item used in the *cohoba* (powerful hallucinogenic made from the seeds of a *Piptadenia peregrina*) ceremonies and ritual feasts. The idea behind its usage was to pass successfully through a stage of a ritual meant to purify the body by vomiting before communing with the *zemis* (spiritual beings).

The province of Higüey seemed to be an important ceremonial center for the eastern-most of the five provinces of the island at the time. Also near the well are four plazas used for public ceremonies, ritual dances, and ball games. That this many ritual places were found concentrated in one area (the greatest number grouped together on the island of Hispaniola) marks La Aleta as a prominent place in the province of Higüey and indicates that its importance was primarily religious. It seems to have been a largely ceremonial center, not a place that people called home on a permanent basis.

Taínos threw the objects (spiritual gifts) in the well, which seemed from the surface to be a bottomless portal into the underworld. Items dropped down the well would disappear from view the moment they hit the sulfuric layer of water, adding to the mystery.

other, more independent-traveler-friendly areas of the Dominican Republic, those who seek unique experiences will not be disappointed either.

PLANNING YOUR TIME

Most who visit the southeast do so with the intention of never leaving the beach or their all-inclusive resort. There is a lot to be said about a vacation where you are pampered at a resort, all food and drink included, amid palm trees and some of the most beautiful and well-maintained beaches around.

But for those who tire of the same atmosphere, this region has much more to offer. Even if you are staying in a resort complex, one way to combat "resort fever" is to check out the excursions desk. They frequently offer exciting activities and day trips that can be added to your vacation for an extra charge. It is yet another worry-free way to vacation in an all-inclusive and get some additional thrills; it won't even take a lot of planning on your part. But check what your options are soon after your arrival as reservations may be necessary, especially if the excursions require you to leave the southeast. For instance, taking a day trip to the Ciudad Colonial in Santo Domingo requires a four-hour bus ride and could be done in one long day or overnight, with a stay in one of the charming hotels in the first city of the New World.

However, if resorts just aren't your cup of tea, *guaguas* are a very cheap and exciting way to travel. Keep in mind that they only run during daylight hours. The towns of **Bayahibe** on the southern coast, **El Cortecito** on the eastern Costa del Coco, and **Miches** or **Sabana de la Mar**, both on the Costa Esmeralda on the southern coast of the Bahía de Samaná, make great stop-offs for the independent traveler who seeks either rest and relaxation or action and adventure.

HISTORY

To the Taínos this area was known as the Higüey province and was the territory of a cacique named Cotubanamá (sometimes referred to as Cayacoa). But in 1503, Bartolomé de Las Casas destroyed much of the area, killing thousands of Taínos and their leader. By 1515 almost the entire population of Taínos was annihilated.

Researchers believe that this area (especially the Parque Nacional del Este) was the site of a major community of Taíno Caribbean civilization. Deep in the forest of the national park, scientists have discovered ruins, artifacts, and cave drawings pointing to the settlement of Taínos that had once called the southeast home. And although there is Spanish documentation of these early events, the cave drawings discovered tell important stories of the first interactions and subsequent altercations between the Spanish and Taíno natives from the Taíno perspective. Additional pictographs were found in the caves of the Parque Nacional Los Haitises.

Bayahibe

Conveniently located near the La Romana airport and flanked to the south by the Parque Nacional del Este, the Bayahibe area is fast becoming a tourist destination. Traditionally, the area has been known as the doorway to the Parque Nacional del Este and the launching point to Isla Saona. But today, it is growing out of its "pit stop" reputation and becoming more of a hub for the resort-weary needing a change of scenery. Bayahibe's calm and low-key vibe provides a nice contrast to the sometimes overstimulating pool-side atmosphere of the all-inclusive resorts.

Until the late 1990s, this little seaside town was nearly untouched by tourism. Now, the resorts that populate the surrounding area are drawing tourists in record numbers. But the publicity has not turned this traditional fishing village into a cookie-cutter tourist trap yet. Bayahibe has been a favorite spot for independent travelers for many years and is still a good location for bargain hotels, cheap meals, and the quaint Caribbean experience that many are expecting when they book their trips to the Dominican Republic. Enjoying the slow pace of village life—hanging out in an open-air seafood restaurant and watching the fishermen haul in their day's catch—is a favorite way to spend time here. But action isn't too hard to find either. If you're not making use of the excursion desks at the mega-resorts, this is the place to find a local company to take you deep-sea fishing, scuba diving, or snorkeling. Some of the best diving in the country can be enjoyed at the offshore coral reefs and islands.

Despite the bulging tour industry waistline of the area, there is still no tourism office and very few services in the town of Bayahibe, but you will find small restaurants, cafés, a church, and some gift shops.

the bay of Bayahibe

© ANA CHAVIER CAAMAÑO

SIGHTS
ⓒ Bayahibe and Dominicus Beaches

These beaches are reason enough to spend time in this part of the country. Whether your main focus is beach bumming or not, denying yourself a trip to this piece of paradise would be a mistake. The portions that have been overtaken by the all-inclusive resorts are meticulously maintained. Fortunately, there is still easily accessible public beach space available at both. **Playa Bayahibe** (right in the town of Bayahibe), with its white sand, has restaurants and food stands overlooking the beach, so you don't have to go far for nourishment. The sand at **Playa Dominicus** outshines that of Playa Bayahibe. It's far plusher, while Bayahibe's is not as luxurious (but still nice!). Playa Dominicus is in the town of Dominicus Americanus and has a public parking lot; you can rent beach chairs.

Isla Catalinita

Just off the eastern shore of the Parque Nacional del Este sits a tiny little uninhabited island very popular for diving and snorkeling excursions. Located where the Atlantic Ocean meets the Caribbean Sea, this is a spot to see bigger sharks, eagle rays, sea turtles, and more marine life. The coral reefs offer waters perfect for snorkeler's delights.

ⓒ Isla Saona

A trip to this island is the most popular excursion for those staying in Bayahibe, Punta Cana, and Bávaro hotels. Isla Saona, which is part of the Parque Nacional del Este just across the Bahía de Catalinita, attracts nearly 1,000 tourists a day.

Even back in the 16th and 17th centuries, Saona was used as a layover location. Spanish sailors struck a deal with Taíno chieftain Cotubanamá that allowed Isla Saona (originally named Adamanay by the Taínos) to be used as a minimart of sorts. The Spanish were allowed to stop and buy *casabe* bread made by the natives, gather firewood, and take a rest. It's not clear what the Taínos got out of the deal.

Today, the most exciting reason to go to Isla

Isla Saona

© ANA CHAVIER CAAMAÑO

Saona is the "getting there." Through your resort or an independent company, you can book a catamaran, sailboat, or speedboat ride to the island for the day (see *Sports and Recreation*). The journey will show you the turquoise magnificence of the waters and the contrasting beauty of the limestone cliffs of the national park meeting the sea. Isla Saona sits in the crossing zone where the Caribbean and the Atlantic meet at the Canal de La Mona. Be on the lookout for dolphins; they've been known to follow the boats in this region!

The beaches of this 22-kilometer-long island are postcard worthy, with white sands and abundant palm trees. If you've booked through a resort, a barbecue-buffet lunch will most likely be provided on one of the beaches designated for the resort's use. The resorts also have open bars on "their" beaches for drinks. Ask a local to crack a coconut open for you for about US$2. Bring along a bottle of water.

A walk along the coast or on the inland trails of Saona is one way to escape the crowd on the beach (sort of) and add variety to your day. You'll need bug spray because the mosquitoes

THE SOUTHEAST

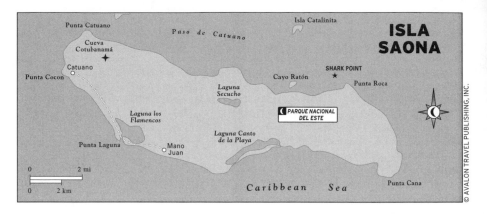

THE SOUTHEAST

and sand flies can be more than bothersome. Saona's mangroves and lagoons are breeding grounds for many birds, including the Hispaniolan parrot, pelicans, and the red-footed booby. Flamingos can be found around the aptly named **Laguna de Los Flamencos** (Flamingo Lagoon) near the southwestern shore. Also on the western half of the island is the **Cueva Cotubanamá,** a cave where Chief Cotubanamá and his family hid out from the Spanish (they was eventually captured). It contains fine examples of rock art and can be reached by foot via a trail.

Mano Juan, a small, picturesque village on Isla Saona's southern shore, used to sustain itself with fishing but has now turned to the more lucrative (albeit less charming) hawking of trinkets to the tourists on the beach. Pastel homes line the beach so take your camera—this is the photo-op you've been waiting for.

Other than for lounging on the beach, Saona is known as a good spot for diving and snorkeling at the reefs just offshore. If you stay more toward shore, you'll see many shells and shrimp. But a little farther out await the giant sponges, coral, and colorful fish.

Unfortunately, the throngs of boats and hordes of tourists coming to spend the day on Isla Saona have done damage to its once serene underwater habitats and unspoiled beaches. Fuel in the water and noise levels of the boats add a congested feeling. With the popularity of this excursion growing, the problems are only increasing.

Reaching Isla Saona is easiest via Bayahibe, where there are a number of independent excursion vendors (see *Sports and Recreation*). Prices among them vary little.

La Piscina Natural

La Piscina Natural, or Palmilla, as it's sometimes called, is a starfish-dotted sandbar in the waters between the Parque Nacional del Este and Isla Saona coastlines. Excursion boats whisking their customers to and from Isla Saona make a stopover in this spot where, more than a kilometer off the coast, one can wade around in clear water that never gets above the waist. It is a unique experience to be able to walk in the Caribbean Sea so far from land.

La Piscina, just like Isla Saona, is no longer a quiet paradise. It is heavily trodden by tourists, but it is easy to see why it's so popular. Under the warm water is a smooth blanket of white sand to walk upon. In some spots, you can sit with the water not even reaching your chin, and the ripples from approaching boats are the biggest waves you'll feel.

Although this site is a rare treat of striking beauty, the large number of boats dumping their fuel into the water here is taking its toll on the natural habitat for the starfish and other sea creatures. Unfortunately, some tour leaders and visitors are not careful when disturbing the red starfish whose home they are guests in; lifting them from the water for anything longer than just a few seconds kills them. If you want photos, get an underwater camera. During high tourist season, La Piscina can sometimes resemble freeway gridlock or a bar in the middle of the sea because of the numerous rum drinks and parties.

Parque Nacional del Este

Declared a national park in 1975, Parque Nacional del Este (National Park of the East, tel. 809/833-0022, office hours 8:30 A.M.–1 P.M. daily) is in the southeastern end of the country in the province of Altagracia between the towns of Bayahibe and Boca de Yuma. Its surface area includes the entire peninsula south of those two towns and is 808 square kilometers, of which 420 are land (including the islands of Catalina, Saona, and Catalinita), while 388 square kilometers are oceanic.

The peninsula is a combination of subtropical humid forest and dry forest with an average rainfall of about 120 centimeters a year. This region is notoriously hot. But if you can stand the heat and are interested in bird-watching, this park is a good location to spot 114 types of birds, including rare ones such as the white-crowned pigeon *(columba leucocephala),* the Hispaniolan parrot *(amazona ventralis),* the brown pelican *(pelecanus occidentalis),* the red-footed boobie *(sula sula),* the magnificent frigatebird *(fregata magnificens),* the barn owl *(tyto alba),* and the herring gull *(larus argentatus).*

Topographically, the changing sea levels over the last million years created the peninsula out of limestone, resulting in a series of terraces and cliffs along the shoreline. Throughout the peninsula, traces of pre-Columbian Taíno life abound in subterranean tunnels and caves where many pictographs have been found. Although there are over 400 caves in the park, only **Cueva del Puenta** can be visited by foot. It holds a small example of Taíno drawings depicting their culture along with many stalactites and stalagmites. To access this cave, first go to the ranger post at **Guaraguao** (about five kilometers past Dominicus Americanus). For the US$3.50 entrance fee, you will get a guide who will walk with you a little over half an hour to the site.

The park's coastline offers a variety of coral formations and is excellent for diving, especially along the western side. The eastern side of the peninsula has more limestone cliffs that drop off dramatically into the ocean. The southern tip has mangroves and saltwater lagoons and is a good spot to find birdlife. Many animals whose existence is threatened live in this protected area. Manatees *(trichechus manatus),* bottle-nosed dolphin *(turisops truncates),* and various sea turtles swim the waters. The rat-like solenodon *(solenodon paradoxus),* the hutia *(plagiodontia aedium),* and the rhinoceros iguana *(cyclura cornuta)* are found on land.

Because the National Park of the East is between the busy tourist destinations of Bayahibe and Punta Cana/Bávaro, it is becoming more popular for excursions. In June of 2005, the La Romana and Bayahibe Hotel Association along with the Ministry of Environment announced they would be working together to open an ecotourism center located in the Valley of La Sabila, near Bayahibe. This visitor's center will be created along with ecological trails allowing access to view the various endemic species of animals and birds that live in the park. This center will also offer opportunities to view pre-Columbian cave art as well as snorkeling and swimming in selected caves.

For now, though, one of the most popular ways to gain access to the park is to hire a boat guide in the Bayahibe harbor. Your guide will take you along the shore, and from there you can hike into the *parque.* If you're coming via car, there are entrances in both Bayahibe on the western edge and Boca de Yuma on the eastern side.

SPORTS AND RECREATION
Diving and Snorkeling

Located in the waters of Bayahibe are some of the country's best sites for diving and snorkeling. The warm Caribbean Sea offers perfect crystalline visibility and warm conditions for experienced and beginning divers. The calmness of these waters and the underwater terrain, compared to the rougher areas off the other coasts of the island, also make it easier for beginners.

The **St. George Wreck** was scuttled in 1999 as an artificial reef off the coast of the port of Bayahibe. It sits upright about 30–40 meters below the surface, and the currents can be rather strong down there, so this is a site for experienced divers only. You will see loads of marine life and have the chance to enter cabins and the cargo room. Another exciting dive site is **Padre Nuestro** cave. Well, it's more of a flooded 290-meter sweet-water tunnel. Again, only experienced divers will be able to explore the stalactites and stalagmites in this subterranean dive.

Excursions and Tours

At all-inclusive resorts, the activity desks offer many excursions, tours, and packages that can be added to your vacation. But for independent travelers, a few establishments in Bayahibe offer similar excursions.

Casa Daniel (Bayahibe, tel. 809/833-0050, www.casa-daniel.de, 8 A.M.–6 P.M. daily) is right on the waterfront at Bayahibe. Daniel and his wife, Susan, have put together a multilingual dive team that leads excursions in German, English, French, and Spanish. While beginners and experienced divers can both enjoy the colorful reef life in depths varying 10–25 meters, special excursions like night dives, wreck dives (St. George), cave trips (Padre Nuestro), and deeper dives are only offered to experienced divers. Without equipment rental, one-tank dives cost US$33. Packages of 6–10 dives are available (US$182–325). Equipment rental costs extra. A full-day snorkeling excursion to Saona and Catalinita costs US$68. In addition to snorkeling at the islands, you'll make stops to see some of the mangrove forest and La Piscina Natural. A better choice for a family trip is the excursion to Isla Catalina. You have the day to snorkel, including lunch on the beach, and on your way back, you'll make a stop at the Río Chavón and the artists' village of Altos de Chavón (US$59). PADI certification courses, refresher courses, and specialty courses are all available. Casa Daniel is perhaps the best choice, if only for its local reputation.

Scubafun (Calle Principal 28, Bayahibe, tel. 809/763-3023, fax 809/833-0085, www.scubafun.info, 7:30 A.M.–6 P.M. daily), in the middle of Bayahibe, offers many excursions, from simple dives (US$65) to boat trips to the islands of Catalina (US$100), Catalinita (US$114), and Saona (US$124). Scubafun excursions are recommended for parties that have both divers and non-divers since they allow non-divers to join.

Dominican-run **Asplaba Boat Trips (Bayahibe)** offers boat excursions and is in a booth on the fringe of the bay of Bayahibe. In typical Dominican style, all you have to do is show up around 8:30 or 9 A.M. any morning to set it all up; if you speak Spanish, call the owner, Freddy Berroa (tel. 809/952-4450), or Estefano, his coworker (tel. 809/710-7336), to arrange for an excursion. It's surely not the most efficient of the three excursion outfitter choices, but the prices are good. A trip to Isla Saona costs you US$151–182 depending where on the island you are dropped off, excursions to Islas Catalina and Catalinita are US$167 each, La Piscina Natural is US$121, and a trip up the Río Chavón is US$106. These prices are per *group,* not per person. So the more, the merrier, if you're splitting the cost with travel buddies. A deep-sea fishing excursion, which is priced *per person,* will run you US$50. On any of these excursions, lunch can be arranged for an extra charge. Make sure to agree on the price before booking the trip, though.

ACCOMMODATIONS
Under US$50

There are many small cabana options in Bayahibe. Since most of these establishments don't have telephones, it is impossible to make reservations. They are typically very low budget and have basic rooms. However, if you show up before dark, you can try your luck by simply strolling through town or (if you know some Spanish) chatting with the locals for ideas on accommodations. Here are some reliable options if winging it isn't your style.

Hotel Llave del Mar (main street, tel. 809/833-0081, cell 809/399-3169, US$27 d

© ANA CHAVIER CAAMAÑO

All-inclusive accommodations line the Bayahibe coastline.

with air-conditioning, US$18 d without air-conditioning) is in the middle of Bayahibe and is a good low-budget alternative to the all-inclusive. Expect a place to collapse after a day on the go and not much more. While this hotel has 25 rooms, many of them are often rented out for fixed periods of time, so reservations are advisable. You must request air-conditioning in order to get it, but most rooms have fans. Rooms have TV and private cold-water bathrooms but do not have phones. Telephones at the front desk are available to guests. From the hotel, the ocean is visible and only a three-minute stroll. Upon your arrival in Bayahibe, turn into town via Calle Juan Brito and you will see signs directing you to the hotel.

Hotel Bayahibe (main street, tel. 809/833-0159, cell 809/224-5804, hotelbayahibe@hotmail.com, US$41 d with breakfast only, US$52 d with breakfast and dinner) is the best bet in the budget category and has been a mainstay in Bayahibe for the independent traveler. Reservations are essential, particularly in peak season, as it tends to fill up quickly. There are 25 rooms, and all are equipped with hot-water bathrooms, air-conditioning, TV, phone, and refrigerator. Some have a kitchenette, which is great if you don't plan to dine out every meal.

Rooms on the lower floor can be noisy, so if possible, request one on the top floor. Hotel Bayahibe is best for access to the sea and dive centers, and it offers free beach towels. Don't want to walk the five minutes to the beach? You can catch a free ride on one of the hotel's *carrozas* (horse-drawn wagons). Four people can stay at Hotel Bayahibe for US$71 a night with breakfast and dinner included—the best bargain in town. Reservations should be made at least two weeks in advance for stays during January and February.

Cabañas Francisca (main street, Bayahibe, tel. 809/556-2742, US$18–25 d) is next to the Hotel Bayahibe. You can get a very basic room for quite cheap. Request air-conditioning for a few dollars more. You will have cable TV, a refrigerator, and your own bathroom, but no hot water (time to hone your speedy shower skills).

Cabaña Trip Town (main street, tel. 809/833-0082, fax 809/883-0088, US$24 d with air-conditioning, US$19 d without air-conditioning) is across from the Hotel Bayahibe. Parking is available for this pink and white, cheery, 14-cabana hotel. All rooms have two beds (one double and one single). The maximum number of people allowed in

THE SOUTHEAST

a room is three, but you pay the same rate as you would if it were just two. Rooms have their own hot-water bathroom and TV. The water is a two-minute walk.

Villa Iguana (Bayahibe, tel. 809/833-0203, cell 809/757-1059, www.villaiguana.de, US$29 d) is a German-owned hotel associated with the scuba excursion company Scubafun. Together, they offer dive and accommodation packages. In the hotel, there are seven standard rooms (with private bath, air-conditioning, fridge, and safe) and three apartments (with kitchenette, private bath, one bedroom, an extra bed for a third person in the living room, and a safe; some have balconies). There is one penthouse suite available, which occupies the entire fourth floor; you can enjoy your ocean view, air-conditioning, fridge, private bath, private pool, outdoor living room, and sun deck for only US$69! All rooms are very clean and a good value.

US$50-100

If neither low-budget options nor mega-complex resorts appeal to you, **Cabaña Elke** (Av. Eladia, Dominicus Americanus, tel. 809/689-8249, www.viwi.it, room US$60 d, apartment US$75 d) might be perfect. Although not in the town of Bayahibe, it is near the beach of Dominicus, just south of town. Guests enjoy clean accommodations (either standard rooms or apartment style), a pool, bar, and restaurant (for lunch and dinner only). Apartments have a sitting area, kitchenette, and a loft bedroom and face the garden and pool area. This is a hotel to escape to since there are no phones or televisions in the rooms. A plus to Cabaña Elke is that it is directly behind the Viva Wyndham Dominicus Beach resort, so Elke guests can purchase a day pass to the swanky Wyndham grounds for US$40/day, thereby enjoying the best beach in the area without having to commit to the giant all-inclusive style or price.

US$100 and Up

In the last five years, all-inclusive resorts have begun to sprout up near the town of Bayahibe; prior to that, most all-inclusives in this region

were relegated to the Punta Cana/Bávaro area. But with the popularity of this type of vacation package, coupled with the pristine beauty of the beaches near Bayahibe, these plush resorts can't help but be manicured, luxurious, and pampering. After all, they are all fighting for your business and the competition is stiff. The surreal part of it is that in this all-inclusive rat race, they can end up like cookie-cutter replicas offering accommodations and amenities similar to one another. Most resorts' rooms have two double beds or a king-size bed, minibar, air-conditioning, fan, hair dryer, iron, cable TV, phone, hot-water bathrooms, and terrace. In-room security boxes are available, but usually for an extra charge. And as with most things in the Dominican Republic, if you tip your chambermaid you're likely to get better service such as more towels in your bathroom or a fully stocked minibar refrigerator.

Prices for all-inclusives in this section are based on double occupancy of a standard room per night in high season. Traveling in low season will reduce the cost. If wheelchair accessibility is a priority for your room, make reservations far in advance as many only have a few rooms specifically designed to suit your needs.

(Iberostar Hacienda Dominicus (Playa Dominicus, Dominicus Americanus, tel. 809/688-3600 or 888/923-2722, fax 809/221-0921, www.iberostar.com, US$360 d) about five kilometers south of Bayahibe, has one of the best beaches around, complete with a lively lighthouse bar right on the sand. The impressively luxurious lobby is the tip-off for the extreme comfort of the entire resort. The grounds are perfectly maintained, where flamingos and peacocks wander around the many fountains and tropical foliage. There are five restaurants (one buffet and four à la carte) to choose from, a variety of bars (including a disco for nighttime entertainment), three swimming pools (plus one kiddie pool), various shops, and nightly entertainment in the resort's theater. Amenities include Internet access, health care, massage (extra charge), fitness room, and daytime poolside entertainment. Hacienda Dominicus has almost 500 rooms, all of which are very comfortable (huge showers, too!) and meet the high demands of their growing American clientele. It claims five-star hotel quality, and indeed gives you most everything you need. However, the food is where the five-star claim gets only *a bit* exaggerated. Despite the number of restaurants to choose from, the choices can get a bit repetitious if you are there for longer than a week. **Sunscape Casa del Mar** (Playa Bayahibe, tel. 809/221-8880, fax 809/221-2776, sunscaperesorts.com, starting at US$214 d), with its blue-roofed buildings, offers accommodations and activities similar to those of the Iberostar. There are three restaurant choices, one buffet style. The Metamorphosis Spa offers body and facial treatments featuring a massage in their outdoor "magic gardens." The beach is small and competitive for lounge chairs, especially in the shade. However, just a few hundred meters out is a reef where snorkeling reveals a rainbow of fish varieties. Can't stand the idea of missing football while you're away? In October 2005, the Casa del Mar started a Monday Night Football beach party. Tailgating never felt like this. A giant screen is set up on the Caribbean sand, and you're in a beach lounger (ice-cold beer in hand, of course) with all the American-favorite football foods, like wings, popcorn, burgers, and pizza—it's definitely a unique way to watch football. The folks back home will be jealous!

In the 532-room **Canoa Coral by Hilton** (Coral Canoa Dr., tel. 809/682-2662, fax 809/688-6371, www.coralbyhilton.com, from US$380 d), you will find spacious rooms with all the comfortable amenities of an all-inclusive resort. This is a popular resort with the European traveler, so expect the food in the buffet to be more suited to their tastes and traditions. There are four restaurants (Italian and Tex Mex are among the specialties) and five bars, including a sports bar, swim-up pool bar, and in-house disco, where the music seems to pack more punch than the drinks. But it's the beach that puts a happy smile on the guests' faces. The water is a magnificently clear blue, and oddly enough, there's not much of a fight

for beach chairs. Other on-site amenities include tennis, scuba lessons, a full-service spa at extra charge, baby-sitting service, fitness center, and all nonmotorized water sports, which are included in the cost of your stay. Children under the age of five stay free.

The **◖ Viva Wyndham Dominicus Beach** (Playa Dominicus, Dominicus Americanus, tel. 809/571-0402, fax 809/571-9550, www.vivaresorts.com, starting at US$240 d) and its sister resort, the **Viva Wyndham Dominicus Palace** (Playa Dominicus, Dominicus Americanus, tel. 809/686-5658, fax 809/687-8583, www.vivaresorts.com, starting at US$270 d), share a glorious three-kilometer expanse of Bayahibe beach, perhaps the best of the area. It is big enough so that the lively events (volleyball, beach aerobics, and merengue) happening at one end of the beach won't disturb your hard-earned afternoon siesta under the hundreds of palm trees.

The bigger of the two, Dominicus Beach, has a whopping 530 rooms available as standard, superior, or bungalows. Aside from the fantastic beach, there are three pools and four diverse restaurants, four bars, daily and nightly entertainment, a supervised kids' club, dive center, and many sports (four tennis courts, a basketball court, and even a soccer field) and activities to squelch any boredom that might occur. Guests of Dominicus Beach can use the spa at Dominicus Palace for an additional fee. Take your own snorkel gear, though; the hotel doesn't rent the equipment out because there aren't any sections of water blocked off for snorkelers and boats tend to speed by carelessly. The reef is beautiful nonetheless, and worth the effort if you play it safe. The Dominicus Beach is very popular with the Italian travelers, so it has a livelier atmosphere, and dressing up at night is common.

Dominicus Palace is the smaller of the two sister properties, with just 330 rooms within several colonial-style buildings and one pool. Seven restaurants offer many choices, including the open-air, oceanfront buffet where the cuisine is served up accompanied by a refreshing breeze rolling in from the Caribbean Sea. Not a bad

THE SOUTHEAST

way to wake up in the morning. Also on-site are two bars, a disco, a dive center, tour desk, a kids' club, and entertainment programs.

Dominicus Palace offers a full-service spa. You have full access to facilities at Viva Wyndham Dominicus Beach and its amenities, such as the lighted tennis courts and multiple pools, just a stroll in the sand away.

FOOD

With a view of the bay of Bayahibe, **Restaurante Mare Nostrum** (Calle Principal, tel. 809/833-0055, Mon.–Sat. for lunch and dinner, US$15–25) offers a first-rate Italian dinner in a chic setting. Homemade pasta, risotto, seafood, and a tasty wine selection are begging to be enjoyed.

 Restaurante La Punta (Calle Principal 20, tel. 809/833-0082, 11:30 A.M.–9 P.M., US$10–25) is a long-time favorite with tourists. The seafood is the best in town, very fresh, and a great break from the all-inclusive food, which can be bland and repetitious. It is right on the beachfront and serves seafood dishes and Caribbean-style cocktails. Grilled lobster is tops here.

Casual **Playa Restaurante Bar Pub/Pizza** (tel. 809/426-4645, US$3–15), right on the point of Bayahibe, has a wide variety of pizzas for a low cost.

Lively **Big Sur** (Playa Bayahibe, tel. 809/915-8127, noon–11:30 P.M. Tues.–Sun., US$7–18) is popular with tourists and locals alike, serving Italian (pizzas, pastas, flavorful meat dishes), salads, and seafood. You want to eat good food at a good price and then get your groove on? This is a casual, open-air (that means no air conditioner), thatch-roofed restaurant during the week and a restaurant/discotheque on the weekends. Big Sur is right on the point of Bayahibe.

Café Restaurante Leidy (right on the point, tel. 809/543-0052, US$5–15) serves breakfast, lunch, and dinner on the eastern side of Playa Bayahibe. Seafood, pasta, chicken, pork, and beef choices are numerous, all to be enjoyed in a breezy atmosphere.

Restaurante Yssamar (right on the point,

no phone, US$10–20) is the definition of unpretentious dining. Renowned for its seafood, casual atmosphere, and location right on the point in Bayahibe, Restaurante Yssamar places its tables directly on the sand under a thatched roof. Especially good is the lobster or squid in typical Dominican sauces.

 Colmado Billy (Bayahibe, no phone, 7:30 A.M.–10 P.M. Mon.–Sat., 7:30 A.M.–7 P.M. Sun.) is a typical Dominican *colmado* (small grocer). Standard staples include canned and dried goods, rum, bread, and cheese.

INFORMATION AND SERVICES

In 2005, the Bayahibe Hotel Association and the Ministry of Environment were planning to work together to build the Ecotourism Center of Padre Nuestro in the Valley of La Sabila of the National Park of the East, to open in 2006. A visitor's center and ecological trails to various springs are scheduled, allowing viewing of endemic species, birds, butterflies, and animals that live in the park, and to give passage to various caves where pre-Columbian artwork can be enjoyed. Tourists will be able to snorkel in some of the crystalline waters of select cave springs; a highlight will be an underwater archaeological museum re-created on the bottom of a subterranean lake.

Even with tourism expanding every year, there is no tourism office yet in Bayahibe or Dominicus Americanus. Nor are there many services. With any luck, and the building of the ecotourism center, more services will shortly follow.

Money

To change U.S. dollars, euros, or traveler's checks, you don't have a choice where to go since **Agencia de Cambio Sanchez** (Calle Principal, Bayahibe, tel. 809/833-0201, 8 A.M.–10 P.M. Mon.–Sat., 8 A.M.–6 P.M. Sun.) is the only exchange center in Bayahibe. It's right next to Hotel Llave del Mar.

There are **ATMs** in many of the big resorts like the Iberostar Hacienda Dominicus; they dispense pesos only. It is best to bring cash with you if you need small bills for tipping since the dollar is more appreciated in today's economy than the Dominican peso.

BanReservas may have a small branch next to Hotel Bayahibe open by the end of 2006.

Communications

Just off the big parking lot in a group of buildings facing the bay sits **Bayahibe Tele.com** (Bayahibe, 8:30 A.M.–7 P.M.), offering the only DSL Internet connection in town (US$4 per hour), fax services (international and within the DR), and long-distance calling (calls to the U.S. are US$0.32 per minute, and calls to Europe are US$0.67 per minute).

Laundry

New Generation Laundry (Bayahibe, 8 A.M.–6 P.M. Mon.–Sat.) will launder and press your clothing for less than US$1. It is located on an unnamed street that runs parallel to the main street.

GETTING THERE

Bayahibe is only 25 minutes east of La Romana and 40 minutes from Higüey. La Romana international airport is the most convenient arrival port for Bayahibe and Dominicus Americanus. Highway 3 will lead you to a southbound road about two kilometers long that forks off leading you to the two beach towns. Go right, and you'll get the dirt road to Bayahibe. Choose left, and you'll get the paved road to Dominicus Americanus.

A *público* from La Romana to Bayahibe will cost you US$2.50. A *guagua* from La Romana is US$1.50 and from Higüey will run you US$1.75.

Taking a taxi is a more expensive option: From La Romana it's US$17; Higüey, US$25; Las Américas international airport, US$75; Punta Cana airport, US$75. Prices can vary from taxi to taxi, so definitely settle on the rate and if you'll be paying in dollars or pesos before getting into the car. It is best to have correct change. There is a taxi stand in the center of Bayahibe called **Bayahibe Taxi** (tel. 809/833-0206).

If you are staying at one of the big resorts, arranging transportation with their shuttle services is a breeze, and the cost is usually included in your package. Ask while booking your trip.

GETTING AROUND

Bayahibe is a very manageable town to walk. Your feet are free transportation, and everything is within a *plátano*'s throw. A few *motoconchos* that hang out in the center of town can take you where you need to go for about US$1. Most people only use them for transport to the main highway, where they can flag down a *guagua* to La Romana or Higüey.

Higüey

A bustling town with a population of nearly 150,000, Higüey is best known for the Basilica de Nuestra Señora de la Altagracia, which contains a shrine to the Virgin Mary that draws religious pilgrims from all over the country seeking forgiveness and miracles. Although Higüey doesn't have much to offer tourists, the basilica is indeed worth a visit if you happen to be passing through.

Higüey is the hub town for the southeastern corner of the Dominican Republic. In the heart of La Altagracia province, Higüey is a nucleus for agriculture. Sugar, coffee, tobacco, cacao, rice, and corn are significant contributors to local economy, as are the cattle and pork industries. Transportation converges here as well. If you are taking any bus within the eastern half of the country, you are likely to catch a connection in this dusty town. Buses coming from Sabana de la Mar, Bávaro, La Romana, and Santo Domingo all join here to swap passengers.

The Taínos referred to this region as the

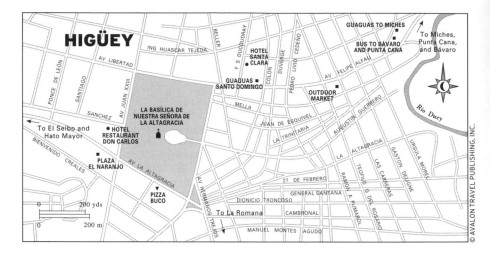

"land where the sun was born." And indeed the sun's rays feel ultra-strong here—sunscreen is a must-have when visiting this town.

SIGHTS

La Basilica de Nuestra Señora de la Altagracia

The basilica (8 A.M.–6 P.M. Mon.–Sat., 8 A.M.–8 P.M. Sun.) is definitely the focal point of Higüey and an important structure in the predominantly Catholic Dominican Republic. It is the house of the patron saint of all Dominicans, Our Lady of Altagracia, the Virgin Mary. Construction began during Trujillo's dictatorship in 1954, was inaugurated by Pope John Paul in 1971, but wasn't actually completed until Balaguer's presidency in 1972. The basilica sits on 40,000 square meters, and the basilica itself is about 4,600 square meters. Its signature, enormous concrete arches loom 80 meters into the Higüey sky, signifying the shape of praying hands, and were designed by the French team of Pierre Dupré and Dovnoyer de Segonzac. The eclectic design allows a harmonious mixture of the traditional Catholic footprint shape of a cross, coupled with a modern rising form. Inside, parishioners hear mass under the multiple arches that lead to the altar and frame a magnificent stained glass wall behind it.

Even more famous than the celebrated architecture of the basilica itself, is the encased, framed painting of the Virgen de La Altagracia (Virgin of the Higher Grace). This depiction of the Holy Mother draws pilgrims from all over the country, who form a line to one by one worship and ask for healing miracles. Prepare to stand in line as some have much to say to her.

The basilica also has artwork on either side of the altar by the Spanish muralist José Vela Zanetti. On the edges of the massive parking lot and across the street from the basilica are various memorabilia stands and shops where you can purchase a wide assortment of trinkets such as candles, plastic rosaries, and photos of the Pope. Wear clothing that respectfully covers your knees and shoulders or you won't be allowed to enter the basilica.

Mercado de Higüey

Higüey is the center of the southeast's very fertile agricultural region. Why go to a grocery store when this is the place to shop for avocados the size of a toddler's head? The produce of this outdoor market (Av. La Libertad, between Guerrero del Rosario and Las Carreras, 7 A.M.–3 P.M.) is overflowing and the crowd is buzzing with life. This is a great way to experience zippy Higüey life with the locals and buy fresh fruit and vegetables at very low cost, all while supporting the local farmers and economy.

There are many snack and lunch stands at the major intersections. You can get treats like *pastelitos* (a fried, meat-filled puff pastry), sweets, freshly squeezed fruit juices, sandwiches, and cold beverages.

FESTIVALS

On January 21, **Día de la Altagracia,** thousands of devoted pilgrims from all over the Dominican Republic come to La Basilica de Nuestra Señora de la Altagracia to fulfill promises made in prayer to the Virgin Mary, the Dominican patron saint, and touch the painting of her that hangs behind the altar.

But it's not only Catholicism that draws people to Higüey for Altagracia Day. As with anything in the Dominican Republic, where there is a gathering, there is dancing in the streets to blaring merengue music and flowing rum. Oranges, conveniently in season this time of year, are abundantly for sale in honor of the legend

© ANA CHAVIER CAAMAÑO

La Basilica de Nuestra Señora de la Altagracia

that the Virgin Mary appeared in an orange tree to a sick little girl, miraculously healing her.

ACCOMMODATIONS

While not a destination city, Higüey has a couple of options for a good night's sleep. **Hotel Santa Clara** (Lic Felix Servio Ducoudray 9, tel. 809/554-2040, US$15 d with fan only) has 31 very clean and comfortable, albeit small and simple, rooms (US$22 d with air-conditioning, and in Higüey it is a good investment). All rooms have TV and private baths with hot water. There is a small kitchenette on the main floor off the central courtyard where you can make coffee or heat up food. Parking is available across the street.

Hotel Restaurant Don Carlos (Calle Juan Ponce de León at Sánchez, tel. 809/554-2344, fax 809/554-4219, US$26–35 d, front desk open 24 hours) has 62 rooms. Although it's older and, therefore, not as well kept as the Hotel Santa Clara, it is a good bet for availability and has a startlingly splendid restaurant. All rooms have air-conditioning, hot water bathrooms, and cable TV. The hotel consists of two buildings; one is older than the other, and the price difference depends on which side you get. Request a room in the "newer" of the two wings. It is cleaner and definitely less run-down. The Don Carlos has a bar that stays open until 2:30 A.M. and offers light *picaderas* (appetizers).

FOOD

Need to grab a quick meal? **Pizza Buco** (across from the basilica, tel. 809/554-5795) serves sandwiches, pizza, and fresh juice. Also available is the "plate of the day," which will cost you about US$3.

Hotel Restaurant Don Carlos (Calle Juan Ponce de León at Sánchez, tel. 809/554-2344, fax 809/554-4219, 7 A.M.–11:30 P.M., US$2–18), two blocks behind the basilica, serves traditional Dominican and foreign dishes in a casual environment and has long been popular with travelers and locals alike. Breakfast, lunch, and dinner are all available. For lunch and dinner, the plate of the day is only US$2, which usually consists of chicken, rice, and

THE PAINTING OF THE VIRGIN MARY

The painting of the Virgin Mary on the altar in the Basilica de Nuestra Señora de la Altagracia is encased not only in glass but also in a fog of legend and folklore. There are many tales of how the painting came to be depending on whom you ask. How did the painting make it to the basilica? Who brought it? Renditions and versions swirl around in the oral-tradition mixer of Dominican culture.

In one version, a merchant was asked by his daughter to get a portrait of Our Lady of Altagracia on his next trip to Santo Domingo. He'd never heard the title and was discussing it while staying overnight at a friend's house just as an old bearded man happened by. The old man pulled a painting out of his satchel and said that it was what the merchant had been searching for, the Virgin of Altagracia. The merchant and his friend gave the old man a place to stay for the night, but by morning he was gone and they never saw him again. The merchant took the painting to his elated daughter. They placed it on the mantel in their home, but it kept disappearing, whereupon they would find it again outside. They finally placed it in a church.

Another legend says a sick child from Higüey gave an old man (thought to be an apostle) a meal and a place to stay, so the man healed her and in the morning left the portrait for her.

Perhaps the most popular story is the one where a sick little girl was visited by the Virgin Mary, who appeared to her in an orange tree that once stood in the place of the original basilica. (In yet another version, it was three children!) A portrait of the Virgin Mary appeared under the tree, so the child/children took it home; by morning, the portrait had disappeared and was found back under the tree. The painting is now built into the basilica.

To this day, orange trees are a major theme in the artwork throughout the basilica, and on January 21 oranges are prominent, sold in piles for the Día de la Altagracia festival.

---

beans, or *la bandera dominicana* (chicken, rice and beans, and fried plantains).

The Dominican fast-food chicken joint **Pollo Victorina** (Plaza El Naranjo, Av. La Altagracia, tel. 809/554-5616) is not a culinary marvel, but it is an option for a quick, cheap meal on the go. It is conveniently located near Plaza El Naranjo and the basilica.

INFORMATION AND SERVICES

Avenida La Libertad is the main commercial street in Higüey. Driving or walking along it, you will come across markets, restaurants, and shops. If you're passing through and only need a few provisions, **Plaza Comercial El Naranjo** (Av. La Altagracia at Av. Juan XXIII) is a strip mall near the basilica where you can find fast food at **Pollo Victorina,** gas and snacks at **Tiger Market,** Internet access at **Tropical Internet Access Center** (tel. 809/554-3576, 8:30 A.M.–10:30 P.M. daily), an ATM at **Banco Popular** (8:15 A.M.–4 P.M. Mon.–Fri., 9 A.M.–1 P.M. Sun.), and a long-distance call center called **Centro de Llamadas Yenny** (tel. 809/554-8019, 8 A.M.–10 P.M. Mon.–Sat., 4–8 P.M. Sun.).

The Higüey **post office** is on Calle Agustín Guerrero (8 A.M.–3 P.M. Mon.–Fri.), but use the services at a resort instead since postal services in the Dominican Republic are generally poor to horrible.

GETTING THERE AND AROUND

From Santo Domingo, you can catch a 2.25-hour bus ride at the **Sichoprola** station (Parque Enriquillo, tel. 809/686-0637, 6 A.M.–6 P.M. daily, US$5.10) to Higüey, making stops along the way. Once in Higüey, it makes various stops including in front of the basilica and at other bus stations where you can transfer to another bus if your final destination is not Higüey. Buses from Sabana de la Mar, Bávaro, La Romana, and Santo Domingo all connect here. Tell the bus driver where you need to go and you'll be taken to the right spot. When boarding and purchasing your ticket, ask where the bus is going; some have signs displaying their destinations, but not always. The connecting buses have frequent departures during the day, but after sunset it is very limited. Start out early if traveling by bus.

The Mella Highway connects Santo Domingo and Higüey. Once in Higüey, eastbound Avenida La Libertad becomes Highway 105, which leads to a connection to Bávaro and the rest of the Costa del Coco. Southbound Avenida Hermanos Trejo becomes Highway 4, which leads you to Boca de Yuma and the La Romana turnoff. Alternatively, west-running Avenida La Altagracia becomes Highway 4 outside of town and will take you to El Seibo and Hato Mayor.

To get around town, simply flag down a taxi. Higüey is filled with them during all hours.

AROUND HIGÜEY
La Otra Banda

A few kilometers north of Higüey is the eccentric town of La Otra Banda, known for maintaining its gingerbread architecture, which the founding fathers brought from the Canary Islands. This is a photographer's opportunity to get photos of the pretty little houses you see on postcards.

As if not to appear "too cute," though, La Otra Banda is also known for its butchers and meat since the livestock industry supports this area. It is common to see cuts of meat and freshly made strings of *longaniza* (sausages) hanging in market windows; this can be an odd sight. Exercise caution in buying these meats; they've often been sitting out for quite some time and (unfortunately) might not be entirely safe for the fragile stomachs of foreigners.

Coming from Higüey on Highway 105, you'll reach a fork in the road where you can choose to stay the course on Highway 105 toward El Macao or take a right onto Avenida Macao, which becomes Highway 106 toward the Bávaro/Punta Cana resort area on the Costa del Coco.

San Rafael de Yuma

South of Higüey along Highway 4 is San Rafael de Yuma. This dusty and simple little town is the site of the home-turned-museum of Spanish conquistador Ponce de León. This museum is the only attraction, making the town a poor choice for overnight stays. The **Casa Ponce de León** (7 A.M.–5 P.M. Mon.–Sat., US$1.50) is an important historical landmark containing many artifacts that were previously owned by Ponce de León and his family, including some of their furniture, household wares, and even a suit of armor said to be his.

The home was built in 1505–1508 by Taíno slaves for de León when he was lieutenant governor of Higüey. The home has been brought back to nearly its original glory and is in good condition.

No signs lead you to the museum, but if you're coming from the west, once in town turn left onto the dirt road right before the town cemetery. After a kilometer, you'll see the entrance on the right-hand side with the rectangular, two-story, stone museum at the end. A bus will drop you off at the station near the cemetery. You can either walk the rest of the way (a little over one kilometer) or hire a *motoconcho*. All tours and signage in the museum are in Spanish only,

Boca de Yuma

Farther south along Highway 4, at the mouth of the Bahía de Yuma and near the entrance to Parque Nacional del Este, is the rather uneventful town of Boca de Yuma. Before Hurricane Georges blasted through in 1998, leaving hotels in ruins and seafood restaurants upturned in its wake, Boca de Yuma was a quaint fishing village that annually hosted an international deep-sea fishing tournament. Even though those days are gone, you can still get some great seafood here.

The main reason to visit this town is a limestone cave, **Cueva de Berna** (8 A.M.–2 P.M.), just west of Boca de Yuma, which has an impressive deposit of Taíno rupestrian art. Unfortunately, there is some graffiti mixed in at the mouth of the cave, but the cave is now under protection to preserve the historic pictograms within. Set aside about a half hour to explore the drawings. Although you don't have to have a guide to enter, one can be hired for about US$0.50 so that you can be sure to not miss any of the artwork—a tip is appreciated.

Also just west of Boca de Yuma is the northeastern gateway of **Parque Nacional del Este** (admission US$3.50), marked by a small cabin, which leads to a long scenic trail where you can enjoy views of the ocean and Isla Saona, birdwatching, and various flora and fauna.

La Costa del Coco

The extreme eastern coast, known as the Costa del Coco (Coconut Coast) is best known for its all-inclusive resorts. Undoubtedly, this is due to marketing jargon. The all-inclusive resorts of the Punta Cana and Bávaro areas have spent much time and money to portray their venues as the only choices along the coast. This is not the case. While there is indeed an overwhelming number of luxurious and affordable all-inclusive choices, there are also independent and less tourist-packed options (mostly farther north).

The Bávaro and Punta Cana area resorts are especially popular with spring breakers, who raise the volume around the pools and party all night long at the big resort complexes, which offer many nighttime entertainment options. On the other hand, the all-inclusives are also especially wonderful for families looking to satisfy their myriad needs for less cost than other Caribbean vacations. These resorts are like mini cities. Child care and kid-friendly activities give parents worry-free vacations and perhaps even some alone time for unwinding from a life otherwise consumed with car pools, PTA meetings, and laundry.

Some resorts cater to those who want child-free surroundings. This is especially popular with couples seeking the one-stop wedding and honeymoon vacation, where the ceremony, accommodations, food, flowers, cake, and honeymoon are bundled in one convenient package simple to arrange. Just bring your dress (or white bikini) and tuxedo (or Speedo) and say "I do."

While the all-inclusives stretch for many kilometers along the coast, it is a long coastline that still has plenty to offer beyond the walls of the resorts. Farther north, along the coastlines of the El Seibo and Hato Mayor provinces, await virgin beaches, wetlands, Taíno cave drawings, and the sky-combing coconut trees that give the coastline its nickname. The independent traveler has much to explore.

A vast majority of travelers to this coast are visiting the all-inclusive resorts and arrive via the Punta Cana airport. Most resorts have shuttle services that take guests directly from the airport to their compounds, making it a very worry-free arrival.

Combined, the **Punta Cana and Bávaro** areas are the gem of the southeastern tip of the Dominican Republic, mainly known for their fantastic beaches. While Punta Cana does have some resorts and is the name that is tossed about as the major resort area, in reality, there are many more choices for all-inclusives and other accommodations nearer to Bávaro.

Europeans have been traveling to the Coconut Coast for decades, and most resorts try to make them comfortable by offering European comforts in the tropics (such as food choices in the buffets), but with a burgeoning American influx, resorts are beginning to fold in American tastes and needs to their accommodations.

For any services, there are plazas near Bávaro, but the only real town in the area is a small beach town called **El Cortecito;** it's a great place for a break from the all-inclusive resort.

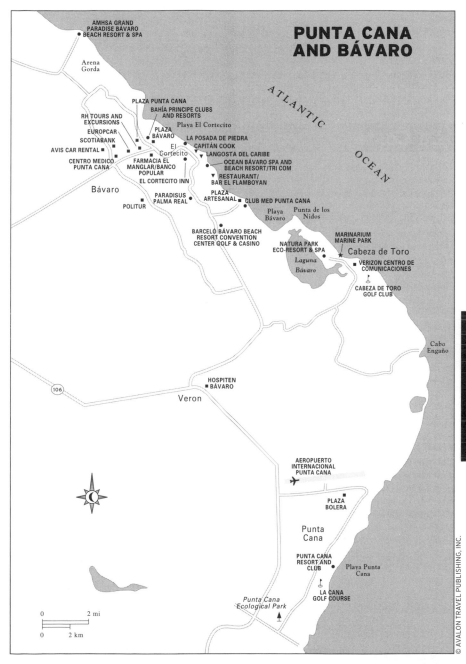

PUNTA CANA
AND BÁVARO

AMHSA GRAND
PARADISE BÁVARO
BEACH RESORT & SPA

Arena
Gorda

ATLANTIC OCEAN

PLAZA PUNTA CANA
BAHÍA PRINCIPE CLUBS
AND RESORTS

RH TOURS AND
EXCURSIONS   Playa El Cortecito
EUROPCAR   PLAZA
SCOTIABANK   BÁVARO   LA POSADA DE PIEDRA
AVIS CAR RENTAL   CAPITÁN COOK
                  El   LANGOSTA DEL CARIBE
CENTRO MEDICO   Cortecito
PUNTA CANA   FARMACIA EL   OCEAN BÁVARO SPA AND
              MANGLAR/BANCO   BEACH RESORT/TRI COM
              POPULAR
              EL CORTECITO INN   RESTAURANT/
Bávaro   BAR EL FLAMBOYAN
              PARADISUS   PLAZA
              PALMA REAL   ARTESANAL   CLUB MED PUNTA CANA
      POLITUR   Playa   Punta de los
                              Bávaro   Nidos

              BARCELÓ BÁVARO BEACH
              RESORT CONVENTION   MARINARIUM
              CENTER GOLF & CASINO   NATURA PARK   MARINE PARK
                              ECO-RESORT & SPA   Cabeza de Toro
                              Laguna   VERIZON CENTRO DE
                              Bávaro   COMUNICACIONES

                                          CABEZA DE TORO
                                          GOLF CLUB

                                                  Cabo
                                                  Engaño

106

              HOSPITEN
              BÁVARO
      Veron

                              AEROPUERTO
                              INTERNACIONAL
                              PUNTA CANA

                                      PLAZA
                                      BOLERA

                          Punta
                          Cana

                          PUNTA CANA
                          RESORT AND   Playa Punta
                          CLUB   Cana

                              LA CANA
              Punta Cana   GOLF COURSE
              Ecological Park

0   2 mi

0   2 km

THE SOUTHEAST

SIGHTS

Beaches

Beaches in the Dominican Republic are, in theory, open to the public. Of course, that hasn't stopped the mega-resorts from trying to restrict their beaches to just their paying guests. Many of them offer day passes for about US$40 if you would like to freely enjoy their grounds, including "their" portion of beach. By law, though, everyone has the right to be on any stretch of beach they want; if you're not a guest of the hotel, you may have to just park yourself on the sand.

The beaches along the southeastern shoreline are arguably the best in the country. **Playas Punta Cana and Bávaro** are wide, white-sand beauties lined with tall coconut trees and laced with resorts. The beach at **Cabo Engaño,** between the beaches of Punta Cana and Bávaro, offers near idyllic conditions for surfing and windsurfing. But be warned; the wind can be rather rough. **Playa El Cortecito** is an often-crowded public beach where local fishermen still bring in their boats, but more on the mark, it is a haven for souvenir shops and wandering vendors. It is a good access spot for a nice long walk along the coastline.

The beaches north of El Cortecito have shabby roads that are best traversed by trucks or SUVs. **Playa El Macao** is about 15 kilometers up the coastline. It is a sandy-bottomed spectacular beach that has a drastic drop-off, not the best for children. Since it is so beautiful, though, it has become a popular stop-off for four-wheeler excursions coming from the nearby resorts, taking away a lot of the peaceful charm. The beaches at **Boca de Maímon** and **Playa del Muerto** are deserted stretches that offer seclusion at its best and are well worth the effort even if the roads are terrible.

Punta Cana Ecological Park

About a kilometer from the Punta Cana Resort and Club, Punta Cana Ecological Park (tel. 809/959-8483, www.puntacana.org, 8 A.M.–4 P.M. daily) is a natural refuge for local flora and fauna, including many rare plants and endangered animals. A guided tour (US$10 adult, US$5 child) through the portion of the park called the **Parque Ojos Indígenas** (Indigenous Eyes Park) takes you through thickly vegetated trails of natural and cultivated gardens. You'll pass natural freshwater lagoons, and kids especially will like the petting farm, where Dominican domesticated animals are available to touch and feed. The iguana habitat has examples of the rhinoceros iguana, which is a species endemic to the island of Hispaniola. Agricultural exhibits have Dominican crops like the cacao bean, coffee, and tobacco, including a display of a traditional Dominican farm or *conuco*. Guided tours are given in English, Spanish, German, and French. Self-guided tours are possible by purchasing a booklet at the visitor's center.

Horseback tours (US$20 for one hour, US$30 for two hours) are a fun way to see the park and all it has to offer, along with an extended ride along the coast. They must be arranged ahead of time.

Supporting this park is a great way not only to have fun and learn something about the country you are visiting, but also to give back through sustainable tourism. The Punta Cana Resort and Club created the Punta Cana Ecological Foundation and the Coastal Marine Project. They are nonprofit organizations that work to protect the ecosystem and sustain the health of the coastal zone and coral reefs. It has made significant headway in promoting the growing sustainable tourism industry in the Dominican Republic.

Marinarium Marine Park

This is another simultaneously fun, educational, and sustainable tourism-minded activity. A half-day cruise with the **Marinarium** (Cabeza de Toro/Bávaro, tel. 809/689-5183, www.marinarium.com, US$72/adult and US$36/ages 2–12) starts with your "Safari Express" from your hotel to the launching point along the coast at Cabeza de Toro. After boarding what looks like a giant pontoon boat with a viewing chamber on the bottom (watch the fish and coral go by!), you'll take a short ride to the controlled section in the ocean, which stretches for some 40,000 square meters and reaches depths of three meters. You'll snorkel with sharks, rays, and much more tropical marine life. Even though it is a little spendy, it is a good excursion for families. Cost includes drinks, snacks, and snorkel gear. Kids also enjoy the educational trip back to shore with a chance to win a free T-shirt. English, Spanish, and French are spoken. Reservations are necessary and can only be made through hotel excursion desks.

ENTERTAINMENT

On the grounds of the **Barceló Bávaro Beach Resort** (tel. 809/686-5797) there are many choices for nighttime entertainment. The **Tropicalissimo** (10:30 P.M. Mon.–Sat.) show is a lively cabaret featuring all Dominican music, dancing, and singing. The talented dancers and singers wear colorful costumes and headdresses in flashy Las Vegas–style pizzazz. This is a lot of fun to watch. Try to get there early so that you can get good seats. It's held in the air-conditioned Salón Mallorca with free drinks served during the show.

Just outside the theater is the **Black Jack Piano Bar,** where the drinks are tasty and the atmosphere is relaxed. The **Barceló Casino** (open 24 hours) is the best in the area. Try your luck at the game tables and slot machines. Free appetizers and drinks are offered.

Want more action? The **Bávaro Disco** (11 P.M.–5 A.M.) is the most popular disco in the area for the younger, and often single, crowd. It's the place to go if you've been craving a party atmosphere and want to dance to some loud pop music.

Entrance to the venues within the Barceló complex is free to guests and US$45 for non-guest entrance to the complex.

SHOPPING

Most of the huge all-inclusive resorts have their own gift shops, sometimes many, as at **Bahía Principe Clubs and Resorts.** Outside of the mega-resorts, the other plazas are somewhat limited. Expect trinket shops, not high fashion.

Plaza Artesanal Bibijagua

This plaza (8 A.M.–midnight daily) is a collection of stalls positioned directly on the sandy shore between Bávaro and Cabeza de Toro. Here you'll find all the standard Dominican gift-shop trinkets: sarongs, T-shirts, jewelry, bottles of Mamajuana, rum, and cigars. The atmosphere is rife with the sounds of haggling and the not-so-distant roar of the ocean. Parking is available.

Plaza Bávaro

This shopping complex comprises a few plazas: Plaza Punta Cana, Plaza Bávaro (across the street), and Bávaro Shopping Center (on the south side of Plaza Punta Cana). They are mainly tourist-oriented with trinket shops, cigar shops, a pharmacy, a photo shop, a bank, and other services.

SPORTS AND RECREATION
Tours and Excursions

RH Tours and Excursions (El Cortecito, tel. 809/552-1425, www.rhtours.com, 9 A.M.–7 P.M. daily) is a one-stop paradise for choices in excursions. It's in El Cortecito near the Capitán Cook restaurant. This long-established and trusted company offers excursions such as helicopter tours (US$70–200/person), caving expeditions (US$106), a Santo Domingo day trip (US$50), Parque Nacional Los Haitises tours (US$79), deep-sea fishing (US$80), and even trips into the central mountains. Languages spoken are English, Spanish, German, and French.

Walk down toward the north end of El Cortecito to find other independent excursion companies. Kiosks offer a bevy of choices from catamaran rides, snorkeling, and flying boats to windsurfing, sailing, and banana boat rides.

The **Punta Cana Express Bus Bar** (Punta Cana, tel. 809/686-9290, cell 809/481-1469) is an all-day excursion package. You are picked up at your hotel at 8 A.M. in a large "party bus," and the tour passes sugarcane fields and coffee and cacao plantations. You'll see a cockfight, then move on to a ranch for some horse riding along the beach. Lunch is provided at the ranch. You are returned to your hotel around 4:30 P.M. Two vehicle choices are available depending on the size of your party. The jeep for four people is US$80 per person, whereas booking a truck to hold 18–20 people is US$75 per person. Everything is included.

Golf

La Cana Golf Course (Punta Cana Resort and Club, tel. 809/959-2262, fax 809/959-4650, www.puntacana.com, tee times 7 A.M.–4 P.M.) is both challenging and beautiful. Designed by Pete B. Dye, this 18-hole, par-72 course opened in 2001 and has 14 holes with views of the Caribbean Sea and 4 that run alongside it. If you are going to go all out and splurge for a round, this is the best in the area. This course is part of one of the best hotels in the area, and the beauty, service, and prices indicate this. Greens fees for 18 holes are US$144 for nonguests of the hotel, US$88 for 9 holes. Caddies cost US$6 for 9 holes or US$12 for 18 holes. Golf club rental is available for US$40/round.

Cabeza de Toro Golf Club (Bávaro Catalonia Resort, tel. 809/412-0000, fax 809/412-2001, tee times 7 A.M.–4 P.M.) has two 9-hole courses, one is a regular 9-hole course (par 35) and the other is a 9-hole executive course (par 3) that opened in 2000. While they are short courses, it's a stimulating and enjoyable play for both novice and experienced golfers, with its five lakes (adding water obstacles), numerous shade trees, and wide fairways. Greens fees are considerably less than at the La Cana course. Greens fees are US$45 for a round on the 9-hole course (cart US$20 extra) and US$65 for two rounds (cart US$25 extra).

The **Cocotal Golf and Country Club** (El Cortecito, tel. 809/221-1290 ext. 2000, fax 809/686-5427, www.cocotalgolf.com) has been carved out of what used to be a coconut plantation. Spanish golf champion José "Pepe" Gancedo designed two courses (18 and 9 holes)

by using what nature already afforded the lush and rolling landscape. Lakes, tactical placement of trees and bunkers, generous fairways and greens, and the peaceful surroundings can fool a golfer. This is a challenging course. Winds run opposite of play direction, waters wrap greens, and just when you thought you had the wind figured out, it is at your back. Greens fees plus cart rental for the 18-hole course are US$135. Fees for the 9-hole plus a cart are US$80. Lessons are offered through the Cocotal Golf Academy for US$60 per 45 minutes.

ACCOMMODATIONS
Under US$100

If the all-inclusive scene doesn't appeal to you, here are some options for independent accommodations under US$100.

El Cortecito Inn (Av. Melia Fiesta, El Cortecito, tel. 809/552-0639, fax 809/552-0691, US$60 d per room w/breakfast), a 70-unit hotel right on the main strip of El Cortecito and only 40 meters from the beach, offers very basic rooms, each with its own private bath. Don't expect pampering. The location is convenient, just paces from shops, restaurants, the beach, and excursion offices. Children up to seven years old stay free. This hotel has seen better days, with dated decor and poor maintenance, but it has a pool and a bar/restaurant where the food portions are generous. If you are traveling with your laptop, the hotel will let you use its hookup for free. Free parking is available.

At **La Posada de Piedra** (Playa El Cortecito, Bávaro, tel. 809/221-0754, www.laposadadepiedra.com, US$35–45 d) it's all about location, location, location (for an extremely low price). This very small (five rooms, to be exact) family-owned hotel offers low-maintenance, independent travelers the accommodations they've been looking for. Two of the rooms are actually in the owner's home, where you'll have your own private bath, a ceiling fan, and a shared balcony overlooking an amazing view of the ocean. The other three rooms are in very basic cabanas on the beach. Meals and drinks are available in a family-style atmosphere. It's a short walk to the shops and restaurants of El Cortecito.

US$100-200

Natura Park Eco-Resort & Spa (Cabeza de Toro,Punta Cana, tel. 809/221-2626, fax 809/221-6060, www.blau-hotels.com, US$135 d) sits next to Laguna Bávaro amid a beautiful estuary and a spectacular stretch of white-sand beach great for long walks. This is a good choice if you are an ecoconscious traveler who wants to be pampered at the same time. It is known for its efforts to minimize impact on the environment, such as using only reusable cups and biodegradable soap in your bathroom. There are 510 rooms and 20 suites; the pool has a swim-up bar and a children's area, and there is a luxurious spa with massage and beauty treatments available. If you don't speak a word of Spanish, communication might be a challenge since much of the staff does not speak English. Rooms are not luxurious but are more than comfortable, and all have a terrace or balcony.

Just the name of **Ocean Bávaro Spa and Beach Resort** (El Cortecito, Bávaro, tel. 809/476-2326, fax 809/221-0814, www.ocean-hotels.net, US$110–210) can evoke a heavenly emotion of relaxation and escape. Situated on the gorgeous Playa Bávaro, this resort offers comfortable and nicely decorated standard rooms with regular amenities. Junior or deluxe suites are very pleasing upgrades—often these rooms are a little more "cared for" and there is less chance of the pesky mustiness that seems to have afflicted some of the rooms. The resort as a whole is kept very clean, from the gardens to the restaurants to the rooms. One of the overwhelmingly obvious reasons to come here (aside from the beach—need it be mentioned again?) is for the Metamorphosis Spa, where you can enjoy a massage by the beach for US$30 an hour or buy packages consisting of massage, exfoliation, European algae wraps, and beauty services in the ocean-view spa.

There are five à la carte restaurants, one buffet, and two snack bars (serving snacks 24 hours a day). No shorts are allowed in the à la carte restaurants.

It's a long name—**Barceló Bávaro Beach Resort Convention Center Golf & Casino** (Playa Bávaro, Punta Cana, tel. 809/686-5797, fax 809/686-5797, www.barcelo.com, from US$110 d)—but for a complex of five all-inclusive resorts (Bávaro Palace, Bávaro Beach, Bávaro Caribe, Bávaro Golf, and Bávaro Casino) within its almost 13-square-kilometer confines, it is only fitting. All but the Bávaro Casino are situated along the ocean. This complex is best for those who want a great number of choices for entertainment in addition to their beloved beach time. It can be a rather lively party scene, especially during spring break. As a guest, you have access to most of the rest of the complex's amenities as well, including some restaurants, the casino, discos, the Tropicalissimo show, and golf. Make no mistake, though; this is an excellent location for families. The myriad food choices within the entire complex are reason enough; there are water sports galore, kids' clubs, minigolf, sporting courts (basketball, soccer, tennis), and baby-sitting as well.

The Bávaro Palace (from US$240) is the newest in the family and therefore has the biggest and most comfortable rooms in its six buildings, all with elevators making accessibility easier. It has a buffet, five à la carte restaurants, and five bars (one in the pool). If you plan on exploring the rest of the grounds, make sure to ask for a map and catch one of the free shuttles that make frequent tours and stops.

When it comes to all-inclusive affordable luxury, the Iberostar hotels—**Iberostar Bávaro, Iberostar Dominicana, and Iberostar Punta Cana** (Playa Bávaro, tel. 809/221-6500, fax 809/688-6186, www.iberostar.com, US$115–171)—hit a home run. Located right next to one another, all have ingredients for a tasty cocktail of relaxation and entertainment, offering huge pools, excursion options, open-air buffets as well as à la carte international-themed restaurants, very comfortable rooms, and some of the best beach stretches around.

THE SOUTHEAST

The Iberostar Bávaro is an all-suite resort. Each junior suite has a sunken living room and balcony or patio; with the cost of your stay, you have access to the other Iberostar hotels. It has nine restaurants and a lake-like pool surrounded by palms with a swim-up bar and separate area for the kids. Also available are children's programs, a casino, billiards, archery, and even a teen disco among the so many other amenities.

In comparison to other all-inclusive resorts, **Amhsa Grand Paradise Bávaro Beach Resort & Spa** (Carretera Macao, Playa Arena Gorda, tel. 809/221-2121, fax 809/221-2181, www.amhsamarina.com, US$181 d, children ages 7–12 stay for US$91) is more compact and, therefore, is a very family-friendly choice. From your room to the beach to the pool to the restaurants, nothing is a long walk. Also, the Kiko's Kids Club is a great way to entertain the kids and steal some quiet time for yourself. While the rooms are nothing fancy, they are comfortable and clean. There are six bars, one buffet, and five à la carte restaurants available. The main menu in the à la carte restaurants is included, but there are special menu items at an extra charge, so be careful how you order. The beach at the Grand Paradise is wonderful, with plenty of loungers to go around. However, the water is a bit on the rough side with a strong undertow.

The main attraction at **Club Med Punta Cana** (Playa Punta Cana, Punta Cana, tel. 809/687-2767, www.clubmed.com, US$125–240) is its variety of activities: many water sports, aerobics, horseback riding, flying trapeze, kickboxing, yoga, tennis, and much more. Children will be kept quite happy with the myriad kid-geared activities, like rollerblading, educational fun, circus lessons, and dancing. Guests are international, mostly from Europe.

For the utmost in tranquility for your vacation, **(Punta Cana Resort and Club** (Playa Punta Cana, Punta Cana, tel. 809/959-2262, fax 809/959-3951, www.puntacana.com, US$93–185 d depending on season) is a welcome oasis, even if traveling with the entire family. Although there are some things to keep you busy, it is definitely not a party scene. Families and older couples are happiest here. Enjoy a daytime tennis match (night tennis costs US$10/hour). If getting out into the "big blue" is your idea of paradise, you can rent a boat, scuba dive, or go deep-sea fishing at the resort's full-service marina. Booking these activities ahead of time is highly advised.

Just a quick jaunt to the right of the beach area, by the hotel's marina, is Punta Cana Resort and Club's 240-hectare private ecological reserve. Fighting the heat of the Caribbean midday is a joy while taking a dip in the Manantial Yauya natural spring. Guided tours, bird-watching tours, and educational workshops are available at the Parque Ojos Indígenas.

The resort accommodations themselves are set on more than a hectare of lush gardens along five kilometers of powdery coastline. Rooms are very nicely decorated, but lunch and drinks are not included in the price. There are many excursions to choose from, at extra charge, and they can be arranged in the hotel's own travel agency.

US$200 and Up

(Bahía Principe Clubs and Resorts (Arena Gorda–Macao, Bávaro, tel. 809/552-1444, www.bahia-principe.com) is a complex home to the **Gran Bahía Principe Punta Cana** (US$268) and the **Gran Bahía Principe Bávaro** (US$250). Don't let the names fool you; they are side by side along the same amazing pearl-white beach of Playa Bávaro. The grounds are very well tended, lush, and vast enough to offer frequent-running shuttle services to take you from one end to another. Down by the beach, there is one large pool that can get quite lively, but in the middle of the complex there are two other pools reserved for quieter sun worship. The rooms are spacious with very nice bathrooms. Nightly entertainment is abundant at the Principe resorts. Cabaret-style shows, a piano bar, and karaoke night (it's fun to hear singers from many nations) are relaxing ways to pass the evening. For more lively nights, head over to the Pueblo Principe (the resort's "small town") and listen to live music, watch a dance contest, groove the night away in the disco, or test your luck in the casino. The excursion office offers many attractive ways to spice up your vacation. But, for those who would rather stay put, this complex has everything you need. You'll find a pharmacy, along with shops (albeit quite overpriced) with trinkets, jewelry, clothing, and anything else you want in the Pueblo Principe.

If you've been on a search for a hotel that doesn't have a kids' club as a major selling point, here it is: **Secrets Excellence Punta Cana** (Playas Uvero Alto, Punta Cana, tel. 809/685-9880, fax 809/685-9990, www.secretsresorts.com, US$249 d). Secrets is an adults-only (18 or older) resort, making it extremely popular as a honeymoon resort. There are two huge pools, with the biggest one stretching longer than a football field and containing a swim-up bar. At the beach, you'll find perfectly powdery sand for kilometers, great for long walks with your honey. The waves are strong, which makes it great for boogie boarding, but the strong undertow doesn't make it a peaceful swimming spot. If you walk to the right of the resort and around the bend, the water can be calmer. In Secrets' spa you can enjoy many soothing treatments, including a couple's massage. There are seven different restaurants, one of which includes a seaside candlelight dinner. At night you can enjoy the piano bar, take in nightly stage performances, go dancing in the disco, gamble in the casino, or (and this is the best part) take a moonlit horseback ride along the ocean! Romance is in the air at Secrets Excellence. All 446 rooms have a four-poster bed and Jacuzzi for two. Couples celebrating honeymoons or anniversaries receive complimentary special treatment (you must mention when booking and show proof when you arrive). Special honeymoon and anniversary packages are available for US$699/couple and include items like arrival fruit basket, breakfast in bed, private beachfront dinner, and a spa treatment. There is even a complimen-

tary wedding package, but wedding packages that offer services above and beyond start at US$1,500.

Paradisus Palma Real (Playa Bávaro/Punta Cana, tel. 809/686-7499, fax 809/686-7699, www.solmelia.com, US$267) is a new 554-suite luxury resort in operation in the new so-called six-star category. Among its amenities are six restaurants serving international cuisine, a kids' club, three more-than-generous-in-size pools, tennis, and a fitness center including trainers and yoga, tai chi, and pilates classes. Each guest gets unlimited greens fees at the Cocotal Golf and Country Club, and there is a casino and live shows for nightly entertainment. Each beautifully appointed suite boasts a Jacuzzi for two, a private terrace, flat screen TV, 24-hour room service, and minibar.

FOOD

Most people who vacation in this part of the Dominican Republic do so in the all-inclusive resorts and will stay in those compounds for the duration of their trip. Therefore, independent restaurants that last are rare. But there are a few and one is a top pick.

Capitán Cook (El Cortecito, tel. 809/552-0654, noon–midnight daily, US$11–45) is well known for its freshly grilled seafood, ambience, and amazing location. Super-fresh fish is grilled to order in the outdoor kitchen. The chefs bounce around one another, adding to the already vibrant atmosphere of this (mostly) outdoor restaurant. At tables under thatch-roofed gazebos, food and drinks are served in front of the azure ocean to the tune of wandering *bachata* musicians. Should you choose to sit inside, there is a more formal indoor dining area overlooking the ocean. Grilled fish and other meats come served with salad, potatoes, or fries. Other delights include entrées like seafood spaghetti or an appetizer mix for the table to share. A meal plan that comes complete with transportation from your hotel can even be arranged. For US$40 per person during the day, you'll be picked up by boat. At night, for US$45

THE SOUTHEAST

per person, you'll receive a taxi ride. They will travel the entire coastline to get you, but reservations are required.

The much less exciting but reliable **Restaurant/Bar El Flamboyan** (El Cortecito Inn, Av. Melia Fiesta, El Cortecito, tel. 809/552-0639, fax 809/552-0691, 11 A.M.– 2 A.M. daily, US$5–22) is just across the street from Capitán Cook's in El Cortecito Inn. The restaurant serves international and Dominican food in generous portions, including lobster for US$22. Dress is casual.

On the beach in the town of El Cortecito, at ⟨ **Langosta del Caribe** (El Cortecito, tel. 809/552-0774, fax 809/552-1898, www .restaurantebavaro.com, US$11–20) you'll sit under umbrellas with your feet directly in the sand. Langosta del Caribe has a complimentary boat pick-up service from wherever you are staying in the Bávaro area. Its specialty is grilled seafood. You can choose your own lobster, and cooks will prepare it on the barbecue or however you desire. After you eat, you can swim at the beach or rest on some of their beach loungers. This is a great way to enjoy a lazy afternoon on the beach.

INFORMATION AND SERVICES

When you are staying in an all-inclusive resort, many services are located within the walls of the complex. Otherwise, the best places to go for most services are the small town of El Cortecito and the plazas making up the **Plaza Bávaro** area.

Communications

In El Cortecito, the only public Internet connection is at **Tri Com** (9 A.M.–11 P.M., US$3/ hour). It is also a call center. Calls to the U.S. run US$0.42/minute, calls to Europe are US$0.70/minute.

Verizon Centro de Comunicaciones (Cabeza de Toro, 8 A.M.–9 P.M. Mon.–Sat., 8 A.M.–4 P.M. Sun.) has a call center and Internet connection.

Internet Tropical Café (Plaza Punta Cana, Bávaro, tel. 809/552-1229, 8 A.M.–11 P.M.

Mon.–Sat., 9 A.M.–11 P.M. Sun., US$5/hour) offers sandwiches and drinks and the use of the Internet, phones, fax, copy machines, and even games.

Banks and Money Exchange

All of these banks will exchange U.S. dollars, euros, and traveler's checks and have ATMs.

Banco Popular is in Plaza Punta Cana (tel. 809/959-1021, fax 809/959-1019, 9 A.M.– 4 P.M. Mon.–Fri.).

Banco del Progreso has three locations in the Bávaro/Punta Cana area: in the Aeropuerto Punta Cana (tel. 809/221-9690, fax 809/221-9695); inside El Cortecito Supermarket (El Cortecito, 9 A.M.–9 P.M. Mon.–Sat.); and in Plaza Bolera (Bávaro, 9 A.M.–4 P.M. Mon.–Fri.).

ScotiaBank is in Plaza Brisas (Bávaro, tel. 809/552-1500, fax 809/552-1504, 9 A.M.–5 P.M. Mon.–Fri., 9 A.M.–1 P.M. Sat.).

For money transfers, there is a **Western Union** (Plaza Bávaro, tel. 809/532-7381, 8 A.M.–5 P.M. Mon.–Sat.).

Health and Emergencies

All-inclusive resorts have small clinics that can treat you for minor ailments and concerns for an extra cost, but if you have other more serious concerns, there are some rather nice choices available in this heavy tourist area.

Hospiten Bávaro (Carretera Higüey– Punta Cana, tel. 809/686-1414) is the best bet for care should you need it. Doctors here speak English, French, and German, and the emergency room is open 24 hours. This 70-bed hospital opened in 2000 and has the latest medical and surgical technology, an intensive care unit, a blood bank, and X-ray machines. Hospiten Bávaro is on the highway in between Punta Cana and Bávaro, just before you turn to Bávaro.

Centro Médico Punta Cana (Bávaro, tel. 809/552-1506) is another reliable and good choice for medical care in the area. The name is a bit confusing since it is actually in Bávaro about a kilometer before the turn off to El Cortecito, near the bus station. The ER is open 24 hours.

It is absolutely best to take medications with you from home as they can be overpriced in the resort pharmacies, even over-the-counter medications. However, there are pharmacies in El Cortecito and the plazas of Plaza Bávaro. **Farmacia El Manglar** (Plaza Punta Cana, Bávaro, tel. 809/552-1533, 8 A.M.–midnight daily) will even deliver what you need to your hotel.

Politur (Tourist Police, tel. 809/686-8227) has two locations serving the area, both open 24 hours: next to the bus terminal in Bávaro and in the Plaza Bolera in Punta Cana near the airport.

GETTING THERE
By Bus
The entire southeastern region, especially the Costa del Coco, is best served by the **Aeropuerto Internacional Punta Cana.** Catching a taxi to your hotel is no problem and can be quite inexpensive, costing under US$30. Make sure to agree on the price before getting in the cab or letting them help you with baggage. Most people staying in all-inclusive resorts arrange for a ride on one of their resort's free shuttles. Inquire about it when booking your vacation.

Guaguas are an option for independent travelers who arrive during the day. Once the sun disappears, so does this mode of transportation. Just stand on the side of the road for the direction you want to travel and flag one down. Let them know where you are going before getting aboard; they won't let you on if they're not going in your direction. A ride on one of these small public "buses" is about US$1.50 but could be more depending on how far you're going.

Coming from Santo Domingo, you can catch an **express bus** in the Gazcue neighborhood bus station at the Plaza Los Girasols (Juan Sanchez Ramírez 31, tel. 809/682-9670, US$7) to the major resorts of the Punta Cana/Bávaro area. They all pass through Higüey two times a day (7 A.M. and 4 P.M.).

Buses also leave from Santo Domingo's Parque Enriquillo for a two-leg trip connecting in Higüey. In Higüey, you must transfer to an-other bus. Most have signs in them displaying their destinations, but it is best to ask which one you should board. For each leg of the trip, you'll pay on board the bus (US$5 from Santo Domingo to Higüey and US$2 from Higüey to Bávaro).

By Air
Although the country is easy to drive around and few fly between destinations within the Dominican Republic, air travel is a growing trend. **Takeoff Destination Service S.A.** (Plaza Brisas de Bávaro 8, Bávaro, tel. 809/552-1333, fax 809/552-1113, www.takeoffweb.com) has flights between Punta Cana and Santo Domingo (US$89), Puerto Plata (US$119), and Samaná (US$99). It can also arrange excursions, charter flights, shuttle transfers, and hotel pickups; it has a flight school.

By Car
From Higüey, travel northeast along Highway 105 to the town of La Otra Banda, where you turn off onto Highway 106 to get to the Bávaro/Punta Cana area.

GETTING AROUND
Taxis are easy to get through your hotels. Many resorts post the cost in menu form at the front desk or at their front gates. You can also call the **Siuratural** (tel. 809/552-0617) company for 24-hour service.

Car Rental
Most visitors who come to the Costa del Coco don't rent cars because they are staying in resort complexes and don't consider leaving them. Still, one would think it would be relatively easy to rent a car right at the airport in this high-tourist area. That's not the case, but, never fear, there are car-rental places scattered throughout the Punta Cana/Bávaro area. It is a wonderful way to break out of the mold and see the less touristy Dominican Republic. Book a rental online if you can; prices can be more reasonable that way (they are rather pricey in this part of the DR). Cost fluctuates here in a very haphazard manner in all

seasons. Expect to pay anywhere from US$35 to US$90 a day for an economy car. **Avis Car Rental** (Arena Gorda, Carretera Friusa-Riu, tel. 809/688-1354), **National Car Rental**

(Plaza Bávaro, tel. 809/221-0286), and **Europcar** (Calle Gustavo Mejía, near Plaza Punta Cana, tel. 809/686-2861) all rent cars in the area.

La Costa Esmeralda

MICHES AND SURROUNDING AREA

The seaside town of Miches is tucked into a small bay at the southern mouth of the Bahía de Samaná. The town itself doesn't offer a lot to a traveler and is mainly a stop-off point for transfer to Sabana de la Mar, a town located west along the same shore. This coastline, stretching from the easternmost edge of El Seibo province and over to Sabana de la Mar in the west at the junction to the National Park Los Haitises, is sometimes referred to as **La Costa Esmeralda** and is home to two lagoons, Redonda and Limón. The beaches near here are less manicured and more on the wild side.

Highway 104 leads you away from Bávaro to the absolutely stunning **Playa Limón** (turn off in the town of El Cedro in a northerly direction) and **Punta El Rey** (turn off in the town of La Mina). Playa Limón is three kilometers of unparalleled beauty that draws tour groups occasionally but, for the most part, is not overcrowded. In fact, near Playa Limón is the scientific reserve at **Laguna Limón,** a freshwater reserve that meets up with Playa Limón at the coast and is well known for the fantastic birdwatching within its wetlands and mangroves. Just around the curve of the coastline, into what becomes the southern edge of the mouth of the **Bahía de Samaná,** is Punta El Rey, truly a breathtaking beach.

Accommodations and Food

Although there aren't a lot of choices in the area since tourism is still quite relegated to the Bávaro area, this could be good news for the independent traveler. It means there are smaller hotels where you can stay for a frac-

tion of the cost of the mega-complexes in the Punta Cana and Bávaro areas. The two listed are in or around Miches and are run by the same Swiss group.

Coco Loco Beach Club (Playa Miches, Miches, tel. 809/980-7908, www.puntaelrey .com, US$35 d) is a 10-cabin hotel right on the beach that offers simple but clean accommodations, each with two double beds, bathroom (no hot water), fan, table with chairs, and a private porch. Cabins do not have a TV, phone, or air-conditioning. This area is particularly good for kids; there is no traffic and the plush grass is great to jump, play volleyball, or run around on. The main building is a two-story structure with an open-air lounge and restaurant serving fish, shrimp, pasta, salads, and sandwiches. A pizzeria boasts 20 different kinds of pizza (US$5.50–9). Meals are not included in the price.

The main selling point of **Hotel La Loma** (Miches, tel. 809/980-7909, US$50 d) is its view, without a doubt. You can enjoy the panorama of the breathtaking Bahía de Samaná, where sunsets are amazing. The rooms are simple and quite comfortable, each with one kingsize and one twin bed, air-conditioning, TV, a private bath, and balconies looking down over the small pool and the vista. The hotel's restaurant is open for all meals, and breakfast is only US$5 per person, served with the same amazing view as a backdrop.

Guests of either of the above hotels are encouraged to ask about the interchangeable rate plan, where paying one multinight fee enables you to stay in both hotels should you choose to divide your time between the two. Guests also get a free boat transfer for a day trip to the gorgeous Punta El Rey beach. Just ask the very

© ANA CHAVIER CAAMAÑO

grazing in the southeastern countryside

accommodating and hospitable management at the front desk.

Services

If you are looking to find all the comforts of home during your vacation, this is not the spot. Despite the beautiful beaches and breathtaking vistas, Miches is not set up to receive tourists. There is no hospital or Internet access. Street signs aren't always in place, but one to keep in mind is Calle Mella.

BanReservas (Miches, 9:30 A.M.–3 P.M. Mon., Wed., and Fri.) has an ATM and you can exchange money. It's in the center of town about a block south of Calle Mella.

Go to **Verizon Centro de Comunicaciones** (Miches, Calle Mella, 8 A.M.–7 P.M.) to make international calls to the U.S. (US$0.40/minute) and Europe (US$1.30/minute).

SABANA DE LA MAR

Although it's not a tourist attraction town, most travelers pass through Sabana de la Mar to get to the Parque Nacional Los Haitises or to catch a ferry to Samaná. There are very few services, accommodations, or places to eat in Sabana de la Mar.

The resort 【 **Paraíso Caño Hondo** (Sabana de la Mar, tel. 809/248-5995, cell 809/889-9454, www.paraisocanohondo .com, website in Spanish only, US$59 d with all meals included) is really the only recommended place to stay in the area. Located right at the foot of the Parque Nacional Los Haitises, it is a fantastic choice as a base to explore the park. This small hotel offers very comfortable rooms decorated with rustic elements of the area, containing two or three full-size beds, a ceiling fan, and private hot water bath. Room service is available upon request. Six of the 12 rooms have a private balcony; in the quiet surroundings, you can hear the sounds of the nearby river and the native birds from the park. Nature lovers will fall hard for this place. Rates are less expensive in low season and less expensive if you choose to not include all meals in your plan, although keep in mind that food choices outside the hotel are sparse.

Children under 2 years old stay for free and ages 2–8 pay 50 percent of an adult fee. There is a weekend minimum stay of two nights. At El Cayuco, the hotel's bar and restaurant, you can enjoy plates of native Dominican fare. Stone pathways lead to various river-fed pools where, amidst the waterfalls and thick vegetation, you can take a dip in the heat of the day. If you're looking for the ultimate privacy, try to book for midweek; most excursions and student groups pass through on the weekends. If you're just in the area for the day, ask about a pass so that you can enjoy a swim in the pools without staying the night. Boat and hiking excursions are available.

Besides being a great hotel choice, the Paraíso offers ecological excursions ranging from walking tours (US$18), camping, horseback riding, and moonlight and other boat rides (US$15–33) to excursions to the park's caves. During humpback whale season you can go on a whale-watching tour in the Bahía de Samaná (US$57 per person).

Services
As in Miches, don't expect a lot of variety or services in Sabana de la Mar.

BanReservas (Calle Duarte, 9 A.M.–5 P.M. Mon.–Fri., 9 A.M.–1 P.M. Sat.) has an ATM. **Verizon Centro de Comunicaciones** (Calle Duarte, 8 A.M.–10 P.M. Mon.–Sat.) offers international calls to the U.S. (US$0.32) and Europe (US$0.74).

◖ PARQUE NACIONAL LOS HAITISES
The Dominican Republic is blessed to have a great deal of ecodiversity for such a small country, and the Parque Nacional Los Haitises (Land of the Mountains National Park) is one of the most distinctive of its national reserves, comprising nearly 160 kilometers of mangroves, estuaries, coves, and bays that together embrace the southwestern curve of the Bahía de Samaná.

Over 700 species of flora (17 are endemic to the area) thrive in the subhumid tropical forest due to its great amount of annual rainfall. Roughly 110 species of birds nest here, including the blue heron, the great white egret, the brown pelican, the roseate tern, and the rare Hispaniolan parakeet. The park's fauna includes scores of bats, tortoises, and manatees, which reside in the mangrove systems along the coast and various caves throughout.

The extensive limestone cave system is a major attraction for its examples of stalactites, stalagmites, and Taíno pictographs and petroglyphs depicting animals, rituals, faces, and divine beings.

Considering the rugged topography and its remoteness, the park is best conquered by boat excursions. They will take you through mangrove rivers, islets, and caves along the coast.

Coming from Highway 103 or 104, you'll see a park service sign in the south end of Sabana de la Mar. Excursions for the Parque Nacional Los Haitises are best done through various companies in Sabana de la Mar, Samaná, and Sánchez.

Getting There
There is a *guagua* stop at the convergence of Highways 103 and 104 in Sabana de la Mar. A ticket to Santo Domingo (via Hato Mayor) will cost you about US$4; buses leave every half hour 6 A.M.–4 P.M. A ticket to Miches will cost US$2.50, and buses leave every half hour.

Transportation Maritimo (tel. 809/538-2556, US$3.50) is the only choice to get across the bay to Samaná and, surprising, is the most direct way to get to the Costa Ámbar (via Samaná). The ride takes about an hour, leaving at 9 A.M., 11 A.M., 3 P.M., and 5 P.M. daily.

Getting Around
Walking is easiest in Sabana de la Mar because it is so small. *Motoconchos* tool around the area, and it will run you US$2–3 for a ride to the park. The best place to look for a taxi is the bus stop or the ferry dock. Secure a price before getting in.

LA PENÍNSULA DE SAMANÁ

Dense with coconut trees, bromeliads, other tropical vegetation, and some of the country's most beloved beaches, La Península de Samaná, roughly 40 kilometers long and 15 kilometers wide, has been a long-time favorite destination for the independent and backpacking tourist. In general, the Dominican Republic has a laid-back vibe, but on La Península de Samaná that mentality is encouraged. Mom-and-pop businesses and budget accommodations thrive on the peninsula, whereas in other parts of the country they are being drowned out by commercialism and big business.

Las Terrenas, Las Galeras, and Samaná are the three small towns worth visiting. Along the northern Atlantic coast, the town of Las Terrenas is the busiest, offers the most variety for accommodations and restaurants, has long sandy stretches of beach, and has the best nightlife of the three towns. Las Galeras, on the eastern tip of the arm, is by far the most quiet and remote, and the beaches are, without doubt, the most beautiful on the peninsula—especially the famous Playa Rincón, with its gently curved white-sand beach backed by a thick coconut grove. Santa Bárbara de Samaná, the capital of the province of Samaná, is on the Bahía de Samaná and is best known for its excursions to see the humpback whales in their natural habitat in the waters right offshore. The humpback whales arrive every winter to give birth and mate in the waters of the Bahía de Samaná.

PLANNING YOUR TIME

La Península de Samaná is a major destination for the tourist who doesn't want to be

© ANA CHAVIER CAAMAÑO

HIGHLIGHTS

◖ Cayo Levantado: Sweep over the turquoise waters of the Bahía de Samaná aboard a catamaran to this island. Enjoy a light lunch served right on the beach and float in the warm, shallow water. During whale season, this is a great way to wind down after the excitement of visiting the huge mammals in their natural habitat (page 127).

◖ Salto El Limón: The trek to this waterfall is an ecotourist's dream. Ride a horse through some of the country's most beautifully rainforested mountains, climb down the heavily vegetated trail, and take a dip in the pool that the 52-meter-high waterfall empties into (page 127).

◖ Whale-Watching: Humpback whales put on an exhilarating display in the Bahía de Samaná. These 30–50 ton creatures travel from as far away as Iceland every year to the waters just off the northern shore and proceed into the Bahía de Samaná for breeding and calving rituals. See them crest and splash just meters from your boat (page 128).

◖ Playa Rincón: Enjoy the striking beauty of this remote beach, known as one of the top 10 beaches in the Caribbean. With the clear water of the Bahía de Rincón on one side and a thick palm grove on the other, this beach feels like a level of heaven (page 135).

◖ Cabo Cabrón: Arguably the best dive site on the northern coast, Cabo Cabrón has stunning underwater walls, home to myriad corals and other marine life. Experienced divers should not miss this opportunity to dive in one of the Dominican Republic's best spots for scuba (page 136).

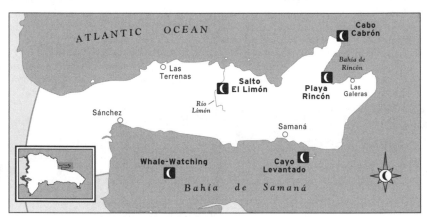

LOOK FOR ◖ TO FIND RECOMMENDED SIGHTS, ACTIVITIES, DINING, AND LODGING.

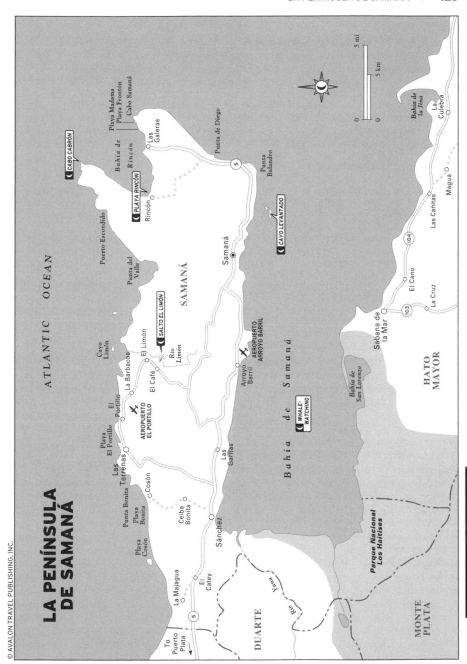

LA PENÍNSULA
DE SAMANÁ

ATLANTIC OCEAN

Cabo Cabrón

Playa Madama
Playa Frontón
Cabo Samaná

Bahía de
Rincón

Las
Galeras

Punta de Diego

Bahía de
la Jina

La
Culebra

Magua

Punta
Balandro

Puerto Escondido

PLAYA RINCÓN

Rincón

5

CAYO LEVANTADO

Las Cañitas

104

Punta del
Valle

Samaná

SAMANÁ

El Cano

La Cruz

103

Cayo
Limón

El Limón

SALTO EL LIMÓN

Río
Limón

AEROPUERTO
ARROYO BARRIL

Sabana de
la Mar

HATO
MAYOR

La Barbacoa

El Café

Arroyo
Barril

Bahía de
Samaná

El Portillo

Playa
El Portillo

AEROPUERTO
EL PORTILLO

WHALE-
WATCHING

Bahía de
San Lorenzo

Punta Bonita
Las Terrenas

Playa
Bonita

Cosón

Las
Galitas

Bahía de Samaná

Playa
Cosón

Ceiba
Bonita

Sánchez

Parque Nacional
Los Haitises

La Majagua

El
Catey

Río Yuna

MONTE
PLATA

5

To
Puerto
Plata

DUARTE

5 mi

5 km

0

0

© AVALON TRAVEL PUBLISHING, INC.

LA PENÍNSULA DE SAMANÁ

SETTLING INTO SAMANÁ

When Christopher Columbus attempted to settle the peninsula, he fell under the vicious attack of the Ciguayo natives; he immediately retreated (after having killed and enslaved many), naming the bay the Gulfo de las Flechas (Gulf of the Arrows).

However, with the exception of a motley assortment of pirates, the peninsula was nearly uninhabited until the 18th century, when settlers from the Canary Islands began to populate the area. In 1820, while this portion of the island was under Haitian control and together with U.S. abolitionists, land was gifted to 2,500 former slaves of the United States. Still visible today are their contributions to the culture of the area. The descendants of · the former slaves — "Los Ingleses" (The Eng-

lish), as they were called — still speak a sort of English/Spanish mixture. There is an ever-present sizzle of frying *yaniqueques* (johnny-cakes), which the settlers introduced to the present-day Dominican culinary fare. And the Methodist religion is still practiced.

In 1946, Santa Bárbara de Samaná was destroyed by a major fire. Most of its original wooden houses and buildings fell to the destruction, rising in a puff of black smoke, while one building stood in the midst of the ashes: the Methodist church or **La Churcha**. It was originally donated to the ex-slaves by the Methodist church and imported from England. To this day, "La Churcha" stands as a beloved heirloom of the family history of the region.

---

confined behind the walls of an all-inclusive resort. It is chock-full of independent hotels, mom-and-pop restaurants, and small tour operators. Since it is a small sliver of land that is relatively easily traversed in a doable amount of time, it is possible to spend your entire vacation on just the peninsula and find plenty to keep you occupied.

If you're flying in to Puerto Plata or any other airport in the Dominican Republic, plan on using your first day for travel and getting settled in. The three major towns on the peninsula—Samaná, Las Galeras, and Las Terrenas—while close to one another on the peninsula, are remote compared to the rest of the country. You'll need four hours of travel time from Puerto Plata and the other airports are farther away than that. Once you've gotten to your hotel, though, especially if you're staying in one of the towns, walking around is the easiest way to get your bearings and explore.

Next up, decide if you're going to do any excursions. For instance, if you're going to go whale-watching in the Bahía de Samaná or take a horseback ride to **Salto El Limón**, but you're staying in Las Terrenas, arrange for res-

ervations and transportation right away since tour spots could fill up.

HISTORY

The Samaná Peninsula, on very old maps, is sometimes shown as an island. That is because where the Río Yuna's estuary now flows into the Bahía de Samaná, there once was a channel that reached all the way up to the northern coast, creating a marshy waterway across the stretched neck of the peninsula.

Crafty pirates used this channel as an escape route to evade the Spanish. Back then, buccaneers loved Samaná for just the sort of escapist vibe the channel evoked. It seems that to this day, Samaná acts more like an island unto itself because of this history. It has a tradition of being the adopted home of invaders, violators, expatriates, and those with wanderlust.

From the Spanish, French, and Germans to the English, Haitians, and Americans, everyone has wanted to own the Peninsula of Samaná. Hundreds of years later, the former marshy waterway is now a fertile stretch of land on which rice grows easily, the pirate ships have all buried themselves in the waters offshore, and the expats have opened businesses.

Santa Bárbara de Samaná

For the majority of the year, the seaside town of Santa Bárbara de Samaná (commonly referred to as Samaná) is mainly quiet. Then in January, Samaná's population dramatically skyrockets with tourists from all over the world who have come to see the humpback whales that migrate to the waters of the Bahía de Samaná. A fresh energy fills the area. In the bay, the huge beasts lob their tails and breach just meters from the tourist-filled boats. In the town, the normal tranquility of is replaced with the drone of *motoconchos,* tour buses, and vendors.

Since 2005, Samaná has evolved into a cruise-ship stopover port. This new identity has caused an explosion in the local tourism industry there, multiplying the amount of visitors and services offered in Samaná.

The popularity of Samaná during whale-watching season cannot be denied. It is truly a remarkable natural event that must not be missed.

SIGHTS AND RECREATION
(Cayo Levantado

This island, though choked with tourists, has a beautiful white-sand beach. Due to the island's protected positioning in the bay, the waters are calm, shallow with a plush sandy bottom, and warm. This is an enjoyable place to take the family.

It's easiest to obtain a ride to Cayo Levantado by going directly to the Port of Samaná, where boats will take you there for US$5–10 per person. Alternatively, about 10 minutes from town up the Carretera Las Galeras, on the right-hand side, is a parking lot with a big sign that says Al Cayo; here you can make a deal to go to either Cayo Levantado or to Los Haitises. Along the same route, farther up the hill and on the right, is another boat-launching point called Simi Baez. A fair price for these boats to ask is US$25–30 per boatload (eight people). Make sure you agree on the price before boarding.

After disembarking on Cayo Levan-

tado, follow the crowd to the left and you'll eventually see dozens of booths selling crafts; past there is a beach where you can rent loungers for US$3. Food vendors sell ice-cold beers (US$3) and plates of freshly fried fish with rice and salad for US$9. Beware: The trinket-hawkers are *everywhere* and rather persistent. In 2005, there were no hotels on the island, but plans and construction have begun for one.

(Salto El Limón

Nestled in a thickly forested area in the middle of the Samaná Peninsula, northwest of the town of Samaná, is Salto El Limón (Lemon Waterfall). This 52-meter-high cascade falls into a swimming hole, giving a most refreshing end to the somewhat difficult, and at times hair-raising, trek it takes to get there. Most people go to the waterfall by horseback. *Paradas* (literally "stop," but in this instance it

© ANA CHAVIER CAAMAÑO

Make the trek to Salto El Limón.

LA PENÍNSULA DE SAMANÁ

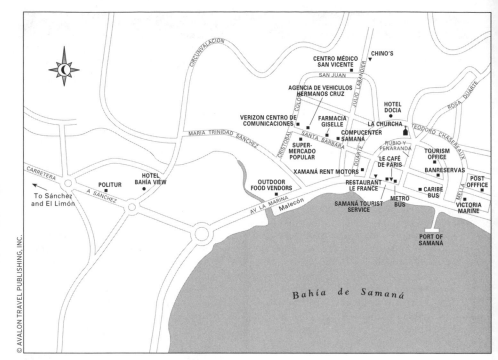

© AVALON TRAVEL PUBLISHING, INC.

means a horseback-riding tour operator) line the highway that cuts across the peninsula from El Limón to Samaná. These outfitters' routes vary, but most will provide your party with a horse, a guide who will walk beside you up the mountain, and the option of a lunch prepared for you upon your return. It is an awesome experience that shouldn't be missed when you visit the peninsula.

Parada Ramona y Basilio (El Café, tel. 809/491-0561, US$15, US$20 with lunch). While the trail that this *parada* follows is one of the longer ones, it is a very enjoyable and scenic ride. Ramona and Basilio are the two very hospitable hosts of this well-organized operation, and you'll find them along the road from El Limón to Samaná marked with a big sign in front of the thatch-roofed pink house. While Ramona is the head chef for your meal, Basilio will give you an education on cacao and coffee production. The horse ride portion of your trek takes you

through the small village of El Café, over the Río Limón in two different spots, and up the mountainous passes where you'll see clear over to Cayo Limón on the northern shore of the Bahía de Samaná. You take a break at a small hilltop rest stop. It is a wonderful place to take photos of the waterfall from a distance and you can also purchase refreshments before you continue on to the falls on foot. The hike down can be rather steep in spots (don't forget—you have to climb back up!) and it's not easy after a rain has come through. Your guide will wait at the top of the hill to return you to the *parada* on horseback again. The guides walking your party up and down the mountain depend heavily on your tips.

◖ Whale-Watching

One of the major reasons the town of Samaná is on the tourism map is because it is one of the best places in the world to observe doz-

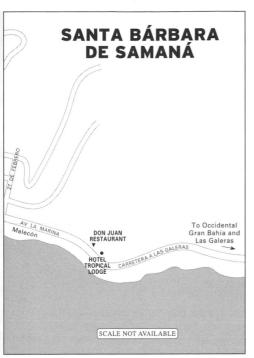

SANTA BÁRBARA DE SAMANÁ

27 DE FEBRERO

AV LA MARINA
Malecón

DON JUAN RESTAURANT

HOTEL TROPICAL LODGE

CARRETERA A LAS GALERAS

To Occidental Gran Bahía and Las Galeras →

SCALE NOT AVAILABLE

lations set in place to minimize the impact on the whales, such as the number of boats observing the whales at one time, distance to the whales, time limits, and speeds in the bay and around the animals. Kim keeps a record of the whales that pass through the bay and asks that anyone who snaps a photo of the tail markings, which are like a whale fingerprint, to email them to her.

Free refreshments are provided on the boat, and information about the whales is given over a speaker. Tours are given in French, English, German, and Spanish. Be sure to ask about the optional stop at Cayo Levantado after observing the whales. This option gives you a couple of hours to swim at the beach and then enjoy a catamaran ride back to Samaná.

Also offering whale-watching excursions is the **Samaná Tourist Service** (Av. La Marina 6, tel. 809/538-2848, samanatour@verizon.net, US$65, tours 8:30 A.M.–12:30 P.M. and 2:30–6:30 P.M. Mon.–Fri., 8:30 A.M. –12:30 P.M. Sat.).

ACCOMMODATIONS

Despite the huge burst of tourism during the whale-watching season, accommodation choices within the town of Samaná remain surprisingly limited, no doubt in part due to the fact that most people visiting the area do so only to take part in a whale-watching cruise for a few hours.

Under US$50

The prices at the simple **Hotel Bahía View** (Francisco de Rosario Sánchez 15, tel. 809/538-2186, US$20 d w/ocean view balcony, US$23 d w/air-conditioning) vary depending on whether you have a balcony and/or air-conditioning or not. However, all nine rooms have ceiling fans and hot water and are kept clean. There's no TV. The rooms with a balcony are more comfortable, if only for that extra little bit of space. The restaurant below is good, but not included in the rate. This hotel is a good value, but keep in mind that the strict checkout time is at 11 A.M. or they charge you for another day.

ens of humpback whales in their natural environment. This awe-inspiring activity will take you near Cayo Levantado amidst turquoise waters of the Bahía de Samaná, where the giant, white-finned humpbacks practice their mating rituals. Every year, thousands of these huge mammals come from the faraway waters of Greenland and Iceland to the Bahía de Samaná.

Victoria Marine (Calle Mella at Av. La Marina, tel. 809/538-2494, www.whalesamana .com, US$45/adult, US$28/ages 5–10, free age 4 and under) tours leave at 9 A.M. and 1:30 P.M. Canadian marine mammal specialist Kim Beddall was the first to offer whale-watching tours in Samaná back in 1985, and through the years she has been sharing her considerable knowledge with a vast majority of the tourists that come to Samaná. Experience and respect for the whales results in a highly recommendable tour group. Victoria Marine adheres strictly to the whale-watching regu-

LA PENÍNSULA DE SAMANÁ

TWO-TON DOMINICAN BABIES

Most humpback whales that live in the northern Atlantic Ocean are Dominicans. It is here that female humpback whales are courted by males, where they mate, and where the babies are born 12 very long months later. The balmy waters of the Bahía de Samaná are the perfect "delivery room" for baby humpback whales. Shallow waters create warmer temperatures and therefore cause less shock to the calf upon delivery.

Each female will have only one baby every 2–3 years, a baby that can measure 3–5 meters in length and weigh up to two metric tons. *"¡Que grande!"*

Within 2–3 months the calves must be ready to accompany their mothers on the long migration back to the northern Atlantic Ocean, where humpbacks feed for the summer before they return to the Caribbean to start the process all over again. For that journey, the baby swims below its mom to suckle her nutrient-rich milk, thereby building up its own blubber. Calves can be dependent on their mothers for food for a whole year, until the next time they return to the Caribbean. In that time, the baby will have doubled in size. But this year is treacherous. If something should happen to the mom, the calf is doomed. No other female whale can nurse it since they only have enough milk for their own calves.

Every year, around December, the humpbacks start coming back, tourists get their cameras out, and the boats circle, hoping to catch a glimpse of mom and baby practicing the acrobatics that humpbacks are famous for. Seeing a 40-ton adult whale leap high into the air and land with a enourmous splash is an amazing display of grace and power. But seeing a baby attempt to mimic what mom has just done is a stunning illustration of nature and the circle of life.

a female humpback whale and her baby

© ANA CHAVIER CAAMAÑO

Just a few blocks from the sea-front, in a quiet part of town, is **Hotel Docia** (Teodoro Chasereaux at Rosa Duarte, tel. 809/538-2041, fax 809/538-2458, US$17 d), perfect for the backpacker who doesn't expect bells and whistles. You do get a very clean room with a private bathroom and free coffee in the morning. With the town center just a short walk away, there are plenty of options for food, but there is a small kitchen in the hotel available for guests to do light cooking.

US$50-100

If you're looking for a place with spectacular views, **Occidental Gran Bahía** (Carretera Samaná, tel. 809/538-3111, fax 809/538-2764, www.occidentalhotels.com, US$100 d) is the hotel for you. This Victorian-style all-inclusive is situated on a point overlooking the Bahía de Samaná and Cayo Levantado. A daily shuttle to the island is built into your rate; just sign up at the front desk. The rooms are colorful, spacious, and clean, but they are a bit dated and in need of some repair. Make sure to request one with an ocean view. Unfortunately, the food is dull. It is not a lively place—no disco or nightly entertainment—but great for a quiet rest. You can take scuba lessons in the pool or walk down the dramatic steps to the beach that is for hotel guests only. All rooms have air-conditioning. Amenities include a beauty parlor, boutique, excursion desk, and tennis.

While not in the thick of the "action" of Samaná, **(Hotel Tropical Lodge** (Av. La Marina, tel. 809/538-2840, fax 809/530-2068, juan.felipe@verizon.net.do, www.samana-hotel.com, US$40 d in low season, US$70 d in high season) is still within reasonable distance of all the amenities of the town. Its quiet garden has a pool and Jacuzzi that face the Malecón and the Bahía de Samaná. The rooms to ask for are the ones that open onto their own balcony. All are nicely appointed and comfortable with private bathrooms. The front desk can help you arrange

excursions throughout the peninsula. In addition to the hotel's restaurant, the on-site **Don Juan Restaurant** serves hand-made pizzas and other fast food.

FOOD

Many of Samaná's restaurants are along the Malecón (Avenida La Marina). Since Samaná has been a favorite expat residential area, there is a good assortment of cuisine including French, American, Italian, Chinese, and of course Dominican. In a region surrounded by the sea and teeming with coconut groves, one must simply try a typical regional dish with any kind of fish in coconut sauce.

(La Hacienda (Av. La Marina, tel. 809/538-2383, 5–11:30 P.M. Thurs.–Tues. for dinner, grill and bar open at noon, US$8–15) has a great reputation and for good reason. The food varies from international choices to specialty French cuisine dishes and is wonderful. The menu is in three languages, making ordering easier. For dinner try the steak in peppercorn sauce, experiment with seafood like octopus, or go for some traditional Dominican chicken.

Restaurant Bambu (Av. La Marina, tel. 809/538-2495, US$3–10) is directly in front of the Victoria Marine excursion office. While it is not a culinary delight like La Hacienda, it is a suitable choice for a quick lunch after your whale-watching excursion. It serves international favorites like sandwiches and pasta.

Le Café de Paris (Av. La Marina, tel. 809/538-2488, 8 A.M.–11 P.M. daily, US$4–12), across from the Port of Samaná, is an open-air restaurant and bar (serving drinks only from 10 P.M. onward). It doesn't have speedy service, but it does have good crepes and breakfast. For lunch and dinner pizzas and salads are good choices.

Restaurant Le France (Av. La Marina, tel. 809/538-2781, 10 A.M.–11 P.M. Tues.–Sun., US$5–15), right next to Le Café de Paris, despite its name offers Dominican fare along with French dishes in a relaxed atmosphere.

Have a meal in the fresh breeze and watch Samaná go by.

Chino's (Calle San Juan 1, tel. 809/538-2215, 11 A.M.–11 P.M. daily, US$5–15) is on the top of a hill (just behind the Hotel Docia) with a fantastic view. The thing about the food in Samaná is that it reflects the number of expats that live there. Here you can get everything from French crepes to Italian pizzas to American burgers and now Chinese food. Stir-fry, egg rolls, wonton soup, it's all here. Dominican dishes are served too.

Don Juan Restaurant (Av. La Marina, adjacent to the Hotel Tropical Lodge, tel. 809/538-2480, noon–10 P.M. Wed.–Mon., US$5–20) serves a variety of dishes, but the main focus is pizza cooked in big outdoor ovens.

Supermercado Popular (Calle Santa Bárbara 1, tel. 809/538-3220) is just one block from the main drag, on the western end of Calle Santa Bárbara where it meets with Calle Cristóbal Colón. You'll find locally grown fruits and vegetables, a butcher shop, delicatessen, canned products, and beverages.

Around dinnertime, small food stands along the waterfront serve cheap eats and ice-cold beers. It's a good place to grab a casual meal, watch the boats, and ask the locals where the best place for merengue dancing is, since it seems to change constantly.

ENTERTAINMENT AND EVENTS
Nightlife
Tourists in Samaná tend to make a night of their dining experience and then plant themselves wherever the lively atmosphere is on that particular night. Samaná does not have the same hopping nightlife scene of Las Terrenas, but fun can usually be found at the numerous open-air stalls that are set up at dusk on the weekends along the Malecón.

At night **Le Café de Paris** (Av. La Marina, tel. 809/538-2488, 8 A.M.–11 P.M. daily) transforms into a lively outdoor bar with a great variety of drinks and plenty of pumping music.

Naomi's (Av. La Marina, 9 P.M.–4 A.M. Fri.–Sun., US$2), on the waterfront above the Restaurant Le France, is the local favorite for merengue and *bachata* dancing. As the only disco in town, it can get pretty packed.

Festivals
There are few times that Dominicans stray from their loyalty to dancing the merengue or the *bachata,* but if you're in the area on October 24 for the **Festival of San Rafael** or on December 4 for the **Patron Saint Day,** you'll see the traditional dances *bambulá* and *chivo florete* being performed in the streets. Their roots are from the African slaves and the immigrating American freed slaves who populated the area. Processions, open-air music, dancing in the streets, and stalls selling food, beverages, and local crafts are all part of these festivals.

INFORMATION AND SERVICES
Tourist Information
At the **Oficina de Turismo** (Calle Santa Bárbara, tel. 809/538-2332, 8:30 A.M.–3 P.M. Mon.–Fri.), you can get maps and some information about the peninsula. It's not the most efficient office, but with tourism booming in Samaná, that will hopefully change.

Communications
CompuCenter Samaná (Calle Lavandier, tel. 809/538-3146, 9 A.M.–12:30 P.M. and 3–6 P.M. Mon.–Fri.) offers Internet service for US$2.50 per hour.

Verizon Centro de Comunicaciones (Calle Santa Bárbara, tel. 809/536-2133, 8 A.M.–10 P.M. daily) is sometimes closed 1–2 P.M. for a lunch hour. It is both an Internet and international call center. The Internet connection costs US$1.75, and long-distance calls are US$0.35 per minute to the U.S., US$0.75 per minute to Europe.

The **post office** (Calle Santa Bárbara, 8:30 A.M.–5 P.M. Mon.–Fri.) is not the most reliable way to communicate with the rest of the world.

Health and Emergencies

Centro Médico San Vicente (Av. María Trinidad Sánchez 1, tel. 809/538-2535) offers emergency medical care 24 hours a day.

Farmacia Giselle (Calle Santa Bárbara 2, tel. 809/538-2303, 8 A.M.–10 P.M. Mon.–Sat., 8 A.M.–noon Sun.) is the most reliable pharmacy in town, with a bigger selection of meds and other potential needs. It's one block past Duarte at Calle Julio Labandier.

Most **Politur** (Francisco de Rosario Sánchez, tel. 809/754-3066, 24 hours) employees speak another language, but it is best to go there with a Spanish dictionary just in case.

Money

Banco Popular (Av. La Marina, tel. 809/538-3666, 8 A.M.–4 P.M. Mon.–Fri., 9 A.M.–1 P.M. Sat.) is the bank with the best location, right in the thick of it all, across from the Port of Samaná. It has an ATM.

One block off the Malecón is **BanReservas** (Calle Santa Bárbara, 8 A.M.–5 P.M. Mon.–Fri., 9 A.M.–1 P.M. Sat.) and also **ScotiaBank**

(Calle Francisco del Rosario Sánchez 111, tel. 809/538-3151, 8 A.M.–4 P.M. Mon.–Fri.).

GETTING THERE

By Car

From Puerto Plata, after the town of Cabarete Highway 5 starts its southward bend toward the town of Sánchez, where it continues along the southern coast of the Samaná Peninsula. This is the best driving route. The terrain throughout the peninsula is lush and the drive is a difficult one due to the steep mountainous passes, breakneck speeds that Dominicans are comfortable driving, and road conditions in general. That said, following Highway 5 is still the best bet, via the southern edge of the peninsula rather than trying the northern route via Las Terrenas. After Highway 5 runs east through the town of Samaná, it curves upward along the eastern coast of the peninsula to end in Las Galeras.

By Air

There are two airports on the peninsula,

© ANA CHAVIER CAAMAÑO

life on La Península de Samaná

LA PENÍNSULA DE SAMANÁ

Aeropuerto Internacional Arroyo Barril on the southern coast and **Aeropuerto Internacional El Portillo** just outside of Las Terrenas on the northern coast. The former airport is more for private charters, while the latter serves the entire peninsula with its one landing strip (planes from Europe and inter-Dominican flights land there). Construction is underway for a bigger one, **Aeropuerto Internacional Samaná,** expected to be finished in 2007. It's near El Catey and will hopefully make travel and tourism blossom to an even greater extent on the peninsula.

For now, the airport at El Portillo has a few companies that have regularly scheduled flights departing and arriving every day. **Takeoff Destination Service S.A.** (Plaza Brisas de Bávaro 8, Bávaro, tel. 809/552-1333, fax 809/552-1113, www.takeoffweb.com), located in the southeast, has a flight between Punta Cana and Samaná for US$99 with regular flights every Tuesday, Thursday, and Saturday. **Aerodomca** (Aeropuerto Internacional de Herrera, Santo Domingo tel. 809/567-1195, Las Terrenas tel. 809/240-6571) offers flights from the airport at El Portillo to Santo Domingo (US$65) and Punta Cana (US$85) as well as other airports in the Dominican Republic and throughout the Caribbean. Reservations are required with a 24-hour advance notice.

Both of these companies also offer taxi services.

By Bus

The station of **Caribe Tours** (Av. La Marina, tel. 809/538-2229) is directly across from the Port of Samaná. Rides (4.5 hours) are offered to and from Santo Domingo at 7 A.M., 8:30 A.M., 10 A.M., 1 P.M., 2:30 P.M., and 4 P.M. (US$7.50).

Another bus company, **Metro** (Av. La Marina, tel. 809/538-2851), just a block away, offers the same ride to Santo Domingo for US$8 but only twice a day (8 A.M. and 3 P.M.). Both of these companies' routes stop in Sánchez, Nagua, and San Pedro de Macorís along the way.

If you're coming from Santiago, **Transporte Pepe** (Santiago, Calle Pedro Francisco Bono at Lili, tel. 809/582-2134) offers a direct bus once a day (1:15 P.M.) to Samaná.

The Samaná *guagua* terminal (Av. La Marina near Ángel Mesina, no phone) has rides to Las Galeras (US$2), El Limón (US$2), and Sánchez (US$2) nearly every 15 minutes 6 A.M.–6 P.M. *Guaguas* to Sánchez stop at 4:30 P.M.

By Ferry

Traveling from Samaná to Sabana de la Mar is possible via the Bahía de Samaná. At the **Transporte Maritimo** (Av. La Marina, tel. 809/538-2556, US$3.50), you can catch a ferry for a one-hour ride across the water. They leave at 7 A.M., 9 A.M., 11 A.M., and 3 P.M.

GETTING AROUND

Samaná is easiest on foot. It is small and most of the restaurants and other locations are just a stroll away. Like in other towns in the Dominican Republic, though, *motoconchos* are everywhere. Many of the *motoconchos* of Samaná are special in that they can accommodate more than just one passenger and are perfect for when you've got armloads of souvenirs to haul back to your hotel room. They hang out around the entrance to the Port of Samaná and can be hired for US$1–3 depending on distance to be traveled.

If you plan on doing any driving throughout the rest of the peninsula and want to rent a car, there are rental places in town. Consider spending the extra money for a four-wheel-drive as many of the roads can be rough and uneven.

It is only a matter of time before the international car rental companies come to set up shop in Samaná, but for now, these are some local companies that offer pricing similar to one another (starting at US$50 a day): **Sama Rental Moto** (Av. La Marina, tel. 809/538-

© ANA CHAVIER CAAMAÑO

motoconchos in Samaná

2380, 8 A.M.–noon and 2–6 P.M.), **Agencia de Vehiculos Hermanos Cruz** (Calle Santa Bárbara, tel. 809/751-5687, 8 A.M.–noon and 2–6 P.M. Mon.–Sat.), and **Xamaná Rent Motors** (Av. La Marina, tel. 809/538-2380, 8 A.M.–noon and 2–6 P.M. daily).

Las Galeras

While La Península de Samaná is a magnet for independent travelers seeking the uncommon track in the Dominican Republic, Las Galeras is for those who seek an even more potent version of that. Those who like small village life as an alternative to their regular hectic lives at home will fall in love with the coconut plantations, numerous secluded and private beaches, and the tropical lushness of the undulating hills throughout this region. Las Galeras went virtually unnoticed until the early 1990s. Its remarkable beaches (some that you'll have to reach by boat or hike to in order to enjoy), remote location on the Samaná Peninsula, and the slow-paced tranquility of the village have created a following among independent travelers from Europe and Canada over the past two decades.

BEACHES

Las Galeras is known for its untouched beaches. Walking the white sands, you might find yourself on a secluded beach, surrounded by tall palms. These beaches have been hailed by many Dominicans as the most gorgeous in all of the Dominican Republic. Certainly, if you are not staying overnight in Las Galeras, their splendor alone is reason for a day trip.

(Playa Rincón

If the beaches of Las Galeras are the jewels of the beaches in the Dominican Republic, then Playa Rincón goes even beyond that. *Condé Nast Traveler* voted Playa Rincón one of the top 10 beaches in the world—you will surely see why. As if on a stage, it is surrounded by

LA PENÍNSULA DE SAMANÁ

the 600-meter cliffs of Cape Cabrón and a thick curtain of palm trees that run into the plush white sand and clear sapphire water. Sound too perfect for reality? It is not: Playa Rincón is one of those beaches that you thought you'd never find. It is not perfect in the manicured, raked-sand way, but in the wild and deserted-in-paradise way with fallen coconuts and twigs from trees scattering the ground. And, there is plenty of sand space for all who go there. There are even several spots to buy freshly caught seafood and rent beach chairs.

Playa Rincón's remoteness and terrible roads are probably keeping it from being overcrowded. To reach Playa Rincón by car, a four-wheel-drive (like a jeep) is strongly recommended. The eight-kilometer trip from Las Galeras to the town of Rincón takes 40 minutes, and then you turn off for a two-kilometer, very rough ride to the beach. But the best way to reach Playa Rincón is by boat. At the main beach in Las Galeras you can find local boat captains with whom you can make arrangements for a departure and pick-up time to Playa Rincón or any of the other beaches in the area (US$12–15 per person).

Playa Las Galeras, Playa Cala Blanca, and Playita

At the north end of Highway 5 is Playa Las Galeras, a perfectly good beach where you can catch boats to other beaches or simply while away the afternoon enjoying the white sands and calm waters, with lunch from a small fish stand.

Adjacent Playa Cala Blanca, a short walking distance away, is a tranquil beach perfect for families with small children. The coral reef offshore prevents big waves from making it to the beach, creating a shallow, warm, and tranquil pool.

Playita can be reached by foot or from the main road just south of Las Galeras; turn west onto a dirt road that is marked for the beach and the Hotel La Playita. The beach itself has tranquil surf, a wide sandy area, and a coconut grove. You can get some fresh fish and a cool drink from the stands here.

Playas Madama and Frontón

These adjoining beaches are a bit harder to get to, but their beauty will give a huge payoff to those who make the effort. East of Las Galeras are the rocky shores and high bluffs surrounding Playas Madama and Frontón. Playa Madama is wonderful for snorkeling, and it is not unheard of to find these beaches with few to no other people on them. These beaches are best reached by boat. Negotiate a price with the Playa Las Galeras local boat captains.

◖ CABO CABRÓN

Experienced divers will enjoy the sites at Cabo Cabrón, one of the best dive sites on the northern coast; it's known for its walls. In the reefs, you'll see many creatures including turtles, barracudas, tuna, and dolphins. Special highlights are **The Cathedral,** a colossal underwater cave, and **The Tower,** which is a deep 24-meter diameter underwater summit rising from 50 meters to within 5 meters of the water's surface. This pinnacle is covered in gorgonian fans, sponges, and corals and is home to a wonderful array of marine life. In the fissures of the wall you'll encounter spider crabs and lobster, while swarms of colorful tropical fish swirl around you in search of food.

SPORTS AND RECREATION
Diving

The diving along the eastern coast of La Península de Samaná is an exciting adventure, especially at Cabo Cabrón. Water visibility ranges 30–45 meters, and January–March whales migrate to the Bahía de Samaná for the yearly mating season.

Dive Samaná (Playa Las Galeras, tel. 809/538-2000, 7 A.M.–6 P.M.) offers dive excursions to some remarkable drop-offs where you'll see eels, rays, barracudas, and sea turtles. Dive Samaná is at the end of Casa Marina Bay's stretch of beach. Dives run US$60 for a one-tank dive (includes all equipment) and other packages are also available for up to four tanks. PADI certifications are available. Reservations are recommended.

Horseback Riding

A great way to experience the countryside and get to the secluded beaches of the area is to go on horseback. Discover beautiful vistas looking down to the country's most beautiful beaches or wind you way through coconut groves and the Dominican countryside.

Enzo's Rancho (Las Galeras, tel. 809/427-3468, fax 809/538-0066, www.enzos-rancho.com, US$12/hour or US$36–55 for excursions) offers half- and full-day packages to the area's beaches and lakes. Definitely don't forget your bathing suit on this ride; the water will be a wonderful cool-down after a sunny ride on the back of a horse in this region. The owners of this rancho, Enzo and Petra, also offer diving, snorkeling, and boat trips. You'll find Enzo's Rancho on the main road in Las Galeras at the Casa Marina Bay Resort.

Tours and Excursions

Aventura Tropical (Calle Principal, tel. 809/538-0249, 8 A.M.–7 P.M. Mon.–Sat., 8 A.M.–1 P.M. Sun.) has excursions including hikes to secluded beaches, whale-watching, boat trips through Los Haitises, and even a tour that will take you through a village where you'll get an in-depth glimpse at rural Dominican life.

Nightlife

Las Galeras is not known for its nightlife. If you're looking for wild nights of spirited dancing and mingling, head to Las Terrenas. There are, however, two places to get in a little *bachata* or merengue dancing in Las Galeras. **V.I.P.** (Calle Principal, 9 P.M.–late, free) and **Chez Manuel** (Calle Principal, 9 P.M–late, free) are both popular clubs that draw locals from all over the surrounding area to dance on the weekends.

ACCOMMODATIONS
Under US$50

Casa ¿Por Qué No? (just north of the main intersection in town, tel. 809/538-0066, US$35 d) is a small bed-and-breakfast with only two rooms; it is only open November–April but is a lovely and economical choice. Each room is clean and nicely appointed, has a private bathroom, and includes a patio overlooking the flourishing garden. Rates include breakfast.

Villa Casa Lotus (Playa Las Galeras, tel. 809/538-0119, www.casalotus.ch.vu/, US$40 per person and up) is a quaint guesthouse next to the sea, moments from the center of Las Galeras. It sits under a canopy of palm trees and has three double bedrooms and one single-bedroom apartment. All of the rooms have a private hot-water bathroom, and the apartment has a kitchen and can accommodate up to four people. Decor includes with wood furnishings, mosquito-net canopies over the beds, exposed beam ceilings, and French doors to the lush tropical garden. The owner will prepare vegetarian meals for those who request them.

The seven clean and simple cabins of **Paradiso Bungalow** (Calle Principal, tel. 809/967-7295, US$25 d) each have their own cold-water bathroom, small porch with patio furniture, double bed, and ceiling fans. The bungalows are all in a plush garden 60 meters from the beach.

Hotel Moorea Beach (Playa Las Galeras, tel. 809/538-0007, www.hotelmooreabeach.com, US$45 d) has eight hotel rooms and one apartment that all have fantastic sea views. The three-story, colonial-inspired white building is 150 meters from Playa Las Galeras, where you can catch boat rides to the many beaches of the area. The rooms are simple but very comfortable and tastefully decorated, each with a bathroom with hot water. The apartment has a sofa bed and direct access to the pool on-site. A restaurant is on-site, open during peak season only, and wireless Internet is available. When you reach the main intersection in town, take a left; after 100 meters, you'll see the Hotel Moorea Beach on your right-hand side. Rates decrease during low season.

US$50-100

Apart Hotel La Isleta (tel. 809/538-0016, www.la-isleta.com, US$65), 100 meters from the center of Las Galeras, has six very captivating apartments, each with its own complete kitchen, private hot-water bathroom, and porch with a magnificent ocean view. Tastefully decorated with tropical colors, these cabin-like apartments with loft bedrooms offer a spaciousness that you just can't get in a standard hotel room, making it particularly well suited to families. Each unit has a water cooler and TV. Weekly and monthly rates are available. Amenities include a barbecue, Jacuzzi, and bar.

There are 10 apartments of varying size in **Apart-Hotel Plaza Lusitania** (Calle Principal, tel. 809/538-0093, fax 809/538-0066, www .plazalusitania.com, US$40–100 per apartment). The smallest is a one-room flat with two beds, and the largest is a two-room flat with six beds. All apartments have small kitchenettes, private baths, and tile floors throughout, and are decorated with island furniture and art. All have balconies and are kept very clean. This hotel is on the second level of a shopping area that includes a grocery store and a restaurant that serves Dominican and Italian. Rates include breakfast. Parking is free.

Juan y Lolo Bungalows (Calle A 313, tel. 809/538-0208, www.juanylolo.com, US$35–120) is one of the best bungalow rental companies in Las Galeras. All bungalows are tastefully decorated and have kitchens, bathrooms, and patios. The style of the bungalows varies considerably, from Caribbean thatch-roofed simplicity to a Columbus-era bungalow complete with Queen Isabella–inspired furniture. All have incredible rates for what you get.

US$100 and Up

Club Bonito (Playa Las Galeras, tel. 809/538-0203, fax 809/538-0061, www .club-bonito.com, US$80–140 d) is a chic beauty right on the beach. The building is made of stone, palm thatch, and other local natural materials, with many ramps built into the design to aid wheelchair accessibility. The rooms are decorated with stylish simplicity and are very comfortable. All 21 rooms are spacious, and 15 have terraces with ocean views (priced accordingly); six overlook the gardens where bougainvillea blooms amid coral-rock formations and palm trees. Three luxury rooms offer extra comfort with a king-size bed, Jacuzzi, fridge, and minibar. Not all the rooms have air-conditioning, so be sure to request this if you want it. For a low-key and relaxing vacation, this is a perfect spot, whether taking a swim at the gorgeous Playa Las Galeras or strolling to the other pristine beaches within walking distance, or lazing by the pool in the garden, or making use of the hotel's massage service. Visitors looking for activity won't be disappointed as excursions can be arranged at the front desk, and guests can borrow snorkeling gear free of charge.

On the curved bay of Playa Las Galeras is the plush oasis at **Villa Serena** (tel. 809/538-0000, fax 809/538-0009, www .villaserena.com, US$160 d w/air-conditioning in peak season), a white, two-story, Victorian-inspired hotel. One of the most charming things about the hotel is that all 21 rooms are decorated differently, adding to the unique experience. All rooms have private balconies and face the ocean. Not all the rooms have air-conditioning, but those on the second floor receive a very refreshing sea breeze. This hotel is a very romantic honeymoon spot (ask about the free honeymoon package when staying a minimum of five nights) and is great for those wishing for tranquility. A small pool surrounded by natural stones sits between the hotel and the sea among the garden's color-bursting tropical plants and palm trees. The other fantastic reason to spend the rather hefty rate on this hotel is the restaurant. Guests can enjoy Dominican and French cuisine at one of the best restaurants in the town of Las Galeras. Rates include breakfast. Tours can be organized, and free bicycles and snorkel gear are available for guests.

FOOD

Many great meals can be had at the shacks found at the entrance to Playa Las Galeras. Fish and shellfish are caught daily and cooked right on the beach. It is a great, low cost way to go.

Expats who've settled here have turned Las Galeras (much like the rest of the Samaná peninsula) into a culinary pleasure. And although many hotels have their own restaurants, there are good choices in town as well. Just a stroll down the main drag will reveal many options.

For nearly two decades now, **◖ Chez Denise** (Calle Principal near the main intersection, tel. 809/538-0219, 9 A.M.–11 P.M. Mon.–Sat., US$5–15) has been a darling of the expats and tourists. In this casual and open-air restaurant, both French and Dominican dishes are served. Crepes are a delectable specialty, as is the fresh fish in coconut sauce. No credit cards are accepted.

El Pescador (Calle Principal, tel. 809/538-0052, 4 P.M.–midnight Tues.–Sun., US$7–17) is often called the best seafood in town by locals. When in the Caribbean on vacation, seeking the freshest seafood can become an obsession. Just as the name would suggest, "The Fisherman" specializes in the freshest catches of the day. The grilled fish is always a good bet, but more experimental dishes like stewed crab, paella, and lobster beg to be tried. No credit cards are accepted.

◖ Patisserie Boulangerie Français (Calle Principal, 7 A.M.–7 P.M. Tues.–Sun., US$2–5) is the place to come for a perfect espresso drink, French pastry, or loaf of bread made from scratch. This is a sweet-tooth's dream. Breakfast options are available.

I'm not sure if it's the sauce, the cheese, the many ingredients, or the fact that vacations bring taste buds alive, but the pizza is fabulous at **Pizzeria** (Calle Principal, 11 A.M.–3 P.M. and 6 P.M.–midnight Wed.–Sun., US$6.50–9)—crispy-crusted slices of paradise.

There are two supermarkets in town.

Supermercado 1 (Calle Principal, 7:30 A.M.–9:30 P.M.) has the best selection of fresh and canned foods.

INFORMATION AND SERVICES

The services are offered in Las Galeras are mostly near the main intersection in town. While there is no tourism office in Las Galeras, there are many expat business owners and English-speaking visitors who can direct you if you need help.

Las Galeras Tourist Service (Calle Principal, tel. 809/538-0232, fax 809/538-0066, lgts@katamail.com or sdol@dr.com) in the center of Las Galeras is a one-stop service center offering money exchange, safety deposit box rental, a gift shop (with cigars, souvenirs and art), Internet access, and motorbike and car rental. The **Farmacia Joven** (Calle Principal, tel. 809/538-0103, Mon.–Sat. 8 A.M.–9:30 P.M.) is centrally located and has a good variety of general medications.

Communications

Internet Las Galeras (Calle Principal, 8:30 A.M.–8 P.M. Mon.–Sat., 9 A.M.–12:30 P.M. and 2:30–8 P.M. Sun., US$6.25/hour) offers Internet connection, although it's expensive. They also sell stamps and will mail letters for you.

Located on the first level of the **Plaza Lusitania** is **Verizon Centro de Comunicaciones** (Calle Principal, 9 A.M.–noon and 1–6 P.M. daily, US$0.40 per minute to the U.S., US$0.80 per minute to Europe) is the best bet in town for long-distance calls.

GETTING THERE

Las Galeras enjoys its remote location on the peninsula, and therefore transportation options are limited. *Guaguas* are the only public transportation that will get you here and take you away. Where Highway 5 intersects with Calle Principal, right at the entrance to the beach, is where all *guaguas* stop to pick up passengers

LA PENÍNSULA DE SAMANÁ

traveling to and from Samaná. A one-way trip between Las Galeras and Samaná costs US$2 for the 45-minute ride. You can expect to find one leaving every 15 minutes 7 A.M.–5 P.M.

GETTING AROUND

Las Galeras is very walkable, with all services near or around the main Calle Principal and where that intersects with Highway 5 coming from Samaná. But with so many beaches in the area, renting a car is an option worth considering. The roads can be pothole-ridden messes, so a four-wheel-drive is optimal. Make sure to ask for a map. Most rental places have staff that speak English.

Hermanos Cruz Agente de Cambio and

Rent-a-Car (Calle Principal, tel. 809/341-4574, 8 A.M.–6 P.M. Mon.–Sat., 8 A.M.–noon Sun.) rents four-wheel-drives for US$70–100 a day. Incidentally, as the name suggests, they also exchange money.

Xamaná Rent Moto (Calle Principal, tel. 809/538-0208, 9 A.M.–noon and 3–6 P.M. Mon.–Fri., 9 A.M.–noon Sat. and Sun., starting at US$25/day) has cars and also rents motorcycles for a more adventurous way to traverse the countryside.

Caribe Fun Rentals (Calle Principal, tel. 809/538-0109, 9 A.M.–6 P.M. Mon.–Sat., 9 A.M.–noon Sun.), across the street from Xamaná, rents motorcycles (US$25) and vehicles (US$50–70) by the day.

Las Terrenas

Las Terrenas is a humming hive of activity. Slow-strolling tourists and speeding *motoconchos* coexist somehow. The flaxen-colored sand and indigo waters of the beach, fringed by palm trees, stretch for kilometers and remind us that Las Terrenas is still a place to relax and enjoy paradise despite the frenzy that swirls around, even into the early morning hours. This is the best place to come on the peninsula if you're wanting a vacation of both slow days in the sun and a fun-filled nightlife. The other towns on the peninsula just don't have the same vibe.

In the late 1970s, tourists traveling to the small town began falling in love with it and started staying for good. These expats, mostly from European countries like France, Italy, and Switzerland, have opened many hotels, restaurants, and other businesses that continue to thrive and give new tourists plenty of appealing options.

BEACHES

Las Terrenas is known for its beaches. The road from Samaná to Las Terrenas turns into the main drag, Avenida Duarte, in town. Once it runs into the town's cemetery, a sharp

left turn will take you to Avenida Francisco Alberto Caamaño, which leads you to **Playa Las Terrenas,** where you'll find many restaurants and bars in the **Pueblo de Los Pescadores.**

Continuing west, some of the area's best beaches can be reached either by *motoconcho* (about a 10-minute ride) or by foot along the coastal road or on the shore itself. If you decide to walk along the shore, a pair of water shoes is a good idea, since you have to cross a rather marshy area.

Playa Las Ballenas and **Isla Las Ballenas** offer good snorkeling and diving opportunities. Advanced divers head to the offshore shipwreck and the underwater cave of Isla Las Ballenas, as do snorkelers for the tiny island's coral reefs.

Playa Bonita, or Pretty Beach, is a nice alternative to Playa Las Terrenas, not because it is more beautiful but because this stretch of golden sand is consistently less crowded. Some of the hotels that reside along the shore of Playa Bonita manicure the strips of beach near them, but the rest of Playa Bonita, although nice, tends to be scattered with natural debris. Farther west along the coast, the delightful and untouched **Playa Cosón** appears thick with vegetation over six kilometers of golden sand.

SHOPPING

Compared to Las Galeras and Samaná, Las Terrenas has more to offer to those who want to spend their money on things to take home. Three shopping plazas all have the same hours of operation (9 A.M.–8 P.M. Mon.–Sat., 9 A.M.–3 P.M. Sun.) and are very close to one another along Avenida Duarte. **Plaza Taína**, across from the cemetery, holds a *cambio*, **Mini-Market Ray**, a newsstand, and clothing and other stores. The shops of **El Paseo** include a film store, **Farmacia Hemaopatia** (for sunscreen and medications), **Deci's** (shoes and clothing), an ATM, **La Cave á Vin** (wine shop), and an Internet access center. **Casa Linda** has yet more souvenir and clothing shops.

Haitian Caraibes Art Gallery (Av. Duarte 159, tel. 809/240-6250, 9 A.M.–1 P.M. and 4–8 P.M. Mon.–Sat.) offers a fantastic selection of good quality Haitian paintings, cigars, art, clothing, and jewelry.

La Cueva de Los Indios (Plaza Taína, tel. 809/240-5168) has typical artwork from the island as well as a nice array of amber, larimar, and black coral jewelry. Visa and Mastercard are accepted. English, French, German, and Italian are spoken.

SPORTS AND RECREATION
Diving and Snorkeling

A number of diving centers are located in Las Terrenas, and two of the best are **Stellina Dive Center** (Kari Beach Hotel, tel. 809/868-4415, 9 A.M.–1 P.M. and 3–5 P.M. daily), which offers dive packages starting at a one-tank dive for US$46 (with equipment), and **Tropical Diving Center** (Av. Italia, tel. 809/240-9619, www.tropicaldivingcenter.com, 8:30 A.M.–6 P.M.), which has a variety of courses for beginner and advanced divers and even specialist training.

Water Sport Rentals

Pura Vida (Calle Libertad 2, tel. 809/862-

0485, www.puravidacaraibes.com, 10 A.M.–5:30 P.M. daily) is right near the beach. It is a wonderful location for renting kitesurfing and windsurfing gear. Also available are mountain bikes, bodyboards, and surfboards. Kitesurfing lessons go for US$80 for two hours. Mountain biking, kitesurfing, and windsurfing expeditions can be arranged.

Tours and Excursions

Although there are many water sports and things to do in Las Terrenas, you have even more exciting options. Las Terrenas excursion operators offer a good variety of activities from which to choose.

Bahia Tours (Av. Duarte 237, tel. 809/240-6088, www.bahia-tours.com, 9 A.M.–1 P.M. and 3:30–7 P.M.) offers day trips and local excursions throughout the peninsula as well as overnight excursions to other locales in the Dominican Republic. Local excursion prices are per person and include transportation, like whale-watching in the Bahía de Samaná (US$66), a horseback ride to the waterfall of El Limón (US$25), lunch and a catamaran ride to Cayo Levantado (US$78 per adult, US$38 per child), an excursion to Los Haitises National Park (US$60), or a jeep ride to beautiful Playa Rincón (US$70).

Safari Quad Excursions (Av. Duarte, tel. 809/240-6056, cell 809/869-8031, safariquad@verizon.net.do), across from Plaza Taína, rents quads for exploring the region's countryside and beaches. They'll lead you on an all-day expedition, leaving at 9 A.M. and returning at 4:30 P.M., through enchanted hills and landscapes, along deserted beaches, and to a typical Dominican household of El Limón.

ACCOMMODATIONS

Las Terrenas has a wider assortment of hotel options than Samaná but is not nearly as inundated with the big company all-inclusives like on the southeast or northern coasts.

Under US$50

The 16-room **Hotel Papagayo** (Carretera

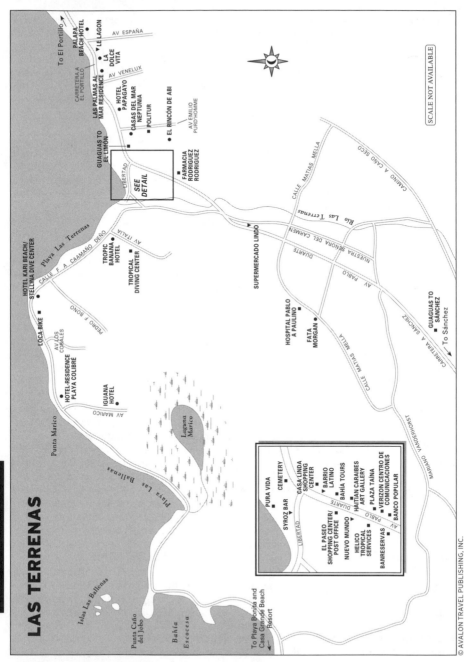

LAS TERRENAS

SCALE NOT AVAILABLE

© AVALON TRAVEL PUBLISHING, INC.

El Portillo, tel. 809/240-6131, fax 809/240-6070, US$28), right on the beach, has nicely furnished and clean rooms. Ask for one of the four rooms that have a terrace with an ocean view. Rooms have fans and private hot-water bathrooms. Breakfast is included. **Casas del Mar Neptunia** (Av. Emilio Prud'Homme, tel. 809/240-6617, fax 809/240-6070, www.casas-del-mar-neptunia.com, US$40 d) is half a block from the ocean, on a street perpendicular to the highway leading to El Portillo. It offers a serene atmosphere even though it is close to the center of town. The spacious and charming bungalows are set in a garden around a thatched-roof cabana where breakfast is served every day. Since all bungalows have large doors that swing open onto their own private terrace, you have the option of enjoying your breakfast there as well. All units have a fan, private bathrooms, daily maid service, and a refrigerator. Cabanas sleep up to four people. Two apartments can sleep up to six people and offer air-conditioning-optional bedrooms (starting at US$55/night). English, French, and Spanish are spoken.

The bungalows at **Fata Morgana** (La Ceiba, tel. 809/836-5541, www.samana.net/fatamorgana, US$15) may be just the budget accommodation for those travelers who enjoy sinking into the rural culture of their surroundings. Fata Morgana is about five minutes from the town center and beach. With the distance comes peacefulness. Enjoy a quiet read in the rocking chair of your own bungalow. You can even borrow a book from the library. The cheerfully decorated bungalows are clean and have fans and private bathrooms. The owner, Edit Dejong, can give you tours of the area, and you can even borrow a bicycle if you need transportation, although *motoconchos* are easy to find.

El Rincón de Abi (Av. Emilio Prud'Homme, tel. 809/240-6639, US$28 d) has six rooms and one two-bedroom apartment (US$45) in a quiet neighborhood. Rooms are clean and a good value. Guests are welcome to use the out-door kitchen, but breakfast is already included in the rate and other meals are US$6–10.

US$50-100
Palapa Beach Hotel (Carretera a El Portillo, tel. 809/240-6797, www.palapabeach.com, US$70 without air-conditioning in high season) is a stylishly designed small hotel with 16 bungalows, all of which are uniquely and tastefully decorated with natural appointments. The multilingual staff is very accommodating and willing to work with many special requests. The bungalows are two levels with a loft bedroom, and more beds are available. Below the bedroom is a seating area, which is also kitchenette-capable upon request. The Palapa's excursion office offers exciting packages like fishing cruises, sunset drink cruises, catamaran rides, diving, wind- and kitesurfing, and Jet Ski rental. While the hotel itself is across the highway from the beach, the Palapa has an area of the beach quartered off where they serve breakfast, lunch, and drinks on the sand. On the second level of the hotel is a new trendy lounge with an amazing view of the ocean; Japanese delights like sushi and other international favorites are served. The hotel's Internet office is open 7 A.M.–7 P.M. Arrangements can even be made for you and your friends to have a private party by the pool—think fresh lobster grill—with a one-day advance notice. The pool is small but located in a tropical garden brimming with vegetation.

Iguana Hotel (Calle Playa Cacao, tel. 809/240-5525, fax 809/240-6070, www.iguana-hotel.com, US$60–70 d) has eight very small, sparsely but sweetly decorated Caribbean-style bungalows in a serene (and we do mean serene) garden. Think cheerful colors and thatched roofs. Follow the sandy path 150 meters to the beach, where you'll find a coral bed lying just offshore, great for snorkeling. Each bungalow has one or two bedrooms, so this hotel is a good choice for families. Each has its own private bathroom, safe, and fan. A restaurant and bar are on-site, and guests can use the fully equipped kitchen and barbecue. Babysitting and children's beds are available at extra cost. American breakfast is included in price. Excursion arrangement is available, as well as car and bicycle rentals.

The best thing about **El Portillo Beach Resort** (Carretera a El Portillo, tel. 809/240-6100, www.portillo-resort.com, US$80–100) is its surroundings. This all-inclusive is four kilometers away from Las Terrenas, placed on lush grounds on a marvelous beach. As it stands, this resort is not a "throw-down party," despite their efforts with the nightly entertainment. No, instead what you will find is a relaxing environment where on the porch of your room you can hear the busy sounds of the tropical nights. The rooms are spacious enough, and comfortable, but definitely showing their age. The food, mostly geared toward European and Dominican tastes, was only available for three meals a day and one snack. A Spanish company bought the resort and closed its doors in January 2006, with promises to reopen by November 2006 for the winter season. If this is achieved and El Portillo is restored to its former glory, this will be a top contender for accommodations in the area.

La Dolce Vita (Carretera a El Portillo, tel. 809/240-5069, fax 809/240-5072, www.ladolcevitaresidence.com, US$78 per night per one-bedroom apartment) has apartments with ocean views, and all come with a fully equipped kitchen, TV, DSL Internet connection, and safe. This is a good residence for many travelers staying together or for families. One-, two-, and three-bedroom apartments are available, all very nicely appointed, clean and comfortably sized, with their own porch. The three-bedroom apartments have three bathrooms, one of which has a Jacuzzi in it! Air-conditioning is extra. There is a restaurant next to the medium-sized pool. The beach is just across the highway to El Portillo.

Hotel-Residence Playa Colibrí (Calle Francisco Alberto Caamaño Deño, tel. 809/240-6434, www.playacolibri.com, US$75–130) has 45 apartments in four different layouts (priced accordingly), all offering fully equipped kitchenettes, TV, ceiling fans, terraces, in-room safe boxes, and daily cleaning service. Layouts go from a two-person studio to a very spacious split-level apartment with two bedrooms and two baths. Colibí is less than two kilometers from the center of Las Terrenas and right on the beach with countless palm trees on white sand and a coral reef offshore. The pool has a Jacuzzi, and there is a restaurant/bar. This is a great find for families and traveling groups looking to settle into a comfortable place.

To a great amount of public scorn, **Cayo Limón Hotel Beach Resort** (Carretera de la Playa, tel. 809/374-3111, from US$125 d per night in high season) braved to open its doors as the first exclusively gay all-inclusive resort in the entire Dominican Republic. Even though not all the details have been worked out, the doors are still open. The grounds and accommodations are beautiful. Rooms are nicely appointed, have a minibar and private bathroom, and open onto a terrace with a view of the pool. A restaurant and bar are also on the premises. Bottom line: If you're looking for an all-gay resort in the Dominican Republic where you can freely express yourself, this is it. It's not always full, so it is best for couples, and it's good to rent car since it is not located in Las Terrenas. The approach road from the main highway to the resort is a jostling, pothole-ridden hazard, but it's clearly marked with a sign. It is not the best hotel in the area of Las Terrenas, but its existence is worth mentioning for the LGBT community looking for exclusively LGBT accommodations.

The rooms in the **Hotel Kari Beach** (Calle Francisco Alberto Caamaño Deño, tel. 809/240-6187, www.karibeach.com, US$58 d) are brightly decorated, clean, have vaulted ceilings, and are well ventilated. Only 3 of the 24 rooms have air-conditioning, but all have private bathrooms and TV. Hotel Kari has one of Las Terrenas's dive shops, which makes the hotel a good base for divers. Good Italian and international fare is served in the restaurant. Rates include breakfast.

© ANA CHAVIER CAAMAÑO

The El Portillo Beach Resort is on Playa El Portillo.

Casa Grande Beach Resort (Playa Bonita, Calle F Peña Gomez, tel. 809/240-6349, www.casagrandebeachresort.com, US$70 d in high season) is a charmer. Located directly on Playa Bonita, this small 13-room hotel has gone to great lengths to make your vacation memorable. Each room is decorated uniquely with brightly painted accents, throw pillows, gauze curtains, and other touches to remind you that you're not vacationing inside of a machine-made hotel. The restaurant appeals to the same idea that ambience is half the fun. Presentation is superb, as is the taste of their unique mixture of Mediterranean, Asian, and Creole cooking.

US$100 and Up

Las Palmas al Mar Residence (Carretera a El Portillo, tel. 809/240-6292, fax 809/240-6089, www.laspalmasalmar.com, US$120 per cottage/night in high season.) has a collection of 12 two-level cottages placed in a neatly manicured setting. The pool is small, but the beach is located just across the street.

The cottages have a kitchenette, seating area with a fold out couch, one bedroom with a double bed, one with two single beds, two bathrooms, and lovely wrap-around porches with a BBQ. This is a wonderful place to stay if you want comfortable and clean accommodations, but are willing to stock up the refrigerator and dine out because Las Palmas doesn't have a restaurant. No matter though, it is within walking distance to a great many choices. Other amenities include: purified water, cable TV with DVD player, safe, and DSL Internet hookup. Price doesn't include air-conditioning and discounts given depending on length of stay.

Tropic Banana Hotel (Calle Francisco Alberto Caamaño Deño, tel. 809/240-6110, www.tropicbanana.com, US$100 d). Situated on three hectares of tropical landscape abutting the golden sands of Playa Las Terrenas. Even though the hotel was opened in the 1970s, it has been well maintained. Rooms are small and medium sized and all are pleasingly adorned and comfortable, each with their own

LA PENÍNSULA DE SAMANÁ

bathroom. Upper level rooms have private terraces. Suites are even more comfortable with roomier bathrooms (US$140). The restaurant serves French and international fare (see *Food*). Other features include a moon-shaped pool, billiards tables, tennis, ping-pong, and Internet. Rates include breakfast and overall rates dramatically decrease in the low season. Tropic Banana is popular at night with live merengue music.

FOOD

Where the Río Las Terrenas meets the Atlantic Ocean is a cluster of fishing shacks known as **El Pueblo de Los Pescadores** that have become the most popular dining spot in town. Most open to the road and have waterfront seating.

At 🌀 **Wasabi** (Pueblo de Los Pescadores, tel. 809/977-4936, open nightly except Mon. at 7 P.M., US$8–25), that hankering for some Zen will get satisfied. This small and chic seaside Japanese cuisine restaurant serves fresh sushi, sashimi, noodles, and soups, prepared and served with care.

The young and hip enjoy traditional Mediterranean grilled fish and meat, fresh gnocchi, and pasta to the soundtrack of international tunes at seaside **Etnie Restaurant and Music Café** (Pueblo de Los Pescadores, tel. 809/849-7733, www.etniecaraibi.com, open for dinner only, US$9–20). But just as the name suggests, the music is on the menu too, and on Saturday nights it is a lively place to be with a DJ spinning funk, house, hip-hop, and world beats.

Basque-owned 🌀 **Casa Boga** (Pueblo de Los Pescadores, tel. 809/240-6321, email casaboga@terra.es, 12:30–11 P.M., US$12–25) comes highly recommended as one of the best seafood places in town. Don't blink, though, you might miss it. This very small restaurant is hidden down a small walkway between two other restaurants and in front of Paseo de la Costanera. It serves a great variety of seafood and fish from the Dominican coast, such as fried fish served with a mixed salad and fried *yuca* or *plátano*. The fish soup is a specialty.

El Cayuco (Pueblo de Los Pescadores, noon–11 P.M., US$5–15) is a Spanish restaurant that will serve you an eye-catching paella filled with fresh seafood and tantalizing tapas. It is a casual restaurant and a good value for the prices.

A French restaurant, **La Salsa** (Pueblo de Los Pescadores, tel. 809/240-6805, cell 809/816-2970, 7 P.M.–midnight, US$11–20) transforms local products like lobster and fresh fish into tasty dishes. There is a good selection of red meat dishes as well.

Le Lagon (Av. 27 de Febrero, tel. 809/240-6603, noon–late daily, closed Thurs. in low season, US$7–20) serves appetizers and main dishes right on the sand. Specialties include pizza, meat, fish, and lobster cooked in a wood oven. Look for the plate of the day on Mondays and Fridays.

Barrio Latino (Calle Francisco Alberto Caamaño Deño, tel. 809/240-6367, 7:30 A.M.–midnight daily, US$2–13) is a great place to go if you need to please a lot of different tastes, as it's popular with both Europeans and Americans for breakfast. Other satisfying dishes include burgers, pizzas, salads, and sandwiches. Häagen-Dazs ice cream for dessert or a fresh fruit juice might help cool you down. The restaurant is open-sided and a great place for people-watching.

Cafeteria Comedor Mami (Av. Duarte, 9 A.M.–6 P.M. daily, US$3–18) is a very casual place, a good venue for Dominican and international favorite dishes. This mom-and-pop place offers a nice variety of meat, seafood, sandwiches, and pasta.

If you're looking for a classy dinner at one of the best restaurants in town, go to **Tropic Banana Hotel** (Calle Francisco Alberto Caamaño Deño, tel. 809/240-6110, 8 A.M.–midnight daily, US$15–25). In a white tablecloths and candlelit setting, the menu offers standard favorites and some memorable, unique dishes like fish fillet in cream of sea urchin, or pasta with squid. Good wines from California, Chile, and France adorn the wine list, making a night at the Tropic Banana hard to compete with.

You've had your seafood, your Italian pizzas, your steak and cocktails, now what? Craving something sweet? **Sucré Salé** (Plaza Taína, Av. Duarte, tel. 809/860-0863, 7 A.M.–7 P.M. daily) has beautiful hand-made French bread and pastries that will make your toes curl. Coffee and pastries all can be enjoyed in the streetview terrace. This is a great way to watch the buzz of Las Terrenas as it unfolds.

Super Mercado Rey (Av. Duarte, tel. 809/240-6010, 8 A.M.–10 P.M. Mon.–Sat., 8 A.M.–2 P.M. Sun.) has basic provisions like canned goods, bread, and water. It's a good place to buy long-distance phone cards. There may be a small fresh fruit vendor on the other side of the grocer's parking lot.

Supermercado Lindo (Plaza Rosado, 8 A.M.–9 P.M. Mon.–Sat., 8 A.M.–6 P.M. Sun.) is yet another market with canned goods, produce, and more.

NIGHTLIFE

Roaming from one bar to the next is effortless when sticking to **Pueblo de Los Pescadores.** After the dinner hours, most restaurants turn into bars and lounges, and they're lined up like dominoes. Here are a few outside of that area that are worthy of exploration as well.

Nuevo Mundo (Av. Duarte, 9 P.M.–4 A.M. Wed.–Sun.) is a disco popular with Dominicans because it plays mostly merengue and *bachata*. It has turned into a spot for the tourists wanting to experience more of the culture's music and dance.

Swanky **Syroz Bar** (Calle Francisco Alberto Caamaño Deño, tel. 809/866-5577, 5 P.M.–4 A.M. Mon.–Sat.) sends you into a reality melt-down as you listen to live jazz on the beach. Really, what could be better for jazz lovers outside of a corner booth at the Blue Note in New York? Swaying to the tunes under the stars with a cocktail on the deck facing the ocean or inside in the candlelit ambience doesn't sound too shabby.

El Mosquito Art Bar (Pueblo de Los Pescadores, tel. 809/857-4684, 6 P.M.–midnight), at the entrance of the Pueblo de Los Pescadores, is the perfect place to enjoy a cock-tail from the gigantic drink menu or a plate of tapas. You can sit and listen to the great music on couches on the patio overlooking the ocean.

INFORMATION AND SERVICES
Health and Emergencies

Farmacia Rodriguez Rodriguez (Av. Duarte, tel. 809/240-6084, 8 A.M.–8 P.M. daily) is a good pharmacy on the main drag, right near the Banco Popular. It offers a good selection of meds and other necessities.

Hospital Pablo A. Paulino (Calle Matias Mella, tel. 809/274-6474) has an emergency room open 24 hours.

Politur (Av. Emilio Prud'Homme, tel. 809/754-2973, open 24 hours) officers are there to help you with emergencies. Most tourism police speak another language, but a Spanish dictionary would be helpful just in case.

Communications

For the best long-distance rates and service in Las Terrenas, head to **Verizon Centro de Comunicaciones** (Av. Duarte, 8 A.M.–10 P.M. daily), on the main drag near Plaza Taína. Calls to the U.S. are US$0.32 per minute, to Europe US$0.74 per minute.

Don't need to communicate but just want word that the outside world still exists? Head over to the **Newsstand of Plaza Taína** (Av. Duarte 9 A.M.–8 P.M. daily) and grab a paper. The newsstand has a good (albeit very expensive) selection of newspapers from all over the world.

The **post office** (El Paseo shopping center, Calle Francisco Alberto Caamaño Deño, 9 A.M.–1 P.M. and 3–5 P.M. Mon.–Fri.) is not the best, fastest, or most trusted way to communicate from the DR, but it is acceptable for those postcards to send home.

Internet Access

The nice thing about vacationing in Las Terrenas is that you can escape your daily life without falling off the planet. Many of the hotels are jumping on the cyber bandwagon by offering Internet hookups as an amenity. Additionally, in town there are a number of options.

Conveniently located **Cyber Heladeria** (El Paseo shopping center, Calle Francisco Alberto Caamaño Deño, 8 A.M.–9 P.M. Mon.–Sat., 8 A.M.–3 P.M. Sun.) offers connections and ice cream.

Verizon Centro de Comunicaciones (Av. Duarte, 8 A.M.–10 P.M. daily), in addition to being a telephone call center, offers cheap connection fees—the best rates in town.

L'entract.com (Plaza Taína, Av. Duarte, 9 A.M.–1 P.M. and 3:30–7:30 P.M. Mon.–Sat.) is another well-located cybercafé. Plaza Taína is at the center of activity, and this cybercafe has air-conditioning and fast connections.

Money

Fort Knox Money Exchange (El Paseo shopping center, Calle Francisco Alberto Caamaño Deño, 8 A.M.–1 P.M. and 4–8 P.M. Mon.–Sat., 10 A.M.–1 P.M. Sun.) exchanges euros and American dollars. There are many other *cambios* along Av. Duarte, or you can exchange money in the banks.

Banco Popular (Av. Duarte, 9 A.M.–5 P.M. Mon.–Fri., 9 A.M.–1 P.M. Sat.), just next to the Farmacia Rodriguez Rodriguez, has a 24-hour ATM.

BanReservas (Av. Duarte, 9 A.M.–6 P.M. Mon.–Fri., 9 A.M.–1 P.M. Sat.), right across the street from the Banco Popular, also has a 24-hour ATM.

Banco del Progreso (Av. Duarte, tel. 809/240-6409, 9 A.M.–3:30 P.M. Mon.–Fri., 9 A.M.–1 P.M. Sat.) is in the El Paseo shopping center.

GETTING THERE
By Air

Las Terrenas is only a few kilometers from **Aeropuerto Internacional El Portillo,** which receives flights mainly from Europe and some inter-Dominican flights. It is a very small operation with no terminal nor phone, just a landing strip. A couple of companies serve the Samaná peninsula: **Takeoff Destination**

© ANA CHAVIER CAAMAÑO

the end of the day for a shrimp fisherman in La Península de Samaná

Service S.A. (Plaza Brisas de Bávaro 8, Bávaro, tel. 809/552-1333, fax 809/552-1113, www.takeoffweb.com), in the southeast, has a flight between Punta Cana and Samaná for US$99 with regular flights every Tuesday, Thursday, and Saturday.

Aerodomca (Aeropuerto Internacional de Herrera, Santo Domingo tel. 809/567-1195, Las Terrenas tel. 809/240-6571) offers flights from the airport at El Portillo to Santo Domingo (US$65) and Punta Cana (US$85) as well as other airports in the Dominican Republic and throughout the Caribbean. Reservations are required with a 24-hour advance notice.

Helico Tropical Services (Av. Duarte, tel. 809/240-6607) offers helicopter trips from the airport at El Portillo to Las Américas in Santo Domingo for US$65 per person or to the Herrera airport in Santo Domingo for US$55 per person. Ask about excursion flights, including romantic sightseeing, golf flights, or even medical assistance flights. For other trips, they charge by the half hour for however long you want to go.

By Bus

Guaguas make stops in Las Terrenas along Avenida Duarte. To catch one going to Sánchez, go to the stop along the highway to Sánchez (US$1.50 leaving every 20–25 minutes 7 A.M.–6 P.M.). The stop for a *guagua* going toward El Limón (US$1.75 leaving every 15 minutes 7 A.M.–5 P.M.) is more centrally located near the intersection of Avenida Duarte and the highway to El Portillo.

By Car

If arriving from the west, make a left turn out-side the town of Sánchez for a beautiful drive up over the **Cordillera Samaná.** It is a curvy, steep road that gives spectacular views of the Bahía de Samaná and the Parque Nacional Los Haitises. Las Terrenas is 17 kilometers northeast of Sánchez.

If you are coming from the east, perhaps from Las Galeras, you must first go through Samaná, then turn right on the road toward El Limón and El Portillo. It is another 30–45 minutes to reach Las Terrenas.

GETTING AROUND

You will never come up empty trying to flag down a *motoconcho* in Las Terrenas. There seem to be hundreds buzzing throughout the town. But really, walking is incredibly easy, a lot safer, and completely free.

To get to the area's other beaches, either a *motoconcho* (US$2–7 depending on distance) or taxi (US$10–20) can get you there. Secure the price before hopping on or in.

Car and Bicycle Rental

Kanesh Rent-car and Motor (Calle Francisco Alberto Caamaño Deño, tel. 809/974-3966), across from Barrio Latino restaurant, rents jeeps (US$60), motorcycles (US$28), quads (US$54), and scooters (US$25). All rentals have options of half-day to 15-day rentals. Prices given here are for full-day rental.

Loca Bike (Calle Francisco Alberto Caamaño Deño, tel. 809/889-3593, 8 A.M.–noon and 2–6 P.M. daily, US$11/day) rents bicycles, which can be a fun way to get around town and keep your dependence on public transport down.

Sánchez

Back in the 1800s, Sánchez was a major fishing village. To this day, there is a lot of shrimping here, catching some of the biggest and best in the country. Now, however, what Higüey is to the southeast, Sánchez is to the Samaná Peninsula: a transportation hub. Those who stop in Sánchez are mainly doing so to get to other places on the peninsula or to catch a boat to Los Haitises (Sánchez is the closest launching point to the national park). If you find yourself in Sánchez and have some time, take a stroll through town and notice the brightly colored Victorian homes or wander down by the sea where the ruins of the old port (leftovers from the early 20th century) are lying in their rusty state, jutting out into the water.

© ANA CHAVIER CAMAÑO

locals helping a fisherman with his boat in Sánchez

Getting to La Península de Samaná

This is where buses from Santo Domingo and Puerto Plata stop to exchange and pick up passengers whose final destination is to either Samaná or Las Terrenas. Two bus companies serve this area. The trip to Santo Domingo takes four hours.

Caribe Tours (tel. 809/552-7434, www.caribetours.com, US$7.50) has buses to and from Santo Domingo at 7:30 A.M., 9:30 A.M., 2:30 P.M., 4 P.M., and 5 P.M.

Metro (tel. 809/552-7332, US$7.50) has service twice a day at 8:30 A.M. and 4 P.M. to Santo Domingo.

Getting to Parque Nacional Los Haitises

Most who visit the *parque* are doing so through tour agencies from other towns. However, local boats in Sánchez can take you as well.

Augusto Tours (tel. 809/249-3038 or 809/249-0122, US$28 without lunch, US$34 with lunch and drink) is a very small Dominican family-owned operation that will take you to Los Haitises on a four-hour round-trip excursion leaving at 9:30 A.M.; it takes you through mangroves and to select caves of the park. The launching point is at their restaurant, **Las Malvinas,** right by the rusting remains of the old port.

LA COSTA ÁMBAR

Those who visit La Costa Ámbar (The Amber Coast) will find that its menu of activities is as varied as its topography. At the northwestern corner of the country lagoons rest peacefully amidst mangroves and thick vegetation, mountainous tropical forests reach to blue skies, and arid cliffs fall steeply into the ocean's breakers. And whether you are an adventure junkie, a history buff, or a sun-seeking beachcomber, there is something in this region to satisfy your needs.

When Christopher Columbus made his second journey to the New World in 1493 he founded the second European settlement in the New World on this stretch of coastline at La Isabela in the northwest. All that now remains of that settlement are the ruins of their destroyed encampment, which can be seen in the Parque Nacional La Isabela. After the miserable failure of La Isabela, Columbus and his men moved to Santo Domingo and the north coast became mainly an import-and-export shipping yard for hundreds of years. But the mountainous tropical forests with no real passageways caused the area to be secluded from the rest of the country and unsettled for many years. Tourists didn't even start visiting this region until the late 1900s.

Although much of this region still has wide expanses of undeveloped land, many people associate La Costa Ámbar with the all-inclusive resorts of the Playa Dorada region. But there is so much more here to experience along the north coast: Windsurfers and kitesurfers recognize Cabarete's prowess as a major port of call for water sport lovers,

HIGHLIGHTS

◖ **Playa Grande Golf Course:** Although your golf game may suffer because of your attention to the views rather than your game, this golf course slopes and sprawls in all the right places. Keeping your eye on the ball might be harder than it's ever been (page 157).

◖ **Kiteboarding and Windsurfing in Cabarete:** Glide across the water at top speed where world champions ride. All, from beginner to pro, agree that Cabarete has some of the premier conditions for water sports in the entire world (page 162).

◖ **Diving and Snorkeling in Sosúa:** Explore the coral gardens, walls, wrecks, and

reefs off the coast of Sosúa in supreme diving conditions (page 171).

◖ **Museo del Ámbar Dominicano:** This museum has the most impressive display of the ancient resin in the country. Here, 40-million-year-old bugs lie frozen forever in a golden casing (page 177).

◖ **Cayo Arena:** Just off the coast of Punta Rucia, this picturesque sandbar fits no more than 100 people at a time and offers up fantastic snorkeling. The constantly shrinking and expanding ultra-white sand of this tiny sandbar can be your Paradise Island for the afternoon (page 190).

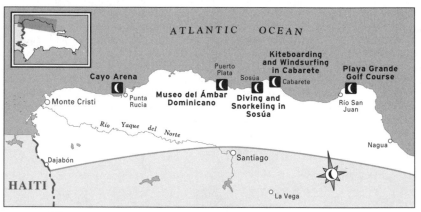

LOOK FOR ◖ TO FIND RECOMMENDED SIGHTS, ACTIVITIES, DINING, AND LODGING.

Sosúa has emerged as a scuba diver's dream, and untouched beaches are scattered all along the curvaceous coastline.

PLANNING YOUR TIME

It is said that 95 percent of travelers who visit this coast fly in to Puerto Plata, find their resort shuttles, and spend the rest of their vacation within the confines of its walls. If you are prone to "resort fever" or have adventure on your mind, then you will want to budget your time for the many things to see and do along the Amber Coast. Deciding how and where to concentrate your time is a daunting task with so many options available. Choosing your main focus before arrival is essential. For instance, if you want to spend most of your time kiteboarding, then Cabarete is the place to focus your vacation. Will you be taking a *guagua,* renting a car, or depending on the bus schedules to get you from location to location? If you are at the mercy of public transportation, leave time in your itinerary for missed connections.

Days on the beach are a given. It's what the northern coast does best. But an afternoon saved for visiting the Museo del Ámbar Dominicano and the Fuerte San Felipe in Puerto Plata or getting a tour of the first settlement of the New World in La Isabela is all you need for a break from the sand.

If you fly in to Puerto Plata and drive east toward Río San Juan, save at least a day for snorkeling in Sosúa and a couple of days for water sports in Cabarete.

Choosing to go west from Puerto Plata is a decision that requires more time. Perhaps that is why tourism wanes the farther west you travel. Not that there isn't a lot to see and do, but that there is a lot of ground to cover between stops. Driving from Puerto Plata to Monte Cristi, there is an opportunity for that afternoon in historic Puerto Plata, or to spend the night and visit Ocean World the next day. In Luperón, spend the night mixing and mingling over beers with expats and in the morning take an early swim at Playa Grande before heading off to see the ruins of La Isabela and the Templo de Las Américas. Continuing west, you'll have to budget a few days for a full visit to Monte Cristi and even more if you choose to detour to Punta Rucia.

All in all, the north coast offers a great variety of activities in many different locales. No matter which direction you go, or if you stay put in one locale, book tours and excursions either prior to arrival or in the first days of your stay to avoid the disappointment of not getting a spot.

While traveling according to an itinerary, you may find paradise along the way and can't bring yourself to move onward. If you truly want to experience the Dominican way of life, then do as the Dominicans do and wing it. If you suddenly feel like scrapping your plans to stay at one beach, then spread out your towel and relax.

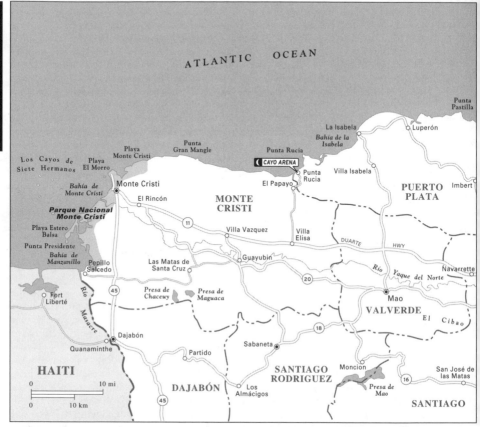

ATLANTIC OCEAN

Punta Pastilla

La Isabela   Luperón
Bahía de la Isabela

Playa Monte Cristi
Punta Gran Mangle
Punta Rucía   CAYO ARENA
Villa Isabela

Los Cayos de Siete Hermanos   Playa El Morro
Bahía de Monte Cristi
Monte Cristi   El Rincón
Punta Rucía
El Papayo
PUERTO PLATA   Imbert

MONTE CRISTI
Villa Vazquez   Villa Elisa
DUARTE   HWY

Parque Nacional Monte Cristi
Playa Estero Balsa
Punta Presidente
Bahía de Manzanillo   Pepillo Salcedo
Las Matas de Santa Cruz
Guayubin
Río Yaque del Norte   Navarrette

Fort Liberté
Presa de Chacuey   Presa de Maguaca
Mao
VALVERDE   El Cibao

Río Masacre
Dajabón
Sabaneta
18
SANTIAGO RODRIGUEZ   Moncion   San José de las Matas

Quanaminthe
Partido
Presa de Mao
SANTIAGO

HAITI
0   10 mi
0   10 km
DAJABÓN   Los Almácigos   16

Río San Juan

This is one of only a few towns along La Costa Ámbar that maintain their small-town peacefulness. There isn't much in the way of nightlife and there aren't many choices for hotels. What Río San Juan is blessed with, though, are some spectacular beaches that make for fun diving and snorkeling.

SIGHTS
Laguna Gri-Gri

This mangrove-blanketed area with its marine caverns is what put Río San Juan on the

tourism map to begin with, but since the huge media push of Playa Grande, it has fallen from its previous glory and suffers from lack of upkeep. However, tours are still given and can be quite a relaxing excursion.

Look for the **Laguna Gri-Gri Tour Booth** (tel. 809/859-2277) at the entrance to the lagoon, which is at the end of Calle Duarte. There you can arrange for a boat to take you for the two-hour ride through a kilometer of mangroves to Swallows Cave, where hundreds of the birds nest, onward for a swim in the

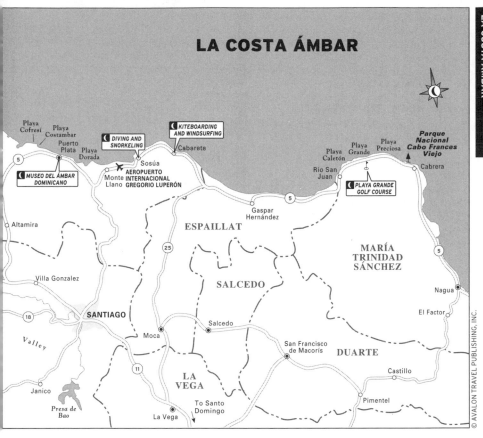

LA COSTA ÁMBAR

Natural Swimming Pool. If you like, you can extend your trip for a two-hour layover at Playa Caletón. For a boatload of 3–7 people the trip will run you about US$28.

Playa Caletón

Known locally as La Playita, this beach is a petite slice of paradise. Golden sand meets clear blue water, and palm trees give shelter from the sun. It's the perfect place to spend an afternoon, quietly reading, swimming, and enjoying lunch at one of the food stands. The turnoff is marked from the main road, and if you take a *guagua* or *motoconcho,* it will most likely drop you off there and you'll have to hoof it the rest of the way; no worries, it's not even a kilometer to the water.

Playa Grande

Recently, this beach has been all over the tourism development news. Companies have bought up land to develop the area and soon it will be crowded. This is a gorgeous and gigantic beach. "Big Beach" is aptly named in that everything about it dwarfs you. Tall cliffs surround the area and its band of golden sand is wide, backed by a thick coconut grove that continues for miles. If you walk east, you'll keep finding more hidden spots where you can get more privacy than on the main stretch. Even the water seems bigger here—it is definitely stronger. The wind whips into this area and creates a robust surf with a strong undertow. It's not the

© ANA CHAVIER CAAMAÑO

entrance to the mangrove lagoons of Río San Juan

beach for children or people who aren't strong swimmers.

There are quite a few food stands where you can get lunch and drinks, and various stalls with bathing suits, jewelry, and trinkets. Vendors proffer beach chairs (US$2/day), snorkeling gear, bodyboards (US$5/hour), and surfboards (US$25/day).

The entrance from the main road is clearly marked. It leads down to a parking lot in the trees at Playa Grande. To get there, you have to pass through a gate that's been put up by hotel developers. If it is closed, it doesn't mean the beach is closed. The beach is open to the public by law. If the gate is open and you take a *guagua* or *motoconcho*, ask the driver to take you all the way down to the parking lot. It is about a 1.5-kilometer walk from the turnoff to the beach.

Playa Preciosa

Although this beach, whose name translates as "Beautiful Beach," is truly that, it is also a scary display of strong water—not a place for

a leisurely swim. If you want to sit and watch some daring and very experienced surfers brave the waters, this could be entertaining. It is less than a kilometer east of Playa Grande and can be accessed by the same entrance road from the main highway.

SPORTS AND RECREATION
Diving and Snorkeling

For divers that are new to the sport, the Natural Swimming Pool is perfect in that many fish can be seen in shallow clear waters. For more experienced divers, there are many coral reefs and canyons with caves and swim-through holes. **Gri-Gri Divers** (Calle Gastón F Deligne, tel. 809/589-2671, www.grigridivers.com, 8 A.M.–5 P.M. Mon.–Sat.) has been in business for over 10 years and is the best dive shop around. Diving packages and certification courses range from beginner to challenging and expert. Dives start at US$45 with equipment rental, and the more dives you book, the bigger the discount. For instance, 10 dives are US$30 per dive with

ATLANTIC OCEAN

RÍO SAN JUAN

Mangroves

GRI-GRI DIVERS

Laguna Gri-Gri

LAGUNA GRI-GRI TOUR BOOTH

SÁNCHEZ

EL CORRAL DEL POLLO

LE CAFÉ PARIS

VERIZON CENTRO DE COMUNICACIONES

PLAYA GRANDE RENT-A-CAR

TOURIST OFFICE

JANDR.NET

CHEO'S CAFÉ

TAXI STAND

FARMACIA REYES

BUSES

BANCO PROGRESSO

POLITUR

Mangroves

SCALE NOT AVAILABLE

GASTON FDO DELIGNE · 27 DE FEBRERO · SÁNCHEZ · SAN JUAN ADAMES · LORENZO ADAMES · MELLA · PADRE BILLINI · BELLER · RUFINO · DR. AGOSTO · CAPOTILLO · BALBUENA · PADRE BILLINI · DR. VIRGILIO GARCÍA · LUPERÓN · LIBERTAD · DUARTE · LAS FLORES · CARRETERA RÍO SAN JUAN-CABRERA · CARRETERA RÍO SAN JUAN-GASPAR HERNÁNDEZ

equipment. Discounts are also given if you have your own equipment.

🄲 Playa Grande Golf Course

One of the north coast's best golf courses. Playa Grande Golf Course (Carretera a Nagua, tel. 809/582-0860, US$65 for 9 holes, US$120 for 18 holes) was designed by Robert Trent Jones Sr., who designed some 500 courses, with this one at Playa Grande as one of his last ones. Although he never saw the final result, this celebrated founding father of the American Society of Golf Course Architects would've been exhilarated with the outcome. The sprawling tee boxes and large sloping greens of this par-72 course are precariously placed on the 30-meter cliffs overlooking the awe-inspiring Playa Grande. It is well maintained and the views are amazing from almost every single hole. Caddies and carts are US$15 extra for 18 holes and are a must.

ACCOMMODATIONS

There are no accommodations in the town of Río San Juan. Instead, the choices listed here are nearby at Playa Grande or just east of town.

Hotel La Catalina (Los Farallones, Catalina, tel. 809/589-7700, fax 809/589-7550, www.lacatalina.com, US$98 d) is east of Río San Juan, near the town of Cabrera. This hotel has 30 rooms and apartments, all of which are very comfortable with tropical floral decoration and cool tile floors, and every room has a great view of the ocean and the lush countryside. Tennis court, billiard room, library, and two swimming pools are some of the other amenities. A free shuttle to Playa Grande and breakfast are included in the rate.

All-inclusive **Occidental Alegro Playa Grande** (Carretera Nagua Kilometer 51, Playa Grande, tel. 809/582-1170, fax 809/582-6094, www.occidentalhotels.com, US$98 d) is on the cliffs overlooking Playa Grande, the golf course, and the Atlantic Ocean. Its views are breathtaking and its rooms are spacious and clean. The grounds and gardens are nicely kept, there are three restaurants, and the pool is large and kid-friendly. Really, the best reason to stay here is that it is so close to Playa Grande. Considering that you have to go down many steps to get to the beach, the hotel had good thinking when it put in a snack bar down there for its guests. Once you're down there, you tend to stay for a while.

Bahía Principe San Juan (Carretera Gaspar Hernandez Kilometer 18, Playa Grande, tel. 809/226-1590, fax 809/226-1994, www.bahia-principe.com, US$188 d) is a massive all-inclusive. Its 1,000-plus rooms are spread out over a large, well-manicured area expansive enough to warrant a trolley service to take guests from spot to spot. There are six restaurants, 11 bars, three pools, tennis courts, minigolf, a soccer field, spa, gym, supermarket, bank, excursion desk—the list goes on from there and you get the idea. It is a town. And a nice one. All rooms come with two double beds or one king-size, air-conditioning, private bath, satellite TV, safe, minibar, and balcony or terrace. Water sports are available also, although some cost extra.

FOOD

Just as the accommodations are limited, so too is the restaurant selection.

Le Café Paris (Calle Sánchez, tel. 809/844-4899, 8 a.m.–9 p.m. daily, US$5–18) is a nice place to have a slow meal or a drink outside.

petrified wood sculptures on Playa Grande

© ANA CHAVIER CAAMAÑO

The food is okay but there is plenty to look at since it is right across from where the boats to Laguna Gri-Gri dock. The area has a charming atmosphere with the shade-filled lagoon. The menu has French food, pizza, and some grilled seafood.

El Corral del Pollo (Calle 16 de Agosto, tel. 809/251-2192, 8 A.M.–6 P.M. daily, US$8–20) serves Spanish cuisine like paella in a casual atmosphere.

Locals love to recommend **Cheo's Café** (Calle Padre Billini, tel. 809/589-2290, US$7–17) and the tourists love to eat here. International favorites are available, but so are rabbit in coconut sauce and grilled catch of the day.

INFORMATION AND SERVICES

For such a small town, services are plentiful, and most are along the main drag of Calle Duarte. All are within walking distance.

Banco Progreso (Calle Duarte, 8:30 A.M.–4 P.M. Mon.–Fri., 9 A.M.–1 P.M. Sat.) has a 24-hour ATM at the corner of Duarte and Alvarado. The **post office** is farther toward the Laguna between Mella and Bulbuena.

For communication needs, head to **Verizon Centro de Comunicaciones** (Calle Duarte at Mella, tel. 809/589-2736, 8 A.M.–10 P.M.), where you can make long-distance calls. For an Internet communication option **JandR .net** (Calle 30 de Marzo, 8 A.M.–8:30 P.M. Mon.–Sat., 8 A.M.–noon Sun.) is two blocks southwest of Verizon and offers connections for US$2.20 per hour.

The **Oficina de Turismo** (Tourism Office, Calle Mella at Calle 16 de Agosto, tel. 809/589-2831, 8 A.M.–4 P.M. Mon.–Fri.) is available if you have any more questions or want brochures and maps of the area.

Health and Emergencies

If you travel west on Highway 5, the tourist police office, **Politur** (Carretera a Cabarete, tel. 809/754-3241), is on the left-hand side after you've passed Calle Duarte.

Farmacia Reyes (Calle Duarte, tel. 809/589-2234, 8 A.M.–noon and 2–6 P.M.

Mon.–Fri., 8 A.M.–noon Sat.) has an okay selection of meds and necessities.

Getting There and Around

At the intersection of Highway 5 and Calle Duarte, buses, *motoconchos,* and *guaguas* all stop to pick up passengers.

Caribe Tours (Hwy. 5, tel. 809/589-2644) has a bus leaving for a 4.5-hour trip to Santo Domingo for US$7 at 6:30 A.M., 7:45 A.M., 9:30 A.M., 2 P.M., and 3:30 P.M. every day.

There are usually a few people waiting on *guaguas* at this intersection so you can ask questions, but the ones headed for Cabarete (US$2), Sosúa (US$2.50), and Puerto Plata (US$3.50), leave every 15 minutes 6 A.M.–5 P.M. daily. The *guaguas* going east leave every 10 minutes. To take one to Playa Grande it only costs US$0.50, and to Nagua it is US$1.75, where you can then catch transportation to Samaná.

Two blocks up Duarte at Calle Dr. Virgilio Garcia there is a **taxi stand** where you can hail one to take you to the area beaches or your hotel.

Renting a car is always a great way to see the countryside, and this stretch of Highway 5, all the way to Puerto Plata, is relatively well-maintained. **Playa Grande Rent-a-Car** (Calle Duarte 15, tel. 809/589-2391, 8 A.M.–6 P.M.) has cars for rent starting around US$45 for the day.

Nagua sits quietly on coastal Highway 5, 36 kilometers northwest of Sánchez. It doesn't have anything to offer a tourist (it's rather uninteresting) except that it serves as a gateway and transportation hub between La Costa Ámbar and La Península de Samaná.

Guaguas converge here and can take you to many cities, including: Sánchez, San Francisco de Macorís, Moca, Santiago, and the north coast towns.

Guaguas heading for the northern coastal towns can be hailed on the main highway. Just stand on the side of the road for the direction you need to go and wave one down. They pass quite frequently, about every 15–20 minutes. *Guaguas* heading inland need to be hailed just where they turn off of Highway 5 and onto Highway 132. If you are coming via a *guagua* and need to transfer, tell the driver your final destination so you can be let off at the appropriate spot to flag down the next one. These connections aren't as frequent as the northbound *guaguas,* arriving once an hour.

Caribe Tours (Calle Mella, tel. 809/584-4505, US$6) has a bus that goes from Nagua to Santo Domingo every day at 7:30 A.M., 8 A.M., 8:30 A.M., 10 A.M., 10:30 A.M., 11 A.M., 2 P.M., 3 P.M., 4:30 P.M., and 5:30 P.M.

Metro (Calle Sánchez 71, tel. 809/584-3159, US$6) makes the same trip with fewer departure times. Its buses leave at 7 A.M., 9:15 A.M., and 4:15 P.M. On weekends (Fri.–Sun.) there's an extra departure time at 2:15 P.M. The trip to Santo Domingo takes roughly 3.5 hours.

Cabarete

Known internationally as a top windsurfing and kitesurfing spot, Cabarete has been a choice location for adventure-sport enthusiasts. The area has also appealed to young and young-at-heart travelers, with its many low-budget accommodation options and easy-going nightlife. Charming, hip, and low-key, Cabarete was the sort of place that you'd purposely miss your flight home for so that you could deny that the rest of the world existed for just a little while longer.

But when Cabarete stepped into the world's windsurfing spotlight, people and businesses suddenly started coming in droves. Now the once-small fishing town is a jam-packed, horn-beeping hotbed of tourist activity. There are still budget accommodations and places to eat, but now there are amenities to please every type of traveler.

BEACHES
Playa Cabarete
This is the main beach in town, and it is windsurfing and kiteboarding central. The Bahía de Cabarete is a gradual semicircular stretch that is great for people-watching. On the sand are countless bars, restaurants, and hotels from which to set up camp and witness the acrobatics of the hot shots and bless-their-hearts-for-trying beginners. It isn't an easy surf, but it is close to ideal. All the natural conditions that form this bay play a part to the perfection of the area for water sports. The temperature of

the water is always balmy so forget the wetsuit. There is an offshore reef at the entrance to the two-kilometer-wide bay where the more experienced surfers ride, but the majority of the sea floor becomes sandy once you are in the bay itself. Combine these things with the direction

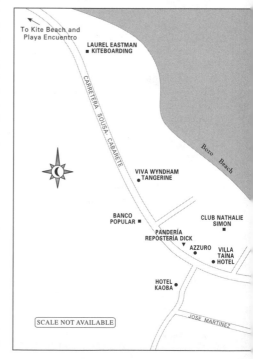

of the eastern trade winds, which start blowing in around noon, and the low-lying hills behind Cabarete and you've got outstanding wave and beach conditions.

The western, downwind portion of Playa Cabarete is called **Bozo Beach,** which is named for the beginning windsurfers and kiteboarders still getting the hang of the sport who get pulled by the wind to this end of the beach.

Kite Beach

This beach is about two kilometers west of Playa Cabarete, just past Bozo Beach, and clearly is named for the sport that it is ideally suited for. The wind is stable here, perfect for kitesurfing, since you need to have good control of your sail as the wind picks you up high into the air above the ocean. This beach can be much more populated on the days when there is a good wind. Everyone—from beginners to

training professionals—finds Kite Beach the best. In fact, the conditions are so perfect that many world kitesurfing competitions have been held on this beach.

Playa Encuentro

What the other beaches are to wind and kite surfers, Playa Encuentro is to regular wave surfers. Big waves, strong tides, and deep water draw crowds of surfers, especially in the morning when the water and wind conditions are prime. It's best if you start before 7 A.M.—it gets blown out fast here. In the beginning, hang back and watch the regulars and locals for a bit to learn the etiquette of the water. After the surfers' prime hours are gone, the windsurfers and kiteboarders join in. The beach break at Playa Encuentro has a strong current, so watch where the locals paddle out. There are quality reef breaks to challenge you, like The Destroyer,

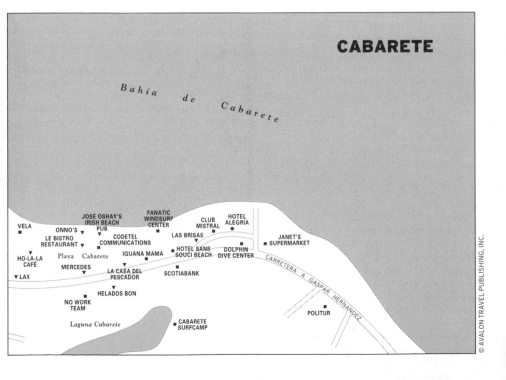

CABARETE

Bahía de Cabarete

VELA
JOSÉ OSHAY'S IRISH BEACH PUB
ONNO'S
LE BISTRO RESTAURANT
FANATIC WINDSURF CENTER
CODETEL COMMUNICATIONS
CLUB MISTRAL
HOTEL ALEGRÍA
LAS BRISAS
JANET'S SUPERMARKET
HO-LA-LA CAFÉ
Playa Cabarete
MERCEDES
IGUANA MAMA
HOTEL SANS SOUCI BEACH
DOLPHIN DIVE CENTER
LAX
LA CASA DEL PESCADOR
SCOTIABANK
CARRETERA A GASPAR HERNÁNDEZ
HELADOS BON
NO WORK TEAM
CABARETE SURFCAMP
POLITUR
Laguna Cabarete

which is fast and shallow (good for short boards), the Coco Pipe, and La Preciosa (The Precious One).

SPORTS AND RECREATION

Cabarete is, without a doubt, the water-sports capital of the Dominican Republic. It could even be why you chose to vacation here. Cabarete is chockfull of outfitters, schools where beginner lessons are given, and places to rent the equipment you will need.

Windsurfing

The sport that started the entire hullabaloo about Cabarete is still, despite the rise in popularity of kiteboarding, very popular and big business here. Playa Cabarete is a good beach for beginners and experienced windsurfers alike due to the strong winds necessary for the sport and the sandy sea floor of the inner bay.

The conditions in the morning are usually good for beginners and children since the wind isn't as strong and the water is flatter, which gives you more time to pull the sail up and get your balance. By about noon, the wind usually starts to pick up and blows parallel to the shore at up to 25–45 kilometers per hour. Additionally, it's calmer toward shore and rougher out where the coral reef breaks the waves. This is where the hotshots go to jump, do their 360-degree spins, and do flips.

You'll find lots of places that offer lessons and equipment rental right on the shore of Playa Cabarete. Generally, boards rent for US$50 per day or US$200–270 per week. Ask about package deals where you can pay a lump sum and you get a set amount of days, but you don't have to use them all in a row. Also ask about damage insurance, which can run you about US$45 for a week. Lessons are a great way to get into the sport. Beginners can expect to pay US$40 an hour for private instruction.

Vela (Playa Cabarete, tel. 809/571-0805, www.velawindsurf.com), on the upwind end of the beach, is a reliable outfitter who has some of the most high-tech and fancy equipment

for rent. You'll look like a pro even if you end up doing a face plant. Vela offers a beginner windsurfer program, private lessons, and free windsurfing clinics. Kiteboarding instruction is also available.

Club Nathalie Simon (Playa Cabarete, tel. 809/571-0848, www.cabaretewindsurf.com, 9 A.M.–6 P.M. daily) is on the west end of the beach. It has very nice equipment for rent for all skill levels. The instructors will only teach 1–3 people maximum, which allows you to progress quicker. Kids as young as five can learn the sport with lessons on the lagoon behind the beach. CNS also rents kayaks and boogie boards.

Fanatic Windsurf Center (Playa Cabarete, tel. 809/571-0861, www.fanatic-cabarete.com) offers rental of equipment at cheaper rates by using older equipment, which is a good deal if you're doing it for the first time. A family package includes lessons for the parents and child care while you're on the water. Or, if your children are ready to learn windsurfing, they can take lessons also.

Kiteboarding

While windsurfing put Cabarete on the map, kiteboarding is gaining in popularity quickly. It is impressive to watch from the shore, let alone try. One moment you're skimming along the surface of the waves, then you suddenly swoop into the air for a hang time above the ocean.

Both Kite Beach and Bozo Beach are good spots for learning, but Bozo seems to be less crowded. This exhilarating sport is best when you have lots of hours of instruction (6–12 is standard), and it is best to choose a quality school. It is a dangerous sport that you'd be wise to learn from the best.

Kiteboarding is more expensive to learn, and beginners should expect to pay around US$250 for six hours of lessons. Try to shop around, though; there are so many instructors around that you should get your money's worth by having an instructor with whom you have a good rapport and who makes you feel safe.

© ANA CHAVIER CAAMAÑO

kiteboarding on Playa Cabarete

Super-cool **Kite Club** (Kite Beach, tel. 809/571-9748, www.kiteclubcabarete.com), at the upwind tip of Kite Beach, offers beginners group (US$25/hour) and individual (US$70/hour) lessons. Lessons are available in English, French, German, and Spanish. If you buy a membership (starting at US$30/week) for the duration of your trip you get special incentives, like use of a locker, use of Kite Club facilities, and access to a rescue boat (could come in handy). An on-site restaurant specializes in tasty food that perks you up after a good run but won't weigh you down so you can get back out there.

Laurel Eastman Kiteboarding (Hotel Caracol Beach Club, tel. 809/571-0564, www.laureleastman.com) offers lessons in many different alluring packages, including kids' classes and women-only classes.

Club Mistral (Playa Cabarete, tel. 809/571-9791, www.club-mistral.com) has the credibility of having many operations worldwide. This German company offers many kitesurfing, windsurfing, surfing, and combo packages.

Surfing

The surfing on Playa Encuentro is some of the best on the island. Reef breaks include Coco Pipe, Encuentro, and The Destroyer. Surfboard rental is quite inexpensive compared to wind- and kite-surfing. Board rental is typically around US$15 for a half day. Beginners and experienced surfers alike might enjoy the surf camps that some outfitters offer. A five-day camp can cost US$150.

No Work Team (Calle Principal, tel. 809/571-0820, www.noworkteamcabarete.com) offers a mini course where you'll learn about the sport and how to handle the equipment, paddle across waves, and catch them (US$35 for three hours). A surf camp costs US$119 for five days.

Take Off (Playa Encuentro, tel. 809/963-7873, www.321takeoff.com) is another outfitter right at the beach.

Diving

While this is clearly not the big sport of this area, **Dolphin Dive Center** (tel. 809/571-3589, www.dolphindivecenter.com, 9 A.M.–1 P.M. and 2–6 P.M. Mon.–Sat.) can arrange for transfer to the nearly 20 dive sites within a 20-minute boat ride. Dive packages start at US$46 for a one-tank dive.

Tours and Excursions

Iguana Mama (Calle Principal, tel. 809/571-0908, www.iguanamama.com) is the best ecotour operator in the Dominican Republic. It has been around for a while and has a great selection of exhilarating tours and excursions like hiking, trekking, canyoning, and cascading as well as some more laid-back choices like catamaran rides. But Iguana Mama is best known for its mountain-biking trips, from one-day to multi-day biking excursions that take you deep into the Dominican Republic that few other tourists see. Some trips even go across the entire country! Hiking and mule trips to Pico Duarte are a good choice through this company as well. Browse the website or stop by the office to look at brochures to get a feel for the limitless possibilities available to you; if you don't see just the right excursion, they will customize one for you. Among the top 10 reasons to choose Iguana Mama as your tour operator is that 10 percent of its net income goes to local schools and parks. Iguana Mama operates truly sustainable and responsible tourism.

ENTERTAINMENT AND EVENTS

Nightlife

Cabarete's surfers and youthful visitors have given the small town a spring-break type of nightlife. Many of the restaurants lining the shore transform into spirited bars after dinner hours where music and drinks flow well into the early morning. The party hearty atmosphere probably owes itself to the fact that most wind- and kitesurfers don't go out on the water until the wind picks up in the afternoon.

LAX (www.lax-cabarete.com, 9 A.M.–1 A.M. daily) is a restaurant that serves a wide variety of items for breakfast, lunch and dinner, but it has become a popular starter venue mainly because of its *re-LAX-ed* atmosphere. Cash only.

Two dueling hot spots right next to one another are **Bambú** (tel. 809/982-4549, 6 P.M.–6 A.M. daily), a large club with comfy sofas, and **Onno's** (tel. 809/383-1448, 9 A.M.–5 A.M. daily), which gets crazy-packed at night. Both offer outrageous drink specials and hours of music-pumping zaniness.

If you can't help but crave a little American bar food, **José Oshay's Irish Beach Pub** (Playa Cabarete, tel. 809/571-0775, 8 A.M.–11 P.M. daily) is the place for you. The owners are an Irish-American father and son team who opened this bar back in 2002. Since then they have been serving fish and chips, bangers and mash, and shepherd's pie right on the beach in Cabarete. An annual St. Patrick's Day bash complete with bagpipes and Irish dancers sends this stretch of beach into a frenzy with upwards of 2,000 in attendance. Other popular dishes are a plate of nachos big enough to feed four, freshly caught seafood, cocktails, and tropical frozen drinks. A live rock band plays five nights a week.

Las Brisas (tel. 809/571-0614, 8 A.M.–5 A.M. daily) is the club to go to if you want to have the Latin experience and try your fancy footwork to the tunes of some great salsa and merengue beats.

Festivals and Events

The **Master of the Ocean** competition, which has happened at the end of February since its inception in 2002, challenges individuals in their mastery of kitesurfing, windsurfing, and surfing. While they are judged in individual categories, the winner is the one who can prove that they've got the chops to master all three categories. The rounds are held at various area beaches, but the final heat is at Playa Encuentro with its big, intimidating waves so as to ensure challenge for the participants and theatrics for the spectators. It is a thrilling event.

Held at the end of October, the **Dominican Jazz Festival** (www.drjazzfestival.com) celebrates jazz with artists that visit from many countries of the world in addition to Dominican talent.

The **International Sand Castle Competi-**

tion is an event that both kids and adults will enjoy. Forget the plastic bucket and shovel kit; these competitors are serious! It's held in Cabarete in the first part of March every year with adult and kid competitions.

Both **Cabarete Race Week** and the **Kitesurfing World Cup** are held in the month of June when the winds are prime. During this time Cabarete is overcome with international windsurfers and kiteboarders ready to compete in the tournaments. This event is fun to witness, but if you plan on traveling here during this time, book your hotel well in advance.

ACCOMMODATIONS

There are plenty of accommodations and a good assortment for all income levels. Cabarete is unique in that there are two peak travel seasons: December to April and mid-June to mid-September, when the winds give good surfing conditions.

Under US$50

◀ **Hotel Sans Souci Beach** (Calle Principal, tel. 809/571-0755, fax 809/571-1542, US$26 per person) is part of a chain of very affordable rooms and apartments. While this one is the best, there are six more to choose from, all located in Cabarete and starting at a mind-boggling US$12 per person. The Hotel Sans Souci Beach is at the far eastern end of Playa Cabarete, directly on the beach. This hotel is nothing fancy, showing its age, but its rooms are clean and spacious with cable TV, safe, and refrigerator; best of all, most have a panoramic ocean view. Parking is free.

In a quiet location by Laguna Cabarete, **Cabarete Surfcamp** (Laguna Cabarete, tel. 809/571-0733, www.cabaretesurfcamp.com, US$20 d with breakfast and dinner) is only a short walk from Playa Cabarete. Rooms are cheerfully decorated and clean. Apartments and studios are also available at very good prices. The garden holds a pool.

Hotel Alegría (Callejón 2, tel. 809/571-0455, www.hotel-alegria.com, US$22 d), tucked into a side road, has cheap accommodations and is relatively comfortable and

acceptable for those on a budget. One three-bedroom, three-bathroom apartment would be good for friends traveling together. This is a good value if you are staying for an extended amount of time. Features include a billiard table and laundry service.

The 28 bungalows at **Hotel Kaoba** (Calle Principal, tel. 809/571-0300, www.kaoba.com, US$40 d) enjoy close proximity to the beach but without being on the main drag. There are also 15 rooms and 10 deluxe rooms available. All rooms have TV and minibars and some have kitchenettes. There is a pool and a restaurant/bar.

The name alone sets a hotel up for high expectations: What **Extreme** (Carretera Sosúa, tel. 809/571-0880, US$45–75 d) offers (not that other places don't) is an in-house kiteboarding school, a surf school, and a skate park (at extra cost to you) called Six Feet Under (named after the reef breaker Six Feet Over, which is just in front of the hotel). The rooms are nice and comfortable, but if you're staying in a hotel that caters to action sport enthusiasts, you probably won't spend a lot of time in there anyway. Free wireless Internet is available so that you can check surf and wind conditions. Plenty of day excursions are available if there's not enough wind. Extreme prides itself on an exercise hard all day, party all night atmosphere. Breakfast is included in rate.

US$50-100

Kite Beach Hotel (Carretera Sosúa, tel. 809/571-0878, www.kitebeachhotel.com, US$66 d) offers comfortable and very clean rooms, with nice and roomy bathrooms, remote control air-conditioning, phone, cable TV, ceiling fan, and safe. Unfortunately, only the suites and apartments have balconies with ocean views (US$100–160 d), and both of those have kitchenettes. The pool area has good views of the goings-on of Kite Beach. A breakfast buffet is included in the rate. It's a good value for kiteboarders because you can get a package deal including lessons.

The rooms at **Azzuro** (Calle Principal, tel. 809/571-4000, www.starzresorts.com,

VILLA RENTALS

Travelers looking for accommodations outside the walls of the ever-popular all-inclusive resorts have quite a few alternatives, and excellent ones at that.

Renting a villa is a great option for the independent-minded tourist. Whether one is seeking exclusivity, privacy, and/or affordability, villas offer an opportunity to personalize your vacation in ways that all-inclusive resorts cannot. Luxury villas are available for those who want to live like a rock star and are therefore willing to pay like a rock star.

The **Sea Horse Ranch** (Carretera Sosúa-Cabarete, tel. 809/571-3880, fax 809/571-2374, www.sea-horse-ranch.com, US$550-3,000 per night) is a 100-hectare development on the north coast between Sosúa and Cabarete. Many villas, all of which have private swimming pools, are available seaside or with private gardens. Particularly of interest is the Sea Horse Ranch Equestrian Center, which offers riding lessons and wilderness and beach tours.

Bea Location (La Ceiba, Las Terrenas, tel. 809/240-5381, www.bealocation.com, US$300-3,600 per week) offers rental villas with hotel services. All located in Las Terrenas along Samaná Peninsula, each villa is of a unique design – from romantic bungalows ideal for a couple to the Casa Lila, which sleeps up to 6 people and features a garden with a swimming pool, to the Villa Loma Bonita, with its second-floor infinity pool, outdoor living room, and accommodations for up to 16 people. Bea Location also offers for rent Caribbean-style seaside apartments with an ocean view and terrace. With so many options to choose from, you really can't go wrong.

If you are feeling on the fence in terms of whether to choose a villa or a resort, the **Excel Villas at Casa de Campo** (La Romana, tel. 305/856-5405, www.casadecampo.com, US$600-1,070) offers the best of both worlds. You get the privacy of a villa but access to resort amenities. In La Romana on the Caribbean coast, the villas range from three to six bedrooms and have either a whirlpool or a swimming pool. With fully equipped kitchens and comfortable furnishings, the Excel Villas truly can be your "home away from home." Plus, you can tell all your friends you stayed at the resort where Michael Jackson married Lisa Marie Presley, where the Clintons have vacationed, and where Oscar de la Renta once lived and Julio Iglesias keeps a home.

If more moderately priced accommodations are more your speed, but comfort and quality are still high on your list of priorities (as well they should be!), the Dominican Republic does not lack for housing options.

Coastal Cottages by the Sea (Cabarete, tel. 809/885-8477, www.coastalcottagesbythesea.com, US$750 per week) is on the north coast in Cabarete. With only four cottages on the premises, it truly offers the feel of cozy seclusion, but its location allows for quick and easy access to a multitude of restaurants and adventure activities right nearby. The cottages share access to a central private pool and a small thatch-roofed beach bar, which serves up everything from breakfast and snack to drinks and ice cream. Yum!

With swinging hammocks for napping and large beds for a good night's sleep, **Natura Cabañas** (Paseo del Sol 5, Perla Marina, Sosua, tel. 809/571-1507, www.naturacabana.com, US$ 80 d) truly is a one-of-a-kind alternative to your typical hotel. First of all, the rooms are individual bungalows. Second, each is designed for maximum comfort and minimal effect on the environment. Overhead fan petals (in lieu of air-conditioning) and hand-crafted bamboo furniture make these ecologically sensitive accommodations accommodating to you and the environment.

Also check out the following for more villa rental information: www.puerto-plata.com, www.a1vacations.com, and www.domini-can-holiday.com.

For choosing a villa in a specific area of the Dominican Republic, go to www.vrbo.com.

US$85–90 d) are comfortable enough, though not outrageously special, with the usual commercial hotel appointments. But with this location, who can go wrong? Azzuro has a rather large pool and great beach access. Try to get an ocean-view room because from your balcony you can watch the sky fill with kiteboarders.

All rooms at **Villa Taína Hotel** (Calle Principal, tel. 809/571-0722, www.villataina.com, standard room US$75 d, standard oceanside $105 d) are equipped with air-conditioning, Internet connection, minibar, balcony or terrace, and nice bathrooms. The pool is small but attractive, there is direct access to the beach, and the restaurant and bar overlook the ocean. A generous buffet breakfast is included with the rate and half-board rate options are available.

US$100 and Up

Viva Wyndham Tangerine (Calle Principal, tel. 809/571-0420, fax 809/571-9550, www .vivaresorts.com, US$200 d) is a good all-inclusive option. The 223 rooms are very comfortable (especially the bed) with large spacious bathrooms—a little plain, but kept ultra-clean. The buffet, while trying to cater to all nationalities, does reasonably well. All the regular all-inclusive amenities are present: nighttime entertainment, large pool, direct access to beach, and disco to name a few. Do try to get a room in the building closest to the ocean; although your view to the water is not completely unobstructed (the restaurant and pool come first), you do avoid a rather disconcerting odor that seems to waft around the buildings closer to the road.

 Natura Cabañas (Paseo del Sol 5, Cabarete, tel. 809/571-1507, www.naturacabana .com, US$160 d), between Cabarete and Sosúa, offers 10 charming bungalows as an alternative to the staid room you get at other hotels. This unique hideaway is a treat. Each separately named (not numbered) bungalow (such as Cabaña India, Mexicali, or Caracol) has a rustic interior of bamboo, wood, and stone coral. The environmentally sensitive use of materials and the design blend this hotel into the environment without disrupting the natural beauty

of the area. Some bungalows have kitchenettes and all have minifridges. A vacation spent in this hotel is one of lazy days in one of the numerous hammocks, healthy meals in the restaurant, sunning yourself by the pool, taking a yoga class by the ocean, and indulging in a spa treatment on-site. Rates include airport transfer, breakfast, and maid service. This is truly a good find.

FOOD

Playa Cabarete is a romantic and charming area, and many of the restaurants here provide that sort of atmosphere as well. Many offer beachfront dining, but be prepared to pay higher prices than at the venues farther from the beach. Some of the restaurants also turn into lively nightlife spots after dinner.

Mercedes (Callejón de la Loma, tel. 809/571-0247, noon–10 P.M. daily, US$3–10) is where the locals are eating. This is good down-home cooking the Dominican way.

Pandería Repostería Dick (on the west end of town, tel. 809/571-0612, 7 A.M.–6 P.M. Thurs.–Tues., US$3–6) is a great breakfast spot very popular with the locals. It serves international breakfast favorites and freshly baked bread. The coffee is phenomenal. Breakfast is served until 1 P.M., so that those late-rising kiteboarders can get some before they go out on the water.

La Casa del Pescador (Playa Cabarete, tel. 809/571-0760, 8 A.M.–11 P.M. daily, US$6–17) might not be much to look at, but the seafood and fish are excellent. This is a celebrated mainstay in Cabarete. Specialties include seafood spaghetti and paella.

Centrally located **Ho-La-La Café** (Playa Cabarete, tel. 809/571-0760, 10 A.M.– midnight, US$10–20) has a classy dining atmosphere and mostly French cuisine in a seaside-facing restaurant. The surf and turf and *paella de mariscos* for two are good choices. A kids' menu is available.

Reservations are essential at **Blue Moon** (Los Brazos, tel. 809/223-0614, noon–midnight, US$15), an East Indian restaurant that requires a minimum of eight people per party. Enjoy your dinner served in the traditional manner on comfy cushions on the floor. Tandoori chicken, curried goat, vegetable curries, and homemade chutneys arrive on banana leaves as plates. Blue Moon is east of Cabarete on the highway to Sabaneta. Turn right toward Jamao al Norte and go through Los Brazos, where you'll see a sign directing you to take a left up a hill.

Le Bistro Restaurant (tel. 809/850-4254, US$4–20), nestled in a passageway between the main drag and the beachfront restaurants, is a quaint French restaurant with a tranquil ambience. Try the lobster and fish fondue or the duck stewed in red wine. Pay in pesos or dollars.

Centrally located **Helados Bon** (Calle Principal, 11:30 A.M.–11 P.M., starting at US$1.50) is open late. Somehow ice cream just tastes better here. Maybe it's the heat or maybe it's the ingredients. One thing is for sure; it is the stuff that Dominican childhoods are made of, with flavors like *bizcocho* (cake) and *mantecado*, which is a rich buttery vanilla.

At **Janet's Supermarket** (Carretera Gaspar Hernandez, 8 A.M.–8 P.M. Mon.–Sat., 8 A.M.–1 P.M. Sun.) you can find almost all of your grocery needs, including dry goods, produce, and sundries.

INFORMATION AND SERVICES
Health and Emergencies

The **Politur** (Carretera Gaspar Hernandez, tel. 809/571-0713, 24 hours) office is at the eastern outside end of town.

Servi-Med Medical Office (tel. 809/571-0964, 24-hour service) is right in the middle of town across from Sky Internet Access, and they'll come to you. English and German are spoken. On staff are four doctors, a dentist, and a chiropractor.

Money

ScotiaBank (8:30 A.M.–4:30 P.M. Mon.–Fri., 9 A.M.–1 P.M. Sat.) has a 24-hour ATM on the east end of town, and **Banco Popular** (9 A.M.–5 P.M. Mon.–Fri., 9 A.M.–1 P.M. Sat.) has a 24-hour ATM on the western end of town.

Money exchange offices are along the main drag and will all change euros, U.S. currency, and traveler's checks.

Communications

At **Codetel Communications** (9 A.M.–9 P.M. Mon.–Sat.) calls to the U.S. cost US$0.32 per minute, and to Europe they cost US$0.74 per minute. Codetel is in a walkway that leads to the beach. You can buy long-distance cards here.

Sky Internet (9 A.M.–3 P.M. daily) offers Internet access for 15 minutes (US$0.70), 30 minutes (US$1.70), and 60 minutes (US$2.60) in a central location across from the Servi-Med Medical Office.

There is no post office in Cabarete, but you can ask your hotel's front desk to post mail for you.

Getting There and Around

Guaguas can be hailed anywhere along the main road that skewers Cabarete. Remember to stand on the side of the road for the direction in which you want to travel; that way you'll be certain to catch the right one. When in doubt, say the name of the town you wish to go to and they either will or will not let you on, depending. Trips to Río San Juan (US$1.75) take an hour, Sosúa (US$1) is a 30-minute ride, and to Puerto Plata (US$1.75) it's a one-hour ride.

There are taxi stands along the main drag and *motoconchos* can always be waved down if you feel like taking part in a more dangerous activity than kitesurfing.

Sosúa

In the early 1990s Sosúa wasn't the vacation mecca that it is now. It was a small fishing village with just a few hotels. But the secret that independent travelers and vacationing Dominicans once guarded leaked out, and the one-kilometer strip of sandy shore began to attract tourists in droves. This emergence of tourism in Sosúa dichotomized the area into two very different neighborhoods, El Batey and Los Charamicos. Abutting the eastern side of the beach is the more popular of the two, El Batey, which is characterized by small hotels, souvenir

and gift shops, manicured gardens, and many excursion companies. On the western end of the beach, Los Charamicos is where the Dominican residents of the area live.

Sosúa's history is unlike that of any other Dominican town. In 1937, Trujillo ordered a massacre of around 20,000 Haitians. His next step was a desperate attempt to clean up his image (not his act) in the eyes of the world. Since World War II was underway, Trujillo offered political asylum to Jewish refugees escaping Hitler's Nazi Germany. Thus, in 1939,

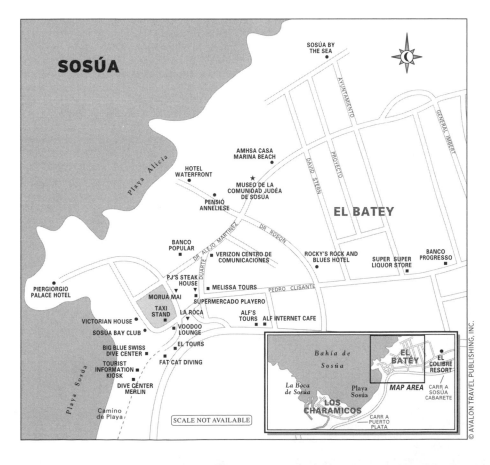

Sosúa was founded by nearly 600 European Jewish immigrants. While some of the Jewish families integrated and stayed in the Dominican Republic, many of them left. About 20 families remain in Sosúa today, and the legacy of their relatives still lives on in the community. A strong dairy and cured meat industry was formed when the first refugees came during WWII. And the synagogue that was built still holds services.

SIGHTS
Museo de la Comunidad Judía de Sosúa

The **Jewish Community Museum of Sosúa** (Calle Dr. Alejo Martínez, tel. 809/571-1386, 9 A.M.–1 P.M. and 2–4 P.M., US$2.50) stands next to the synagogue of Sosúa. Inside you'll see exhibits on the story of the Jewish immigration and influence on the Dominican Republic. Trujillo had hoped that by inviting the Jewish families to immigrate and work on a plantation (few were actually farmers) he could convince the world he was not the anti-Semitic, ruthless dictator he truly was. Trujillo was a self-promoter and the act was simply a marketing ploy. Few Jewish families stayed more than a few years, but in the time that they were here they began a successful meat and dairy industry that survives to this day and is collectively referred to as Productos Sosúa. It is known to be the finest in the country. In the museum you'll see a chronology of the lives of the Jewish settlers during their time in the Dominican Republic. It is a well-maintained museum whose signs are in English and Spanish and is worth a stop to learn about the unique history of Sosúa.

Playa Sosúa

Playa Sosúa is the main beach; it lies in the middle of the two neighborhoods (El Batey and Los Charamicos). The beach's tawny, fine sand is the point where the two worlds combine. Dominicans from Los Charamicos and the tourists from El Batey come together, making for a rather crowded beach. This public space is lined with restaurants, vendors, bars,

food vendors on Playa Sosúa

and excursion desks, all vying for the attention of the tourists. It's a busy place. You can rent beach loungers for US$1.70.

Playa Alicia

To the east of Playa Sosúa is a smaller and definitely less crowded beach called Playa Alicia, most commonly referred to as Playita (Little Beach). It is at the end of Calle Dr. Rosen by the Hotel Sosúa by the Sea, and a staircase leads down the rocky cliff. Since it's harder to get to, you won't find (as many) vendors of trinkets, food, or drink, but you'll find peace and quiet compared to the overly populated Playa Sosúa.

ENTERTAINMENT AND EVENTS
Bars

Easy-going **Rocky's Rock and Blues Bar and Hotel** (Calle Dr. Rosen 22, El Batey, tel. 809/571-2951, 7 A.M.–4 A.M.) admittedly caters to expats and tourists, but it is popular with locals as well. You can grab an ice-cold Presidente or try a Mamajuana shooter to some rock and blues music (obviously). The Canadian-American menu has dishes like fried chicken and homemade pies.

At **Voodoo Lounge** (Pedro Clisante, tel. 809/571-3559, www.voodooloungeonline .com, 1 P.M.–1 A.M.), a cool expat-owned bar, you can listen to live music (Fridays), do a little dancing, or belt out a tune during karaoke (Sundays) in the bar, which is located on the first floor. Upstairs, you can settle down for a drink in the lounge. There's an amazing all-day happy "hour" that lasts from 1 P.M. to 8:30 P.M. The international clientele is friendly.

PJ's Steak House (Calle Pedro Clisante, tel. 809/571-2091, 7:30 A.M.–midnight) is at the corner of Clisante and Duarte. Here you find a gaggle of expats, tourists, and locals enjoying juicy burgers and drinking at night and then, moving a little slower than the night before, having a hearty breakfast at the same joint in the morning. Outdoor seating makes it a great people-watching place, too.

Dominican Republic Jazz Festival

Even though the country is world-renowned for its merengue music, this festival (www .drjazzfestival.com) attracts some of the brightest performers of jazz from all over the world. Concerts are held at the end of every October in Sosúa, Cabarete, and Puerto Plata.

SHOPPING

There are many trinket shops in Sosúa, but for a nice art shop go to **Viva** (Calle Dr. Alejo Martínez, tel. 809/571-2581). It has a wonderful selection of local art and Dominican paintings. It is a good place to buy a traditional Dominican craft gift for someone back home.

Patrick's Silversmithy (Calle Pedro Clisante 3, tel. 809/571-2121) has interesting larimar, amber, and coral jewelry pieces that are affordable and unique.

Shopping along **Playa Sosúa,** you'll be able to find all the regular trinkets in a long line of booths. Haggle your head off for T-shirts, sunglasses, jewelry, and paintings and you'll hopefully get a good deal. Shopping like this might get a little tiresome, being hounded by all the hawkers trying to get you to buy their look-a-like wares, but it is an adventure, and you don't have to leave the beach.

SPORTS AND RECREATION
Diving and Snorkeling

Sosúa is considered one of the premium dive sites along La Costa Ámbar. With the quality comes the popularity and therefore your choices are immense. Numerous dive shops exist, and most are along the Calle Arzeno where it meets the beach entrance.

There are many interesting and exciting dive locations near Sosúa, including Zíngara Wreck, which now acts as an artificial reef; Paradise Island; Coral Gardens and Coral Wall with their varied soft and large types of coral; and Airport Wall with depths of up to 35 meters containing tunnels.

Dives vary between companies but usually start around US$35 for a one-tank dive. Dive packages are always a way to ensure saving money if you plan to go more than once.

Snorkeling is a lower-cost alternative with some excursions as low as US$10. Prices usually include equipment and are always subject to how much equipment you need and how many locations or tanks you choose. All of the dive outfitters offer certification courses and special excursions. One piece of advice: Find one that speaks your language of choice.

Near the entrance to Sosúa beach, **Fat Cat Diving** (tel. 809/222-3456, www.fatcat-diving.com, 9 A.M.–5 P.M. daily) has great deals on courses for beginners and advanced divers. The regular dive site is just offshore and costs US$35 for a one-tank dive. The more tanks you purchase, the more you save per dive. Fat Cat offers many excursions. If you have multiple skill levels in your party, an all-day excursion to Cayo Arena is an excellent choice. It runs US$35 if you are only going to snorkel, US$75 if you choose to dive there. For advanced divers only, there is a dive at the freshwater cave near Cabarete, Cave Du-Du. Here you pay US$95 and you get lunch, transportation, and beverages. Snorkeling with Fat Cat is the most cost effective. For only US$10 they will take you out to the reefs, and that includes the gear you'll need. Transportation from your accommodations at Playa Dorada and Cabarete are possible for extra cost. Victoria, the head instructor, is very nice and speaks English and German fluently.

Located on the same street are **Big Blue Swiss Dive Center** (tel. 809/571-2916, 9 A.M.–5 P.M. daily) and **Dive Center Merlin** (tel. 809/571-4309, 9 A.M.–5 P.M. daily), offering similar packages and courses.

Tours and Excursions

There are many tour and excursion companies in Sosúa. Do a little shopping around and ask a lot of questions about what you'll get for your money. Many tour operators offer local excursions as well as ones that take you as far away as the mountains of the Cordillera Central or the capital city. It is important to find out how long the trip will take including transportation and activity time at your destination. Choose a different company if the other allows you more

or less time (whichever you prefer) at your destination.

As you enter Playa Sosúa, there is a **tourist information kiosk** (tel. 809/571-1868, cell 809/223-5068) that offers glass-bottom boat excursions that take you for a 40-minute tour of Sosúa Bay to show you the colorful and varied coral formations and sea life for which Sosúa Bay is famous (US$12). Tours leave every 45 minutes. The kiosk offers many other excursions.

Melissa Tours (Calle Duarte 2, tel. 809/571-2567, 8 A.M.–5:30 P.M. Mon.–Fri., 8 A.M.–noon Sat.) is a locally owned tour company that offers excursions and tours to various places throughout the country, such as Samaná (US$30), and even one to Haiti (US$65).

El Tours (Calle Dr. Alejo Martínez at Calle Duarte, tel. 809/571-4195, 9 A.M.–5 P.M. Mon.–Fri., 9 A.M.–1 P.M. Sat.) has been offering adventure tours like horseback riding and river rafting since 1999.

Alf's Tours (Calle Padre Clisante 12, tel. 809/571-1013, www.alftour.com, 9 A.M.–6 P.M.) has many trips to choose from, including one all the way to Santo Domingo for US$49. It's next to an Internet café owned by the same company.

ACCOMMODATIONS

Even though Sosúa is very popular, it is still an affordable vacation destination offering both budget and luxurious accommodation options. There are only a few all-inclusive hotels in town and even those are considerably smaller when compared their counterparts in other areas of the country, adding a more personal feel to the facilities.

US$50 and Under

Rocky's Rock and Blues Bar and Hotel (Calle Dr. Rosen 22, tel. 809/571-2951, www.rockysbar.com, US$22/night) is comfortable but not fancy by any stretch. This five-room, Canadian-owned hotel offers private bathrooms, TV in each room, wireless Internet throughout, and 24-hour electricity, and is adjacent to the bar and restaurant, which is quite a popular hangout with expats, locals, and tourists. That said, don't count on it being very quiet. Rocky's also rents condos starting at US$180 per week in a building with a pool, laundry, and maid service. It's a great value with either choice.

Dutch-owned **El Colibrí Resort** (Calle Pedro Clisante 141, tel. 809/571-1847, www.elcolibri.net, US$25 d w/fan only) has very clean and modest rooms. Air-conditioning costs extra, as does a view of the pool, which is a good idea since there is a sliding glass door to the patio that aids air circulation. Although it is showing its age a bit, there is a nice pool with the restaurant right next to it, a laundry, and maid service, and it offers airport transfers. English, German, and Dutch are spoken.

Pensión Anneliese (Dr. Rosen, tel. 809/571-2208, US$25–40) is right near the better, less crowded beach in Sosúa. The rooms are clean and have a small refrigerator and private bath, and there's a pool. It's nothing too special, but the short walk to the beach could make up for it.

◀ Hotel Waterfront (Calle Dr. Rosen, tel. 809/571-2670, www.hotelwaterfrontdr.com, US$40 d), on a six-meter cliff facing the Atlantic Ocean, offers comfort in a simple way. Yes, the 27 rooms are a little plain, but the view from the pool, restaurant (one of the best in town), and patio will all quickly win you over. All rooms have a terrace or balcony looking out over the lush tropical gardens. Cabanas are also available. The hotel is in front of Sosúa's best beach, Playa Alicia. If you don't like the limitations of all-inclusives, this hotel is a good match.

US$50-100

Piergiorgio Palace Hotel (Calle La Puntilla, tel. 809/571-2215, fax 809/571-2786, US$95 d in high season), in a quiet neighborhood and atop dramatic cliffs overlooking the ocean, has some of the best views in Sosúa. The building is of a Victorian style, and rooms are spacious with good light, private bath, and balcony. They're kept very clean and are reasonably comfortable despite the darn chintzy decor. Of

course, you could make up for the decor by insisting on an ocean view room. The hotel is a little aged but is a good choice for that view, a very romantic setting especially at sunset, and a good restaurant. Staff can help you arrange excursions and activities. There's no beach at this hotel, but steps lead you down to the rocks where you can snorkel. Rates include breakfast. Did we mention the view?

Sosúa by the Sea (Calle B Phillips, tel. 809/571-3222, www.sosuabythesea.com, US$70 d) is on a beautiful stretch of beach with magnificent views, just a short walk from town. The hotel is small enough that it doesn't feel like you're just a number. The rooms are clean and comfortable. Facilities include a restaurant, two bars, and a good-sized pool.

US$100 and up

One of Sosúa's nicest hotels, **Sosúa Bay Club** (Calle Pedro Clisante, tel. 809/571-4000, US$145–210) offers optimum service and accommodations with a killer view of Sosúa Bay. This resort can rival the Playa Dorada all-inclusives in that the rooms are just as comfortable and plush. On the cliffs overlooking the bay, two pools are built on two different levels of terraces with ample space and loungers in which to sun yourself. Beach access is limited, so instead a ladder leads from the wooden deck down to the clear teal water, a unique and strikingly beautiful solution.

◀ Victorian House (Calle Pedro Clisante, tel. 809/571-4000, fax 809/571-4545, www.starzresorts.com, US$309 d) is adjacent to the Sosúa Bay Club and run by the same parent company, Starz Resorts. The difference is that this one is considered in its "Boutique Collection" and is therefore much more lavish and expensive. Perched high on the cliffs overlooking Sosúa Bay, this hotel is constructed to mimic the Caribbean plantation-style home from the outside. The rooms are luxuriously decorated compared to other all-inclusives. Also available are split-level penthouses in case you didn't feel pampered enough.

AMHSA Casa Marina Beach (Calle Dr. Alejo Martínez, tel. 809/571-3635, www.amhsamarina.com, US$120 d) is on Playa Alicia, one of its only positive aspects—not that anything is particularly bad, just not striking. It offers the same things that most all-inclusives do. Standard rooms are equipped with two beds, air-conditioning, TV, telephone, private bath, and garden, pool, or ocean views. It is comfortable and clean and a good value if you plan on dining in the hotel most nights. Cuisine is Creole and international.

FOOD

Many of the restaurants can be found on Calle Pedro Clisante and are quite varied. **La Roca** (Calle Pedro Clisante, tel. 809/571-3893, US$7–12) serves fresh seafood that is quite good. If you like barbecue, you'll enjoy the Friday all-you-can-eat special for US$8, or try one of the shrimp dishes sold by the pound, sandwiches, pastas, or select Mexican dishes. There's both indoor and outdoor seating on a patio.

La Puntilla de Piergiorgio (Calle La Puntilla, tel. 809/571-2215, noon–midnight, US$9–15), the restaurant on the roomy, multi-leveled terraces of the Hotel Piergiorgio, cooks up Italian cuisine. Under the stars and high above the Atlantic, you will enjoy such dishes as freshly caught fish, cannelloni, steak in peppercorn sauce, and wood-fired pizzas. The food is good, but the view is amazing. It is a powerfully romantic place at sunset with the orange, red, and yellow sky burning over the immense ocean. Exercise caution when choosing your dining partner—you might be engaged to each other by dessert.

Piergiorgio doesn't have the market cornered on sunset dinners. **On the Waterfront** (Calle Dr. Rosen 1, tel. 809/571-3024, 7 A.M.– 10 P.M., US$4–20) does it very well and with even better food. Popular dishes include filet of sole in orange sauce, sea bass meunière, conch, or a hefty filet mignon flambéed in pepper sauce. The ambience (aside from the sunset) is casual elegance under an open-beam thatched roof and open to the breeze.

One of the more expensive places to dine in Sosúa is **Morua Mai** (Calle Pedro Clisante, tel. 809/571-2966, 8 A.M.–midnight, US$7–17). The international cuisine includes steaks, seafood, and pork. Try the linguini with clams in a white wine sauce or the generous seafood paella, and real homemade cheesecake or the "anything flambéed" for dessert. Dine inside with white tablecloths or out on the sidewalk café under the palm trees. Morua Mai has a nice collection of wines, cigars, and cocktails, too.

Supermercado Playero (Calle Pedro Clisante, tel. 809/571-1532, 8 A.M.–10 P.M.) offers a good selection of necessities and is centrally located near Calle Duarte.

At **Super Super Liquor Store** (Calle Pedro Clisante, 8 A.M.–8 P.M. Mon.–Sat.) you'll find the requisite Brugal and Presidente, some wine, and cigars, but not a huge selection.

INFORMATION AND SERVICES

Near the intersection of Calles Duarte and Pedro Clisante you'll most likely find every-

La Puntilla de Piergiorgio

© ANA CHAVIER CAAMAÑO

thing you need. It is the main commercial sector of El Batey.

Health and Emergencies
On the road to Cabarete, **Centro Médico Bella Vista** (Carretera Sosúa–Cabarete, tel. 809/571-3429, 24 hours) is the best place to go for medical attention. For emergencies, though, dial 911 like you would in the United States. **Farmacia Sosúa** (Calle Pedro Clisante 10, tel. 809/571-2350, 8 A.M.–9 P.M. Mon.–Fri., 8 A.M.–8 P.M. Sat.) is conveniently located near the supermarkets and other storefronts, offering a good selection.

Money
Banking options are **Banco Popular** (Calle Dr. Alejo Martinez, tel. 809/571-2555, 8:15 A.M.–4 P.M. Mon.–Fri., 9 A.M.–1 P.M. Sat.) and **Banco Progreso** (Calle Pedro Clisante, tel. 809/571-2815, 8:30 A.M.–4 P.M. Mon.–Fri., 9 A.M.–1 P.M. Sat.).

Communications
ALF Internet Cafe (Calle Pedro Clisante 12, tel. 809/571-1013, www.alftour.com, 9 A.M.–10 P.M. daily) is run by a tour agency that is right next door. Rates are US$0.75 per minute and US$2.25 per hour.

At **Verizon Centro de Comunicaciones** (Calle Duarte, tel. 809/571-2001, 8 A.M.–10 P.M. daily) you can make a call to the U.S. for US$0.32 per minute and to Europe for US$0.75 per minute.

GETTING THERE
Most people fly in to Puerto Plata (Aeropuerto Internacional Gregorio Luperón) and then take a cab, *guagua,* or hotel shuttle to their accommodations in Sosúa. Expect to pay around US$20 for a cab and US$1 for a *guagua.*

Caribe Tours (Carretera a Puerto Plata, tel. 809/571-3808) is in the Los Charamicos neighborhood. From Sosúa you can catch a bus to Santo Domingo (US$5.70) leaving every hour 5:15 A.M.–5:20 P.M.

GETTING AROUND
Walking is easiest in Sosúa. If you need a ride to some further away spots, you can either flag down a *motoconcho* (US$3 on average) or catch a taxi at the taxi stand (tel. 809/571-3027) on Calle Pedro Clisante at Calle Dr. Rosen.

Puerto Plata and Playa Dorada

Named Puerto Plata in 1493 by Columbus because of the way the sun shone on the water, creating the illusion of a mass of silver coins *(plata),* this port was originally used as a stopover for ships carrying loads of silver on their way to Spain from Mexico. But of course in those days, where there were riches, there were pirates. Things got so bad that the Spanish crown insisted that the port be abandoned, only to revisit and move in again 100 years later. The town remained a trading port until it built up its tourism industry beginning in the 1960s. The area experienced its most lu-

crative years in the 1990s when the economy swelled from the revenue that tourism created, far surpassing the tobacco, sugar, and cattle industries that had sustained it for so long. However, with the more recent birth of a lucrative tourism industry in the southeast of the country, the economy here is once again slightly declining.

Even though the name Puerto Plata and the term all-inclusive are still synonymous, the real seedbed of the resort scene in the area is east of Puerto Plata on Playa Dorada. Long stretches of golden sand lure tourists to these

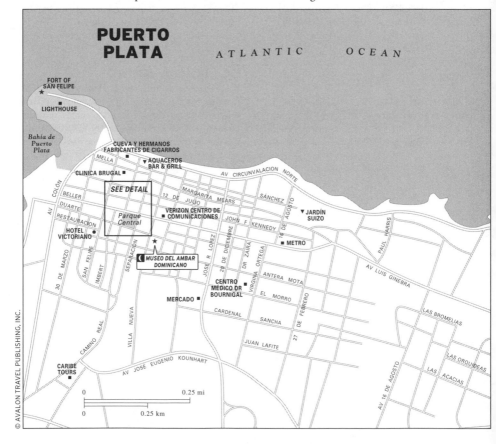

worry-free sanctuaries where all their needs are met in one place.

Aside from the beautiful beach here, Puerto Plata's charming town square lined with restored Victorian homes offers plenty of reasons to wander outside of the resort complex. The town features two reputable amber museums, a colonial fortress, and a cable-car ride up the verdant and plush mountainside of Pico Isabel de Torres. Puerto Plata also presents an annual jazz festival and Carnaval celebration.

SIGHTS

Finding sights in Puerto Plata is easy if you remember certain streets for directional pur-

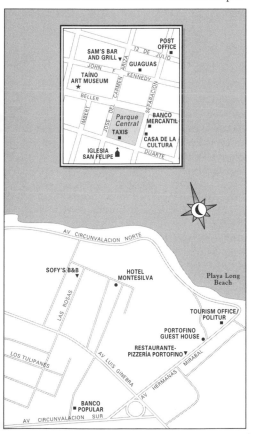

poses if you're walking or driving around on your own. Puerto Plata's **Malecón** (the street that runs along the sea) is called Avenida Circunvalación Norte and Avenida General Luperón as it gets closer to the end where it meets up with the Fuerte San Felipe. Six blocks to the southwest (inland) is the **Parque Central** (actually called Parque Independencia), which is sandwiched between Calle José del Carmen Ariza and Calle Separación. A main street to keep in mind is **Avenida Beller.** It is the road immediately to the north of the Parque Central and runs east–west. Following Avenida Beller to the east will take you toward Playa Dorada and then the airport.

Playa Dorada is the gated resort complex containing many all-inclusive resorts located 2.5 kilometers east of Puerto Plata.

Museo del Ámbar Dominicano

The Dominican Amber Museum (Calle Duarte 61, tel. 809/586-2848, www.ambermuseum .com, 9 A.M.–6 P.M. Mon.–Sat., US$1.75), in an old Victorian mansion, houses a stunning array of amber pieces; some of them are quite rare. The most celebrated find is that of a 40-centimeter lizard perfectly conserved, dating back 30–40 million years. There are many other impressive pieces in the collection, which is well displayed with good signage and can be described to you personally by a guide in English or Spanish. On the first floor of the mansion is a gift shop that has a gorgeous display of amber jewelry in a variety of price ranges. It's a wonderful place to buy a take-home present.

Galeria de Ámbar

The Amber Gallery (Calle 12 de Julio, tel. 809/586-6467, www.ambercollection.itgo .com, 8:30 A.M.–6 P.M. Mon.–Fri., US$1), not to be eclipsed by its competitor, has an impressive collection of amber pieces, but also adds a very important and educational exhibit of Dominican products. After you've seen the amber, you'll be lead by a guide through rum, sugar, tobacco, coffee, and Taíno artifacts exhibits—an excellent way to learn about the history of these products and the way they have shaped

Dominican culture through the ages. Guides speak English, French, German, and Spanish. Signage is in English and Spanish.

Casa de La Cultura

This **Cultural Center** (Calle Separación, tel. 809/261-2731, 9 A.M.–noon and 3–5 P.M. Mon.–Fri., free), on the first floor of one of the renovated homes that sit around Parque Central, often hosts cultural and literary events as well as exhibitions of Dominican artists.

Iglesia San Felipe

The Iglesia San Felipe (Puerto Plata, Calle Duarte, 8 A.M.–noon Mon.–Sat., 7 A.M.–8 P.M. Sun.) was devastated by Hurricane Georges in 1998. The uniquely two-steepled church is a picturesque sight just off the Parque Central. In 2005 the church finally underwent a face-lift to repair the damage from the storm. In addition, various Puerto Plata families donated beautiful Italian stained-glass windows to further beautify the church.

© ANA CHAVIER CAAMAÑO

Parque Central in Puerto Plata

Museo de Arte Taíno

The Taíno Art Museum (Puerto Plata, Calle Beller, Plaza Arawak, tel. 809/586-7601, free) is an odd little museum that houses *replicas* of Taíno artifacts. To make things weirder, it has incredibly erratic hours of operation, and signage is in Spanish only. This is worthy of a stop only if you are completely enraptured by Taíno history, no matter how inauthentic the exhibit may be. Some reproductions are sold.

Fuerte San Felipe

The Fort of San Felipe (Puerto Plata, Av. Circunvalación, 9 A.M.–5 P.M., US$0.50), unlike the very visible ruins in the Ciudad Colonial of Santo Domingo, is sadly the only remaining structure from Puerto Plata's colonial days. Built between 1564 and 1577 as a line of defense from invasion by sea, for much of its life its hulking walls and deep moat were put to use as a prison instead. Today, it houses a slightly disappointing museum. The building itself is remarkable, but the contents within are rather uneventful. Cannonballs and bayonets make

up a majority of the artifacts. The views of the **Bahía de Puerto Plata** and the Atlantic from on top where a couple of cannons still stand guard and the surrounding grounds are very nice and provide for some attractive photo-ops. Tours are given in English, French, German, and Spanish.

Also on-site is a **lighthouse,** which was built in 1879 and restored a few years ago. It originally employed a unique revolving light and shadow system of illumination, fueled by kerosene. *El faro* was a beacon to ships and a symbol of the then industrial progress of Puerto Plata. An octagonal cupola sits high upon the yellow I-beams but is no longer in service.

Pico Isabel de Torres and Teleférico

Rising nearly 800 meters above Puerto Plata is Isabel de Torres Peak, which Christopher Columbus named for the queen who helped fund his expeditions. You can ride to the top of the mountain via the Teleférico (Camino a los

Dominguez, tel. 809/586-2122, 8 A.M.–5 P.M. Thurs.–Tues., US$10), which you board at the base of the mountain; it takes you up to the flat top and to the Christ the Redeemer statue (a smaller version of the one in Brazil), where you can enjoy a very beautiful view of the Bahía de Puerto Plata and surrounding area. While you're there, amble about in the 13.5-hectare **botanical garden** and its multiple trails. The subtropical vegetation is home to 15 brooks and streams and is especially beautiful in the morning when the sun isn't as hot and the air is cooler.

Brugal Rum Bottling Plant

This bottling plant (Carretera a Playa Dorada, tel. 809/586-2531, 8 A.M.–4 P.M. Mon.–Fri., free) has an important role in the lives of many Dominicans. Rum is ingrained into all social events and festivities and the industry employs many. Its product is one of the few uniformly appreciated and utilized

---

DOMINICAN AMBER: NOT JUST A PRETTY FACE

A substantial amount of the world's amber comes from the Dominican Republic. Formed over millions upon millions of years (we're talking anywhere from 30 to 80 million), Dominican amber is among the most pure and widely sought due to its translucent quality, making it one of the most valuable in the world. In fact, in terms of commercial availability, Dominican amber is second only to that from the Baltic region of Europe.

FORMATION IS A STICKY SITUATION

Amber is a fossilized resin, formed when the sap from trees – produced as a protection against potentially invading insects – was carried away by streams and re-deposited into the earth, polymerizing the substance over millions of years. In the Dominican Republic, this tree was the locust, genus *Hymenaea*. Occasionally, living creatures, like insects, were picked up along the way by the oozing sap, resulting in the fossilization of these animals inside the amber.

Although amber was discovered thousands of years ago, it really only became popular starting in the 1960s. The industry of mining amber can be a dangerous one, as most deposits are found buried deeply in mountains and hillsides.

VALUE: IT'S WHAT'S ON THE OUTSIDE AND INSIDE THAT COUNTS

While amber is not a mineral, it is widely considered to be a gemstone – in fact, it's one of the few non-mineral gemstones allowed to be called such. Even prehistoric people valued it; it is believed that amber was one of the first substances used for ornamentation. To this day, amber is a highly sought jewelry material.

Called amber because of its golden color, the gemstone can come in many different colors ranging from yellow to orange to red, to syrupy brown, to blues and blacks. The more rare the color, the more valuable the stone.

An "inclusion" – the suspension of a tiny fossilized animal in the nugget – also adds value to amber. Though it is quite rare, occasionally the preserved bodies of flies, ants, small termites, or beetles are found embedded in the amber. Most difficult to find, and therefore the most valuable, are inclusions of large spiders, scorpions, and even small frogs and lizards. Contrary to the ideas made popular in the film *Jurassic Park*, mosquitoes, too, are an uncommon find.

JURASSIC PARK: COULD IT REALLY HAPPEN?

Speaking of the rarity of finding a mosquito buried in a nugget of amber, the chance of a real-life Jurassic Park happening is close to zilch, but, well, never say never. It won't be from any mosquito buried in amber found in the Dominican Republic, though, as the fossil resin here is not old enough to contain one that might have fed on a dinosaur.

items bridging a very wide gap between all Dominican walks of life. And yet what could be a potentially very interesting and culturally significant topic and tour instead is a woeful swing and a miss. Upon arrival with throngs of other tourists pouring off of buses, you are led into a standing-room-only theater where you watch a very short film about rum and the Brugal company that fills you with anticipation of what is to come. Then, you are given a few moments to watch the bottling process. And then it's over. It's short and un-

---

RUM

If merengue is the national music and dance of the Dominican Republic, rum is the country's national drink. Dominican rum, or *ron*, is widely considered one of the smoothest, most distinguished rums in the world. More than four million cases of rum are produced in the Dominican Republic each year.

The rum industry has its beginnings in the 18th century, when sugarcane brought over from Africa found a place in the Dominican (and world) market. Sugarcane juice is extracted from the stalks and heated to boiling until it takes on the thicker consistency of syrup. Mixed with water and left to ferment, a rum is born. Of course, with modern technology, the refining processes have become a little more complex. Rum producers in the Dominican Republic are known for their particularly natural processes of distillation, and the liquor is often left to age in imported American white oak kegs.

There are three types of basic rum: light (*blanco*), amber (*amarillo*), and dark (*anejo*). Light rum has the highest alcohol proof and tends to be more popular for use in mixed drinks. Amber rum has been aged for at least a year, during which its distinct flavor develops. Dark rum is the smoothest and is often consumed on its own or on the rocks.

There are many locally produced rums in the Dominican Republic, but the most popular brands are Barceló & Co., Brugal, and Bermúdez.

---

eventful. Afterward, you're given a drink and the opportunity to buy the product and other articles bearing the Brugal insignia.

SPORTS AND RECREATION

All the Playa Dorada resorts offer countless excursions like diving, snorkeling, fishing, and even some farther-reaching tours that will take you all the way to Santo Domingo. It is best to check with the excursion desks at your resort for these options.

The main sporting attraction off the beach is the 18-hole championship, par-72 **Playa Dorada Golf Club** (Playa Dorada, tel. 809/320-3472, www.playadoradagolf.com, 7 A.M.–7 P.M.). Designed by Robert Trent Jones Jr., it wraps around the entire Playa Dorada resort complex and along the coast. Anyone can enjoy the on-site restaurant and bar, golfer or not. Greens fees are US$53 for 9 holes and US$76 for 18 holes. Caddies (US$7 for 9 and US$14 for 18 holes) are obligatory, whereas carts (US$18 for 9 holes and US$24 for 18 holes) are optional. It is best to book your tee time through your resort since many of them offer special rates.

ENTERTAINMENT AND EVENTS
Bars and Dance Clubs

Hemingway's Café (Playa Dorada Plaza, tel. 809/320-2230, noon–2 A.M., US$4–19) is a popular hangout right in the middle of the Playa Dorada resorts. It looks unlike any other venue in the complex, decorated like Papa Hemingway just cleaned out his boathouse, with nautical equipment everywhere. The good variety of food includes bar food favorites like burgers and quesadillas. It's air-conditioned to the max and has a lively atmosphere at night with live rock and karaoke nights.

Mangú (Playa Dorada, tel. 809/320-3800, www.occidentalhotels.com, 8 P.M.–2 A.M., US$5) is a very popular dance club on the grounds of Jack Tar Village. Music is a mix of Latin and international pop. The dance floor starts to crowd between 11 P.M. and midnight. Playing the same mix of music is the **Crazy Moon** (Playa

Dorada, tel. 809/320-3663, 10 A.M.–4 P.M., at the Paradise Beach Resort. It's popular.

Festivals

Festivals are what Dominicans do best. In Puerto Plata three festivals are held annually.

The Cultural Festival is held in the third week of June. It is a celebration of Dominican customs and arts with performances held at the Fuerte de San Felipe of folk music, traditional African dances, salsa, and merengue. Art exhibits are displayed in the Parque Central.

The **Dominican Republic Jazz Festival** (www.drjazzfestival.com) is held annually throughout the entire month of October in Puerto Plata, with performances in area hotels and other venues by many recognizable talents from the international landscape of music as well as from the Dominican Republic.

Perhaps the most beloved festival of all is the **Merengue Festival.** Though the festival is not yet even 10 years old, merengue has been the dance and a way of life in the Dominican Republic for generations. It is the soundtrack to which your vacation will most likely take place. It blares out of car windows, on the corners of *colmados,* on the beaches, or is simply carried through the air on the voices of the Dominicans, who always seem to be singing. The festival is a four-day extravaganza held in the first week of October. The Merengue Festival is celebrated in many locations throughout the country. In Puerto Plata, the entire length of the three-kilometer Malecón (Puerto Plata and Avenida Circunvalación) is shut down to make way for food stalls.

SHOPPING

The **Museo del Ámbar Dominicano** (Puerto Plata, Calle Duarte 61, tel. 809/586-2848, www.ambermuseum.com, 9 A.M.–6 P.M. Mon.–Sat.) has the best selection of amber jewelry on the north coast. There are many unique pieces to choose from, so ask the staff for guidance should you have questions. The shop also has larimar, gold, and silver pieces. And as an added bonus, there is a special section for the purchase of rum and cigars. This is a one-stop shopping experience for many memorable and quality Dominican pieces.

Goods at the **Mercado** (Puerto Plata, Av. Isabel de Torres and Calle 2, 8 A.M.–5 P.M. Mon.–Sat.) are not as plentiful as at the Mercado in Santo Domingo, but it has a great selection of Dominican and Haitian art, the usual trinkets along with fresh produce. The vendors inflate prices expecting that you'll haggle or in the hopes that you'll actually pay them.

If you're a cigar aficionado, you'll love **Cueva y Hermanos Fabricantes de Cigarros** (Puerto Plata, Av. General López, tel. 809/970-0903, 1–6 P.M. Tues.–Sun.). This company's main factory is in Santiago, but this branch has a good assortment of cigars to choose from, all at distributor prices. Ask to sample one if you want to purchase a box. Prices range from about US$5 per cigar to about US$100 per box.

Playa Dorada Plaza (Playa Dorada, tel. 809/320-6645, fax 809/320-4013) is a good bet for anything you might need, services or shopping, in the area. Here you'll find bars and restaurants, jewelry stores, tour operators, Internet access, and gift shops galore. From the main road, take the western entrance into the Playa Dorada complex.

ACCOMMODATIONS
Under US$50

Not many options exist in the area by way of satisfactory low budget accommodations. These moderately priced alternatives could work, though.

Portofino Guest House (Puerto Plata, Av. Hermanas Mirabal 12, tel. 809/586-2858, fax 809/586-5050, US$28 d) has 20 comfortable rooms that are kept very clean and come with a private hot-water bathroom, cable TV, and air-conditioning. The pleasant garden is shady and has a refreshing pool. You are a short walk from the beach.

Hotel Montesilva (Puerto Plata, Calle La Estancia, tel. 809/320-0250, US$35 d) is a good value. It's on a quiet street and offers clean rooms with comfortable beds. All have a private hot-water bathroom, fan, and cable TV. Not all have balconies.

Centrally located **Hotel Victoriano** (Puerto Plata, Calle San Felipe 33 at Restauración, tel. 809/586-9752, US$28 d) gives clean rooms and is within walking distance of many restaurants. It's a backpacker's favorite. Rooms have fan or air-conditioning and cable TV.

$50-100

Viva Wyndham Playa Dorada Resort (Playa Dorada, tel. 809/686-5658, www.vivaresorts.com, US$82–140) is a short but very pretty walk from the beach, and the landscaping overall is especially pretty with a waterfall by the pool. Rooms are spacious and very clean (the entire resort was updated in 2005), and all have nice balconies. While it is a smaller resort, it is one of the nicer and gets rave reviews. Specialty restaurants include Asian and Mediterranean ones that are especially good.

The 386-room **Puerto Plata Village Caribbean Resort** (Playa Dorada, tel. 809/320-4012, www.ppvillage.com, US$94

d) is the furthest resort from the beach. To make up for it, though, a shuttle goes from hotel to beach every 15 minutes and it is only a 5-minute ride. On the sand, in the section set aside for this resort, are a bar and a grill. The resort is done in a faux-Victorian-style design in pastel colors, and the rooms are clean and comfortable. This is a good resort for kids since they have lots of activities and there are two pools. It's a wheelchair-friendly environment. The food is basic but good.

US$100 and Up

The Playa Dorada beach is a very pretty golden sand stretch of heaven. The water tends to get deeper quicker here than on the southern coast of the country and tends to be colder. Children should be monitored.

While beaches in the Dominican Republic are technically public property, resorts do everything they can to try to keep "outsiders" away. All-inclusive guests are tagged with colored plastic bracelets that have their hotel's insignia on them. If you are a nonguest and have

Victorian architecture in Puerto Plata

© ANA CHAVIER CAAMAÑO

somehow found your way onto Playa Dorada, hide your wrist and act normal; it is not uncommon for resorts to employ security guards to patrol the beach.

It is regular all-inclusive practice to have available in a standard room the following amenities: either two double or one king-size bed, air-conditioning, cable TV, telephone, private balcony or terrace, full private hot-water bath, optional safety box (usually at extra cost to you), and often a small refrigerator or minibar. Any variations on the regular theme will be pointed out. Strange hidden cost: Sometimes you have to pay a deposit for a remote control for your television. Make sure to keep your receipt or you will not be given that deposit back.

The resorts usually have a buffet for breakfast, lunch, and dinner, but you have optional specialty restaurants to choose from for dinner. Make sure these are included in your all-inclusive package before you book a reservation (which you have to do at the guest services desk), or you will end up with an unexpected cost at the end of your trip.

Jack Tar Village (Playa Dorada, tel. 809/320-3800, fax 809/320-4161, www.occidentalhotels.com, US$115–140 d) was the first resort to open in Playa Dorada back in 1983 (since then it has been remodeled). It sits directly adjacent to the Playa Dorada golf course, and the beach, which is one of the most well-maintained, is just a few short steps from the pool area. There are two pools, one for adults only that has a waterfall and swim-up bar, and the grounds are lush and beautiful. The standard rooms, dubbed "superior" here, all have a garden or golf course view, but if you opt for the "superior premium" room, you'll be placed closer to the ocean and swimming pools. The Jack Tar Village is home to the Mangú discotheque and a very nice casino. The cuisine at this resort is well known to be some of the best in all of the Playa Dorada resorts.

By far the most luxurious and elegant resort in Playa Dorada **Casa Colonial Beach and Spa** (Playa Dorada, tel. 809/320-2111,

www.vhhr.com, US$350–550 d) is designed in the architectural style of a colonial mansion and decorated with contemporary and colonial accents. Its 50 suites are gloriously chic with marble floors, plush linens, and canopy beds, Amenities include Roman-style tubs and separate showers, high-speed Internet, flat-screen cable TV, bathrobes and slippers, and very good-sized balconies. The spa has 13 treatment rooms, including a couple's treatment room, and pilates and yoga classes. A rooftop infinity pool and four (yes, four) Jacuzzis overlook the Atlantic in a dramatic sweeping panorama. The cuisine is top rate and served in two exquisite dining rooms. The Casa Colonial is not all-inclusive.

FOOD
Puerto Plata
Restaurante-Pizzería Portofino (Calle Hermanas Mirabal 12, tel. 809/261-2423, US$5–12) offers some of the best pizza and pasta in town along with other Italian favorites like eggplant parmesan. Next to the Portofino Guest House, it's a good choice for a casual night out in the open air.

Sofy's Bed and Breakfast (Calle Las Rosas, tel. 809/586-6411, www.popreport .com/sofybb.htm, US$4–8) has three rooms, but it is really the breakfasts that have put it on the map. It's a regular expat rendezvous, for those craving a bit of home—omelets, French toast, and pancakes, all the good stuff. The popularity of this place makes it very busy and there isn't much seating, but it's worth it.

Tex Mex is the specialty at 🆒 **Aquaceros Bar & Grill** (Malecón 32, tel. 809/586-2796, 10 A.M.–2 A.M., US$7–14), but dishes also include fresh barbecued fish, lobster, and burgers. The distinctive Dominican ambience along the Malecón, with the fresh sea breeze and merengue music, makes it a favorite.

Sam's Bar and Grill (Calle José del Carmen Ariza 34, tel. 809/586-7267, 8 A.M.–11 P.M. daily, US$4–12) is an institution with the local expats for dishes like meatloaf, chili, Philly cheesesteaks, pancakes, chicken cordon bleu, and a great many other American diner favorites. You'll often find a sporting event of some kind on the televisions, and it is a lively place for drinks around dinnertime.

Jardín Suizo (Av. Circunvalación 13A, tel. 809/586-9564, 11 A.M.–3 P.M. and 6–11 P.M. Mon.–Sat., US$8–19) is a wonderful place to take in a lunch or dinner and the tropical breeze coming from the ocean. The mainly Dominican and Swiss cuisine is very enjoyable and fresh, although other international dishes appear on the menu as well. Beef stroganoff, chicken curry, pork in mushroom sauce, and pasta are but a few of the varied choices. The view is nice, as is the ambience with checkered-cloth-draped tables and big sliding windows. A particularly good dish is the fish of the day in garlic sauce.

Playa Dorada

Hemingway's Café (Playa Dorada Plaza, tel. 809/320-2230, noon–2 A.M., US$4–19) is a good hangout and a good restaurant. This maritime-decorated bar in the plaza serves mostly American and Mexican food. It's air-conditioned inside with umbrella tables out front for alfresco dining.

Canadian-owned **Café Cito** (Carretera a Playa Dorada, tel. 809/586-7923, www .popreport.com/Cafe_Cito_Web_Page.htm, 10:30 A.M.–midnight daily, US$4–17) is a favorite for expats and a nice respite away from all-inclusive buffet doldrums. Menu items include international items like filet mignon, burgers, nachos, and moussaka. Jazz music and a good cigar can be thoroughly enjoyed on the open-air terrace.

◖ **El Manguito** (Carretera a Playa Dorada, tel. 809/320-1025, US$5–15) serves traditional and outstanding Dominican cuisine with excellent service and gets great reviews. Try a plate of *la bandera dominicana* (chicken, beans, rice, and fried plantains), very fresh seafood, or, if you're feeling adventurous, some tripe stew. From the Iberostar resort, it is about a 10–15 minute walk. It's across the street from Café Cito and hard to see from the road—worth the hunt.

INFORMATION AND SERVICES

When staying in a resort in Playa Dorada, any services you may need can be found at **Playa Dorada Plaza** (tel. 809/320-6645, fax 809/320-4013), which is in the middle of the entire complex. Services include Internet and call center, medical service, pharmacy, and banks.

Health and Emergencies

Fortunately, Puerto Plata has some of the best medical services around. **Clínica Brugal** (Puerto Plata, José del Carmen Ariza 15, tel. 809/586-2519) has 24-hour emergency service and a doctor who speaks English, German, and Spanish. **Centro Médico Dr. Bournigal** (Puerto Plata, Antera Mota, tel. 809/586-2342) is a highly recommended hospital and has a pharmacy (tel. 809/586-8821) on the premises. Staff speak many languages and there is 24-hour service in the clinic.

For pharmaceutical needs, go to **Playa Dorada Farmacia** (Playa Dorada Plaza, tel. 809/320-6226, ext. 2500, 9 A.M.–9 P.M. Mon.–Fri., 9 A.M.–7 P.M. Sat. and Sun.).

The tourism police office, **Politur** (Puerto Plata, Hermanas Mirabal, tel. 809/320-0365), is open 24 hours a day near Long Beach. This agency was set up to help tourists with their concerns.

Communications

For Internet connections in Puerto Plata, your best choice is the air-conditioned **Verizon Centro de Comunicaciones** (Beller at Padre Castellanos, tel. 809/586-4393, 8 A.M.–10 P.M. daily), where you can get online for US$1.70 per hour or make a long-distance call (to the U.S. for US$0.30 per minute).

Internet Flash (Separación and Margarita, 8 A.M.–9 P.M. Mon.–Sat., 10 A.M.–2 P.M. Sun.) has a friendly and knowledgeable staff and good facilities.

Money

Banco Popular (Av. Circunvalación Sur, 9 A.M.–5 P.M. Mon.–Fri., 9 A.M.–1 P.M. Sat.)

is near Avenida Hermanas Mirabal and has an ATM. If you're downtown near the Parque Central, go to the more conveniently located **Banco Mercantil** (Separación, 8:30 A.M.–5 P.M. Mon.–Fri., 9 A.M.–1 P.M. Sat.); it has an ATM as well.

Tourist Information
The **Oficina de Turismo** is above the Politur office on Calle Hermanas Mirabal at the Malecón. The very friendly staff speak English, Spanish, and German and have lots of maps and brochures.

Post Office
The Puerto Plata **post office** (7 A.M.–5 P.M. Mon.–Fri., 7 A.M.–noon Sat.) is on Calle 12 de Julio where it meets Separación, but don't rely on Dominican postal services for communication.

GETTING THERE
By Air
The **Aeropuerto Internacional Gregorio Luperón** (tel. 809/586-0107) is about 18 kilometers east of Puerto Plata and Playa Dorada. A **taxi** to or from the airport to this area costs US$20.

This is the airport that most travelers fly into if they are visiting Cofresí, Maimón, Luperón, Puerto Plata, Playa Dorada, Sosúa, Cabarete, Playa Grande, and Cabrera hotels. Some of the airlines that serve the airport are: **American Eagle** (tel. 800/433-7300), **American Airlines** (tel. 800/200-5151), **Continental** (tel. 809/200-1062), **Air Canada** (tel. 809/541-5151), **Lufthansa** (tel. 809/200-1133), and **Martinair** (tel. 809/200-1200).

By Car
Coming from the south, take Autopista Duarte 1 northward to Via Santiago, then take Exit 5 to the right, which is the route to Puerto Plata.

Driving from the east simply take the coastal and very scenic Highway 5, which runs all the way from Las Galeras on the Península de Samaná to Puerto Plata and then curves south.

By Bus
Caribe Tours (Puerto Plata, Camino Real at Eugenio Kunhardt, tel. 809/586-4544) has service to Santo Domingo (US$7) with stops in Santiago (US$2.50) and La Vega (US$3.15). A bus leaves every hour for the four-hour ride from Puerto Plata to Santo Domingo.

Metro (Calle 16 de Agosto, tel. 809/586-6061) offers service to Santo Domingo (US$7.50), and with just one stop in Santiago (US$2.65), you'll shave half an hour off your travel time. Buses leave at 11 A.M., 2 P.M., 4 P.M., and 6:30 P.M.

Guaguas are low-budget option. Eastbound ones line up on the northern end of the Parque Central; they'll stop at the gate to Playa Dorada and then onward along Highway 5 with stops in Sosúa, Cabarete, and finally Río San Juan. If you're heading to Nagua you'll have to transfer and then in Nagua transfer again for Samaná. You can be dropped off anywhere and flag them down anywhere. It really is a very efficient mode of transportation.

GETTING AROUND
Car Rental
Should you choose to rent a car to do some exploration on your own, you can find them via kiosks in the airport, along the highway between Playa Dorada and Puerto Plata, or along the Malecón in Puerto Plata. Rates start around US$50 a day and of course depend on the type of car you get. You can also ask your hotel's front desk if they can help you secure one.

Companies include **Avis** (Carretera a Puerto Plata, tel. 809/586-4426, www.avis.com; at the airport, tel. 809/586-7007; Playa Dorada Plaza, tel. 809/320-4888), **Budget** (tel. 809/586-0214 or 800/527-0700, www.budget.com), and **Hertz** (tel. 809/586-0200 or 800/654-3001, www.hertz.com). All have offices at the airport.

Taxis
Beware the inflated tourist price. Cabs are not metered here, and if you don't speak any Spanish and don't agree on a price before

you get in, you'll get taken for a ride in more ways than one. A good rule to go with is, just don't pay more than US$10 to go a distance that is about the length of Playa Dorada to Cofresí. You can find taxis around Parque Central. If you need a taxi for a two-way trip, consider reserving the driver to return and pick you up at an agreed upon time for the return.

Motoconchos

This is your cheapest option by far. You can expect to pay about US$1 for a short ride. But be mindful that these are not safe by any means. Consider other forms of transportation.

Costambar and Playa Cofresí

Adjacent to Puerto Plata are the two very small communities of Costambar and Cofresí. Costambar is an open beach protected by coral reefs abundant with almond trees, very pretty and way less tourist-ridden than Playa Dorada. For the most part, Costambar consists of timeshares, villas, townhouses, and not much else.

Playa Cofresí, five kilometers from Costambar, is not much different. Although the beach isn't as pretty as that of Costambar or Playa Dorada, it does have a couple of resorts and many villas and homes. It is also home to the large and very commercial **Ocean World** (Playa Cofresí, tel. 809/291-1000, fax 809/291-2255, 9 A.M.–6 P.M. daily, ages 13 and up US$55, ages 4–12 US$40, under 4 free). You can snorkel in a tank with tropical fish and a faux (although done quite well) coral reef, visit two aviaries with native and nonnative species of tropical birds, swim in the same pool as a tiger (with a glass wall partition), and view stingray and shark feedings. But for additional cost, you can take a step closer to interact with some of the animals. Swim with the dolphins (US$125 per person), have a dolphin "encounter" that involves getting "kisses" and "dancing" with our frisky friends (US$100 per person), enjoy a sea lion encounter (US$80) or a shark or manta ray encounter (US$55 per person). Also on-site are lockers for your personal belongings, a restaurant, and a big Ocean World souvenir shop, of course. You can arrange for pick-up and drop-off from your hotel; don't forget your sunscreen. Reservations (3–6 months in advance) are necessary for the special programs, especially the dolphin swim. Kids who love animals have a lot of fun at Ocean World.

ACCOMMODATIONS

For a regular hotel, stay in Cofresí. Costambar is made up of short-term rentals, condos, and time shares (see the sidebar *Villa Rentals*).

Sun Village Beach Resort (Playa Cofresí, tel. 809/970-3364, US$120 d) offers standard and deluxe rooms, suites in varying sizes, and villas. There are eight bars (two are swim-up), a spa, nighttime entertainment, activities for kids, and lots of activities for adults. The standard rooms are typical of all-inclusives: clean, roomy, and comfortable. The resort is not actually on the beach.

Lifestyle Hacienda Villas and Beach Resorts (Playa Cofresí, tel. 809/970-7777, fax 809/970-7100, US$90–120 d) is a complex of three all-inclusive hotels: the Hacienda Tropical, Hacienda Garden, and Hacienda Suite. All have spacious rooms with balconies. The decor is showing a bit of age. The Hacienda Tropical is a four-star accommodation done in Mediterranean style while the other two are considered three-star hotels. None is directly on the beach, although there is easy access. The Sun Village is a better value.

FOOD

The open-air thatched-roof seaside restaurant **Chris and Mady's** (Playa Cofresí, tel.

809/970-7502, chrismadys@yahoo.com, US$6–20) is a popular hangout. Seafood is the best thing going here—it's super fresh and cheap. There are sandwiches and a good selection of international options. There's a 3.5-meter big-screen TV on which they show major sporting events. If you're there in March, they celebrate St. Paddy's Day the right way, with green beer and everything.

Austrian-owned **Restaurant Los Dos** (Cofresí, tel. 809/970-7638, 8 A.M.–11 P.M. Mon.–Sat., US$9–15) serves Austrian and international specialties like weinerschnitzel and barbecue. Sometimes it has special menu nights like Greek Night. It's a casual atmosphere and very friendly environment.

Right across the way from Restaurant Los Dos is **Le Pappillon** (8 A.M.–11 P.M. daily, tel. 809/970-7640, US$12–25), which is slightly more pricey. Fresh seafood is a specialty but it also serves steaks and even a couple of vegetarian entrées.

Jenny's Market (Costambar, Calle Principal, tel. 809/970-3028, 8 A.M.–9:30 P.M.) is a good place to get your supplies if you're doing a short-term rental. It has a delivery service and an Internet café adjacent to the market.

INFORMATION AND SERVICES

There's no need to go all the way to Puerto Plata, although the services are better there; the two big resorts here have medical services in each. **Sun Village** (tel. 809/970-7518) and **Hacienda Resorts** (tel. 809/586-1227) have 24-hour emergency clinics and multilingual staffs; the latter has a pharmacy as well.

The **Farmacia de los Trópicos** (Cost-ambar, Calle Central, tel. 809/970-7607, 8:30 A.M.–7:30 P.M. Mon.–Sat.) has a full array of medications.

For Internet services check out **Dot Com Internet Café** (Costambar, Calle 12 de Julio, tel. 809/261-6165, 8:30 A.M.–9 P.M. daily). **Jenny's Cyber Café** (Costambar, Calle Central, tel. 809/970-3028, 9:30 A.M.–12:30 A.M. daily) is a great find because not only can you get on the Internet, you can order Mexican food and other favorites. Jenny's Market is directly adjacent.

Costambar Rent Car (Costambar, Calle Central 2, tel. 809/970-7005, cell 809/757-3744) not only rents cars but also is the only place to get cash in town. It's right across from Jenny's Market.

GETTING THERE AND AROUND

To get to this area from Puerto Plata a taxi will cost US$5–7. Agree on the price before getting in. Unfortunately, *guaguas* don't go to either Costambar and Playa Cofresí. They exit onto the highway toward Santiago before Costambar. Once there, walking is the best option for getting around within the villages themselves. To go to a neighboring community, you'll need a *motoconcho* or taxi.

Car Rental

Within Costambar or Cofresí, you won't need a car, but to get out beyond town limits you might want to rent one. **Costambar Rent Car** (Costambar, Calle Central 2, tel. 809/970-7005, cell 809/757-3744, 8 A.M.–6 P.M. Mon.–Sat., 8 A.M.–10 P.M. Sun.) rents regular and four-wheel-drive vehicles.

West of Puerto Plata

As La Costa de Ámbar stretches past Puerto Plata to the west, the concentration of tourist areas and visitors declines enormously. It is partially because of the popularity of the all-inclusive resort vacationing trend that keeps them grounded in Playa Dorada, partially because there is a lot to do east of Puerto Plata, and partially because visitors have not been made aware of the offerings of the western half of La Costa Ámbar. Those who do venture over visit a few select places for a short amount of time, perhaps on a guided tour for the day with a tour package from their all-inclusive resort.

Whatever the case may be, it is well worth the effort to check out this half of La Costa Ámbar. Whether it is to check out the beautiful beach at Luperón, do some world-class diving in Monte Cristi, go canyoning in Damajagua, or go to the Haitian market in the border town Dajabón, excitement and individuality await but crowds and mass tourism do not.

DAMAJAGUA

In the forested hills near the town of Imbert about 22 kilometers southwest of Puerto Plata, 27 waterfalls (some as high as 15 meters) connect through a series of canyons, tunnels, caves, and natural pools. In this area you can take heart-pumping leaps off cliffs, slip and slide through naturally formed water slides, and dunk into waterfall pools. The hike to get to these waterfalls can be demanding. Visitors interested in seeing this set of cascades should be able to swim and have good upper-body strength. While no technical experience is needed, an experienced guide is necessary for this hike. Many hotels arrange excursions, but the most reputable adventure-tour company in the country, **Iguana Mama** (Cabarete, tel. 809/571-0908, www.iguanamama .com, 8 A.M.–5 P.M. daily, US$60 per person), leads regular trips to Damajagua and will take you as far as the 12th waterfall. Many of the other tour companies will only lead you to the seventh waterfall. Iguana Mamma also provides transportation to the area, breakfast, and lunch.

LUPERÓN

Luperón is a quiet and inviting little town with a lot of expats, yet it's still steeped in traditional Dominican small-town ways. Example: Once when I was there, a road was closed down to traffic and a man was redirecting cars; upon being asked why, the man replied, "because there is a sick woman who lives on this street." Traffic had been prevented from passing her house out of respect for the dying. It is the kind of town that still knows its neighbors and still watches out for one another.

Luperón is on the Bahía de Luperón, which is about 50 kilometers west of Puerto Plata. In this town of 20,000, inhabitants still make their living through fishing. It is well-known for its marina, Marina Puerto Blanca, one of the only safe harbors in the Dominican Republic, where many boats moor themselves in order to stock up on supplies or simply take a break from the sea. Yachts from all over the world stop here because the natural shape of the bay makes it a shelter from hurricanes. Still, there are not a lot of services and, thus, not a lot of tourists despite a rather sizable expat community.

Sights

After discovering La Navidad, Columbus returned to Spain, leaving about 40 of his men in charge of the settlement, thinking that it would all be under control. But upon his return a year later, he found all of his men dead and La Navidad completely obliterated. Columbus then sailed 110 kilometers east and founded a new settlement and named it after Spain's Queen Isabela. The new settlement, La Isabela, would not survive long either. Life was hard on the settlers. Lawlessness became a way of life, hurricanes blew through, and disease ran rampant, all claiming the lives of many. Some simply gave up the search for gold (their main reason for being there in the first place) and returned to Spain. Eventually, anyone remaining gave up entirely and went to the thriving new town, Santo Domingo.

Today, only ruins and a general layout of the original settlement can be seen at **Parque Nacional La Isabela** (8 A.M.–5:30 P.M. daily, US$1.50), which once included Christopher Columbus's original house, a cemetery with both Spanish and Taíno graves, and what is thought to have been the first City Hall of the New World. The archaeological remains used to be more plentiful, but Trujillo asked a local official to "clean up" the area so that he could bring visiting dignitaries to visit. The local official then made a grave mistake by misunderstanding "El Jefe" and had a majority of La Isabela bulldozed and shoved into the water of the Atlantic Ocean, losing copious amounts of archaeological and historical grandeur, not something Trujillo could forgive. It was a mistake that cost the official his life.

Many Dominicans refer to La Isabela, now a national park, as the first settlement of the New World. Perhaps the reason they consider it the "first," practically ignoring that La Navidad even existed, is that more of a community was built in La Isabela. Most importantly, though, the first Catholic mass was said by Fray Bernardo Boil in 1494, thereby blessing the settlement.

A museum houses some artifacts uncovered in the area. The entrance fee affords you a personal guide to take you through the site and the museum. It is customary to tip. Getting to La Isabela is easiest if you drive (just follow Carretera La Isabela from Luperón) or take a taxi. From Luperón, a taxi will cost about US$25.

Templo de Las Américas (7 A.M.–6 P.M. daily, free) was built as a replica of the church where Fray Bernardo Boil said the first mass on January 6, 1494. It was built using some of the rubble from Columbus's first home, the original church, and the first City Hall. On January 6, 1994, a mass was said to commemorate the 500-year anniversary of that historic mass. Inside you'll see pieces of art donated

by every Latin American country and a statue from Genoa, Italy (Columbus's home town), of Columbus praying to the Virgin Mary to protect his sailors.

Recreation

In a bay as popular as Bahía de Luperón, there are bound to be **sailing** opportunities. Unfortunately, it is not quite as prevalent as one might hope. If you go down to the **Marina Puerto Blanco** (tel. 809/299-4096) or any of the restaurants and bars in town, and ask around, you can find someone who is willing to take you out on the water. Prices vary greatly. Agree on a price before committing.

If you thought that beautiful beaches of the north stop at Playa Dorada, you'll be pleasantly surprised to find **Playa Grande,** with its beautiful long stretch of golden sand and blue water. The sea bottom is sandy in spots and rocky in other parts farther offshore. A majority of the beach is lined by an all-inclusive, but beaches are public property by law, and there are a couple of public entrances so you can enjoy it even if you're not staying at the resort. One entrance is next to the **Luperón Beach Resort** and another is marked by a sign along the highway about 700 meters from the resort.

Accommodations

Hotel Dally (27 de Febrero, tel. 809/571-8682, US$18 d), in the middle of Luperón, has clean rooms with fans and hot-water bathrooms. It is right next to Restaurant Letty's.

Luperón Beach Resort (Carretera de Las Américas, tel. 809/571-8303, www.besthotels.es, US$90–125 d) and **Tropical Luperón Beach** (Carretera de Las Américas, tel. 809/571-8303, www.besthotels.es, US$100–150 d) are two spacious resorts next to one another on the same beach. They are very similar in amenities. Accommodations are roomy and comfortable with balconies. Suites have a big seating area. The pool is nice and the beach is long and not overcrowded, with plenty of shady areas. While the food at the regular buffet is good and varied, the food at the beachside grill is substandard. At night there is entertainment either in the pool-side open-air dance floor with live music, or in the amphitheater for shows. All in all, don't expect the luxury accommodations that you'd find elsewhere, but they're a good value.

Food and Nightlife

Captain Steve's Restaurant and Bar (Calle Duarte at 27 de Febrero, US$4–12) serves good pizzas and sells provisions. It's a popular and laid-back thatch-roofed, open-air restaurant popular with the growing expat crowd.

Gina's (Calle Duarte at 27 de Febrero, 11 A.M.–11 P.M. Mon.–Sat., US$4–9) is one of those places that became well known to pleasure-boaters the world over by word of mouth. It serves good bar food like cheeseburgers and nachos and is a favorite of locals and expats alike. Poker nights, pool tournaments, live music, and a four-hour happy "hour" keep regulars and returning visitors coming back.

Mi Sueño (27 de Febrero, 9 A.M.–2 A.M., free) is a lively place to dance to Latin and rock music.

Information and Services

Any services you may need, you're bound to find along Calle Duarte. **Politur** (Calle Duarte, tel. 809/581-8045) is open 24 hours. **BanReservas** (Calle Duarte, 8 A.M.–5 P.M. Mon.–Fri., 9 A.M.–1 P.M. Sat.) is right across the street from the Politur office.

Verizon Centro de Comunicaciones (Calle Duarte, 8 A.M.–10 P.M. Mon.–Sat., 8 A.M.–6 P.M. Sun.) has telephone, fax, and Internet services.

Getting There and Around

Entering Luperón from the south, the highway becomes Calle Duarte, which leads you to Avenida 27 de Febrero; this is the main drag where you'll find Luperón's commercial district. From here, the port is east. To get to Playa Grande and Parque Nacional La Isabela, stay on 27 de Febrero; this will turn into the Carretera de La Isabela, which you will follow for 19 kilometers to reach the national park. Walking is the best option for getting around this small town.

PUNTA RUCIA

Punta Rucia is a small fishing village that is a very quiet place, no raucous party-town here. But when the tour groups come, they descend in droves. Most people who visit here do so on a day excursion from any number of all-inclusive resorts along La Costa Ámbar to visit Cayo Arena. There are no services in Punta Rucia, so if you plan on staying a night or so, come very prepared.

🄲 Cayo Arena

Cayo Arena is a beautiful sandbar 10 kilometers into the middle of the Atlantic off the coast of Punta Rucia. It's often called **Paradise Island** by tour guides, and it is easy to understand why. Ultra-white sand gently slopes into the mind-bendingly clear turquoise water, where snorkeling and diving are exceptional because of the coral reefs. It is difficult to say how big the "island" is because it shrinks and expands depending on the season and the ocean's currents. On the island there are small food shacks and that's it—there is no room for anything else. In fact, tour operators have to alternate times to be there in order to have enough space on the island for their guests. If you're an independent traveler and you speak Spanish, ask around Punta Rucia or talk with the fishermen to see if anyone else can take you. Perhaps you can beat the mad rush.

Accommodations, Food, and Tours

Cayo Arena Tours (Punta Rucia, tel. 890/656-0020, www.cayoarenatours.com) offers rooms, excursions, and a restaurant. A trip to Cayo Arena (US$30) leaving in the morning and returning around 1 P.M. includes drinks while there and a buffet lunch after you're back on the main island. A catamaran trip (US$45) includes a snorkel stop. The room rental costs US$30 per room, with two beds and a private bath (cold). Don't expect a lot of bells and whistles, just the very basics. A beachfront restaurant and bar serves decent food.

El Paraío Tours (tel. 809/612-8499, www.cayoparaiso.com) offers rooms, a restaurant, and excursions as well, and strangely, it is right next door to Cayo Arena Tours. A speedboat adventure (US$30) will take you to Cayo Arena for snorkeling and through mangroves to see a completely different environment. But the luxurious VIP yacht tour is the crème de la crème. Cruising along the coast like a movie star, you'll visit La Isabela, share a snack of oysters and champagne, go for a swim at Punta Rucia with lunch served on the beach, then head out to Cayo Arena for an afternoon of snorkeling and return through the mangroves, all for US$145. Rooms with El Paraío are US$30.

Both companies give very good discounts for tours if you are renting rooms with them, and both companies' rooms are in the same apartment-style complex and are therefore the same in caliber. They are at the beach right next to one another. So if one is booked up, just walk next door.

Getting There and Around

Since there is no bus service of any kind to this area the only way to get here independently is by driving. Highway 1 is the best route to travel north from Villa Elisa. Since you'll have a car, you can either drive around or walk. Walking is so much easier in this small village.

MONTE CRISTI

Monte Cristi is about 135 kilometers west of Puerto Plata and is the capital of the arid and desert-like province of the same name. There isn't a lot of tourism here, but those who do come enjoy beaches and wonderful diving. It is said that the surrounding waters have about 180 sunken galleons whose treasures still quietly rest in the sea. Others come to see the Parque Nacional Monte Cristi and its subtropical dry forest, its lagoons, and the 274-meter-high mesa. Off the coast is a collection of islands where sea turtles lay their eggs. Most of the residents of Monte Cristi still make their living farming the land, fishing, or from the salt flats in the north.

The town was founded in the early part of the 16th century and for many years was an important trading port for cattle and manufactured goods. But in 1606, the Spanish crown ordered the northwest corner of the country to be evacuated and moved to Santo Domingo, when it had become clear that pirates were gaining control of trading with the colonists after having bullied the Spanish galleons from the shores.

And for 150 years, Monte Cristi was a ghost town. That is, until the French began moving into the territory. Concerned about losing control of the land, the Spanish moved 100 farming families from the Canary Islands and settled them into the area. Once again, it became an important port with its perfect positioning at

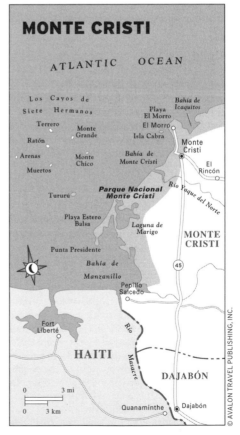

the mouth of the Yaque del Norte river basin. Timber and tobacco were floated down from such towns as Santiago and La Vega to be exported from Monte Cristi. The timber industry began to attract Europeans, who settled the area, and the economy flourished.

But the prosperous time came to an end when, in 1860, the four-year Restoration War, in which the Dominicans fought the Spanish for their independence, ruined the city. But the European influence was still present as they rebuilt in their Victorian architecture, some of which survives to this day.

On Avenida Mella is the former house where Máximo Gómez (Cuban military commander) and José Martí (leader of the Cuban independence movement) signed the Montecristi Manifesto for Cuba's independence on March 25, 1895.

Sights

The town of Monte Cristi is hugged on three sides by the **Parque Nacional Monte Cristi,** which is made up of lagoons on either side of the town, beaches, a cluster of islands called Los Cayos de los Siete Hermanos, and one hill (El Morro) rising 239 meters above sea level and shaped like a camel's back. Living in the mangroves are more than 160 species of birds and more than 10 species of reptiles; both the ever-elusive manatee and rare solenodon call this national park home.

At Monte Cristi's main beach, **Playa Juan de Boloños** (located at the end of Avenida San Fernando where it meets the sea), you can find some hotel accommodations and restaurants, but the beach itself is not grand.

Playa Detras del Morro, just as the name suggests, is behind the hill that looks like a camel's back. It's worth seeking it out, because it is the best in the area. It's a beautiful half moon of sand surrounded by the rocky cliffs. Following Avenida San Fernando to the national park will take you right to the beach. The steps leading up the hillside are in serious need of repair. It is a marvelous view from the top, although it's incredibly windy.

If you're up for a short boat ride, catch one

out to **Isla Cabra,** where there is a nice and very private beach. Just ask one of the boat captains at Playa Juan de Boloños and negotiate for a round-trip boat ride. Make sure to get a flat rate for the entire boatload of you, rather than per person, and have it agreed upon before you get in. Here you can also find a boat to take you snorkeling.

Los Cayos de los Siete Hermanos are about a kilometer from shore and are part of the national park. The white beaches of these uninhabited islands are beautiful, and there are many dive spots in the offshore reefs.

La Casa de Máximo Gómez (Av. Mella, 9 A.M.–noon and 3–7 P.M.) was once the home of the Dominican who was instrumental in Cuba's independence and the Dominican restoration, Máximo Gómez. Inside are photos and mementos.

Parque Central or, as it's sometimes called, Parque Reloj, is at the corner of Calle Duarte and San Fernando. The clock tower here is notable. Made by a French designer, it was inaugurated in Monte Cristi in 1895 and in the late 1990s it was restored. Lining the park are some run-down Victorian homes, some of which have been restored (a little). They all stand in testament to the European influence that the third wave of settlers had on Monte Cristi.

Festivals

On January 21, the **Día de la Virgen de la Altagracia** (the protector of the hearts of all Dominicans), nearly 2,000 pilgrims climb up to the top of El Morro to pray and camp out overnight. Simultaneously, many pilgrims are on their way to Higüey to pray.

Carnaval in Monte Cristi is a particularly legendary one. It is one of the oldest Carnaval celebrations in the country, having started 471 years ago. On Sundays during the entire month of February, spectators have the opportunity to witness a competition between the *toros* (the bulls) and the *civiles* (the civilians). It is an aggressive spectacle but popular nonetheless. Around two in the afternoon the Monte Cristi streets fill up with music, costumes, and the colorful crowds of Carnaval. The *toros* wear costumes with elaborate bull masks and wield whips. The *civiles* are undisguised and unprotected, and yet, they taunt the *toros*, which the *toros* gladly take on. What happens then seem a strange custom to visitors: The *civiles* voluntarily accept furious whip lashes from the *toros*. If you want to see the tradition, don't step into the street—it is sometimes seen as a challenge. Stay clear but enjoy this very old and exciting festival's tradition.

Sports and Recreation

Divers can explore the colonial galleons offshore or go diving around Los Cayos de los Siete Hermanos. If you're not planning on staying in the Monte Cristi area but are still interested in diving here, many of the dive companies along the north coast offer day trips to Monte Cristi, so you won't miss out on the opportunity to see its coral reefs and sunken ships.

Other sporting options, like **deep-sea fishing** and excursions to Haiti, can be booked through the **Restaurant El Bistrot** (Calle San Fernando 26, tel. 809/579-2091, www.elbistrot.com), a hotel and restaurant that has rental equipment and excursion options. Starting price for all excursions is US$45.

Hostal San Fernando (road to El Morro, tel. 809/964-0248) offers half-day tours to all seven of the islands at Los Cayos de los Siete Hermanos, where you can snorkel at a couple of spots (US$320 per group of up to 12 people) or take a ride through the mangroves (US$175 per group).

Accommodations

Aparta-Hotel Cayo Arena (Playa Juan de Bolaños, tel. 809/579-3145, US$53–88) is a great value. Two-bedroom apartments have attractive balconies, fully equipped kitchens, living rooms, cable TV, and bathrooms with hot water. Amenities include a small pool and bar.

For those who want a great place to stay within walking distance of the national park, **Hostal San Fernando** (tel. 809/964-0248,

US$50 d) is a wonderful choice. Situated near El Morro, these spacious rooms are comfortable and clean with a patio. It's one of the best choices of the area.

Hotel Montechico (Playa Juan de Bolaño, tel. 809/579-2565, US$20 with fan), conveniently located on the beach, has clean and pleasant rooms with a balcony, some with an ocean view. If you want air-conditioning, request it; the price is higher although not by much (about US$10 more).

Los Jardines (tel. 809/579-2091, hotel .jardines@verizon.net.do) is next door to the Aparta-Hotel Cayo Arena. Choose between two basic bungalows each with two rooms and bathrooms. Keep in mind they don't have kitchen facilities, so it is better for just a night or two. Los Jardines arranges for excursions to various places in the national park at additional cost.

Food

Want to order something traditional to this region? Try *chivo liniero;* it is a spicy goat dish that achieves its exquisite taste because the goats of this region feed on wild oregano, so the meat has been naturally seasoned.

The restaurant of **Hostal San Fernando** (road to El Morro, tel. 809/964-0248, 8 A.M.–late, US$5–20) has traditional chicken, beef, and fish choices as well as good breakfasts. This enjoyable spot is on the road out to El Morro.

Comedor Adela (Juan de la Cruz Alvarez 41, tel. 809/579-2254, US$10 and under) offers an inviting, casual atmosphere, and you can order good renditions of traditional Dominican favorites, like *la bandera dominicana*.

Not only is the seafood a great reason to come to **El Bistrot** (Calle San Fernando 26, tel. 809/579-2091, www.elbistrot.com, 11 A.M.–2:30 P.M. and 6 P.M.–midnight Mon.–Fri., 10 A.M.–midnight Sat. and Sun., US$5–20), but the ambience is worth it as well. You can sit either in the open air of a courtyard or inside. Other dishes include regional goat, sandwiches, and various pastas. It's a very welcoming establishment.

Information and Services

Calle Duarte is the main commercial area of Monte Cristi. Everything is either on or very near there. The **Politur** (Playa Juan de Bolaños, tel. 809/754-2978) is open 24 hours for any emergencies, and **Hospital Padre Fantino** (Av. 27 de Febrero, tel. 809/579-2401, 24 hours) is a basic hospital facility but it does have a 24-hour emergency room.

Unfortunately, there are no Internet services offered in town. **Verizon Comunicaciones** (Av. Benito Monción, 8 A.M.–midnight) is simply a call center, and the **post office** (Calle Duarte, 8 A.M.–5 P.M. Mon.–Fri.) is not a good option for communication.

To access money, **BanReservas** (Calle Duarte, 8 A.M.–5 P.M. Mon.–Fri., 9 A.M.–1 P.M. Sat.) has a 24-hour ATM.

Getting There and Around

Highway 1 (Autopista Duarte) coming into Monte Cristi from the southeast becomes Calle Duarte (the main drag) in town. Highway 45 into town from Dajabón becomes Avenida Mella. Incidentally, this is a notoriously dangerous highway to drive at night. Many Dominicans advise highly against it as robberies are very common.

Caribe Tours (Calle Mella, tel. 809/579-2129) is a block north from Calle Duarte. You can catch a bus to Santo Domingo (US$7.50) leaving at 7 A.M., 9 A.M., 10:45 A.M., 1:45 P.M., 2:45 P.M., and 4 P.M. This same bus makes a stop in Santiago (US$3.50).

There is a *guagua* terminal on Calle Duarte between 27 de Febrero and Benito Monción. They go to Dajabón and Santiago (US$1–4) and generally depart every 20 minutes.

Walking is best in Monte Cristi, but as usual, *motoconchos* are readily available if you're feeling adventurous.

DAJABÓN

A trip to Dajabón is not on the itinerary of many tourists. This Dominican–Haitian border town is a trading post, just as it has been for centuries. Back in the 17th century, most of the northwest, including Dajabón, was evacuated when the Spanish crown regarded its colonists' trading practices with foreigners to be treasonous behavior. After over 100 years, those foreigners began settling the evacuated land, so the Spanish, in fear of losing the areas they had found so hard to conquer, resettled their land. To this day, Dajabón remains a center for trade between Haiti and the Dominican Republic.

Dajabón is best saved for a day visit since there are no services and the only activity there is to go to the Haitian Market. But since the highways around Dajabón are too dangerous to drive at night, should you get caught losing track of time, there is one hotel worth mentioning.

Hotel Juan Calvo (Calle Presidente Henríquez 48, tel. 809/579-8285, US$10 d with fan only), next to the Parque Central, offers comfortable clean rooms.

Haitian Market

Every day Dajabón is a bustling center of trade as Haitians come over to the Dominican side of the border to sell an unbelievable variety of objects like pots and pans, shoes, perfumes, clothing, and tools. They spread their wares on blankets on the ground, on tables under the shade of a tarp. Dominicans come to the town to purchase these items at rock-bottom prices. The scene is one of a great amount of haggling, lively conversation, and frenzied negotiations. You won't find typical souvenirs, but the experience of rich cultural traditions between the two nations and the photos you'll gather might be all the memento you'll need.

Getting There and Around

Crossing over into Haiti can be a bit confusing. It's hard to say just how much you will pay since it seems to be up to the discretion of whomever you ask at the time. For the most part, though, you'll pay US$20 to the **Dominican immigration office** (8 A.M.–5 P.M. daily) and US$10 to the **Haitian immigration office** on the other side. You shouldn't have to pay a return fee, but sometimes that proves otherwise for tourists.

Caribe Tours (Calle Marcelo Carrasco, tel.

809/579-8554) is at Marcelo Carrasco and Presidente Henríquez. A trip to Santo Domingo (US$7.50) stops in Monte Cristi and Santiago and leaves at 6:45 A.M., 8:30 A.M., 10:15 A.M., 1 P.M., 2:25 P.M., and 3:15 P.M. Buses leave Santo Domingo for Dajabón at 6:30 A.M., 8 A.M., 9:30 A.M., 1 P.M., 2 P.M., and 3:45 P.M., stopping in Monte Cristi and Santiago.

Catch a *guagua* to Monte Cristi at the station by the entrance to town. *Guaguas* leave Monte Cristi for Dajabón every 20 minutes from the terminal on Calle Duarte.

Getting around within Dajabón is best on foot as it is so small. But taxis and *motoconchos* tend to hang out around the border crossing and on the main street in town.

EL CIBAO

The Cordillera Central (Central Mountains) and the Valle del Cibao make up the fertile backbone of the Dominican Republic, referred to by Dominicans as El Cibao. Removed from the lazy beach towns and all-inclusive resorts, this lush region highlights the biodiversity of the country, featuring ranches, vegetable and fruit farms, twisting mountain roads, crashing waterfalls, rushing rivers, and crisp, fresh air. The area is abundant with produce ranging from potatoes, coffee, tobacco, and vegetables to some not-so-typical fruits such as strawberries and apples.

Most tourists who come to the tropics typically head to the beaches. But the adventure-minded independent travelers seeking the antithesis of plastic-bracelet all-inclusive resorts come here to enjoy the backyard garden of the Dominican Republic—it's a getaway favorite for the Dominicans themselves. The area offers a visitor not only a taste of mountain culture but also an insider's view of the Dominican city-folk relaxing and at play, taking a break from their own hectic lives.

Ecotourism and adventure travel have gained substantial momentum in the tourism industry of the Dominican Republic. Every year more tourists become aware of the richness and diversity of the Dominican Republic's topography, and many choose the El Cibao region to create a fun, more adventure-focused vacation. Abundant outdoor activities include rafting, canyoning, and treks to Pico Duarte. Whether you ride a mule or do a five-day hike on foot, the climb to the summit of Pico Duarte is one of the most popular activities here, where the

© ANA CHAVIER CAAMAÑO

HIGHLIGHTS

Centro León: This is easily the best museum in the country. See Dominican culture, art, and history in the state-of-the-art facility. While you're there, watch and learn how cigars are made (page 200).

Carnaval in La Vega: Join in the fun during the pre-Lenten Carnaval celebration often touted as the best one in the whole country. Dance in the streets at one of the best parties thrown in the Dominican Republic (page 206).

Paragliding in Jarabacoa: Get your thrill on while seeing the Dominican Republic from the air! Adrenaline junkies love the variety of adventure sports in the Dominican Alps (page 210).

Pico Duarte: Hike 3,087 meters to the top of the highest peak in the Caribbean. This challenging trek takes you to the summit, where on a clear day you can see all the way to the Atlantic Ocean and Caribbean Sea (page 213).

Parque Nacional Valle Nuevo: Take in the phenomenal bird-watching opportunity in this protected forest and then head over to the Salto de Aguas Blancas for a dip in the pool of the three-tiered waterfall (page 217).

LOOK FOR **(** TO FIND RECOMMENDED SIGHTS, ACTIVITIES, DINING, AND LODGING.

EL CIBAO

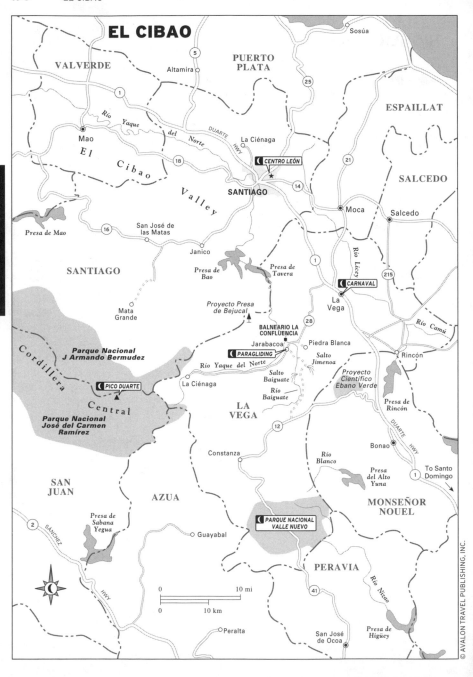

reward is a panoramic view of the Caribbean Sea and the Atlantic Ocean.

PLANNING YOUR TIME

If you are looking to have an action-filled vacation but don't want to move around a lot, Jarabacoa is a fantastic place to make a base camp. Many adventure activities are local, and you can get a lot of action packed into even a three- or four-day vacation. From Jarabacoa you can also book farther-away excursions with local tour companies who will provide transportation. However, if you want to be more mobile, this part of the country is a bit more challenging to get around in via public transportation—it's not impossible, just allow for more time for waiting for buses and *guaguas*. Renting a car is a better idea, but a 4WD is highly recommended for the power needed to get over mountain passes and often rough and rugged terrain.

To hike Pico Duarte, consider going with a tour group. It will alleviate a lot of planning and logistic complications for you, especially if you don't speak Spanish. But if you want to wing it on your own, decide ahead of time which route you'd like to take. That way, you know how many days of travel time and hike time you'll need. For instance, if flying into Santiago (which is best for this area), you should have a day for getting from the airport to your base camp and settling in, booking your trek in the first day or two of arrival with an independent guide. It is best to give your guides a day or two for their own preparations and for yours (you'll need to buy provisions). A minimum of three days should be saved for the actual hike (some can do it in two, but it's best to be safe). After that you'll need your travel time back to the airport.

Santiago

The second-largest city of the Dominican Republic, Santiago de Los Treinte Caballeros (more commonly referred to as Santiago) is an important commercial center in the Valle del Cibao as well as in the Dominican Republic as a whole. The fertile land yields bananas, cocoa, and coffee. Most importantly, the tobacco and sugarcane grown here are turned into rum and cigars, making Santiago a very important and lucrative city for the republic.

It is a bustling city but not as frenetic as Santo Domingo, and it somehow seems more ordered, perhaps because it is steeped in a culture of business and not so much in travel. Therefore, accommodations cater to the international businesspeople who frequent the area. Although there is a good nightlife and arts scene, there are not many sights. As it is the gateway to the surrounding ecotourism of the Cordillera Central, with an international airport just 24 kilometers away and the Autopista Duarte connecting to Santo Domingo, tourists often swing through Santiago for an

afternoon or for a night before they head to the mountains where adventure sports await.

Bartolomé Colón, Christopher's older brother, first founded Santiago in 1495, in the hopes of finding gold. In 1562, it was ravaged and destroyed by a catastrophic earthquake. Eventually the townspeople rebuilt onto what is the modern-day site of Santiago, along the eastern banks of the Río Yaque del Norte. Unfortunately, that was just the beginning of Santiago's long string of difficult times. Pirate attacks, French invasions, three more earthquakes, and a major fire during the Restoration War challenged and all but extinguished Santiago. But it was after that war that the city truly began to thrive. As World War I raged in the rest of the world, prices for products grown in the area so easily (sugar, tobacco, and coffee) rose dramatically, and the city got steadily richer until the 1920s. Today, Santiago's economy has leveled off, but there are still quite a few very wealthy families because of the agriculture and tobacco industries.

EL CIBAO

SIGHTS
(C Centro León

If you can choose only one thing to do in Santiago, make this it. The Centro León (Av. 27 de Febrero 146, Villa Progreso, tel. 809/582-2315, fax 809/724-7644, 10 A.M.– 7 P.M. Tues.–Sun., US$1.75, free Tues.) is the country's finest museum, housing art, anthropological, and cultural exhibitions. It also hosts artistic seminars, workshops, film festivals, and music performances. There are three main-building sections of the museum: contemporary art, a temporary exhibit room, and a Dominican exhibit that focuses on the country's ecology, history, and culture.

The museum was founded by the León Jimenes family, one of the most successful families in the Dominican Republic. They built their fortune in the tobacco, beer, and banking industries, and their story is told in the fourth exhibit, on the second floor of a stand-alone

building on the well-manicured grounds of the center. On the first floor of the same small museum is a small cigar workshop where you can watch the talented cigar rollers work their magic and a store where you can purchase the highly ranked cigars. In the February 2005 edition of *Cigar Aficionado* (www.cigaraficionado.com) magazine, the Aurora 100 años cigar was voted the second-best cigar in the world. Tours require reservations two days in advance and are given in English, German, French (US$5.50), and Spanish (US$3.50), lasting 1–2 hours.

Museo des Artes Folklórico Tomás Morel

This folklore museum (Av. Restauración 174, tel. 809/582-6787, 9 A.M.–noon and 3:30– 6 P.M. Mon.–Fri., free) was the brainchild of Tomás Morel, a celebrated Dominican poet and cultural critic. In its somewhat dusty

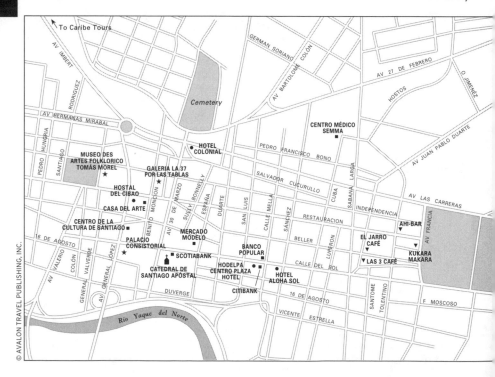

walls is a great abundance of traditional Santiago Carnaval memorabilia, including a collection of ornate handmade masks from the region's celebration of the annual event. This museum provides one of the better keyhole observations into the traditions of the country's beloved event. Here you will learn about all of the different costumed characters of the tradition, like the *lechones* who wear elaborate costumes and were originally meant to keep order by marching ahead of the parade and creating a path through the crowds. They had, at one time, carried small staffs to shoo the onlookers, but they were eventually replaced by sisal rope whips, and later an inflated pig's bladder was attached to the end of the sisal rope.

Palacio Consistorial

In this museum (Calle del Sol, Parque Duarte, 9 A.M.–6 P.M. Mon.–Fri., 9 A.M.–2 P.M. Sat.) you can learn all about the history of Santiago. It is in an attractive Victorian building that once housed city hall. It now contains a highly regarded collection of old and recent works by local artists. As part of the annual Carnaval celebration, colorful masks from all over the country are on display.

Monumento a Los Heroes de la Restauración de la República (Puerto del Sol)

The Monument to the Heroes of the Restoration of the Republic (Av. Monumental, 8 A.M.–5 P.M. Mon.–Sat., free) is hard to miss. Not because it has such interesting features inside or because it has a good exhibit. No, it is literally hard to miss. It is an eight-story tower perched on top of a tall hill overlooking all of Santiago. Trujillo had commissioned that it be built in honor of himself (in classic Trujillo egoism), but when the dictator was assassinated, it was

© ANA CHAVIER CAAMAÑO

Monumento a Los Heroes de la Restauración de la República

rededicated to honor those who died in the Restoration War. A museum inside is a collection of photos and not much else, hardly worth the effort; when I visited, the elevator that used to take you to the top was broken, and there were no plans to fix it. However, this is a wonderful spot to come and watch the sunset and have a beer, which you can buy from the vendors. From here you can see the entire city and surrounding mountains, a truly spectacular view.

Catedral de Santiago Apóstol

The Santiago Cathedral (Calle 16 de Agosto, Parque Central, 7 A.M.–9 P.M. Mon.–Sat., 7 A.M.–8 P.M. Sun.), with its combination neoclassical and Gothic architecture, was built in the latter part of the 1800s. It holds an ornately carved mahogany altar and beautiful stained-glass windows created by artist José Rincón-Morá in the 1980s.

ENTERTAINMENT AND EVENTS

Art Exhibits, Performances, and Classes

If you are visiting Santiago for more than a day, perhaps taking in an art or music class or going to some performances will bring you closer to the culture of the area. Call or stop by and check the schedule of events at each locale since they change often. The **Casa del Arte** (Benito Monción, tel. 809/583-5346, 9 A.M.–7 P.M. Mon.–Sat., free) shows exhibits by local artists and holds cultural events in an outdoor gallery space.

Across the street from Casa del Arte is **Galería La 37 Por Las Tablas** (Benito Monción, tel. 809/587-3033). Here you can enjoy music, dance, and theater performances (also in an outdoor theater), take dance and other kinds of classes, participate in cultural talks, and attend lectures. Admission depends upon the activity or event.

The **Centro de la Cultura de Santiago** (Calle del Sol, tel. 809/226-5222, 9 A.M.–6 P.M. daily) has music and theater performances and classes.

Nightlife

A good place to set out on foot in search of your type of watering hole is around the Monumento a la Restauración. Since it is a busy area, it is a safe area to walk.

Ahi-Bar (Calle Tolentino, tel. 809/581-6779, 4 P.M.–3 A.M.) is a good bar to start out the night because it serves food, but it is most popular as a drinking spot, especially on Friday nights. The large patio is good for open-air conversation, and the bar is quite popular with the blue-blooded youth of Santiago.

The crowd at gay-friendly **Francifol** (Calle del Sol, tel. 809/971-5558) doesn't even get going until midnight or 1 A.M., but it is popular place with the youth of Santiago.

Popular disco **Alcazar** (Gran Almirante Hotel, Estrella Sadhalá, 10 A.M.–late, US$2) is a very hopping place, but it doesn't get crowded until about 1 A.M. and then people stay and dance until dawn! This is not a jeans and tennis shoes bar (outside of the resorts, few in the DR are); you should dress well to get in here.

With the alternative music interplayed with great merengue hits, **El Jarro Café** (Calle Tolentino, tel. 809/971-4942, 4 P.M.–3 A.M.) is a fun bar to hang out in. It's popular with a young crowd that isn't as snooty as at Francifol or Ahi-Bar.

Tailú Bar & Grill (Sabana Larga 166, tel. 809/582-0233) is close to the monument and is frequented by the gay community (mostly men). It's rather discreet. Fridays are good nights for this bar.

Festivals

The *caretas* (masks) of Santiago's Carnaval are especially ornate, making this city's Carnaval celebration a particularly special one to take part in. Competitions for the best mask are held annually in the days leading up to Carnaval.

At the Carnaval parade in Santiago you'll see two character masks that are specific to Santiago, the *lechñn* (piglet) and the *pepin* (a make-believe animal that looks like a duck with spiked horns). Santiago's celebration is special in that you will see a fantastic variety of costumes and cultures represented here that have affected the overall Carnaval celebration of the whole country and throughout history. All of the characters carry the *vejigas* (inflated animal bladders) and hit onlookers with them. If you don't want to be bruised, stay off the street; better yet, try to watch the Carnaval parade from a balcony.

While the most lively and best-known Carnaval celebration in the country is in nearby La Vega (perhaps because it is the most well-organized), Santiago is trying to increase the visibility and popularity of its celebration. Festivities begin around four in the afternoon and go late into the night with live merengue and *bachata* music. At the monument, there is art on exhibit and groups doing folkloric and cultural performances. Making your base camp in Santiago (provided you arrange

CIGARS

Some of the best cigars in the world come from Santiago and its surrounding areas. The Valle de Cibao, where Santiago is located, is particularly fertile, with just the right combination of rich soil, sunshine, and the cool temperature rolling off the surrounding mountains. Though today machines do a lot of the work of creating a cigar, it is – and will always be – the hand-rolled cigar that reigns supreme.

The process starts, of course, with tobacco seeds, many of which are actually derived from Cuban varieties. Once the seeds have been germinated and the plants are harvested (all of which takes approximately six weeks), the leaves are housed in a drying room, where the dehydration results in lowered nicotine levels and eliminates ammonia. Here, the dried leaves are bundled and aged for anywhere from 2 to 10 years. Once the aging process is complete, the hand-rolling begins.

There are three parts to a cigar: the wrapper, the filler, and the binder. A long filler has been produced from whole leaves, whereas as a short filler comes from whatever clippings are left behind after the long fillers have been rolled, or from ground leaves. The long filler (perhaps accompanied by some short filler) is bound by several leaves and the binder and filler together form a cylindrical shape – the cigar shape – at which point the wrapper is applied. After another aging process, the cut and shaped cigar is ready for consumption.

fast cigar rollers in Santiago

© ANA CHAVIER CAAMAÑO

accommodations well in advance) is a great idea so that you can go to both towns' celebrations. All Carnaval celebrations in the country happen every Sunday during the month of February.

SHOPPING

The central and most popular shopping district for Santiago is along **Calle del Sol**. It is a great way to feel the commerce-culture of Santiago and get a feel for this city. Simply strolling along this busy street, you'll find many small stores, vendors, and hawkers.

Much like the Mercado Modelo in Santo Domingo, there is a lot to pick from at **Mercado Modelo** (Calle del Sol, 9 A.M.–5 P.M. Mon.–Sat.): knickknacks, souvenirs, Haitian paintings, jewelry, and all sort of other things to set yourself to haggling over. That is half the fun anyway.

Since you're in the region of serious tobacco production, it would be wise to make your cigar purchases here. At **Centro León** (Av. 27 de Febrero 146, Villa Progreso, tel. 809/582-2315, fax 809/724-7644, 10 A.M.–7 P.M. Tues.–Sun.) you can not only watch the rollers at work, but you can buy some of the world's best cigars.

ACCOMMODATIONS

Although Santiago is the second-largest city in the country, there are very few choices for accommodations.

Under $50

Hostal del Cibao (Calle Benito Monción 40, tel. 809/581-7775, hostal_del_cibao@hotmail .com, US$12 d) is the place to rest the heads of the weary backpackers and budget travelers. Located just a short walk from the Parque Central, there are 14 rooms available. All are spacious with private bath, cable TV, and fan. Enjoy early evenings watching Santiago on your private balcony.

Hotel Colonial (Salvador Cucurullo 115, tel. 809/247-3122, US$13 d) is between Calle 30 de Marzo and España. It offers clean rooms that are a bit small and simple with cable TV,

fan, and private bathroom. The staff here is very hospitable and friendly.

$50 and Up

Hotel Aloha Sol (Calle del Sol 50, tel. 809/583-0090, www.alohasol.com, US$64 d) is close to shopping and other services. There is Internet service, a restaurant, and a piano bar (4 P.M.–midnight). The rooms are very clean and have air-conditioning, cable TV, and a minibar, but you'll be billed if you use anything from it. You can request a room with a fax machine in it if you are here on business. The rooms are all a bit cramped, even the suites, but this is the best hotel in downtown. Breakfast is included in rate.

Hodelpa Centro Plaza Hotel (Calle Mella, tel. 809/581-7000, www.hodelpa.com, US$75) plays a distant second to the Aloha Sol. It has valet parking, but the frills stop there. Although centrally located, it is a basic hotel with outdated rooms.

FOOD

There are many restaurants around the monument and on Calle del Sol. **◖ Pez Dorado** (Calle del Sol 43, tel. 809/582-4051, US$11–20) is a surprisingly nice change from the regular cuisine found in the Dominican Republic; it serves Chinese and other international dishes. They don't let you go hungry and it's a popular place on the weekends.

Kukara Makara (Av. Francia 7, tel. 809/241-3143, 8 A.M.–late, US$5–20) is a Tex Mex, cowboy-inspired restaurant serving thick meals like steak, burritos (including a veggie one), and grilled food. It also has seafood, sandwiches, and burgers. It's very near the monument.

Restaurante Mana (Av. Francia and Calle del Sol, US$3–7) is a small, very casual, cafeteria-style restaurant down the hill from the monument. It's very affordable; for US$3, you can get rice and beans, meat, a side order, and a drink. What a value for the budget traveler! The food is good, too. Just get in line and point to what you want. Dining is on picnic tables under a roof, but open-air.

Las 3 Café (Calle Tolentino 38, tel. 809/276-5909, noon–late, US$6–12) is a very good choice for Dominican *criolla* fare. It's within the bar district and serves wonderful mid-priced meals.

INFORMATION AND SERVICES

Calle del Sol is the main drag, where you'll find many vendors, hotels, banks, and other services. It intersects with Avenida 30 de Marzo at the Parque Central, which is a commercial street also.

For a 24-hour emergency room, go to **Centro Médico Semma** (Pedro Francisco Bonó, tel. 809/226-1053). Also good to know about is a specialty women's care facility, **Hospital de la Mujer** (Av. Imbert, tel. 809/575-8963) that has a 24-hour emergency room; they will treat anyone.

Citibank and **Banco Popular** are good spots for any money needs or concerns, and both are near the intersection of Calle Mella and Calle del Sol. They have ATMs, and **ScotiaBank** (Calle del Sol at 30 de Marzo) has one as well. All banks are open 8 A.M.–5 P.M. Monday–Friday, 8 A.M.–12:30 P.M. Saturday.

GETTING THERE
By Air

The **Santiago International Airport** (Av. Bartolomé Colón, tel. 809/233-8000) is 20 minutes out of town. Airlines that service it are: **American** (tel. 809/233-8401, www.aa.com), **American Eagle** (tel. 809/233-8401), **CaribAir** (tel. 809/233-8270), **Continental** (tel. 809/233-8161, www.continental.com),

and **Jet Blue** (tel. 809/233-8116, www.jetblue.com). Taking a taxi from the airport to Santiago costs US$15–20.

By Bus

There are two bus stations in town. **Caribe Tours** (27 de Febrero at Las Américas, tel. 809/576-0790, www.caribetours.com.do) is in the Las Colinas neighborhood, and has bus service going to many cities. There are 26 Santo Domingo (US$5.50) buses every day leaving 6 A.M.–8:15 P.M. and stopping in La Vega. For Puerto Plata (US$2.50), with a stop in Sosúa, buses leave every hour on the half-hour 8:30 A.M.–9:30 P.M., and Monte Cristi (US$3.50) has six buses 9:15 A.M.–6:15 P.M., stopping in Dajabón along the way.

Metro Tours (Av. Juan Pablo Duarte, tel. 809/587-3837) is a second choice that has service to Santo Domingo (US$7) every hour and Puerto Plata (US$2.50) seven times a day.

GETTING AROUND

If you're driving through, the street to keep in mind is Calle del Sol (the main commercial drag), which runs east into the Monumento a Los Héroes de la Restauración. The main streets that lead in and out of town are Avenida 27 de Febrero, which will take you north, and Avenida Las Carreras, which goes south toward Santo Domingo.

Taxis (US$3–5) are relatively inexpensive, especially if you're just taking them from a restaurant or bar to your hotel. They're a lot safer than *motoconchos* or walking at night.

La Vega

La Concepción de La Vega (commonly referred to as La Vega) sits in the middle of the Valle del Cibao (Cibao Valley). The countryside is plush with vegetation and is an area that is rich in production of tobacco, rice, fruit, and vegetables. La Vega has so very little to offer tourists, it ranks low on the priority list for most. That is, until February, when the small town's streets overflow with hundreds of thousands of Dominicans and tourists for its Carnaval celebration. It is the one thing that keeps La Vega on the map.

SIGHTS
Catedral de la Concepción

This architectural oddity is on the Parque Central and is impossible to miss. The "train-wreck" design was a sincere try at a contemporary version of Spanish Imperial style, complete with castle details. It ended up looking something like a concrete power plant. For those who are admirers of modern architecture, this building does not evoke the genius of Niemeyer sculptural beauty, but rather raises curiosity. So in the spirit of "This I gotta see!," the cathedral is on Avenida Antonio Guzmán at Padre Adolfo. One of the great things about a trip to the cathedral is visiting the *pastelito* vendors that can be found out front. These meat-filled pastries are an absolutely great for a quick snack and an excuse to take a break from sightseeing.

Santo Cerro

Holy Hill is along a road stemming from Autopista Duarte, about five kilometers north of La Vega. Up on the hill with a magnificent view of the Cibao Valley sits **Iglesia Las Mercedes** (open 9 A.M.–noon and 2–6 P.M.), a popular pilgrimage site that contains a hole into which Christopher Columbus is said to have placed a cross given to him by Queen Isabela. The cross that was placed there (and is now "missing") is said to have been involved in a miracle during a Spanish versus Taíno battle. The natives tried to burn the religious symbol, but when it wouldn't catch fire, the Virgin Mary is said to have appeared on it and scared off the Taínos. The Spanish rejoiced and the Dominicans now venerate the spot where the faithful believe it took place on pilgrimage days like September 24 (the patron saint day of Our Lady of the Mercies).

Going to Santo Cerro for the view is a nice side trip. Look for the *níspero* tree near the church. A plaque says it is a descendant of one planted in the late 1400s that was used to build the original wooden church that stood there. Around the church are many stores selling religious items and souvenirs.

La Vega Vieja

"Old La Vega," a few kilometers northeast of present-day La Vega, was founded in 1494 by Christopher Columbus to act as a stronghold for all the gold he assumed he'd find in the region. The settlement gained prosperity, but it was not due to gold. It was the fertility of the valley and the sugarcane industry that began here. But the prosperity ended when, in 1562, a massive earthquake destroyed the town. The **ruins of La Vega Vieja** (9 A.M.–noon and 2–5 P.M., US$1) contain the overgrown remains of the fort, church, and some houses that stood where the original settlement had been, or what was left after the earthquake and a few hundred years.

🌙 Carnaval

Although situated in the picturesque and serene valley of La Vega Real, 125 kilometers north of Santo Domingo, La Vega lacks significant tourist sights, and for 11 months out of a year there really isn't a reason to visit. But for that one month, February, the best reason to come here emerges during the pre-Lenten celebration of Carnaval, when La Vega explodes with energy and activity. Most Dominicans agree that the Carnaval of La Vega is the best, rowdiest, and most fun in the whole country and that no other can rival it.

Every Sunday in the six weeks before Lent,

La Vega virtually doubles in size when almost 100,000 visitors pack the town dancing in the streets and it seems that all hell breaks loose. La Vega's mask (each town has its own) is an ornately decorated and colorful devil with bulging wrathful eyes and teeth. These costumes alone are reason enough to come to Carnaval. These magnificently gruesome devils march along the parade in jingle-bell covered costumes wielding *vejigas* (traditionally, inflated cow or pig bladders) that they use to thwack bystanders on the backside. To stay clear of this tradition, stay on the bleachers set up along the parade route, find a balcony to watch from above, or don't step off the curb into the street—that is a sign that you are fair game.

ACCOMMODATIONS AND FOOD

La Vega is best reserved for a day trip. It is more desirable to stay in nearby Jarabacoa where the accommodation choices are more plentiful. Unfortunately, the accommodations and food options in this town leave much to be desired with some truly dismal choices. But should you decide to stay or simply get stranded, the **Hotel El Rey** (Av. Antonio Guzman, tel. 809/573-9797, US$42 d) is the best choice. Rooms are clean with cable TV and a fan but showing their age. There is free parking and a restaurant serving good *comida criolla* (Dominican food).

INFORMATION AND SERVICES

There are very limited services in La Vega. There is a **BanReservas** (Padre Adolfo, 9 A.M.–5 P.M. Mon.–Fri., 9 A.M.–1 P.M. Sat.); it has an ATM.

There are two pharmacies, **Farmacia Ferreira** (Av. P. Garcia 1, tel. 809/573-2102) and **Farmacia La Mezquita G** (Godoy 1, tel. 809/573-5017), but you'll have to make the trip to Santiago for any medical attention you might need.

GETTING THERE AND AROUND

The odd thing about La Vega is that it is highly accessible by both car and bus, from many directions, and still there are so very few services available.

© ANA CHAVIER CAAMAÑO

Coconut drinks are plentiful at the Carnaval festival in La Vega.

EL CIBAO

Caribe Tours (Av. Pedro A. Rivera, tel. 809/573-2488, 6:30 A.M.–9 P.M.) has a very steady stream of buses coming through its station. Santo Domingo–bound (US$4) buses leave every half hour or so. Northern-bound buses make stops in Santiago (US$1.75), Puerto Plata (US$3), and Sosúa (US$3.50) and leave every hour. A bus for Jarabacoa (US$1.75) leaves at scattered times throughout the day as it is a transfer bus from Santo Domingo.

The north–south-running Autopista Duarte files right past La Vega, making it a major stopover for traffic coming from major destinations on either coast. The main drag, Avenida Antonio Guzmán Fernandez, parallels Autopista Duarte in town and then comes to meet it just north of town. Look for the main plaza near Avenida Guzmán Fernandez and Padre Adolfo; that's where you'll also find the cathedral and the bank.

Jarabacoa

In the heart of the **Cordillera Central** mountains, often referred to as the "Dominican Alps," is the town of Jarabacoa. Its bounty is seen not only in the fertility of its land, but also in what it has to offer visitors.

Thick vegetation surrounds the rich agricultural region, and products such as vegetables, coffee, flowers, and strawberries seem to grow without effort. The delectable red fruit can be seen in brimming-over baskets for sale along the curving road up the mountainside, and the marketplace of Jarabacoa is abundant with produce.

Jarabacoa has long been a popular spot for Dominicans as a summer getaway from their life in the city and the muggy heat of the coastal lowlands. The 500 meters above sea level impart constant spring-like mild days and cool evenings. Foreign visitors come because Jarabacoa presents promises of adventure. It is the launching point for treks to Pico Duarte (the highest peak in the Caribbean), white-water rafting, and canyoning in the waterfalls and rivers (Jimenoa, Baiguate, and Yaque del Norte converge nearby). It is the Dominican Republic that is relatively new to the scene of tourism and the new darling of ecotravel.

SIGHTS

The waterfalls listed here are a fair distance away, so either rent your own transportation or get a taxi to take you. Consider asking your driver to be a round-trip driver for you and establish your time for return. Also, asking a driver to take you around to all three waterfalls for a flat rate is a good idea. Secure prices before beginning your trip.

El Salto de Baiguate

Coming from Jarabacoa, follow Calle El Carmen east; it becomes the Carretera a Pedregal outside of town. There will be a sign for this waterfall in roughly three kilometers; follow the turnoff until you reach a parking lot. Walk along a path in a gorge until you come to some steps that lead to the waterfall. Swimming is nice here, and lots of excursions stop here either on foot or horseback.

Los Saltos de Jimenoa

The two Jimenoa waterfalls are more stunning than the one at Baiguate. The first, and most dramatic, is **Salto Jimenoa Uno.** Follow the road out of Jarabacoa via the road to Constanza. It turns to a dirt road after a bit, so don't be alarmed. Seven kilometers outside of Jarabacoa, you'll pass through a tiny village and then see a small turnoff on your left—this will quickly turn into more of a trail. Follow this path down to the pool at the base of the falls. Salto Jimenoa Uno is about 60 meters high and is fed from a hidden lake above that sends its water crashing in a huge pool at the

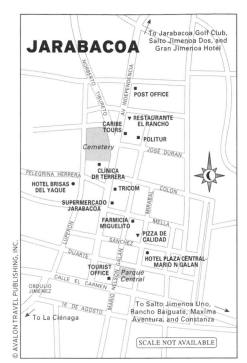

JARABACOA

To Jarabacoa Golf Club, Salto Jimenoa Dos, and Gran Jimenoa Hotel

NORBERTO TIBURCIO

AV INDEPENDENCIA

POST OFFICE

RESTAURANTE EL RANCHO

CARIBE TOURS

POLITUR

Cemetery

JOSÉ DURAN

PELEGRINA HERRERA

CLINICA DR TERRERA

HOTEL BRISAS DEL YAQUE

TRICOM

COLÓN

MIRABAL

SUPERMERCADO JARABACOA

FARMICIA MIGUELITO

MELLA

LUPERON

PIZZA DE CALIDAD

SANCHEZ

DUARTE

HOTEL PLAZA CENTRAL-MARIO N GALAN

TOURIST OFFICE

Parque Central

MARIO NELSON GALAN

CALLE EL CARMEN

OBDULIO JIMENEZ

18 DE AGOSTO

To La Ciénaga

To Salto Jimenoa Uno, Rancho Baiguate, Maxima Aventura, and Constanza

SCALE NOT AVAILABLE

© AVALON TRAVEL PUBLISHING, INC.

bottom. It looks like something from the movies. In fact it was. It was a chosen location for a scene in *Jurassic Park.*

The second is called **Salto Jimenoa Dos** (admittance US$0.60). This is perhaps the most frequently visited of the falls. Coming from Jarabacoa, you'll drive northeast for three kilometers on the road to Highway Duarte. Follow the signs that lead you to the falls at a major fork in the road. After another five kilometers or so, there is a parking lot. Once you've paid the ranger, walk along a trail between canyon walls that includes suspension bridges. These falls are about 40 meters high and splash down into a deep turquoise pool. The water is absolutely frigid, but great for a swim.

SPORTS AND RECREATION

While Cabarete is the extreme sport capital of the north, Jarabacoa is that of the Cordillera

Central. Travelers who are not content with a vacation of being sand-potatoes with a drink in their hand and doing nothing but gathering UV rays come here, to the central highlands, for excitement and adventure in sports such as mountain biking, river rafting, cascading, canyoning, and quad riding.

These are conquer-your-fears sports. They get your adrenaline pumping maniacally through your bloodstream and push you in ways you weren't expecting. The exhilaration of rushing rapids while rafting on the Río Yaque del Norte, the concentration and agility needed for a top-speed bicycle spin down a mountain trail, the "don't look down" butterflies of stepping over that first edge during canyoning—these are only a few of the emotions spawned while taking advantage of all the sports that Jarabacoa has to offer.

Although hiking the waterfalls can be done independently, it is best to go with a guided tour company for your big adventures. There are two main tour operators of this area, and anyone can join in their programs with advanced notice. Give a day or two warning that you're coming so you can reserve your spot and find out the appropriate time of departure.

Adventure Sport Tours

Máxima Aventura, based out of **Rancho Baiguate** (Jarabacoa, Carretera a Constanza, tel. 809/574-6890, www.ranchobaiguate.com) offers an extensive list of excursions, such as local activities like canyoning (US$55), mountain biking, tubing, and a jeep excursion (US$16) that takes you to the local waterfalls and through a flower plantation and coffee factory. Treks to Pico Duarte come in 3–5-day packages and vary in price depending on how many people are in the group. Price quotes and reservations can be made via phone or email.

Iguana Mama (Cabarete, tel. 809/571-0908, www.iguanamama.com, 8 A.M.–5 P.M. daily) is one of the most reputable and highly recommended adventure tour companies in the country. Although it based in Cabarete, they

© ANA CHAVIER CAAMAÑO

Take a dip in the pools of Los Saltos de Jimenoa.

do many tour excursions in Jarabacoa. Programs include guided mountain-biking tours, white-water rafting, and treks to Pico Duarte, among many other excursions and trip packages throughout the country.

◖ Paragliding

Not satisfied with seeing the beautiful Dominican countryside just from the ground? Take flight with **Fly Vacher** (Jarabacoa, tel. 809/882-1201, www.simonvacher.com) and see the mountains, waterfalls, rivers, and even the distant ocean! Fly Vacher is just outside Jarabacoa, on the road to Rancho Baiguate. The daily rate per person is US$65, which includes transportation between fly sites, briefing, and radio assistance. An all-inclusive package for US$95 per person includes lodging and all meals. No worries if you're a newbie—tandem flights are available as well. But if you really want to become a pro, attend the paragliding school for 7–10 days at US$500 per person.

Golf

Jarabacoa Golf Club (tel. 809/441-1940, 7:30 A.M.–7:30 P.M. daily) is a 9-hole uneventful golf course nestled in the pine woods just outside of Jarabacoa. Greens fees are US$30 to go twice around and play a full 18 holes. Caddies and carts are optional. This course is well marked by a sign on the road to Jarabacoa about one kilometer before reaching the town.

ACCOMMODATIONS

Hotel Plaza Central (Mario N Galan, tel. 809/524-7768, US$10 d) offers clean but very basic rooms with ceiling fans and private bathrooms. There are no screens on the big windows, so the mosquitoes can be a bit bothersome, but the air flows freely, as does the noise from the rather busy location (about a half block from Parque Central). The management will let you lock your bags in the office when you're out.

Hotel Brisas del Yaque (Luperón at Peregrina Herrera, tel. 809/574-4490, US$25) is the best deal in town. It doesn't have a restaurant but is close to many in town. The rooms are a little cramped but new and very clean, with brick and wood decor, private bathroom, TV, air-conditioning, and a cool tile floor. Some have magnificent views of the mountains, a big plus!

Rancho Baiguate (tel. 809/574-6890, www.ranchobaiguate.com.do, US$50 d) has been an adventure ranch for more than 10 years, but prior to that it was a camp for kids for 25 years. It is still a good place to bring kids. The ranch is about five kilometers east of Jarabacoa and removed from the noise of the town. This is not "roughing it" at camp, but it is not a luxury dude ranch either. Raw nature lovers will be comfortable here. The rooms vary in style from standard to luxury (ranch-style). The rooms are spacious and clean. The mood is rustic with vaulted ceilings (complete with a quiet ceiling fan!), a porch with chairs, and private, clean hot water bathrooms. There is no air-conditioning (you won't need it); windows have screens but the mosquitoes are relentless in the country when dusk sets in, so bring your bug spray for sure. There's no TV or phone in the room. At night the silence is wonderful, but when the electricity goes out, it is very dark. If you don't find candles in your room, ask for them at the front desk. The ranch is next to a river and has a restaurant, pool, sporting courts, and tons of adventure sport opportunities. The staff is very friendly and speak English well. This is the best place to stay in Jarabacoa if you plan on doing lots of adventure excursions. Many groups and independent travelers come to the ranch in the day to take part in their sporting menu.

Gran Jimenoa (Av. La Confluenza, tel. 809/574-6304, US$50 d) is a fantastic option. Located along the banks of the Jimenoa River, this hotel offers very clean, spacious, and comfortable rooms with private baths and private balconies. Besides a large pool and a Jacuzzi on-site there us a separate open-air, thatch-roofed party hut overlooking the river where they hold events such as karaoke and dances. The restaurant overlooks the river as well and is a very popular spot with the locals.

FOOD

Most people who visit Jarabacoa do so because they want to play hard and be adventurous all day long. By the time dusk sets in, they are ready for dinner and a relaxing evening.

Pizza de Calidad (Calle Hermanas Mirabal, tel. 809/574-4000, Mon.–Fri. 3:30 P.M.–midnight, 3 P.M.–midnight Sat., noon–midnight Sun.) has good basic pizzas in a casual and friendly environment. It is a good place to take kids. It has a small yard with a play area within parental view. If you've had a hard day of activity and can't seem to move a muscle, Pizza de Calidad delivers.

Restaurante El Rancho (Av. Independencia 1, tel. 809/574-4557, US$4–15) has a good assortment of international food and *comida criolla*. Locals say this is one of the best places in town. Local artists' works hang on the walls and the food is made from locally grown products.

Piedras del Río (Hotel Gran Jimenoa, Av. La Confluencia, tel. 809/574-6304, www.granjimenoa.com, 7 A.M.–11 P.M. daily, US$5–15) is a casual hotel restaurant. Its best feature is a fantastic view, as it's situated right alongside the Río Jimenoa's roaring waters. The food is not as good as the view, but it's not bad either. International choices include some very good fish dishes.

Supermercado Jarabacoa (Av. Independencia, tel. 809/574-2780, 8 A.M.–10 P.M. Mon.–Sat., 9 A.M.–1 P.M. Sun.) is a good all-purpose grocery store where you can get provisions for an independent hike or day at the waterfalls.

INFORMATION AND SERVICES

Jarabacoa has an **Oficina de Turismo** (tel. 809/574-7287) in Plaza Ramírez on the second floor.

EL CIBAO

ECOTOURISM

Tourism is no doubt a major industry in the Dominican Republic, which receives around three million visitors a year. Although this boosts the economy significantly, creating jobs for local people and generating a good amount of revenue, relying so heavily upon tourism can exacerbate the strain on the country's natural resources. While it may not be so easy being green, through the collaborative efforts of businesses, government, and communities, the possibilities for sustainability are being fully realized around the country.

The Dominican Republic's Dirección Nacional de Parques has designated conservation areas in the form of six scientific reserves, nine natural monuments, and 16 national parks (parques nacional). Its main objective is to conserve natural resources and ecological inheritances for future generations. Also under protection are a number of panoramic routes and ecological and recreational areas.

Sustainable tourism and ecotourism are movements that seek to support the tourist industry through reducing the negative impact on the environment, and by preserving the integrity of the communities in which tourist accommodations and attractions are located. This includes, in some cases, not just maintaining the communities and economy, but actually pumping new life into them by providing local residents with greater opportunities for a higher standard of living, including educational programs.

Some tour operators, like Iguana Mama, are starting to incorporate this new conscientiousness into their businesses by showing their customers the Dominican Republic that exists outside the all-inclusive resorts that have become so popular. They do this by providing background into the natural history of the country, as well as through fostering interactions between their customers and local folks. Hotels are also starting to get in on the action. Punta Cana Resort and Club is considered the model of the success that can result when private businesses, government, local communities, and educational institutions work together for the good of the country.

Health and Emergencies

Politur (José Duran, tel. 809/754-3216) is open 24 hours.

Clínica Dr. Terrera (Av. Independencia 40, tel. 809/574-4597) offers 24-hour medical care.

Farmacia Miguelito (Mario N. Galan 70, tel. 809/574-2755, 7:30 A.M.–9:30 P.M. Mon.–Sat., 7:30 A.M.–4 P.M. Sun.) has a good variety of different medications, and they deliver too.

Communications

For communication options, try the **TriCom** office on Avenida Independencia to make long-distance calls or the **post office** on the same stretch. The printing shop **Centro Net** (Jimenez, tel. 809/574-4326) is available for Internet services and sells communication cards.

GETTING THERE

Flying in to Santiago is best as it is only an hour's drive to Jarabacoa. The town is equidistant from both Puerto Plata and Santo Domingo at roughly 130 kilometers from each.

Caribe Tours (Calle José Duran, tel. 809/574-4796) has regular service to Jarabacoa from Santo Domingo (US$5.50) with a stop in La Vega (US$1.75) four times a day. However, right next door to this terminal is a *guagua* stop where for about US$0.50 less there is a *guagua* that leaves for La Vega every 20 minutes or so.

GETTING AROUND

Walking is easy within the city of Jarabacoa. But if you are staying out of the town, you'll need some transportation, whether renting a car or hiring a ride of some sort, especially if you plan to be out at night. Taxis usually hang around near the intersection of Duran and Independencia. *Motoconchos* should only be hired during the day.

Car-rental agencies are numerous for such a small town. It is best to rent an SUV for this area since roads can be rough. Expect to pay US$40–50 a day. **Francis Rent a Car** (Carretera a Salto Jimenoa, tel. 809/574-2981, 8 A.M.–noon and 2–6 P.M. Mon.–Sat., 8 A.M.–noon and 2–5 P.M. Sun.) is a reliable choice.

Parques Nacionales Bermúdez y Ramírez

Together the national parks of Armando Bermúdez and José del Carmen Ramírez occupy a whopping 1,530 square kilometers of the central mountainous area which includes the highest point in the Antilles, Pico Duarte, and neighboring peaks La Pelona, La Rucilla, and Pico Yaque. The parks were established in the late 1950s in an effort to salvage what was left of the virgin forest of the island. Since Columbus and his men arrived, it's estimated that nearly two-thirds of the island's forests were destroyed due to fire and development.

The northern **Parque Nacional Armando Bermúdez** is the larger of the two, with 766 square kilometers of protected area. It has both subtropical humid forest and subtropical rainforest temperate zones, giving it a perpetual spring-like climate with temperatures sometimes dipping to a chilly 18°F (-8°C) during December and January nights, leaving a thin layer of frost over the foliage. Flora of the park is varied and depends upon the elevation but mainly consists of local pine trees like the Creole pine *(Pinus occidentalis),* a tree endemic to the island.

The park is home to many birds and other fauna like the Hispaniolan parrot, Hispaniolan trogon, the palm chat (the Dominican national bird), the Hispaniolan woodpecker, the hutia (a rodent), and a wild boar species. In the lower elevations, small snakes are found.

Directly south of Bermúdez is the **Parque Nacional José del Carmen Ramírez,** covering 764 square kilometers of the Cordillera Central. Inside its region are the Yaque del Sur, San Juan, and Mijo Rivers, and its climate is subtropical humid mountain forest. This park is also home to the Valle del Tétero, where you'll find pre-Columbian rock art.

Combined, the two parks have lavish amounts of water running through the region. More than 10 of the country's main river systems flow through them, making them some of the most fertile regions in the nation, irrigating almost 5,000 hectares of land.

Planning a vacation within the national parks alone is a way to experience the Dominican Republic in a way that most tourists do not. If you are hiking, plan on having a couple of days of preparation and at the very least 2–5 days of hiking time, depending on which trail you decide to take.

If your time in the parks is only a leg of your trip within the greater Dominican Republic, save a couple of days for exploration at least. Spending a cool night in the mountain air is a refreshing break from the humidity and sticky heat of the coastal areas. Plus, you'll want a couple of afternoons for exploration of waterfalls, bird-watching, or whatever catches your attention.

◖ PICO DUARTE

The "Dominican Alps" are home to the highest peak in the Caribbean. While Pico Duarte is not the Matterhorn of Switzerland, it does stand tall at 3,087 meters. Surprisingly, while the Matterhorn in the Swiss Alps "weighs in" at 4,478 meters, and was conquered for the first time in 1865, no attempts to climb Pico Duarte occurred until 1944.

EL CIBAO

Not so surprisingly, the peak used to be named Pico Trujillo, when the dictator predictably named it after himself during his tenure. But when he was assassinated, the peak was renamed for the founding father Pablo Duarte.

This challenging climb has been made a little easier since the 1980s when cutting of trails was begun in an effort to increase ecotourism. Currently, nearly 3,000 people hike Pico Duarte and the surrounding peaks every year.

HIKING TRAILS

When choosing a route to take to the top of Pico Duarte, consider how long you've got to spend and honestly ask yourself what sort of stamina or at what athletic level are you able to hike. There are five different routes with varying degrees of stamina needed.

The five routes differ in that the first two routes (La Ciénaga and Mata Grande) leave the Cibao Valley rising upward via the northern slope of the Cordillera Central within the Parque Nacional Armando Bermúdez. Trade winds in this area bring greater amounts of rain, and there are many natural freshwater sources for a large extent of the way. The latter three routes rise via the southern slope of the Cordillera Central within the Parque Nacional José del Carmen Ramírez, where rain is less prevalent, and therefore have a drier climate with fewer potable water sources.

La Ciénaga to Pico Duarte

This route starts in the small town of La Ciénaga just west of Jarabacoa. It is the most popular route to Pico Duarte because it is the shortest and easiest, at 46 kilometers round-trip. Hiring an independent guide is easier in La Ciénaga than in other launching points. Some say to save three days and two nights for this hike, but most can achieve it in two days (with one night in a campground's very basic hut). Beginning a final ascent to the peak well before dawn will reward you with the astonishing sunrise while on top. This route's vertical ascent is about 2,280 meters.

Getting to La Ciénaga from Jarabacoa is as easy as flagging down a *público*, a regular car (usually rather worn down) used as an inexpensive taxi. Or catch a *guagua* for about US$3.

Mata Grande to Pico Duarte

This is the second most difficult route and a popular alternative to the La Ciénaga route. It comes recommended as the most beautiful route of the five. It is a hike of 90 kilometers round-trip that takes three days and has a 3,800-meter ascent, leaving from Mata Grande near San José de las Matas. You'll go over the second-highest peak, La Pelona, too, finally summiting Pico Duarte on the third day. Hiring mules and guides in Mata Grande is similar to in La Ciénaga; secure them two days ahead, and strongly consider hiring a pack mule (the guide may insist) and even a cook (US$10 per day). Your guide and/or cook can help you decide how much food to bring and what to buy.

If you are looking for a more challenging climb than the La Ciénaga one, this is a good choice. Making the trip with organized tours is possible and often easier on you, especially if you don't speak Spanish.

Sabaneta to Pico Duarte

Sabaneta to Pico Duarte (the Sabaneta just north of San Juan de la Maguana—not the one near Dajabón) is the most arduous of the direct routes and takes three days. The vertical ascent is 3,800, just like the Mata Grande trek, but 96 kilometers round-trip. There are two campsites along the way: Alto de la Rosa and Macutico, where you'll stop on the first and second nights. Again, a guide is obligatory and pack mules are highly recommended. The positive aspect about this trek is that since it is the longest, there will be less overcrowding. Take the highway to Sabaneta north for 20 kilometers from San Juan de la Maguana.

Constanza to Pico Duarte

This route is 86 kilometers round-trip and has a 1,600-meter vertical ascent that takes three days to navigate. Constanza is the easternmost departure point. On the first day of your hike via this route, you'll see the impact that humans have had on the area as you will traverse farmland and small towns and onward into more densely vegetated areas on the second day that are recovering from previous human encroachment. The turnoff for Constanza is between La Vega and Bonao.

Padre Las Casas (Las Lagunas) to Pico Duarte

This route is 72 kilometers round-trip and has a vertical ascent of 2,000 meters. It's a three-day trip leaving from Las Lagunas outside of Padre Las Casas in the Azua Province. After about 20 kilometers, it unites with the Constanza route.

ORGANIZED TOURS AND GUIDES

There are tour companies that provide worry-free packages of treks to Pico Duarte, or you can wing it on your own by hiring a guide at the park entrances. The advantage of booking through a tour company is that everything will be taken care of: where you'll sleep, what you'll eat, transportation to the launch point. It is a convenient solution for those who don't have time to plan prior to arrival or are not experienced multi-day hikers. If you've never done it before, there is a lot you could forget, so it is best to leave the details to the professionals so you can concentrate on just having fun.

Máxima Aventura of Rancho Baiguate (Jarabacoa, Carretera a Constanza, tel. 809/574-6890, www.ranchobaiguate.com) has treks in 3–5-day packages that vary in price depending on how many people are in the group. Call or email to reserve your spot and get a price quote.

Although located in Cabarete, **Iguana Mama** (Cabarete, tel. 809/571-0908, www.iguanamama.com, 8 A.M.–5 P.M.) is one of the best trekking companies in the country. For US$450, they'll do all the prep, and you'll just enjoy yourself for three days and two nights

riding mules, spotting rare birds, traversing rivers and creeks, and of course, hiking to the top of the highest peak in the Caribbean.

If you would rather be independent of a tour company, guides typically cost around US$10–20 per day and can be found by asking at the park entrances' ranger stations. Hiring a guide is mandatory. The parks require that for overnight hikes, there is at least one guide for every three trekkers. Most guides take along a mule to carry their equipment, but it is generally a good idea to hire additional mules to assist in carrying your own loads; they cost about US$10 per day. Something else to consider when contemplating the necessity of renting a mule—many hikers find that partway through their journey to the summit, the road gets a little too rough, and that they are not as physically up to the challenge as they thought they were. In cases like these—not all that uncommon, actually—people find that spending part of the journey on the back of a mule is a welcome relief.

Custom dictates that you buy all provisions for the whole journey, for yourself and the guides, and tip them at the end. In making arrangements for your trek independently, it is best to find the guide a couple of days in advance so that preparations can be made with adequate time. Guides are usually willing to tailor trips to your needs and desires (although the cost will vary accordingly).

ACCOMMODATIONS AND FOOD

Most people who come to hike Pico Duarte stay in Jarabacoa or Constanza hotels—that is, until they are on the actual hike. There are about a dozen campgrounds along the way providing very basic shelter. These cabins are basically an empty wooden box and do not have beds (you sleep on the floor). They are free but can be critter-ridden. If you've got the means, a tent that zips closed, pitched outside of the cabins, will, oddly enough, help you get better critter-free rest. It is not possible to reserve a cabin and they are not tended to by the parks on a regular basis.

There are kitchenettes outside of the cabins to cook your meals. Your guide can help you figure out how much food to buy for your entire trip. You'll need to bring bottled water or some sort of purification system.

INFORMATION AND SERVICES

Admission to the park is US$4 and you must be accompanied by a guide at all times. The **ranger stations** (8 A.M.–5 P.M.) are at the start of each of the La Cienaga, Sabaneta, Mata Grande, Las Lagunas, and Constanza trails. Here you can ask for maps (though they never seem to have them) and ask about guides if you are not hiking with an organized tour group.

Preparation

Climbing Pico Duarte is no small feat. Preparing, both mentally and physically, for the (at minimum) two-day hike to its apex can be something of a task in itself. Before you throw on your boots and strap on your backpack, there are quite a few details to consider.

Generally, a trip up Pico Duarte requires a good deal of packing. First off, proper attire is key to enjoying your journey. A variety of clothing will help ensure your comfort through the temperamental climate. The temperature typically ranges 12–21°C (54–70°F) but can dip below freezing, especially in the winter months. Yearly rainfall is between 1,000 and 4,000 millimeters, so waterproof gear is invaluable. Toiletries like sunscreen, toilet paper, and bug repellent will also help make your trip more comfortable and safer. Hiking boots are a must! (Keep in mind, even the top-of-the-line hiking boots will be of little use to you if they are not thoroughly broken in.) Some of the route can be tough going, ranging from dry, rocky terrain to muddy paths to slippery stone, so protect your feet, ankles, and joints as much as possible. A walking stick might also come in handy and make navigating the uneven topography a little easier. Simpler shoes, like sneakers or sandals, are good to wear once you've reached the campsite. If the idea of sharing a cabin with a bunch of strangers is not appealing some camping items you may need are sleeping bags, flashlights, cookware, and tents.

Constanza

Constanza is in a circular valley surrounded by mountains 1,200 meters above sea level. The pastoral scenery offers some of the best views in the country and is what makes it a favorite getaway spot for Dominicans and foreigners. Although it is not a destination filled with many activities, it is a peaceful respite and a jumping off point to one of the routes to Pico Duarte.

The fertile grounds are the livelihood for many families in the region. In the 1950s, Trujillo invited 200 Japanese families to the area to farm the land. His hope was to convert the land into a highly productive agricultural center. Today, many Japanese families remain and the area cultivates a great deal of the country's produce for local consumption and exportation. Although winter temperatures can sometimes dip down to freezing at night, the marvelously fertile ground and pleasant daytime temperatures stimulate the growth of strawberries, cabbage, potatoes, onions, cauliflower, and a great deal of garlic.

SIGHTS

Since most of the sights worth seeing near Constanza are quite far from the town itself, you'll need a good four-wheel-drive to get around and to reach many of the sights and activities.

◖ Parque Nacional Valle Nuevo

Located 20 kilometers south of Constanza is Valle Nuevo National Park. The road to it is horrific, but beautiful views make it worth the work. The park covers an area of 657 square kilometers. This protected forest is 2,640 meters above sea level and the climate can be cool and wet with an annual average rainfall over 2,500 millimeters. It is excellent for bird-watching, with 65 species of birds in the park including the blue-hooded euphonia, the pine warbler, and the white-winged warbler, which is endemic to Hispaniola.

The three-tiered waterfall **Salto de Aguas Blancas** is in the Valle Nuevo park. It is 135 meters high and falls into a very pretty pool.

You'll definitely need a tough 4WD to make the trip to this park.

Reserva Científica Ebano Verde

At one time, the endangered native green ebony (*ébano verde*) tree faced extinction. It was threatened due to its coveted precious wood. But in 1989, a 23-square-kilometer scientific reserve was created by a nonprofit foundation to preserve it and now 621 plant species are protected in its boundaries. There are also amphibious, reptilian, and mammalian species (like solenodons and bats), plus 59 species of birds like the *cotorra* and *el zumbadorcito,* which is the second smallest bird in the world. The reserve is 30 kilometers northeast along the road from Constanza. Once inside you'll find a six-kilometer trail and information posted on trees.

ACCOMMODATIONS

It may feel awkward to pack warm pajamas for a trip to the Caribbean, but if you're sleeping in the cool Dominican Alps climate, you might need them. **Mi Casa** (Luperón at Sánchez, tel. 809/539-2764, US$15 d) has 11 very basic yet clean rooms with private bathrooms; one is a suite that can sleep four people. There's a restaurant on-site.

◖ **Alto Cerro** (two kilometers east of town, tel. 809/539-1553, www.altocerro.com, US$20 d) is on a bluff outside of Constanza. This tourist complex has two- and three-bedroom villas, rooms, and camping facilities, and all have panoramic views of the fertile valley below. The villas are equipped for two, four, five, or seven people with balconies, TV, phone, fireplace, and safe. The rooms are spacious and comfortable and operate on a bed-and-breakfast plan, whereas the suites and villas have kitchens and there is a small market for provisions. But if you don't feel like cooking, there is a restaurant that beats going all the way into town for the next available dining choice. It is a wonderful place for families that offers horseback riding, quad rental, and a large play area for kids. This complex is an excellent value, in town, no matter which accommodation you choose. Meal plans can be arranged.

(C Hotel Rancho Constanza & Cabañas de la Montaña (Calle San Francisco de Macorís 99, tel. 809/539-3268, www.ranchoconstanza .tripod.com/index.html, rooms US$25 d) is a family-run hotel with 11 rooms and two suites (US$55 d). It's clean, with nice hot-water bathrooms and spectacular views overlooking the Valley of Constanza. The suites each have a balcony. Also available are 12 small and basic two-bedroom cabins (US$55) that sleep up to six people, with ceramic tile floors and full kitchens. A conference room can fit up to 150 people, and a restaurant serves *comida criolla.*

FOOD

In the Dominican Republic's garden, Constanza offers fresh local ingredients not typically found elsewhere on the island in such abundance.

Lorenzo's (Luperón 83, tel. 809/539-2008, 8 A.M.–11 P.M. daily, US$5–11) serves fantastic Dominican downhome cooking like *chivo guisado* (goat sautéed and served in a sauce), guinea fowl, or rabbit cooked in wine. Lorenzo's also has an assortment of pastas, pizzas, and sandwiches.

At **(C Aguas Blancas** (Rufino Espinosa 54, tel. 809/539-1561, 10 A.M.–late daily, US$4–10), they like to say that they'll close when everyone goes home. And it is a popular place that comes highly recommended as the best in town. It serves great typical Dominican *comida* for low prices. *La bandera dominicana,* which is a plate of rice and beans with salad and your choice of meat, is always a good choice.

Comedor Gladys (Luperón 36, tel. 809/539-3625, 7 A.M.–10:30 P.M. daily, US$2–8) is a good choice for the budget traveler. You'll get fed well for a very low price. Fresh meat and fish are always available as well as pastries.

Go to **Mercado Municipal** (Gratereaux at 14 de Julio, 7 A.M.–6 P.M. Mon.–Sat., 7 A.M.–noon Sun.) if you need some fresh produce or to see the splendid variety that grows in this very fertile region.

INFORMATION AND SERVICES

For basic tourist information there is an **Oficina de Turismo** (Calle Matilde Viña, tel. 809/539-2900, 9 A.M.–1 P.M. and 2–6 P.M. Mon.–Fri.) in town where they have plenty of information and some brochures to give out.

Health and Emergencies

For health care, you have to go to Santiago since there is no health care at all in Constanza. The **Farmacia Constanza** (Luperón at Libertad, tel. 809/539-2880, 8 A.M.–11 P.M. Mon.–Sat., 8 A.M.–9 P.M. Sun.) has a decent selection of medications and is at the west end of town.

Money and Communications

Banco Léon (Luperón, 8 A.M.–5 P.M. Mon.–Fri., 9 A.M.–1 P.M. Sat.) is centrally located, has an ATM, and exchanges money.

There is a **Tricom** (Luperón 42, tel. 809/539-1015) office that offers international phone service.

GETTING THERE AND AROUND

If you're driving to Constanza, you'll need a four-wheel-drive vehicle for the hills. Be aware that fog can sometimes impair visibility.

The main drag of Constanza is Calle Luperón. On this street is a gas station that doubles as a bus stop at the eastern end. You can catch buses going to Santo Domingo (US$5.50), Santiago (US$5.50), and La Vega (US$2.75).

Guaguas also take off from the same stop (*la parada* to the locals). You can catch one going to Jarabacoa (US$2.80) and El Abanico. From these two stops you can connect to other cities.

La parada (the stop) is also the place to find *motoconchos* and taxis to take you around locally, although Constanza is very easily walked. As with all forms of transportation, make sure you agree on the price before getting on board.

THE SOUTHWEST

Driving through this part of the country, your eyes are met with a spectacular panoply of change: cactus-dotted deserts, lush plantations, towering mountains and cliffs, thriving crops, white-pebbled beaches, and serene lakes. Not many tourists choose to come to this region because it doesn't offer the conventional beach vacation idyll or must-see sights. The majority of the southwest's beaches are carpeted with smooth white rocks along a rough-water, deep shoreline instead of white sand and calm waters. And the closer you get to Haiti, the hotter the climate gets and the more impoverished the towns are. But what is attractive about the southwest is its uniqueness. It is a perfect destination for visitors seeking an off-the-beaten-path experience where you'll encounter gorgeous coastline vistas, a surreal desert terrain, remote and private beaches, flamingo colonies and crocodiles lazing on a river bank, and an extra strong welcome from people who are glad to have tourism come knocking at their door.

The southwest's history, while venerated and celebrated, is not memorialized with museums and grandeur here, but rather, through silent remembrance of its people. It was once the home of the great Taíno cacique Guarokuiá (or Enriquillo, as he was renamed by the Spaniards and is historically referred to), who fought off the Spanish conquistadors through a series of battles for 14 years. Freedom fighter Máximo Gómez, who went on to liberate the republic's sister nation, Cuba, also hailed from here. The black shadow of self-indulgent opulence and egoism of brutal dictator General Rafael Leonidas Trujillo Molina, who killed thousands of

HIGHLIGHTS

🌙 **Reserva Antropológica El Pomier:** This anthropological reserve holds one of the most significant collections of rupestrian art found in the Caribbean. A series of caves features about 4,000 paintings and 5,000 rock drawings by the Taíno, Ingeri, and Carib people (page 224).

🌙 **San Rafael:** Take a dip in the cold and refreshing waters of the *balnearios* San Rafael, then enjoy the breathtaking and photo-perfect views along this highway stretch of the Península de Pedernales, where cliff-top vistas with flowers bloom against the backdrop of white-stone beaches and the azure Caribbean Sea (page 235).

🌙 **Parque Nacional Jaragua:** Take a boat trip to watch the flamingos and 130 other species of birds in their natural habitat of this protected lagoon (page 236).

🌙 **Bahía de las Águilas:** Charter a boat from the fishermen at the Las Cuevas village to one of the most pristine and definitely the most remote beach in the Domincian Republic (page 236).

🌙 **Parque Nacional Isla Cabritos:** Visit the crocodiles and endangered iguanas at Lago Enriquillo, four times saltier than the sea and the lowest point in the Caribbean (page 238).

LOOK FOR 🌙 TO FIND RECOMMENDED SIGHTS, ACTIVITIES, DINING, AND LODGING.

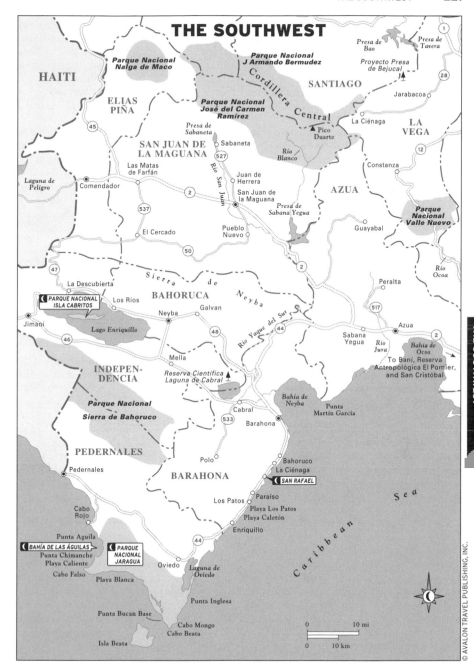

THE SOUTHWEST

Presa de Bao
Presa de Tavera
1

Parque Nacional
Nalga de Maco

Parque Nacional
J Armando Bermudez

Proyecto Presa
de Bejucal

28

HAITI

SANTIAGO

ELIAS
PIÑA

Parque Nacional
José del Carmen
Ramírez

Jarabacoa

La Ciénaga

LA
VEGA

45

Presa de
Sabaneta

Pico
Duarte

12

**SAN JUAN DE
LA MAGUANA**

Sabaneta

527

Río
Blanco

Constanza

Las Matas
de Farfán

Juan de
Herrera

2

Laguna de
Peligro

Comendador

San Juan de
la Maguana

AZUA

537

Presa de
Sabana Yegua

Parque
Nacional
Valle Nuevo

El Cercado

Pueblo
Nuevo

Guayabal

50

2

Río
Ocoa

47

Peralta

La Descubierta

Sierra   de

Neyba

**PARQUE NACIONAL
ISLA CABRITOS**

Los Ríos

BAHORUCA

Galvan

517

Jimani

Neyba

Azua

46

Lago Enriquillo

48

Río Yaque del Sur

44

Sabana
Yegua

Río
Jura

2

Bahía de
Ocoa

Mella

To Bani, Reserva
Antropológica El Pomier,
and San Cristóbal

**INDEPEN-
DENCIA**

Reserva Científica
Laguna de Cabral

Parque Nacional

Sierra de Bahoruco

Cabral

Bahía de
Neyba

Punta
Martín García

533

Barahona

PEDERNALES

Polo

Bahoruco
La Ciénaga

Pedernales

BARAHONA

SAN RAFAEL

S   e   a

Los Patos

Paraíso

Cabo
Rojo

Playa Los Patos
Playa Caletón

Enriquillo

Punta Aguila

44

BAHÍA DE LAS ÁGUILAS

**PARQUE
NACIONAL
JARAGUA**

Punta Chimanche
Playa Caliente

Oviedo

Laguna de
Oviedo

Cabo Falso

Playa Blanca

C   a   r   i   b   b   e   a   n

Punta Inglesa

Punta Bucan Base

Cabo Mongo
Cabo Beata

0   10 mi

Isla Beata

0   10 km

THE SOUTHWEST

people throughout his regime, has stained the otherwise lovely town where he was born, San Cristóbal.

There is a feeling of remoteness from the rest of the Dominican Republic here. It is unlike the rest of the country in geography and most definitely in number of tourism dollars. The southwestern region is a destination for the adventurous visitor, the ecoconscious tourist, and those who want to immerse themselves in the Dominican culture without being separated by the guarded walls of resort complexes.

PLANNING YOUR TIME

To visit the southwest, you could cover some major attractions in just a few days. Perhaps take a three-day weekend away from the city to make your way over the Península de Pedernales or scoop out a driving loop around Lago Enriquillo. Whichever direction, inland or coastal, the best town to look to for a home base is Barahona. It offers the best accommodations options and has some semblance of a nightlife, albeit small.

If you plan a day at the beach, make it Bahía de las Águilas and save a day for it. You'll want to get there midmorning to have a day at the beach, so you'll have to spend your morning gathering provisions and securing the boat ride. The same is true for a loop around Lago Enriquillo, with the tour of the lake being only a couple of hours long.

West of Santo Domingo and the Interior

SAN CRISTÓBAL

Just 25 kilometers west of Santo Domingo is San Cristóbal, known infamously as the birthplace of the brutal dictator Rafael Leonidas Trujillo Molina, who ruled from 1930 until his assassination in 1961.

It is believed that the city was named after the nearby San Cristóbal fortress that Christopher Columbus had built on the Haina riverbank. But in 1934, Trujillo changed the name of the town to Ciudad Benemérita (Meritorious City), supposedly because it was the place where the first legal constitution of the Dominican Republic had been signed in 1844, but it probably had more to do with the fact that it was his birthplace. The name quickly reverted to San Cristóbal when Trujillo was killed and his regime overthrown. Today's San Cristóbal is a good day trip from Santo Domingo and has the ghostly (or ghastly) memories of Trujillo's egoism and "hard-earned" (at the hands of the Dominican people that is) ostentatious wealth in the form of two of his old palaces.

San Cristóbal also has, within a short distance, a series of caves that contain a large array of Taíno cave art.

Sights

Just west of town, on top of a hill, is **El Castillo del Cerro** (Castle on the Hill), one of Trujillo's houses—more of a palace really. Trujillo had the six-story structure built in 1947 for US$3 million and never stayed one night in it when it got back to him that his confidants had criticized it. Trujillo quickly claimed that it was a gift from the townspeople. After Trujillo's death it was looted, and today it sits like an opulently empty shell with some accents still clearly visible as testament to the lavish lifestyle he had: marble staircases, gold leafing, dining rooms, ballrooms with intricately painted ceilings, mosaic tiles, and multiple bedrooms and bathrooms. Perhaps the most surprising thing about El Castillo del Cerro is that it is not even a museum. It simply is locked up and guarded by an armed guard who will open it up and show you around if you tip him. To get there, take Calle María Trinidad Sánchez to Avenida Luperón and take a left at the Isla gasoline station; veer right at the fork in the road, then left and up the hill. It is perfectly acceptable to ignore the Do Not Enter sign; tourists go all the time and the armed guard you'll see at the front door is used to it.

Casa de Caoba (Mahogany House), another of Trujillo's houses, was looted too after his death, and while it appears as though it was probably once a beautiful home, it was ransacked and sits empty. This one is five kilometers north of town. Promises have been made off and on to restore it to its former glory, promises that have not been kept.

Iglesia Nuestra Señora de la Consolación (6–8 A.M. and 5:30–8 P.M. daily) was built on the Plaza Piedra Viva, where Trujillo's childhood home once stood and where he had originally intended to be buried (his remains are elsewhere now). The church is a huge mustard-yellow and white structure that cost an exorbitant US$4 million to build back in 1946. Trujillo spent government funds to build the church and the Plaza Piedra Viva. Inside the church is a large mural from the renowned Spanish muralist José Vela Zanetti.

Food

San Cristóbal is best left for a day trip. There are no satisfactory accommodations choices and what restaurants you find are limited as well. **Fela's Place** (General Leger 55, tel. 809/288-2124, 8 A.M.–midnight) is a very informal place of cheap eats serving Dominican fare and specializing in chicken. To eat a traditional dish from San Cristóbal, look for *pasteles en hoja* (pastry in leaf). They are made from plantain and meat or chicken and the mixture is then wrapped like a present with a banana leaf and boiled. They are a good cheap meal (about US$0.50 each), served with hot sauce on the side.

Information and Services

For health-related matters or emergencies, **Centro Médico Constitución** (Av. Constitución, tel. 809/288-2121) has a 24-hour emergency room.

The **Oficina de Turismo** (Av. Constitución, 9 A.M.–3 P.M. Mon.–Fri.) has limited information but a staff that is willing to help with any questions you may have.

For an ATM or money exchange, head to **Banco Popular** (Av. Constitución, 8 A.M.–5 P.M. Mon.–Fri., 9 A.M.–1 P.M. Sat.) on Parque Colon.

© ANA CHAVIER CAAMAÑO

irrigation aqueduct near Baní

THE SOUTHWEST

© ANA CHAVIER CAAMAÑO

Plaza de Pilones

THE SOUTHWEST

Getting There and Around

San Cristóbal is 25 kilometers west of Santo Domingo and can be accessed easily by driving Highway 2, or you can catch a *guagua* from Parque Enriquillo in Santo Domingo. In San Cristóbal, you can catch a *guagua* back to Santo Domingo about every half hour or so from the Parque Central. If you're headed toward Barahona in the west, you'll need to go out to the main highway to flag down a *guagua.*

Taxis and *guaguas* are readily available in San Cristóbal near Parque Independencia.

◖ RESERVA ANTROPOLÓGICA EL POMIER

In Reserva Antropológica El Pomier (15 kilometers north of San Cristóbal, 8 A.M.–5 P.M. daily, US$3.50) there is a series of 57 interconnecting caves, the most significant collection of rupestrian art found in the Caribbean. The drawings and carvings in this anthropoligical reserve are from not just the Taíno Indians, but the Igneri and Carib as well and are estimated at as much as 2,000 years old. For the Carib-

bean, this is tantamount to what the pyramids of Egypt are for the Middle East. The caves contain over 4,000 paintings and 5,000 rock drawings. Cave One contains 590 pictograms alone. Most of the paintings depict animals and birds with some that are believed to be representative of deities. The caves open to the public (five total) have undergone renovation complete with walkways and electric lighting for viewing. The caves are also home to thousands of bats. The best way to get to the caves is by taxi or *motoconcho* because the turnoff road is unmarked. Try to make sure the driver knows that you need a ride back so that they either wait for you or come back.

BANÍ

After driving past plush fields of sugarcane that wave through the countryside, you'll reach the town of Baní. Sugar is still the main industry here, and during harvest you'll see bands of workers in the fields as well as tractors and oxen-driven cartloads on their way to the mill. Keep your eye out for roadside stalls selling mangoes. The *mango banilejo* has turned Baní into the mango capital of the country, and it is making its way into the international market as well. While they might be the smallest mangoes you've encountered, they will be the sweetest you'll ever eat. Other crops in the area are yucca, plantains, and onions. *Chivos* (goats) are raised here.

A lovely, friendly, and clean town, Baní has few tourist curiosities but is a great place for travelers to stop for the night if they can't make it to their final destination. It was here that the Cuban liberation fighter, Máximo Gómez Báez, was born on November 18, 1836.

Baní is also sometimes called the "city of poets" and was named to honor the Taíno cacique Baní, who is said to have been a very wise man.

Sights

The **Casa de Máximo Gómez** (8 A.M.–5 P.M., free) is Baní's main attraction, really more of a park placed on what was the location of Gómez's childhood home. There is a bust of him, the Dominican and Cuban flags, and a mural with scenes depicting his life. The **Museo Municipal** (Calle Sánchez 1, 8 A.M.–noon Mon.–Fri., free) is on the first floor of the Palacio del Ayuntamiento facing the park and is rather uneventful.

Playa Baní, while challenging to get to, is worth the effort. Both fishing and windsurfing are fantastic here, but very undeveloped. You won't find the windsurfing schools and rentals like in Cabarete. Farther west along the coast, the sand dunes at **Las Calderas** and salt gardens at **Las Salinas** make for surreal yet beautiful views and great photo opportunities.

Plaza de Pilones is not exactly a sight per se, but more of a place to buy a necessary object for cooking Dominican fare. You have your choice of very small to gigantic sized mortar and pestle sets made with the wood from the cambron trees. The Taínos introduced them to the Spanish and they are now found in every kitchen in the Dominican Republic. No kitchen is complete without one. They are a good, authentic gift to take home with you. The more elaborately decorated ones tend to be Haitian; the Dominican ones are basic and sturdy. You can't make an authentic *mofongo* without one (a plantain dish served right in the *pilón*). Plaza de Pilones is an outdoor market on the left side of the highway outside of Baní traveling toward Azua. There is a booth to buy snacks. Look for it after you have passed the Parador Cruz de Ocoa.

Accommodations and Food

Most people simply pass through Baní. But if you find yourself needing a place to rest for the night, there are a couple of choices.

Hotel Caribani (Calle Sánchez 12, tel. 809/522-3871, US$25 d fan only), one block from Parque Duarte, offers clean rooms with hot-water bathrooms, cable TV, and comfortable beds. It is a good location because there are many services close by. This is the best option in town. Also on-site is the restaurant **El Gran Artesa,** which serves Dominican and international food. It is probably the nicest dining option in town with buffet and à la carte service.

Restaurant y Pizzería Yari (Calle Sán-chez, tel. 809/522-3717, 8 A.M.–11 P.M. daily, US$4–10), right next to Hotel Caribani, is a favorite pizzeria of Baní. There is great service in the open-air casual dining room. It has more than pizza; many meat and seafood dishes tend to fare better than the pizza.

Informal **La Casona** (Nuestra Señora de Regla 16, tel. 809/522-3283, 8:30 A.M.–3 P.M. daily, US$4–10) serves classic Dominican *comida criolla* on a big terrace. Cash only.

Parador Cruz de Ocoa (no phone, 6 A.M.–10 P.M.) is outside of Baní on the way to Azua. It is a good place to stop to use a semi-clean public bathroom (take your own toilet paper if you have some), one of the last you'll find for a while if you're traveling west—they're better than some of the ones out there. There is a very large assortment of food in a cafeteria setup, ranging from *comida criolla* to pastry, beer to coffee. There is a clothing boutique adjacent to it. Buses often stop here to let their passengers get provisions and use the bathrooms.

Cafeteria Comedor Abuela is across the street from Parador Cruz de Ocoa and is well known with Dominicans that pass through here for its top-notch *dulce de leche,* a very sweet candy made of condensed milk with a fudge-like consistency. Comedor Abuela is another choice for a "just passing through" snack stop and is in a ramshackle hut on the side of the highway where you can get food, liquor, and sweets.

Information and Services

Banco León (Hwy. Sánchez at Calle Mella, 8:15 A.M.–5 P.M. Mon.–Fri., 9 A.M.–1 P.M. Sat.) has a 24-hour ATM.

Verizon Centro de Comunicaciones (Hwy. Sánchez at Calle Mella, 8 A.M.–10 P.M.) is right next to the Banco León and has long-distance phone services.

Getting There and Around

Guaguas to and from Santo Domingo (US$1.75) are based out of the terminal a half block away from Parque Central every 15 minutes.

At a terminal west of the park on Máximo Gómez, you can find the buses whizzing by

© ANA CHAVIER CAAMAÑO

plátanos en route

headed for Barahona (US$3.50) every half-hour to hour. The ride to Barahona is two hours.

Walking around in Baní is easy and quite pleasant as it is a very small and clean town. As always though, there are *motoconchos* buzzing about if you'd like to flag one down to take you around town or to the beaches, although it's not recommended since the road to the beach tends to be as smooth as a runway on Mars.

AZUA DE COMPOSTELA

Although Azua (as it is commonly referred) is a bustling and fairly large town, it doesn't have much to offer tourists and isn't as charming as Baní. It is an agricultural town that has a healthy watermelon and honeydew melon crop. Most who pass through simply use Azua as a pit stop.

Even though there isn't much by way of tourism here, Azua has an compelling history having briefly been a home base for three infamous Spanish conquistadors.

Azua was founded in 1504 by Diego Ve-lásquez, who came to Hispaniola with Columbus in 1493 on Columbus's second voyage. He later was instrumental to the brutal conquering and governing of Cuba. At one time Azua was also home to a notary public, Hernán Cortés, who fought alongside Velásquez in Cuba and was later key in the conquest of the Aztecs in what is now Mexico. And the third Spanish soldier, Juan Ponce de Léon, also lived in Azua, that is before he went off to look for the fountain of youth in what is present-day Florida. Azua was demolished by fire three times by Haitian soldiers in 1805, 1844, and 1849.

Sights

Modern-day Azua has missed its opportunity, unfortunately, to be a location of interest to tourists as there is only one small monument in the **Parque Central** commemorating a battle that took place 16 kilometers away at **Puerto Viejo,** where the great Taíno leader Enriquillo is said to be buried.

Playa Río Monte, while popular with locals,

© ANA CHAVIER CAAMAÑO

the veggies of Azua

is not a very pretty beach. It has food stalls, is a rather stony beach, and is quite crowded on the weekends.

Playa Blanca is about a kilometer west of Playa Río Monte and has a sandier beach but is best for its vantage point; offshore, dolphins play and manta rays hang out skimming the surface for food. These beaches are in the **Bahía de Ocoa** and are reachable from a marked turnoff six kilometers off the main highway.

Accommodations and Food

Azua is not a good place to stop for the night. It simply doesn't have adequate hotel accommodations. But should you get stuck, **Hotel El Familiar** (Calle Emilio Prud'Homme at Calle 19 de Marzo, tel. 809/521-2272, US$10 d) has bare-bones rooms with a fan only. It really is a last resort and one of the only ones in town at that.

Food is only somewhat easier to find in Azua, and most restaurants are inexpensive. **El Gran Segovia** (Av. Francisco del Rosario 31, tel. 809/521-3726, 8 A.M.–10 P.M. daily) has good authentic seafood in an informal setting. Cash only.

Kevin Sandwich (Calle Duarte, 8 A.M.–1 P.M. and 4 P.M.–midnight daily, US$5) is a very inexpensive sandwich shop with burgers and many other great sandwich choices.

For a great selection of *comida criolla,* head to **Restaurante Francia** (Av. Francisco del Rosario S. 104, tel. 809/521-2900, 8 A.M.–10 P.M. daily) for good traditional food.

Quaint **Cira** (Av. Francisco del Rosario Sánchez 101, tel. 809/521-3740, 8:30 A.M.–11 P.M. daily, US$5–10) has seating in a garden. Its specialty is *chivo* (goat).

Information and Services

For an ATM open 24 hours, go to **Banco Progreso** (Av. Duarte at 19 de Marzo, tel. 809/521-2592, 8:30 A.M.–4 P.M. Mon.–Fri., 9 A.M.–1 P.M. Sat.).

For any pharmaceutical needs you're bound to find what you need at **Farmacia Ramírez** (Calle Emilio Prud'homme, 8 A.M.–10 P.M.) and

SAN JUAN DE LA MAGUANA AND THE TAÍNO *BATEYES*

Founded in the early 16th century, shortly after Christopher Columbus's "discovery" of the west, San Juan de la Maguana is one of the oldest cities in the Dominican Republic. But long before the Spaniards set foot on the island, which Columbus would call Hispaniola, the Taíno walked its earth. However, less than 100 years after Spain staked its claim, the island's entire population of Taínos was destroyed.

Archaeologists, sociologists, and anthropologists have since been able to learn a great deal about the Taíno culture. Much attention has been paid to the cave art discovered in many areas of the island and its spiritual significance to the lives of the Taíno. Also of great religious importance, and the subject of much research, are *bateyes*, or paved courtyards surrounded by large stone blocks and often centrally located in the villages. One particular *batey* – La Corral de los Indios de Chacuey, which is in San Juan de la Maguana – has been the focus of much study and speculation about Taíno life.

The Taíno lived in villages throughout the Dominican Republic – it is thought that the populations of these communities ranged from single families to upwards of 3,000 people. The *batey* was likely used for many purposes, both social and ceremonial, including festivals, markets, dances, and musical ceremonies, which may have included storytelling, dancing, and a ritual ball game.

In the ball game, very similar to soccer, the players were not permitted to use their hands but could use their feet, legs, hips, heads, and bodies to hit the ball, which was made out of a tough and heavy combination of rubber and fiber. It is believed that this game was played

© ANA CHAVIER CAAMAÑO

Taíno *batey*

for more than just fun, as it seemed to be quite dangerous. Teams probably consisted of anywhere from 10 to 30 people. The Taíno may have believed that winning the game meant children and harvest would prosper. And, as the Taíno seemed to have been a mostly peaceful folk who did not believe in confrontation, it is possible the game was played, in part, to work out or avoid disagreements that might occur within the tribe or between tribes.

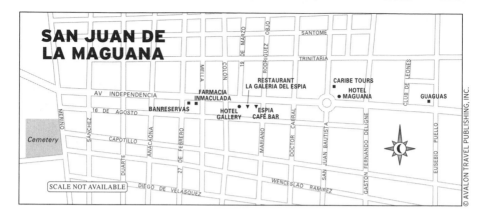

Farmacia Frank (Calle Emilio Prud'homme 70, tel. 809/521-3280).

Getting There and Around

Guagua departures to and arrivals from Santo Domingo (US$3.50) occur every 15 minutes from the corner of Calle Duarte and Miguel Angel Garrido 5 A.M.–6 P.M. You can also catch a *guagua* to San Juan de la Maguana and Barahona every 15 minutes.

Caribe Tours picks up passengers for Santo Domingo at the Parque Central at 7:15 A.M., 7:30 A.M., 10:45 A.M., 11:15 A.M., 2:30 P.M., 2:45 P.M., 6:15 P.M., and 6:25 P.M.

Walking in Azua is easy because of its small size. *Motoconchos* are easily found. They usually all hang out together in front of *colmados* (corner stores).

SAN JUAN DE LA MAGUANA

With a dual-purpose name, San Juan (named for Saint John the Baptist) and de la Maguana (named for a Taíno tribe) honors both of its heritages. This is an old town, simply referred to as San Juan, that was founded in the 1500s by the Spanish in what was an area populated by the Taíno indigenous peoples around the time of the Spanish invasion.

San Juan is a pleasant town that has only one historical tourist sight. It does however, have some interesting festivals that are fun to see if you're in the area while they are happening.

El Corral de los Indios

El Corral de los Indios (free) is 10–15 minutes outside of town (about seven kilometers). It is the Taíno site thought to be a gathering point for games and rituals. Archaeologists believe that at one time, there was a circle of rocks surrounding the field; only a few rocks are left including one large one in the center. In 2005 a government official was making an assessment in order to restore it for tourist purposes. To get to El Corral de los Indios, follow Calle Independencia westbound to Avenida Anacaona and turn north onto Juan Herrera. Good signage will point you to the field.

Entertainment and Festivals

Adjacent to the Hotel Gallery and Restaurant La Galeria del Espia, **Espia Café Bar** (Calle Independencia 7, tel. 809/557-5069, 8 P.M.– until people leave) is a lively and popular bar that has karaoke and dancing. It is an informal bar and a lot of fun.

La Fiesta del Espírito Santo, held around the first Sunday of June, is a procession from the town of El Batey to San Juan. This religious celebration includes carrying a religious icon to drums and chanting. It is a showcase of the Haitian and remaining Taíno influences in the culture of this region. The festival culminates in the plaza of San Juan for another full day.

On June 24, **Día de San Juan,** the town

THE SOUTHWEST

honors its patron saint, John the Baptist, ending a two-week celebration. Two weeks earlier food stands set up, dancing and music in the streets begins, and the festival balloons until the final blowout on the 24th when a live band plays at the archway entrance to town.

Accommodations and Food

Hotel Gallery (Calle Independencia 5 and Monsenor Merino, tel. 809/557-1007 or 809/557-2317, US$19 d) has wonderful service, and even though the 12 rooms are small and boxy, they are very clean and all have air-conditioning, which is a huge plus in this hot region. Rooms come in single, double, or triple. Suites are available that are more like a double room with a king-size bed and a full bed with a small refrigerator. In addition to air-conditioning, all have phone, TV, and a private bathroom. The restaurant serves good Dominican and Mexican food, and room service is available. This is a good value; it's owned by the same proprietors as the adjacent Restaurant La Galeria del Espia and the Espia Café Bar.

Hotel Maguana (Calle Independencia 72, tel. 809/557-2244, US$18 d) has been a mainstay of San Juan since 1947. The rooms are spacious and clean with comfortable beds. All rooms have a private hot-water bath. The restaurant is good.

Restaurant La Galeria del Espia (Calle Independencia, tel. 809/557-2704, 1:30–4 P.M. and 6:30 P.M.–3 A.M., US$4–7), directly adjacent to the Hotel Gallery, is owned by a Dominican and his Mexican wife and serves authentic dishes from each country, like *chivo guisado* and enchiladas. It has a nice atmosphere, clean with wonderful service and a big drink menu and wine list. The odd hours speak to how late-going the adjacent Espia Café Bar can run.

Information and Services

Farmacia Inmaculada (Calle Independencia at 27 de Febrero, tel. 809/527-2801, 8 A.M.–10 P.M.) has a decent selection of medications.

BanReservas (Calle Independencia at 27 de Febrero, tel. 809/557-2613, 8 A.M.–5 P.M. Mon.–Fri., 9 A.M.–1 P.M. Sat.) has a 24-hour ATM, as do most of the banks in town.

rice fields on the road to San Juan de la Maguana

© ANA CHAVIER CAAMAÑO

There is a **Verizon Centro de Comunicaciones** (Calle 16 de Agosto, 8 A.M.–10 P.M.) for any long-distance calls you may need to make.

Getting There and Around

Driving into town on the Carretera Sánchez, it changes into two one-way streets, Calle Independencia (westbound traffic) and Calle 16 de Agosto (eastbound traffic). These are the main drags, and most commercial necessities and hotels are on or very near these streets.

Caribe Tours (tel. 809/557-4520) has buses for Santo Domingo (US$5.25) leaving at 6:45 A.M., 10 A.M., 1:45 P.M., and 5:15 P.M. from its depot which is near the Hotel Maguana. For a bus to Barahona, you'll need to take one to Azua (US$2.25) and transfer there.

Guaguas for Santo Domingo leave from a stop three blocks east of the main archway into town on the eastern side. They depart every 20 minutes 4 A.M.–6 P.M.

Taxis and *motoconchos* can be found hanging around at the Parque Central.

COMENDADOR DEL REY

This is the town of many names: Locals refer to it as Comendador, others call it Elías Piño, and it has had even more names in the past. About the only reason any visitors head to this town is to go to the Haitian Market or cross over into Haiti. It is not a good place to stay overnight.

Haitian Market

This is very easy to find so long as you stay on the main road as you enter town. Just keep driving and you'll run into it. Just as the market goes in Dajabón, so does this one. The Haitian merchants come over and put their wares onto blankets on the ground and shield themselves from the sun with whatever is handy. You won't find tourist souvenirs like the ones in gift shops, but more the likes of pots and pans, housewares, clothes, and produce all for very cheap.

Getting There and Around

You'll find *guaguas* at their terminal on 27 de Febrero at the Parque Central. Buses to Santo Domingo leave every 30 minutes for US$6. If you're going to Barahona, you'll need to board an Azua bus and exchange there.

Crossing the border to Haiti is a bit different here than in Dajabón. At the **Dominican immigration office** (8 A.M.–6 P.M.) they will stamp your passport and you'll pay US$20 to cross over. When you cross over, take a taxi about 2.5 kilometers to the Haitian immigration office, where you'll pay US$10 to enter Haiti. You shouldn't have to pay a return fee.

Taxis and *motoconchos* usually hang around near the Dominican immigration office.

THE SOUTHWEST

Península de Pedernales

BARAHONA

Driving Highway 44 along the coast, the road begins to wind and climb while delivering picturesque vistas of red rock mountains dropping into the coast of the intensely blue Caribbean Sea. Then with the emergence of the **Bahía de Neyba** before you, green fields of sugarcane and bananas begin to brighten the view.

Barahona sits in the western edge of the bay and is the last big town you'll encounter in the southwestern Dominican Republic. With all the beauty surrounding, one has to wonder why tourists haven't been flocking here all along. It is virtually undiscovered. Barahona has a satisfactory variety of accommodation and food choices and a location on a breathtaking coastline within proximity of a number of activities for day trips, so it is a good place, the perfect place, to set up base camp if you want to explore the Península de Pedernales.

While the surrounding area of Barahona is beautiful, the town itself is a little drab. It

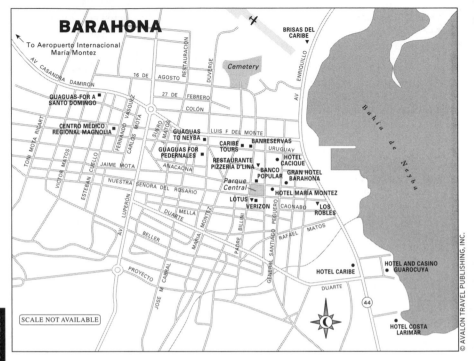

BARAHONA

To Aeropuerto Internacional María Montez

BRISAS DEL CARIBE

AV. CASANDRA DAMIRON

16 DE AGOSTO

27 DE FEBRERO

COLÓN

Cemetery

AV. RESTAURACIÓN

DUVERGE

AV. ENRIQUILLO

GUAGUAS-FOR A SANTO DOMINGO

CENTRO MÉDICO REGIONAL MAGNOLIA

GUAGUAS TO NEYBA

LUIS F DEL MONTE

BANRESERVAS

URUGUAY

GUAGUAS FOR PEDERNALES

CARIBE TOURS

JAIME MOTA

ANACAONA

RESTAURANTE PIZZERIA D'LINA

HOTEL CACIQUE

BANCO POPULAR

GRAN HOTEL BARAHONA

NUESTRA SEÑORA DEL ROSARIO

Parque Central

HOTEL MARIA MONTEZ

LOTUS

VERIZON

CAONABO

LOS ROBLES

MELLA

DUARTE

BELLER

PADRE BILLINI

RAFAEL MATOS

MARIA MONTEZ

GENERAL SANTIAGO PEGUERO

PROYECTO

JOSE M CABRAL

HOTEL CARIBE

HOTEL AND CASINO GUAROCUYA

DUARTE

44

HOTEL COSTA LARIMAR

Bahía de Neyba

SCALE NOT AVAILABLE

© AVALON TRAVEL PUBLISHING, INC.

was founded in 1802 by the Haitian liberation fighter Toussaint L'Ouverture, when the export of wood was a major source of revenue. Then, with Trujillo in power, it became a major sugarcane producer when he had fields planted to make money for himself and his family. Today, the sugarcane gives money to the city, but there is also coffee, bauxite, and gypsum production.

There are no sights whatsoever in Barahona proper, and the public beach of Barahona isn't nice at all, but there are a number of locations within a short drive for some fun day trips, like the Larimar Mines and various *balnearios* (freshwater swimming holes).

Entertainment and Events

At night, most of Barahona's young people hang out along the Malecón, flirting, spinning around on their mopeds, and playing loud music.

Los Robles (Av. Enriquillo and Nuestra Sra del Rosario, tel. 809/524-1629, 9 A.M.–2 A.M.) is a good spot for a beer. You can sit on the outdoor patio or go inside to the brand-new disco and dance to some salsa, merengue, and *bachata*. It's a happening spot.

Lotus (Calle Padre Billini at Nuestra Sra del Rosario, 7:30 P.M.–2 A.M. Wed.–Sun., US$1), across from the Parque Central, has been a main dance club in Barahona for years. It's a good (not seedy) place to go to have fun.

Accommodations

Barahona has turned into a rather popular spot for Dominicans needing respite from the city for the weekend.

Hotel Cacique (Av. Uruguay 2, tel. 809/524-4620, US$9 d) is an amazingly cheap budget option one block away from the Malecón. There are 16 clean rooms with cable TV and private hot-water bathrooms. While this is cheap, the comfort that you'll get at a hotel for just a little more money might be worth the good night's sleep, because you might not get one on these mattresses.

【 Hotel María Montez (Calle Jaime Mota 48, tel. 809/524-6503, US$23 d) was named after the famous Hollywood actress from the 1940s who was born in Barahona. The hotel was built in 2000 and is in a quiet neighborhood. There are shared balconies on each of the three floors where you can enjoy the crisp night air. There was talk of creating a fourth level for a restaurant. All the rooms are similar in size, very clean and comfortable with private bathrooms. All have air-conditioning and cable TV—no phones yet but there is a pay phone in the lobby that you can use. There's a generator for extra power. The owner, Doña Gladys, is very hospitable and friendly. Parking is available.

Gran Hotel Barahona (Jaime Mota 5, tel. 809/524-2415, US$23 d) offers 39 clean rooms with hot-water bathrooms and cable TV. This is a good choice for location's sake, near Parque Central—so restaurants, banks, and other services are near.

Hotel Caribe (Av. Enriquillo and Duarte, tel. 809/524-4111, US$ 30 d), although not as nice as some of the others, does include breakfast in the rate Tuesday–Friday (excluding holidays). The 31 rooms have air-conditioning, telephones, hot-water bathrooms, and TV in each. The restaurant is right next door and is called La Rocca. Hotel Caribe is across from Hotel and Casino Guarocuya.

One of the first hotels in Barahona, **Hotel and Casino Guarocuya** (Av. Enriquillo, tel. 809/524-2121, US$28) is starting to show its age. Unfortunately, it looks like it could have once had wonderful glory days, but now it's in its gloomy days. It is right on the oceanfront, so the rooms facing the water have great views. All rooms have air-conditioning, cable TV, and telephone. The restaurant is open at 7 A.M. and there is a casino that opens at 6 P.M.

【 Hotel Costa Larimar (Av. Enriquillo 6, tel. 809/524-5111, fax 809/524-7063, www .costalarimar.com, US$115 d all-inclusive, US$52 d room only) is Barahona's rather limp attempt at an all-inclusive hotel. The rooms are spacious and have comfortable beds, ceiling fans, working but very loud air-conditioning, and private baths. The windows are nice, but not all of them open to let in fresh air. There is a big pool with a good-sized bar next to it where meals are served along with drinks at night, and sometimes there's live music or karaoke. Although some call it the five-star hotel of Barahona, one should seriously ponder how many stars are possible on that scale. The beachfront was rather a letdown. But if you're looking for a good room in a hotel that has a pool, this might be your only choice in Barahona.

Food

【 Los Robles (Av. Enriquillo and Nuestra Sra del Rosario, tel. 809/524-1629, 9 A.M.–2 A.M. daily, US$5–15) is for sure the most popular spot in town to dine. There is a lot of action at this corner at night, the food is good, and the prices are too. It's on an outdoor patio with a thatched-roof bar and a jukebox that pumps out very loud Latin tunes. For a quieter meal, head to the back garden area where the picnic tables are set up next to an aviary and a pond that has turtles in it. There is also a "take-it-to-go" shack in the back where you can get sandwiches. The pizza is wonderful, as is the *mofongo;* there is a big menu to choose from for international and Dominican fare including grilled meats and seafood. They deliver. After dinner, head to the disco of the same name in the building in the back. It is a small dance floor, but they play great music and its very air-conditioned.

【 Restaurante Pizzería D'Lina (Calle 30 de Mayo at Calle Anacaona, tel. 809/524-3681, US$1–10) has a very loyal following. Pizza is good; there is also seafood, *comida criolla*, appetizers, and sandwiches (the *cubano* was excellent). With so many other restaurants around this area, this one still stands ahead of the others.

Seafood is a specialty at **Brisas del Caribe** (Av. Enriquillo 1, tel. 809/524-2794, 8 A.M.– 11 P.M., US$8), an upper crust yet informal restaurant. Enjoy lobster, shrimp, sea bass, and

THE SOUTHWEST

many more types of fish. It's right on Barahona's Malecón with a view of the sea.

Information and Services

The **Oficina de Turismo** and **Politur** (Calle Batey Central, tel. 809/524-3573) are in the same building on the Malecón as you drive into town from the north.

Centro Médico Regional Magnolia (Av. Uruguay at Francisco Vásquez, tel. 809/524-2470) has a 24-hour emergency room.

Try **Verizon** (Calle Luperón and Calle Padre Bellini, 8 A.M.–10 P.M. daily) for long-distance and computer needs. You'll find another **Verizon** on Calle Nuestro Señora del Rosario across from the Parque Central.

Banco Popular (Calle Jaime Mota at Calle Padre Bellini, tel. 809/521-2102, 9 A.M.–3 P.M. Mon.–Fri.) has a 24-hour ATM and is located at Parque Central.

BanReservas (Av. Uruguay at Padre Bellini, tel. 809/524-4006, 8 A.M.–5 P.M. Mon.–Fri. and 9 A.M.–1 P.M. Sat.) has a 24-hour ATM as well.

Getting There

At **Aeropuerto Internacional María Montez** (Hwy. 44, tel. 809/524-4144), **Caribair** (tel. 809/567-7050) has small planes commuting from Santo Domingo on Monday, Friday, and Sunday, departing at 8:30 A.M. and returning at 5 P.M.; there are also regular flights on the weekend to Haiti from Barahona. **Aerodomca** (tel. 809/567-1984) and **Servicios Aeros Profesionales** (tel. 809/547-3554) service this airport as well.

Caribe Tours (Av. Uruguay, tel. 809/524-4952) has direct service to Azua (US$1.75) and Santo Domingo (US$5.25).

Taking a *guagua* from Barahona to other towns is a bit trickier. For a Santo Domingo–bound ride (US$4.25) head over to Avenida Luis Delmonte between Matos and Suero. They leave every 15 minutes 4 A.M.–6 P.M. For San Juan de la Maguana, take the Santo Domingo *guagua* and let them know where you are going so they let you off at the right connection point.

Guaguas for Pedernales (US$4.25) leave from Avenida Uruguay between Padre Billini and 30 de Mayo every hour from 7 A.M.–3 P.M. For *guaguas* to La Descubierta and Lago Enriquillo (US$2.50) with a transfer in Neyba head over to Avenida Luis Delmonte between Billini and 30 de Mayo.

Getting Around

There are plenty of *motoconchos* and taxis twirling around Barahona, and they can be found at the Parque Central or along Avenida Luis Delmonte. Barahona is a rather sprawling city, but walking around the center part is easy.

AROUND BARAHONA
The Larimar Mines

The Larimar Mines (Mon.–Fri., closed when it rains, free), high up in the lush mountains, are open for viewing, and the drive there is gorgeous. These open-cast mines are where the semiprecious mineral is dug. The Dominican Republic is the only place where larimar is mined; it is then mostly used for jewelry. It is mined by hand, and the men will sell you uncut stones by weight for around US$5–10. Remember that larimar's blue color is enhanced when wet, which is why some will try to sell you pieces that are in jars filled with water. You'll need a four-wheel-drive to get to the mines. Just south of Las Filipinas village (about 14 kilometers south of Barahona), turn right onto a dirt road for 15 kilometers into the hills. Follow this rough road to Las Chupaderos and the mine is at the end of the road.

Bahoruco and La Ciénaga

Located 17 kilometers south of Barahona are the twin towns of Bahoruco and La Ciénaga. Although there aren't really any sights here, or services, there are a few nice places to stay and the people are very nice and known for their very blue eyes.

❰ Casa Bonita (Carretera de la Costa, Km 16, tel. 809/445-8610, US$56 d), high on a hill overlooking Bahoruco and the Caribbean Sea, is a charming and wonderful find. There are 12 thatch-roofed, nicely appointed cabins with sloped ceilings and shuttered windows that open to an amazing ocean view. Next to the pool is a restaurant/bar with a lovely sitting area where you can take in the panoramic views of the ocean and mountains. This is a small, quiet hotel. Sunsets here are very romantic.

Coral Sol Resort (La Ciénaga, tel. 809/233-4882, www.coralsolresort.com, US$50 d) is on the southern end of the two towns. The turn-off is well marked by a sign off the main highway just after you think you've passed it all. There are 10 cabins that are roomy and clean. Each has two beds and two bathrooms. The beach is the typical pebbly kind that you find in this area of the coast, but pleasant. Breakfast and dinner are included in the rate. It's not as charming as Casa Bonita, but a nice place to stay.

(San Rafael

After just a short three kilometers south of Bahoruco and la Ciénaga, you'll reach San Rafael. The things to see here are the *balnearios* (swimming holes) and magnificent vista points on either side of the town.

Balneario La Virgen (8 A.M.–6 P.M., free), right off the main highway, is cleaned often and very cold—but that is the beauty and the experience of swimming in a *balneario*. There is food and drink available in a shack next to this tiered pool. One tier is more for children since it is shallower, and it can get crowded and loud.

Villa Miriam (8 A.M.–6 P.M. daily, US$1.75) is off the highway up a steep road. It is a formed set of several pools and one regular pool. Since this one isn't free, it isn't as popular, but it is quieter and less crowded.

The *mirador* (viewpoint) up the hill from the *balnearios* has a breathtaking panoramic view of the southern coast of the Dominican Republic. The cliffs have blooming azaleas in fire red and orange, set against the blue of the Caribbean Sea; it makes for phenomenal photos.

Los Patos, several kilometers south of Paraíso, has a white-rock beach that is not very safe to swim in as the coastline is incredibly deep. But the adjacent **Balneario Los Patos,** where the Los Patos river meets the sea, is a great place to swim. Its water is crystal clear and frigid with lots of room to splash around.

© ANA CHAVIER CAAMAÑO

white-rock beach of Los Patos

THE SOUTHWEST

It can get crowded on the weekends, but if you come midweek, it should be relatively empty. There are public bathrooms by the pool. The food vendors have gotten together to form an association, and they clean and care for the area because it's the bread and butter of a very poor area. Seafood and drinks are for sale in many booths. They say they can fit 1,000 cars in the parking lot but that is highly doubtful.

Nearby, the town of **Paraíso** has only one decent hotel and a pretty beach. But there are no services save for a **Western Union** (Calle Ana Irma Tejada at Calle Arzobispo Nouel) and a typical *colmado* on the same corner where you can buy food like cheese, sausage, bread, and liquor.

Hotel Paraíso (Av. Gregorio Lupéron and Calle Doña Chin, tel. 809/243-1080, US$14 d fan only) has spacious rooms and they are clean. It's not a spectacular hotel, but a good one in the area.

The beach can be litter-filled in some spots near town, but for the better part, go out past the hotel and you'll find the white-stoned beach in much better shape than the one in town.

Guaguas stop at Calle Enriquillo from both directions.

(PARQUE NACIONAL JARAGUA

Jaragua National Park (8 A.M.–5 P.M., US$1 entrance, US$52 for a tour) is named after a Taíno chief and is the largest park in the nation. In it is a combination of terrestrial, coastal, and marine environments including two continental islands. Its 1,400 square-kilometer expanse includes scrub in a subtropical dry forest. Cacti dominate the flora found here

The park protects flocks of flamingos who spend much of the year on the shore of **Laguna de Oviedo,** where you can also find egrets and black-crowned tanagers, all of which are a part of the 130-some species of bird found in the park. The ricord iguana and rhinoceros iguana, which are endemic to Hispaniola, also call this park home.

For a tour of the park, ask for a guide at the entrance, which is in a well-marked turn-off from Highway 44 just north of the town of Oviedo. The guide will take you by boat for a 2–3 hour ride through the lagoon, showing you the flamingos, three islands, and a cave containing Taíno artwork. Although the cost of the tour was quoted at US$52, this price fluctuates and is easily bargained down.

Birds are better viewed earlier in the day. This is a very sunny and hot area. Bring bug spray, sunscreen, and a hat.

This park makes for a good day trip when you use Barahona as your base. *Guaguas* will drop you off at the entrance. It is best to drive, though, so as not to risk missing the last *guagua* at 4 P.M. You don't want to miss it since there are no hotels nearby.

(BAHÍA DE LAS ÁGUILAS

This is the most pristine beach in the entire Dominican Republic. It is also one of the hardest to get to, in the middle of nowhere. Getting

a local woman with a freshly caught eel from the Bahía de las Águilas

© ANA CHAVIER CAAMAÑO

there is half the adventure, but the payoff is out of this world.

To get to it, first you must travel along the road to Pedernales, but turn off about 12 kilometers before Pedernales at Cabo Rojo (Red Cape), where the land is literally red and surreal against the larimar-blue water of its shallow beach. From the highway, take the marked turnoff for Cabo Rojo, which curves around near where a large American bauxite mining facility has trucks speeding over the road (be very careful). Follow the sign directing you to veer left to Bahía de las Águilas. You'll end up in a tiny fishing community called Las Cuevas (The Caves). The people here have built their homes into the caves of the cliffs in an effort to stay cool in the oppressive heat of the area. They are very friendly, and at a small Ministry of Environment shack you can arrange for a fisherman to take you and your party to the remote beach. Standard cost is around US$1.50 to park your car and US$40 to take up to six people on the boat ride. The beach is completely unspoiled with absolutely no facilities, so make sure to take plenty of water and munchies and return to Las Cuevas with your garbage to help maintain its pristine state for the next visitor. There is a small *colmado* in Las Cuevas where you can buy some things to take. Arrange how long you'd like to be there and where the boat should pick you up. It is possible to arrange for a very fresh fish feast to be cooked for your enjoyment upon return to Las Cuevas. You'll have to be adventurous at heart, though, as it is cooked in a very rough cottage right on the beach.

The threat of commercial development looms constantly, but preservationists thankfully fight against it.

Pedernales

Pedernales is a glum town, the most westerly of the republic, and has very little to see. Passing to Haiti is not possible here, legally, as there is no immigration office. Turning a blind eye for a "fee" is common, but it is not advised that you try.

There is a **BanReservas** (Duarte and Av. 27 de Febrero) and an **Isla Gas Station** (Av. Duarte). Every Friday there is a **Haitian market** that sets up in between the two countries where you can buy clothes and kitchen items.

PARQUE NACIONAL SIERRA DE BAHORUCO

This national park (8 A.M.–5 P.M. daily, US$4) covers over 800 square kilometers of protected and mostly mountainous land. This hard-to-traverse park is home to 1,268 different plant species including 166 orchid species, nearly 55 percent of the total found in the Dominican Republic. The vegetation survives in a variety of climates from dry forest at sea level to humid rainforest up in the mountains. The pines, broad-leafed forest, and mixed forest are home to 49 species of birds, including the Hispaniolan lizard cuckoo, Hispaniolan trogon, the stolid flycatcher, and the white-necked crow.

It was here in these mountains that the great Taíno chief Enriquillo led battles in defiance to the Spanish encroachment. For nearly 14 years, the natives kept the conquistadors at bay, and in 1533, the Spanish decided to back down and made peace with the cacique, making him, to this day, a celebrated figure in the history of the republic.

Without a motorcycle or four-wheel-drive, this park is virtually impossible to explore, making camping impossible as well.

From Highway 44, at the Cabo Rojo intersection, turn north (away from Bahía de las Águilas) and drive for about an hour. Or if you're coming from Barahona, take Highway 46 to Duverge, where you'll then turn south on a pretty terrible road to Puerto Escondido; the ranger station is on the first right. There are no guides at this park.

A day trip to this area is best (if Barahona is your base camp). There are no hotels.

LAGO ENRIQUILLO LOOP

This area of the Dominican Republic has the most unique terrain in the entire country, not what you'd expect to see on a Caribbean vacation. Countless varieties of cacti dot the countryside, crocodiles lie around in the estuaries of rivers, flamingos flock on the salty shores of Lago Enriquillo, and iguanas saunter around like house cats on sedatives. It's a truly distinctive experience. The near-desert environment also brings heat. The heat in this part of the country is intense, so it is best to travel in a rented car with air-conditioning in good working order. And don't forget to take water with you.

As for the entire peninsula, Barahona has your best options for accommodations. From there, travel northwest on Highway 46 (a well-paved road, surprisingly!) until you come to Cabral, about 30 kilometers west of Barahona.

For a strange encounter with mystery (or just plain scientific reasons), follow signs from Cabral to the town of Polo and to a place called **Polo Magnético.** Along this drive your car will feel very heavy like you're going uphill, even though the ground is flat. When you reach the Polo Magnético, a spot where the road appears to rise, roll an item along the ground, and watch it as it appears to roll uphill in a strange optical illusion. Slip your car into neutral (but stay in there ready to brake!) and feel the car independently pick up speed uphill. If you're lucky, Sr. Eugenio Urbáez, who has become somewhat of a self-elected docent to Polo Magnético, will be there to give a demonstration with his Presidente bottle and give his version of the explanation for the strange illusions. Illusion being the key word.

Back on the Highway 46, you may run into soldiers who are trying to hitch rides from their military posts. They tend to wait near the speed bumps so that they can say where they need to go when you slow down. Generally they are harmless and very respectful. You are not obligated to give them a lift; it is all just a courteous exchange. If you have a truck and signal them to get in, they'll automatically hop into the back and tap on the side of the truck when they're ready to get out.

◖ PARQUE NACIONAL ISLA CABRITOS

This national park (7 A.M.–5 P.M., US$1.75) encompasses Isla Cabritos, which is an island

the salty Lago Enriquillo

in the center of the 200-square-kilometer **Lago Enriquillo,** the enormous saltwater lake that is famous for being the lowest part (below sea level) in all of the Caribbean. The lake's water is four times saltier than the ocean and was created when gradual tectonic movements cut it off from the ocean. On the beaches of the lake and the island within, you can find ancient seashells and coral fragments.

If you want to see the island, you'll have to have a guide. The entrance to the park is east of La Descubierta and you'll see the kiosk for the entrance from the road. Plenty of parking is available. Tours cost US$24 for a boatload of 1–8 people. You'll get a two-hour ride out to see the island and the crocodiles and flamingos that inhabit the area. Since it's so miserably hot here most of the time, you'll need sunscreen and a hat, and take water with you on the boat.

One of the most interesting features of the park is its animals. Numerous reptile species including endangered rhinoceros and ricord iguanas and a very large American crocodile

ENDANGERED SPECIES

The Dominican Republic, with its diverse flora and fauna, is home to a number of endangered animal species. There are three classifications of threatened species, each with its own criteria, which are based on the amount of population reduction in the last 10 years or over the last three generations – whichever is longer – or the projected reduction over the next 10 years or three generations. Also taken into account is the "extent of occurrence" or "occupancy" over a given area. Current population of the species is also a factor in categorizing the extent of the threat. Throughout the country, national parks that have been designated conservation lands are home to these threatened species.

"Critically endangered" refers to animals whose populations have been, or are projected to become, reduced by 80 percent over the 10-year/three-generation margins. These species contain fewer than 250 adults with an estimated decline in population of 25 percent over three years or one generation (again, whichever is longer), or only 50 or fewer mature individuals are known to exist.

For species in the "endangered" category, the numbers of reduction drop to 50 percent over the same past or future time periods. The mature individual number rises to 2,500 with a projected consistent drop of at least 20 percent over the next five years or two generations, or the known existence of fewer than 250 adults.

Those on the "vulnerable" list have a sus-pected reduction of 20 percent in the past 10 years or three generations, or in the next 10 years or three generations. The population would contain no more than 10,000 mature individuals and hold an estimation of a 10 percent decline in numbers within 10 years or three generations. Another possibility is that the population just flat out numbers fewer than 1,000 mature individuals.

As of 2004, the Puerto Rican hutia, a gerbil-like rodent that with a bit of luck can be spotted in the Parque Nacional del Este, is on the critically endangered list. The Haitian solenodon is an endangered species. Its characteristics include a small body and a long snout. Like the hutia, the soledonon resides in the Parque Nacional del Este. Among the Dominican species that fall under the category of vulnerable are the American manatee, the humpback whale, and the Hispaniolian hutia.

Other threatened or endangered species that occupy the Dominican Republic, or its surrounding waters, are the West Indian manatee and the bottlenose dolphin, both of which can be spotted along the coasts of national parks or in the Bahía de Samaná. There are thousands of species of birds that live on the island, and among those that are endemic to the country are the white-crowned quail-dove, bay-breasted cuckoo, and the hawk buteo. The rhinoceros iguana, endemic to the Dominican Republic, can be found throughout the country in the drier areas of the national parks.

population live around the lake. Entrance into the park to see the iguanas and just view the lake is US$0.40, and a nice shady path leads down to the water's edge. Here the iguanas heavily pepper the walkways and get surprisingly close; they can be rather big.

In the park, there is a *balneario* for a very frigid dip after a sweltering day of exploration.

Las Caritas is next to Lago Enriquillo and is a free look at some Taíno art in a shallow cave on the north side of the highway. It's vis-ible from the road and you'll have to hike up to see it up close. It's not a very easy hike. You'll need good shoes for both this and the Lago Enriquillo visit.

JIMANÍ

Jimaní is the most trafficked route to Haiti through an authorized crossing point. It is a sprawling town that was once even larger, until the rains of the 2003 hurricane season wiped out nearly 1,500 of its inhabitants. The empty shells of ruined homes are a ghostly reminder on the way into town. The only reason to visit this town is to access the crossing point to Haiti.

Accommodations and Food

The **Hotel Jimaní** (Calle 19 de Marzo 2, tel. 809/248-3139, US$18 d) is a decent place to get a night's sleep and a meal. It's not much on the outside, but the rooms are clean and comfortable with cable TV and a private bathroom (cold water). The restaurant serves all meals in a limited fashion, but it's food. It's not the Ritz, not even remotely, but it'll do in a pinch.

Getting There and Around

Caribe Tours has service that goes from Santo Domingo to Port-au-Prince and it makes a stop in Jimaní. Otherwise, *guaguas* serve this area from Santo Domingo (US$7.50) and Barahona (US$3.50).

On your way from Jimaní to Neyba, it might be refreshing to jump into some ice-cold water. **Las Varias Balneario** in the town of La Descubierta has a nice river-fed swimming hole where they also have food and drink. It is popular with families. It is a nice break on what will most likely be a hot day of driving. There are bathrooms here, albeit nightmarish. If you can, wait until Neyba.

To cross the border to Haiti, you'll need your passport, US$20 for departure tax, and US$5 to pay to immigration. The Dominican side is open 8 A.M.–7 P.M. and the Haitian side is open 9 A.M.–6 P.M.

NEYBA

It might be quite a stretch to call this the Napa Valley of the Dominican Republic, but Neyba is indeed wine country. They sell big jugs of the sweet wine made from regional grapes. Neyba has a nice Parque Central and is a small town with no sights, but it makes for a good spot to stop for a bite to eat on your loop around Lago Enriquillo.

Accommodations and Food

Hotel Restaurant Babey (Calle Apolinar, US$6 d), across from the Parque Central, offers small rooms with fan or air-conditioning (you'll pay extra). It's rather clean and very basic. The restaurant, which is down a long corridor from the sidewalk, serves *comida criolla* at very low prices. The dish of the day (rice and beans and some kind of meat) is about US$2.

BACKGROUND

The Land

GEOGRAPHY

The Dominican Republic's geographical differences are reflected in its diverse landscape, where the roaring surf and sultry heat of the coastlines seem a world apart from the temperately cooler mountains in the center of the country. Here, tropical forests coexist with fertile valleys rife with rivers and fresh springs, only to collide with cactus-dotted semi-arid deserts. The highest point in the Caribbean tapers into the lowest point in the Caribbean. And all of this is on the 48,734-square-kilometer section of Hispaniola that the Dominican Republic occupies.

The island of Hispaniola is positioned in the middle of the Caribbean with the Bahamas to the north, Cuba and Jamaica to the west, Puerto Rico and the Leeward Islands to the east, and South America to the south. The Atlantic Ocean crashes into the northern coast and the southern shore is bathed by the Caribbean Sea. The Dominican Republic occupies two-thirds of Hispaniola, separated from neighboring Haiti by a 388-kilometer border.

Mountains and valleys are natural demarcations dividing the country into northern, central, and southwestern portions. In the northern region, plains hug the coastline from

© ANA CHAVIER CAAMAÑO

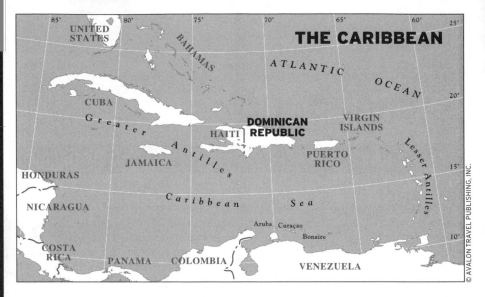

© AVALON TRAVEL PUBLISHING, INC.

Monte Cristi to Nagua and then rise dramatically to form the **Cordillera Septentrional** (Northern Mountain Range), situated just south of the plains and parallel to the ocean. The range's southern face then drops down into the **Valle del Cibao** (Cibao Valley). This valley scoops its path from the northwest corner of the country and stretches all the way to the Bahía de Samaná (Bay of Samaná). The connection of **La Península de Samaná** (Peninsula of Samaná) to the mainland is a swampy area—perfect for growing rice—which then rises up to lushly vegetated mountains up to 600 meters high.

The central region mainly consists of the **Cordillera Central** (Central Range), the nation's spinal column. It begins at 2,000 meters near the Haitian border, rises to the highest point of 3,087 meters at **Pico Duarte** (Duarte Peak), curves southward by the **Valle de Constanza** (Constanza Valley), and finally dips its southern portion, the Sierra de Ocoa, into the Caribbean Sea. The Cordillera Central extends its reach with the Sierra de Yamasá through to the Cordillera Oriental. Just south of these ranges are the Caribbean coastal plains, which extend out from the mouth of the Ocoa River in the midwest to the eastern end of the island. These plains contain limestone terraces that rise to 100–120 meters at the northern edge. The Valle de San Juan (in the west) extends 100 kilometers from the Haitian border to meet up with the Bahía de Ocoa.

In the southwest corner of the country, the Sierra de Neyba extends from the Haitian border to the Yaque del Sur River, with peaks up to 2,000 meters high. On the eastern side of the river is the Sierra de Martín García. The Hoya de Enriquillo is a basin from the Haitian border to the Bahía de Neyba and from the Sierra de Neyba to the Sierra de Bahoruco, a ridge that extends from the Haitian border to the Caribbean Sea.

The Dominican Republic enjoys a diverse topography in its 30 provinces, of lowlands and highlands, rivers and lakes, and includes some offshore islands as well. The islands of Saona, off the southeastern coast, and Beata, south of the Península de Pedernales, are the largest.

Even though the beaches make up only a small portion of the country's 1,633-kilometer coastline and an even smaller portion of what the Dominican Republic has to offer visitors, they are (and justifiably so) the main reason people take their vacations here. Also a part of the coastline are limestone cliffs that reveal cozy coves with small, tucked-away beaches.

Rivers and Lakes

The Dominican Republic has rivers in both the mountains and the plains. The **Yaque del Norte** is the longest river in the country, at 296 kilometers long, and is used for much of the adventure tourism in the central highlands. It rushes and curves through dramatic cliffs and mountains from its home near Pico Duarte in a northerly direction to its emptying point at the Bahía de Monte Cristi. The Río Yuna flows east, serving the Vega Real, and empties in the Bahía de Samaná. Together, these two drain the Valle del Cibao.

In the Valle de San Juan de la Maguana, the Yaque del Sur forms in the southern slopes of the Cordillera Central and flows to the Bahía de Neyba by Barahona, and the Río Artibonito crosses over into Haiti. Much of this water is used for irrigation in the otherwise very dry landscape of the southwestern region.

The Ríos Magua, Soco, Chavón, and Ozama drain the eastern portion of the country.

The very fertile and vegetated landscape of the rest of the nation begins to dwindle in the far western half of the country, where the closer you get to the Haitian border, the more the landscape is characterized by dry scrub and cacti. The Neyba Valley is home to Lago Enriquillo, which is the lowest point in the Caribbean and was once a strait of the Caribbean Sea. The lake has a high level of evaporation, but on average it is 40 meters below sea level and is four times saltier than the ocean. Its drainage basin is made of 10 minor rivers.

CLIMATE

For the most part, the Dominican Republic has a tropical climate. The average annual temperature is 25°C (77°F), and the weather is warm and sunny for a majority of the year.

The seasons have only slight variations. The winter season (November–April) is when humidity is minimal with temperatures lower in the evening than they are in the summer nights.

Coastal areas have temps around 20°C (68°F) in the evening, and in the interior mountain areas, it is much cooler, sometimes dropping below freezing, allowing for a rare frost on the peaks of the mountains. The summer starts in May and goes until October with average daily highs around 31°C (87°F) around the coast, dropping about 10 degrees at night—but the humidity makes it seem hotter.

Whatever the season, the towns of the Cordillera Central enjoy a "perpetual spring" as opposed to the desert region of the southwest, where temperatures can rise above 40°C (104°F). The cool temperatures are what draw the city folk to the mountains during the hotter months on the perimeter of the island.

October through April are the rainiest months for the northern region; in general the west gets the least precipitation, and the south gets the rain heaviest between May and November. Most of the time, the rain falls (150 centimeters on average for the whole country) with excited short bursts, book-ended by sunshine, resulting in quite a pleasant break in the otherwise near perfection of the weather—*near* being the key word. Abnormalities are inevitable, such as overcast skies (marring a sun worshipper's beach vacation) or perhaps unexpected rains (ruining a windsurfer's paradise). But for the most part, it is blue skies and sunshine.

The El Cibao region is fortunate in that it has healthy land and sea breezes that sweep up from the sea to cool the air during the day and then move out again at night, taking the hot air with them.

Hurricanes

The Dominican Republic is prone to tropical cyclones (tropical depressions, storms, and hurricanes), and a majority of them strike the southern part of the country. Hurricane season lasts from the beginning of June to the end of November, but most hit during August or September. Coming all the way from the coast of Africa, hurricanes usually start as tropical depressions that build up their ferocity as they cruise across the Atlantic Ocean, eating up all the warm moist air they can gobble up to fuel their speed as they careen toward the Caribbean islands, producing winds in excess of 200 kilometers per hour and with rainfall sometimes greater than 50 centimeters in a 24-hour period.

In 1998, Hurricane Georges plowed over the Dominican Republic, killing about 300 people. It caused gigantic agricultural losses of staple crops like rice, plantain, and cassava, and caused severe structural damage, leaving thousands homeless. Many people were without electricity for months, and food supplies were minimal after the hurricane.

Even though the Dominican Republic seems to be smack-dab in the middle of a hurricane bowling alley, the chances of getting caught in one are minimal. If you are, though, head inland and stay away from the ocean. It's best to go to a major city so that there are adequate emergency services and shelters. If you're in or near a resort when a hurricane hits, listen to management; they have procedures for evacuation and shelter. Mudslides are a major result of storms in the Dominican Republic, so stay away from all rivers, lakes, and hillsides.

Flora

The Dominican Republic's biodiversity yields a huge assortment of plants and flowers. If you're vacationing only in the metropolitan area of Santo Domingo, the best way to see the full scope of the environment's capabilities is by visiting the Jardín Botánico Nacional in Santo Domingo. But if you're going to the countryside, beaches, mountains, or desert, you'll quickly learn that the Dominican Republic is truly a rich country when it comes to vegetation. No matter what the season, something seems to be blooming, growing, or adding fragrance to the air.

There are over 5,600 species of plants found in the 20 different zones, which is unique for a Caribbean island, and 30 percent of the plants found here are endemic to the Dominican Republic.

orchid

© ANA CHAVIER CAAMAÑO

TREES

Trees native to the Dominican Republic include the mahogany; the ceiba (silk cotton tree), known for its massive stature and long life (up to 300 years!); the Dominican magnolia; the *mamón;* and the *bija* tree. In the semi-arid desert, cacti and agave dominate the terrain. When the Spanish came, they introduced many trees, including the coral tree, the African tulip, and the poinciana.

Perhaps the most prevalent vegetation zone found in the country is the subtropical forest. No true tropical rainforest is found here because rainfall isn't sufficient and, unfortunately, because many of the types of trees found in that sort of environment were hacked away. The subtropical forest is found in the Santo Domingo lowland, in the valleys of the northwest (including Valle del Cibao), and on the Península de Samaná.

Main species of trees found in these moist subtropical forests are royal palms and mahogany. Also found are the non-indigenous capa trees, the jagua palm, lancewood, ground oak, and the yellowwood. The cashew tree *(Anacardium occidentale)* is also found and flowers with the cashew apple (pseudofruit), which looks like a little red, yellow, or orange boxing glove and whose taste punches you in the mouth with bitterness—not too appealing, but when the nut is roasted it is very good; they're sold in jars along the countryside highways.

As you pass the landscape of the country, it would be nearly impossible to miss the scores of hills, lowlands, riverbeds, and shorelines brimming with palms. The coconut palms that line the beaches of the Atlantic and Caribbean are the postcard views that most see of the Dominican Republic palm varieties. However, there are other varieties. While the coconut is mostly found along shorelines, the royal palm, or *Roystonea boringuena* (highly regarded as a national symbol, even appearing on the coat of arms), needs deeper soil and more moisture; it grows in clumps everywhere but high elevations. The sabal palm is found in regions with either environment. Other types of palm, like the cana, guano, and yarey, are all native to Hispaniola and are still used for making things like brooms and furniture.

Subhumid forests have semi-evergreen trees that lose their leaves during the three-month dry season, making for a rather bare landscape, but for the most part they are green leafy regions. A strange mixture of palms and pines characterizes the mountain forests.

cashew apple

Mangroves have woody trees that grow in coastal and estuary areas like those of the Parque Nacional Los Haitises and the Parque Nacional Jaragua. They grow in areas where they are protected from direct wave action and are essential in the protection of the island from strong storms, tides, and erosion because their roots stabilize the sand and mud. Equally important, they provide a stable and protective habitat for wildlife, including fish and flocks of water and sea birds.

FLOWERS AND FRUIT

Plants here are affected by elevation and rainfall, and because of the long spectrum of variables in the Dominican Republic, there is a bewildering array of plants and flowers.

The country is gorged with pineapples, grapefruit, papayas, mangoes, guavas, passionfruit, bananas, and melons. Let us not forget coffee and sugarcane. Breakfast tables have never been this happy. In the morning, start your day with a common breakfast of a milkshake made with fresh *lechosa* (papaya) and mango.

Along the city streets and across the country, fruit and vegetable markets overflow with produce like avocados, *plátanos* (plantains), sugarcane, eggplants, herbs, onions, and yucca.

Tree ferns, orchids, bromeliads, and epiphytes are found in abundance in the humid forests. It is estimated that more than 300 varieties of orchids grow in the Dominican Republic. The Jardín Botánico Nacional in Santo Domingo displays 67 of them. In fact, in the forested highlands of the Sierra de Bahoruco (in the deep southwest of the Península de Pedernales) more than 50 percent of all native orchids are found.

Fauna

Because the island of Hispaniola was never joined to a continent, it doesn't have many land animals. Most of the mammals that you see today were introduced by the Europeans who made the journey. Out of the nearly 500 vertebrate species of animals, 140 are various reptiles, 60 are types of amphibians, and 20 are land mammals. The rest are birds, marine mammals, and bats.

LAND MAMMALS

Before Christopher Columbus and his men showed up, there were an estimated 20 native mammals. Now, there are only two and they are hanging on for dear life. If you see one in its natural habitat, consider yourself lucky; they are rare and tend to hide out.

The **solenodon** is a primitive shrew-like creature about 30 centimeters long with a tail up to 25 centimeters. These insectivores are stout and have an unusually long snout. They're not the cutest kids on the playground (think, rat meets anteater), with long bristly faces and small eyes. They have brown fur but naked tails and huge feet that have long, clawed toes. Still, they are survivors and have been in existence for 30 million years feeding on insects and worms. It's taken scientists a long time to get to know the solenodon, partly because they are nocturnal, burrowing in tents and caves during the day. When they do come out, they scuttle about in a serpentine pattern. Making them even more inaccessible are their grooved incisors that have at the base of each, a gland from which poison runs, fatally wounding any would-be captor in the wild. However, this mean bite was no match for the bigger animals (especially the mongoose) that were introduced. Solenodons are slow, clumsy runners and are not agile. They have had a hard time surviving.

The **hutia**, yet another small rodent, shares many similarities with the solenodon. They both live in tree trunks and caves and are nocturnal. The hutia is, for the most part, an her-bivore. It resembles a prairie dog and likes to climb trees.

Instead of native animals, what most visitors will notice is a remarkable overabundance of stray dogs, cats, and countless chickens.

MARINE MAMMALS

If the Dominican Republic coastal waters were a Broadway play, the **humpback whales** and manatees would have stars on their doors. These top-billed actors draw audiences from all over the world.

Each winter some 3,000 humpback whales migrate all the way from the frigid waters of the arctic circle to mate and calve in the balmy tropical waters off the coast of the Dominican Republic, with the Bahía de Samaná acting as a kind of nursery. Peak "show time" for this event is in January and February. This is a world-renowned venue for viewing these magnificent creatures as they lumber through the water and sometimes breech right before the gape-mouthed camera-clad tourists. It is one of the most glorious spectacles, natural or otherwise, in the country.

This species of whale can grow to be 12–15 meters and weigh up to 60 tons. They are named for the way that they come above the water's surface with an arched back. As they cut across the water's surface, you'll be able to see the signature knobby heads, white flippers, two blowholes, and large tails. For their entire time in the tropics, humpbacks do not eat a single thing. While in the arctic circle they build up their 15–20 centimeters of fat to sustain them on their journey and for the rest of the time they're in the tropics.

The endangered **West Indian manatee** can sometimes be found in the shallow waters of slow-moving rivers, estuaries, bays, canals, and coastal areas. Nicknamed "sea cows," these are very gentle and slow-moving animals that "graze" on plants at the ocean floor. In fact, everything about them is slow. They spend their days feeding and resting at the water's

© ANA CHAVIER CAAMAÑO

Although chickens are not native to the Dominican Republic, they are the most visible animals in the country.

bottom or surface, only coming up for a breath every 3–5 minutes. Females cannot reproduce until they are 5 years old, and males mature at 9–11 years old; gestation is 13 months, and a calf is born every 2–5 years. It's not a hurried lifestyle—perhaps this is why they can live up to 60 years old. Manatees have no known natural enemies, unless you count human interaction. Unfortunately, hunting and tourboat excursions (ironically, to appreciate the mammals) have caused a decline in manatee numbers.

The reefs of the Dominican Republic create a wonderful habitat for a wide variety of sea life, including four kinds of **sea turtles:** the green sea turtle (the kind hunted to make soup), the leatherback (the largest living turtle), the loggerhead (found in lagoons and bays), and the hawksbill. These beautiful creatures can grow up to two meters long and come ashore at night by the Parque Nacional Jaragua from May to October to lay eggs in the sand. Of these four, the hawksbill's survival is in the most jeopardy because of its attractive

shell, which is sold widely in the form of belts, jewelry, and other decorative items.

CORAL REEFS

While diving and snorkeling are two of the most popular activities for tourists vacationing in the Dominican Republic, it might be good to get a handle on some basic knowledge before paddling out to see the splendid colors, to make sure to preserve the delicate ecosystem.

There are three types of coral reefs: the fringe, the barrier, and the atoll. The fringe is a great place for beginners, since it is close to (and connected to) the mainland and therefore tends to be in shallower waters. It has a good variety of coral species.

Just past the fringe reef you'll come to the barrier reef, where the sea life is dialed up a notch from the fringe reef. The type of barrier reef commonly found here is the bank/barrier reef, which is smaller than a barrier reef found in the Pacific Ocean. You'll need transportation to get out to a bank/barrier reef as there are hundreds of meters between it and the shore.

Charles Darwin reasoned that an atoll came to be from a fringing coral reef surrounding a volcanic island that eventually grew upward as the island began to sink, turning the fringe reef into a barrier reef. In time, the old volcano fell below the surface of the ocean and the barrier reef remained, thereby graduating to atoll status. This type of reef is rare in the Caribbean and the closest one to the Dominican Republic is in Belize.

There are two types of coral: hard and soft. While it would seem that the hard corals are the skeleton of the reef and the soft corals merely decorate it, that is not the case. In fact, the creation of a coral reef is very much a team effort. While the hard corals do indeed form the skeletal portion, many types of algae act as the mortar to help bind and solidify the frame. Then crustaceans, mollusks, sponges, urchins, and soft corals all come in to anchor the reef. And just like a community, there are the vandals. Let's cut the snails, crabs, and parrotfish

a little more slack, though; they are, after all, surviving off of the reef.

Scuba diving and snorkeling are vastly popular activities, but so much "flipper traffic" has done tremendous damage to the reefs. Make sure that you follow the simple and very important rules while visiting their habitat: Don't stand on it or touch it. Be careful with your fins; while kicking you can easily accidentally do a lot of damage. And above all, don't take a piece as a memento, even though it is very tempting. Many of the coral reefs have suffered as a result of the tourism industry, which includes individuals who harvest the reefs to make jewelry to sell on the beaches and in the markets.

BIRDS

The Dominican Republic isn't traditionally thought of as a bird-watching destination. But that is changing because, in fact, its environment is a bird's paradise and a bird-watcher's dream. There are 300 recorded bird species, including 27 endemics and a number of Caribbean specifics as well as "vacationing" birds from North America. Species to look for are

© ANA CHAVIER CAAMAÑO

ricord iguana

the Hispaniolan parrot, the Hispaniolan woodpecker, the Hispaniolan trogon, and the Hispaniolan parakeet. Also on the island are owls, egrets, herons, pelicans, parrots, parakeets, and flamingos, just to name a few. The national bird is the **palmchat,** which nests in the royal palms within the coastal plains.

The Sierra de Bahoruco has one of the highest bird densities of the Caribbean and is the only place in the Dominican Republic where you have even a slim chance of seeing 26 out of the 27 endemics. You'll have to go to the mountains to see the white-necked crow or a warbler.

REPTILES AND AMPHIBIANS

While there are snakes and frogs on the island, they are greatly outnumbered by the more than 20 species of lizards.

Lago Enriquillo, with its dry, rocky ground, is the preferred location for the **rhinoceros iguana.** This species of iguana is so named because of the small horns on the males' snouts and their gray color, which make them look like rhinoceroses. A full-grown rhinoc-

eros iguana can be over a meter in length. Although they may look scary, they are indeed rather shy and are herbivores. **Ricord iguanas** are also found at Lago Enriquillo and live only in the Dominican Republic. These red-eyed creatures are omnivorous and can live more than 30 years.

The olive-brown **American crocodile** also makes its home in Lago Enriquillo. In fact it has gotten so comfortable in the Dominican Republic that it represents one of the largest wildlife crocodile populations in the world. With Lago Enriquillo four times saltier than the sea, the crocs tend to lurk near the river inlets to try to catch some fresh water. However, with the diversion of these rivers (for irrigation purposes) the crocodile babies are suffering, since they have not yet developed their tolerance to the briny stew. The average male can grow to be four meters long. The crocodiles mainly feed on fish, turtles, and occasionally goats. They are protected under the Dominican law, and the best time to go to Lago Enriquillo to see them is in the early morning or late afternoon.

Environmental Issues

When Columbus arrived, the forests of the island were plush and vibrant. Over the centuries, it is estimated that nearly two-thirds of those original forests have vanished. Illegal forestation, fires, mass farming without forethought as to how to replenish soils after failed crops, and pollution caused an immense amount of destruction. Over time, fertile and pine-covered hillsides increasingly vanished. In the 1970s, environmentalists warned that by 1990, a majority of the native forest would be destroyed, much like what had begun to occur in Haiti. With that, the Dominican government finally stood up and began an active move toward conservation. Today great amounts of land throughout the country are being protected as national parks.

However, there is still quite a lot going on in the environment. A growing tourism industry picks up more momentum with each year, and the mad rush to create more services, resorts, and activities is only now beginning to be monitored. Thankfully, many ecosavvy travelers have become attracted to the Dominican Republic as a destination. They are not just lying on the beaches anymore. Instead, more visitors are headed inland to raft the rivers and climb the mountains of the central highlands. They are taking boats through mangroves and diving to see the coral beds that fringe the island. While tourism is good for the economy, all of this nature appreciation can take a toll on the environment. An already fragile ecosystem can be crushed under the pressure of so much traffic. Although government programs exist for the protection of these ecosystems, they remain grossly underfunded.

NATIONAL PARKS

In an effort to preserve the ecosystems of the Dominican Republic, 16 national parks, nine natural monuments, and six scientific reserves have been created.

In the center of the country, the northern slopes of the Cordillera Central are protected lands of the **Parque Nacional Armando Bermúdez,** which was founded in 1956 and is home to Pico Duarte at 3,087 meters high. Sliding down the southern slopes is the **Parque Nacional José del Carmen Ramírez,** founded two years later. Together they were created in an effort to protect the remaining pine forests of the Cordillera Central.

The **Parque Nacional Sierra de Bahoruco,** in the southwest, is a forest highland that receives a good deal of rain due to its height compared to the surrounding arid countryside. Almost 52 percent of orchids in the Dominican Republic are found here.

Located on the southern tip of the Península de Pedernales, including the Isla Beata, are the (for the most part) dry forests of **Parque Nacional Jaragua.** Many bird species (flamingos included!) enjoy the habitat created here by mangroves, beaches, and lagoons along the fringes of this park.

The country's second smallest park is that of **Parque Nacional Isla Cabritos.** It is an island in Lago Enriquillo and ranges 4–40 meters below sea level. Perhaps the most fascinating thing about this park is that it has one of the largest populations of the American crocodile and endemic iguanas.

On the eastern shore, tangled in mangroves and swamp land, is the **Parque Nacional Los Haitises,** which forms the southern coast of the Bahía de Samaná. Here, rock formations jut out into the water and caves are homes to bats.

Along with Isla Saona and a portion of the southern coast just below San Rafael de Yuma make up the **Parque Nacional del Este.** The mainland part is made up of limestone terraces and is a dry and hot environment.

In the upper northwest corner of the country is the **Parque Nacional Monte Cristi.** It comprises a land portion that is subtropical dry forest with cliffs dropping dramatically into the sea (like El Morro at 239 meters above sea level), numerous coastal lagoons, and a collection of small islands (Los Cayos de Siete Hermanos).

Parque Nacional Submarino La Caleta, just east of Santo Domingo, is the country's smallest national park, weighing in at just 10 square kilometers. Its offshore coral reef (and its shipwreck) gets top billing in this park, which is frequented by divers exploring its marine life.

ETHICAL ECOTRAVEL

What is this "eco" that is getting thrown around everywhere? The term "ecotourism" was coined in the 1980s and was meant to describe responsible tourism in natural areas (like national parks and forests), making sure to conserve the environment and improve the well-being of local people. Emphasis has been put on areas where the flora, fauna, and culture are the primary attraction. Besides simply paying attention to the environmental and cultural factors of an area, it means that the businesses touting the ecofriendly claims should be taking initiative to promote recycling, energy efficiency, water re-use, and economic opportunities for local communities. Unfortunately, the prefix "eco" has become a sort of marketing gimmick in the tourism industry lately, and the Dominican Republic is guilty of it, too. Be wary of establishments that claim ecofriendliness while behaving in environmentally irresponsible ways. For instance, simply placing a resort in a beautiful landscape does not make it ecofriendly.

Tourists with the best of intentions in seeing the Dominican Republic in an ecoconscious manner can actually do more damage than they realize if they don't adhere to some basic practices. Just going there and spending your money doesn't quite do it. If you really want to help out in an effective way for the Dominicans and their natural environment, there are a few ways to go about it.

Giving Dominican-owned independent businesses your money rather than big corporations helps keep the money in the Dominican economy rather than being sent overseas. Many all-inclusive resorts are foreign owned (mainly Spanish, French, and American). Dominican-owned establishments are relatively rare or short-lived ventures (sad but true). One great Dominican-owned choice is the **Paraíso Caño Hondo** resort in Sabana de la Mar, where you can also book tours of the Parque Nacional Los Haitises.

Consider planning your trip for a lower tourist season. In the case of the Dominican Republic, this means *not* December–March. This will minimize congestion in small towns and spread the influx of tourist money more evenly throughout the year, especially for those mom-and-pop organizations whose livelihoods depend on foreign money. Also, visiting in smaller groups (like 4–6 people) is much less shocking to the cultural environment.

Spending the night out in wilderness is a great idea, but make sure to set up camp in designated areas or on durable surfaces like rock, gravel, and dry grasses. Use existing trails for hiking and don't venture from the trail. Build fires only where it is permitted and burn everything down to ash.

If you're visiting an area that is pristine, it's best to try and inhabit areas that have not been visited so that you don't help to create campsites and trails. Right now Bahía de las Águilas (Bay of the Eagles) is pristine. In 2006, a French development company was proposing building four 70-room hotels along its untouched shoreline. Environmentalist groups like the Coalition for the Defense of the Protected Areas are fighting hard to create other options for true ecofriendly establishments for the area's incredibly fragile ecosystem.

Whatever you take into a natural area, bring back with you when you exit. Packing out all trash, leftover food, toilet paper, hygiene products, and litter is a small task that has a huge impact on the ecosystem. Dig holes for solid human waste (15–20 centimeters deep and at least 60 meters from any water, camp, or trail). While most Dominicans living in the country have no objections to washing themselves and their clothing in rivers, streams, or lakes, it is not good for the environment. Carry water 60 meters away from the source and use biodegradable soap. The philosophy, "When in Rome ..." should not apply here.

Marveling at the rich culture and historical artifacts is part of the fun. But don't touch them or take them! Hard to believe and sad examples of people not adhering to this rule are the Taíno drawings found in some caves that have been completely ruined by graffiti. This goes for plant life too. While the country is dazzling with phenomenally beautiful orchid species, picking them is not cool; in fact it's against the law.

Appreciate the wildlife from a distance and don't feed them. While there aren't many big mammals in the Dominican Republic, you should never approach or follow any if you see them. The same goes for etiquette while diving: If a big sea turtle swims past, don't chase it down—just appreciate it as it passes.

Be courteous to other visitors and they will more than likely be courteous to you. Hiking Pico Duarte can be a very populated venture. Yield to others on the trail and you'll avoid confrontations, which have been known to occur. Keep noise levels down. Everyone is there to hear nature, not you.

History

INDIGENOUS PEOPLE
Pre-Columbian Amerindians

Time didn't start with the arrival of Christopher Columbus. For at least 5,000 years before his appearance Amerindians had settled throughout the Caribbean and eventually on the island he later named Hispaniola. First was a group called the Ciboney. Two tribes immigrated after them from South America, one from the Yucatán (the Caribs) and the second from a tribe in the Amazon (the Arawaks), who became the ancestors to the Taíno Indians, the tribe that ultimately welcomed Columbus.

The Arawaks were skilled seafarers who built long canoes able to carry 50–80 people in order to hunt for a new land to call home. Moving north through the Caribbean, they settled on various islands, scattering themselves around. They were an agricultural and fishing society, so they tended to live near the coasts, eating sea turtles, manatees, and fish. They planted vegetables like cassava, yams, sweet potatoes, and gourds; harvested fruits; and hunted animals like iguanas and birds. They were smart traders and often went from island to island trading what they had.

Hot on their heels were the Caribs, thought to be an extremely aggressive bunch, especially against the Taínos. They attacked them often, killing most men and enslaving the rest. The Caribs and the Arawaks had similar languages, but their social and political organizations were different enough to refer to them as separate nations.

Although the Arawaks were highly organized and smart, they were not warlike and were no match for the tyrannical Caribs, so they escaped and found themselves face to face with the Ciboney on the island of Hispaniola. The Ciboney were engulfed as slaves into what was, by then, Taíno life.

The Taínos

After the Arawaks made their home (over the stretch of about a thousand years) in what is modern-day Dominican Republic, their farming and gathering society evolved into a highly organized one with complex agriculture, art, politics, leisure activities, and rituals. From about A.D. 900 until 1492, the nation lived a blissfully happy existence. Conflicts were resolved peacefully through a game called *batu,* like soccer. They lived communally in *bohios* (round structures that held 10–15 families) and sometimes practiced polygamy. For the most part they were an agricultural society but hunted and fished as well, using nets made of hemp, cotton, or palm. They used words like *barbacoa, hamaca,* and *tobacco,* words that have been incorporated into modern Spanish and English. In their own language, their name, *taíno,* meant "good" or "noble."

They had large settlements of about 1,000 people, and each had a cacique who acted as a shaman-like priest and a law-maker, and he (or she; though rare, it was not unheard of to have a woman be a cacique) was born into the role. There was a second level to politics—the council of elders. All settlements were part of a larger district, of which there were five at the time of Spanish arrival. These districts' caciques were headed up by the most important regional cacique.

The Taínos were a religious people, and this is the most well-understood aspect of their culture. At the center of their dogma were the ideas of respecting life and worship of ancestors and the dead. They referred to spiritual beings as *zemís* and often depicted them in their art as turtles, snakes, and abstract faces. Some of their ceremonies involved a hallucinogenic snuff called *cahoba,* which they prepared from the beans of a tree. Inducing vomiting with ornately designed spatulas was a way to cleanse themselves of any corporeal impurities to symbolize their spiritual purging before the ritual of receiving a communal bread or other rituals.

Although they had no written language, they created extensive cave drawings and petroglyphs in various caves around the island that depicted much of their culture, beliefs, and events. One such drawing in the Parque Nacional del Este is said to depict the trade agreement between a Spanish galleon and a Taíno community.

Tobacco is perhaps their most notable contribution to the Spanish, which they rolled and smoked much in the same way as the cigars of the Dominican Republic today.

Whatever discord there was in Taíno life, there was no misery compared to what was about to happen. There is much controversy regarding how many Taínos were living on Hispaniola when Columbus arrived. Figures are all over the map and range from 200,000 all the way up to eight million, although an estimate closer to one million is more likely. Regardless of how many there were, they knew no disease like the horrible smallpox "gift" that the Spanish brought. By 1530, the numbers had shrunk to an estimated 3,000, due to disease, suicide to escape slavery, or genocide.

COLONIALISM
Columbus Arrives

Christopher Columbus, sailing for the Spanish throne, was expecting to reach Japan and instead stumbled across modern-day Cuba and the Bahamas. But when gold was not to be found on the Bahamian island of Guanahaní, he redirected and found what he dubbed "La Isla Española." After he ran the *Santa María* into a coral reef, it was the Taíno who helped the Spanish salvage every last board and nail so that they could build their fort, named for the day they landed: Christmas Village, or Villa La Navidad. The Taíno generosity and hospitality didn't stop there. They gave the sailors gold as gifts and helped them to build their new home. Columbus wrote to the Spanish crown about the glorious world he'd "discovered," exclaiming that there was gold to be had practically for nothing and remarking how gentle and wonderful the "Indians" were.

Soon after he arrived and set up camp at La Navidad, Columbus felt so confident that he

© ANA CHAVIER CAAMAÑO

ruins of Hospital San Nicolás de Barí

LAS MARIPOSAS

The rise of Rafael Trujillo to the Dominican presidency in 1930, followed by his subsequent destruction of his supposedly beloved country, led to a growing discordance between the Dominican people and their government. The economy suffered greatly as Trujillo's own wealth flourished. People started living in fear of Trujillo and his secret police – the Servicio de Inteligencia Militar (Military Intelligence Service) or SIM – who would descend upon any individual who gave off even the slightest hint of dissent. But in addition to those who lived in fear of the dictator were those who lived in defiance of him, and among them were the Mirabal sisters – namely Patria, Minerva, and María Teresa – who, in their strength and determination to help their country break free from such a repressive and dangerous regime, became known as Las Mariposas (The Butterflies).

The Mirabal sisters grew up in a well-to-do family. They were educated and strong-willed. Patria was the oldest, born in 1924, on February 27, the anniversary of the Dominican Republic's independence from Haiti. Dede, who was not directly involved in the anti-Trujillo movement of which the others became an active part, was born on February 29, 1925.

Minerva was born on March 12, 1926, and María Teresa, the youngest, on October 15, 1936.

Minerva was the first of the sisters to get involved in the resistance. She studied law at the University of Santo Domingo, where she met her husband, Manuel Aurelio Tavares Justo. On January 14, 1959, the Dominican Liberation Movement, which consisted of exiled Dominicans, tried to take down the Dominican government. This attempt, which became known as the Luperion Invasion, was thwarted by Trujillo's military. However, it did spawn the Movement of the Fourteenth of January, an underground anti-Trujillo coalition, of which Minerva's husband became the president. Patria, the most religious of the sisters, and María Teresa, who was an aspiring mathematician, followed their sister into action, and together the three became widely known and admired throughout the country.

The sisters' steadfast opposition to Trujillo led to the dictator lashing out against them (as he did to anyone whom he felt was a threat to his rule). Early on, their family's possessions were confiscated by the government; Trujillo ordered Minerva kicked out of the university because of a paper she wrote in which she detailed what was wrong with the way the

---

left the settlement to go back to Spain with the understanding that some of his men would hold down the fort. What happened when he left was the bloody beginning to a long story of genocide and slavery. When Columbus returned two years later, he found La Navidad burned to the ground; his men had either died or abandoned their posts, setting sail again in their insatiable hunger for the gold they had been promised. Columbus grew bitter and moved his fort 110 kilometers east, where he built a settlement and named it La Isabela, after the queen of Spain. But this was an unlucky venue as well. Plagued with disease and death, it was abandoned five years later and moved south to the east side of the Río Ozama and eventually to the west bank of the river, where it is now called the Ciudad Colonial, or Santo Domingo.

Genocide of the Taínos

With the establishment of the first settlements of the New World came the establishment of the genocide of the Taíno people. They were forced to work in mines, were horribly mistreated, and died of disease or accidents; many committed suicide rather than continue their new lives at the hands of the Spanish.

In addition to being overworked in the mines, they were murdered. Governor Nicolás de Ovando, who came to Santo Domingo and began building it up with stately buildings and homes, pampering the colonists with beautiful surroundings, took the exploitation of the

country was being run – she included several suggestions for improvement. (She eventually returned to school.) Over the years, the sisters and other members of their family – including their mother, father, and husbands – were arrested and sent to prisons, some known for torturing their inmates, where they would be held for up to months at a time. Still, the women did not back down. And in the meantime, the rest of the country was growing more and more disillusioned with Trujillo.

In a final effort to rid his country of the rising influence of the Mirabal sisters, Trujillo ordered several of his men to silence the women for good. On November 25, 1960, the sisters were on their way back home to Salcedo after a visit to Patria's and Minerva's imprisoned husbands. Their car was stopped by Trujillo's devoted thugs, and the three women, along with their driver, Rufino de la Cruz, were ordered out of the car. They were taken into a nearby sugarcane field where they were beaten and killed.

The killers returned the bodies to the car and pushed the vehicle off a cliff.

Despite the attempt to make their deaths appear accidental, when word got out that Las Mariposas were dead, the Dominican people were fooled. They knew Trujillo was behind the women's demise. Now, the influence of Las Mariposas was more powerful than ever. Discontent and rage among the Dominicans was at its apex. Six months after Trujillo had ordered Patria, Minerva, and María Teresa killed, the dictator was assassinated at the hands of his own countrymen.

Today, Las Mariposas live on. In Santo Domingo, an obelisk that Trujillo had originally commissioned in honor of himself has been dedicated to the women and re-painted to depict their likenesses. It is entitled *The Song to Liberty*. In Ojos de Agua, just outside the city of Salcedo, Dede has created a museum out of the last home the sisters had shared, to honor the three women's memory. Patria, Minerva, María Teresa, and Minerva's husband, Manuel, are all buried on the property, which is open to the public. In 1995, Julia Alvarez wrote a fictionalized account of the Mirabal sisters. The title of the novel is *In the Time of the Butterflies*, and in 2001 it was made into a major motion picture of the same name. Now, the entire world commemorates Las Mariposas; November 25 – the anniversary of the women's deaths – has been designated International Day Against Violence Toward Women.

Taínos to a whole new level. He instituted a system of slavery called *encomienda,* in which entire Taíno villages along with their caciques were forced into a type of feudal serfdom. Determined to squash the Taínos, de Ovando devised a horrible plan. In 1503, he invited the female cacique, Anacaona (the widow of the revered cacique Caonabo who died while in Spanish captivity), to a "meeting" along with 80 other caciques. As Anacaona looked on, de Ovando ordered that all the tribal leaders be burned alive because he suspected them of conspiracy. A horrified Anacaona fled but was eventually captured by de Ovando and hung.

Diego Columbus (Christopher's oldest son) arrived with a sense of entitlement; he was appointed governor (1508–1515) of Santo Domingo and then viceroy of the Indies (1520–1524). He set up his friends and supporters with the best digs and slaves, and started one of the first sugar plantations on the island. Like de Ovando, he beautified the city even more and laid the foundation for the first cathedral in the New World. This was the era of the "firsts"—the first cathedral, the first hospital, and even the first mint. It seemed that Santo Domingo was to be a place of great wealth and power.

But outside the walls of the rich gem, Santo Domingo, lay the outback of Hispaniola, completely ignored by Diego and his cronies, as they let smallpox nearly wipe out the entire Taíno population. That resulted in a severe shortage of slaves.

THE SLAVE TRADE

The Spanish saw the potential for a "cash cow" in European's insatiable need for the sweet stuff, so it was the development of the sugar industry that fueled the slave trade. But with the Taíno population dwindling, the Spanish turned to Africa and began importing slaves. In 1522, the first slave revolt took place, right on Diego Columbus's plantation. Unfortunately, the slaves were horribly massacred. Nearly a half million slaves were brought to Hispaniola between 1520 and 1801. They made the trip in the bellies of galleons, chained together for a horrendous three-month voyage to the Caribbean—a trip that would leave many dead before arrival. Then they had to suffer the incomparable horrors of slavery, being denied their culture and identities, all for the gain of European wealth.

The slave trade was a triangle, literally. Boats set out from various European ports toward Africa's west coast with goods they would use in a trade for people. Once they loaded their slaves onto the ships, they would journey to the Caribbean, where the ones who survived were sold. The ships then returned to Europe with sugar, coffee, tobacco, rum, and rice, all produced by slave labor.

Spanish fortunes were made through the sugar and triangular trade industry, and England and France got jealous. As pirates and buccaneers got wind of the riches, they went with the blessings of (and sometimes funded by) their countries to impede the successes of the industry. One famous incident was when Sir Francis Drake and his 18 ships of men, sent by England, took over Santo Domingo and held it for ransom for a month. When the Spanish finally paid, he looted and burned the entire city before leaving.

The French, on the other hand, in a bold move sent over 13,000 men (farmers and African slaves) to populate the poorly guarded western half of the island. Eventually, the population of their colonies greatly outnumbered those of the Spanish side, making the Spanish incredibly uneasy; in fear of losing control of the rest of the island they agreed to a border treaty called the Treaty of Ryswick (1697), which officially ceded the western portion of Hispaniola to France and was named Saint-Domingue and the Spanish side was named Santo Domingo. The border that was created is more or less the same today.

THE OCCUPATIONS

By 1789 Saint-Domingue was a very wealthy colony, heavily coveted by England, which then overtook Port-au-Prince. It was in this moment of unrest in 1793 that the slaves, led by a brilliant ex-slave, Toussaint L'Ouverture, allied with the Spanish to revolt against the French. But when the French government made a counter-offer to the slaves that slavery would be abolished if they joined again with the French to defeat the enclosing British forces, Toussaint returned to the French side along with his army.

With the French, Toussaint and his men successfully defeated both British and Spanish forces. The British finally withdrew from the island entirely in 1798 and in 1801, and Toussaint (without direction from the French government) took control of Santo Domingo for the French Republic. In 1802, Napoleon's French Imperialist forces invaded to try to reinstate the pre-revolutionary climate. Toussaint was eventually captured by the French and sent to Paris where he died of pneumonia in 1803.

The revolutionary war continued under Toussaint's successor, Jean Jacques Dessalines, and in 1804 Haiti won its independence. It was the second independent country and the first black republic in the New World.

While the French were forced out of the western side of the island, they remained present in Santo Domingo until 1809 when they finally returned it to Spanish control. At that point the colony of Santo Domingo declared their independence and requested to join the Gran Colombia Federation, a South American anti-colonial movement run by Simón Bólivar. But that request was never realized because Haiti jumped in and invaded in 1822 and stayed for 22 years under the Haitian President Jean-Pierre Boyer. The 22-year Haitian occupation is still a sore spot between Dominicans and Haitians even to this day. Boyer was a hard-handed leader that expressed outrage and discontent for the former Spanish colony.

On February 27, 1844, Juan Pablo Duarte, with the help of his seperatist movement La Filantrópica (The Philanthropy), captured Santo Domingo at the Puerto del Conde and claimed their independence. Duarte, who was widely supported to be the president of the new republic, was then forced into exile by Pedro Santana who led the troups that were in favor of returning to Spanish rule. Two decades of Spanish rule ensued.

Finally, in 1865, independence fighters reclaimed control in what is now called the La Guerra de la Restauración (The War of the Restoration). And on March 3, 1865, the queen of Spain finally withdrew all her soldiers from the island entirely.

TRUJILLO DICTATORSHIP

After the American occupation ended, the Dominican Republic saw a short period of hopeful growth. And then Rafael Leonidas Trujillo reared his head.

Trujillo had joined the National Guard when the Americans were occupying the country and was trained by the United States Marines to "maintain order" once they vacated. In reality though, the training just ignited his greed and obsessive need for power. Having risen through the ranks, he held a sham election in 1930 and, as the only

EL JEFE AND RÍO MASSACRE

One of the most notorious, devastating events in Dominican history was the slaughter of tens of thousands of Haitians at the aptly named Massacre River. The river seems to have derived its name from a battle back in the colonial period, when a number of French buccaneers lost their lives at the hands of the Spanish. In October of 1937, its waters ran red once again.

The man who ordered the massacre was Dominican president Rafael Trujillo, also known as El Jefe (The Boss). In an effort to "whiten" the Dominican population, known as *blanquismo*, Trujillo ordered soldiers to kill any Haitian attempting to cross over the border into the Dominican Republic. The soldiers tried to distinguish the Haitians from the Dominicans by telling anyone who crossed their paths to say the Spanish word for parsley – *perejil*. The soldiers' thinking – or, rather, Trujillo's – was that those from the wrong side of the border, coming from a French background, would be unable to pronounce the trilled "r" in the word. Of course, this theory was rather faulty in that many Haitians, having grown up in such proximity to the Spanish-speaking Dominican Republic, could pronounce the word "properly." Still, in the end, this did not save most of them.

It is thought that Trujillo admired Adolf Hitler and was heavily influenced by what he was trying to accomplish in Europe at the time. In fact, not long before the slaughter began, Trujillo played host to a delegation of Nazis. Paradoxically, after receiving loads of criticism for his murderous attempt to cleanse his country of Haitians, Trujillo invited 100,000 Jews fleeing Hitler to settle in the Dominican Republic. And while this was a blatant attempt to clear his reputation and current standing as a murderer of thousands, it is also thought that by inviting these Europeans to take refuge in his country, Trujillo was in fact trying to further his campaign to whiten at least the eastern two-thirds of Hispaniola.

Despite the amount of disgust and mortification the world felt toward him at the time, Trujillo remained in power until 1961, when he was assassinated by a group of wealthy Dominicans who had had enough of his destructive leadership. Through his efforts at ethnic cleansing, Trujillo succeeded only in befouling his name and his memory. To this day, and no doubt far into the future, the anniversary of Trujillo's assassination is celebrated as a national holiday in the Dominican Republic.

candidate, "won" the presidency. Very quickly, the Dominican people were introduced to the first true totalitarian (and egomaniacal) dictator in the Caribbean. He changed the name of Santo Domingo to Ciudad Trujillo and renamed the highest mountain Pico Trujillo. By 1934 he was the richest man on the island, having seized sugar plantations and ranches for himself. Tying his personal wealth to the wealth of the country, he set it up so that the country flourished, even achieving the support of the United States. The economy soared, as did agricultural production, as did industrial progress, as did his own personal spending; he even built homes that he never lived in.

And the high cost was being paid by the people in the currency of repression. Under Trujillo, all households had to have portraits or plaques stating their allegiance to "El Jefe" (The Chief), children recited daily prayers for him, and anyone who was thought to be against him could suffer torture or death. His secret police would follow and question, perhaps even jail anyone they wanted. Trujillo trusted no one, and spies were everywhere.

Trujillo was obsessed with creating "whiteness" in the Dominican Republic. *Blanquismo,* as it was called, was the driving force behind his order to massacre around 20,000 dark-skinned Haitian sugarcane workers in a river now named Río Masacre (Massacre River), although he claimed it was a response to the Haitian government's support of exiled Dominicans who were plotting against him. In a mad dash to clean up his image, he promptly invited Jewish immigrants to relocate and escape the horrors of Hitler. This act and the anti-communist policies he adopted put him in the good graces of the U.S. government, but that relationship would eventually be his demise.

With his blatant attempt on the life of the Venezuelan president, Rómulo Betancourt, and his murder of the revolutionary Mirabal sisters, resentment grew and he was assassinated by members of his own regime on May 30, 1961. It is widely believed that the CIA in the United States provided the weapons to his assassins in fear of having "another Cuba" on their hands.

After his death, Ciudad Trujillo and Pico Trujillo, along with a host of other places, reverted to their original titles, Santo Domingo and Pico Duarte.

POST-TRUJILLO

After Trujillo's death, Joaquín Balaguer was president. But it was not a presidency that was supported by the people. He was merely a puppet. Soon, a council took control until elections could be held, at which point the first free elections in the Dominican Republic in years took place and Juan Bosch Gaviño won the presidency. A liberal man, he was a scholar and had a soft spot for workers and students. He enacted many liberal concepts, like separation of church and state, and wanted very much to instill economic and social justice. He went so far as to give Trujillo's estates to peasants (what was left of them after Trujillo's family took off with a majority of the money). After only seven months in office, Bosch was ousted by conservatives. Eventually a civilian triumvirate ruled the nation and did away with his constitution (saying Bosch's ideas were outlawed), declaring it nonexistent.

But Bosch, with the aid of a group called the Constitutionalists, started plotting for his return.

U.S. Occupation

The United States decided to back the conservatives, but even that didn't deter the Constitutionalists, who on April 24, 1965, led by Col. Francisco Caamaño Deño, rose up against the triumvirate to restore Bosch's office. They seized the National Palace and radio stations, asking people to take to the streets and demand Bosch's return. Lawlessness ensued; both sides were heavily armed.

Twenty-three thousand U.S. Marines were sent by Lyndon Johnson, ordered to restore peace and elections. Balaguer eventually was put back into power (no doubt with bribes) and won the elections again in 1970 and 1974, lost in subsequent elections but won yet again, in 1986. In that term, he supported the need for a healthy tourism industry, set up the industrial free zones, and basically spent a lot of public money. Food and power were in short supply. And still, in 1990, he ran again. He won the 1994 election (by this time totally blind and 86 years old), but under the pressure from the military, cut his term short.

Dominican Republic Today
In 1996, Leonal Fernández (born and raised in the U.S.) won the presidency over José Fran-cisco Peña Gómez (a liberal), and he brought a change of economic growth. But with the dawn of the new millennium came Hipólito Mejía, who promptly sank the peso to a hurt-ful RD$52 to the U.S. dollar.

In 2004, Fernández won again, defeating the incumbent Mejía. His win was likely in direct reaction to the severe economic crisis that was the signature of Mejía's presidency, when food costs quadrupled and debt doubled and unem-ployment soared. It was a significant election in that it was the first time Dominicans abroad were allowed to vote in the national election.

Government and Economy

GOVERNMENT
The Dominican Republic has a democ-racy with executive, legislative, and judicial branches. The executive power is the presi-dent, who appoints a cabinet, is the com-mander-in-chief of the armed forces, and executes laws passed by the legislative branch. The president and vice president both hold four-year terms.

The National Congress consists of the Sen-ate (32 members) and the Chamber of Depu-ties (150 members). The judicial system has a Supreme Court consisting of nine judges elected by the Senate.

The three main political parties in the Do-minican Republic are the PRD (Partido Rev-olucionario Dominicana or the Dominican Revolutionary Party), the DLP (Partido de la Liberación Dominicana or Dominican Libera-tion Party), and the PRSC (Partido Reformista Social Cristiano or the Social Christian Re-formist Party). The current president, Leonal Fernández, is a member of the DLP.

With one of the first free elections occurring in 2004, a new generation of "clean" politics has the opportunity to strengthen. But cor-ruption, which has always been a problem, is not gone yet. With each election, government workers fear for their jobs, since most who gain power reward their supporters and oust the previous staffs, and this goes through all levels of government, not just the top seats.

ECONOMY
In 2003, a major banking scandal tipped the economy on its ear, ending in the collapse of the bank Baninter. Confidence in the govern-ment's ability to handle the economy plum-meted, hitting rock bottom along with the peso. As the peso lay cold on the economic floor, then-president Mejía's spending and borrowing habits (US$1.1 billion) added even more insult to injury and brought the inflation rate to around 25 percent—prices rose and wages didn't—and the poor got even poorer.

The Dominican Republic has long been de-pendent on agriculture (especially sugar) for the economy, but it is no longer a one-trick-pony as the cigar production industry has stepped up its game.

But for exporting, mining (gold, silver, fer-ronickel, and bauxite) is number one, with agriculture behind it. Dominicans living abroad—sending money home—are huge sup-porters of the economy, offering about US$3 billion a year.

Perhaps more controversial are the manufac-turing plants called industrial free zones (like the one in San Pedro de Macorís) that were set up to specifically make goods for the U.S. market. These plants offer tax concessions and supply extremely cheap labor under harsh conditions. In 2005, under the Bush administration, the CAFTA-DR agreement was signed between the United States and Costa Rica, El Salvador, Guatemala, Honduras, Nicaragua, and the Dominican Republic, in the hopes of strengthening and developing economic relations and encouraging trade between the countries by reducing and eliminating barriers of trade in goods and services. Major opponents to this bill say that the supposed benefits of globalization don't make it down to the citizens (doing the work) with proper work environment guidelines and benefits.

A huge boom in tourism helped what seemed to be an ongoing economic sinkhole. Since the 1960s, tourism had been gaining on sugar, which was the main provider for the nation's economy. But now, tourism brings in the most foreign currency (about US$2 billion each year) and has created many jobs (about

150,000), but not nearly enough. About half of the Dominican Republic's population lives in poverty and about a third of the people don't have secure jobs. The inequality between rich and poor is obtrusive. And so it goes; the middle class (what little one there is left after the recent economic turbulence) holds on feebly.

Tourism

Its unclear why the Dominican Republic arrived so late to the tourism game. Perhaps it was a controlling dictator who didn't like foreigners in his own backyard, or perhaps it was the political and civil unrest of the 1960s. Whatever the reason, tourism did begin to take hold later on, but then 9/11 happened in the U.S. and people stopped traveling for a little while. As tourists started arriving again, it was the American contingent that picked up because of the U.S.'s proximity to the Dominican Republic. Vacationing closer to home became very desirable to Americans, and the DR was benefiting and continues to do so.

The tourist industry has focused on budget

farmland near Baní

travel, with special attention to the all-inclusive scene. Tourism is highly concentrated in the complexes along the coasts, which are mostly foreign owned. This type of vacation caters to the sun-worshipping visitors who rarely leave the confines of the resort's walls. When they do, it is most often only to go to the metropolitan area of Santo Domingo.

The potential for ecotourism has risen dramatically over the years. Born to oppose the practices of mega-resort complexes, which mistreat the environment with their pesticides to kill mosquitoes and their blind eye toward the ecosystem, ecotourism, with its emphasis on environmental sensitivity, has inadvertently shined a spotlight on the center of the country, where adventure sports are really taking off and becoming a viable competitor for the "best-kept secret in the Caribbean."

Agriculture

The real face of the Dominican Republic is the one of its countryside, where the produce grows and where the sugarcane waves through the breeze in magnificent green fields. Agriculture was the supporting structure of Dominican economy for centuries. In the 1960s, it encompassed about 60 percent of the labor force and yielded about 80 percent of exports. By the 1980s those numbers dramatically dropped. Even sugar production dropped down the list of important economic producers. In large part, the transformation paralleled the trend of the population moving to more urban areas. At the same time, the United States reduced its call for sugar quotas, thereby depressing the production of the crop, which was the backbone of the economy for a very long time.

Culture

It is often said that the Dominican people are some of the friendliest and most hospitable in the world. In fact, most discussions about Dominicans begin this way because it is so true. They are fierce believers in making a visitor feel welcome and included in the Dominican experience. The Dominican experience is to walk lightly through life with a smile for everyone to see and a polite demeanor. Whether you are purchasing something from a stranger or talking with someone you know, polite behavior is to chitchat for a bit first and be complimentary. In other words, don't be in too much of a hurry to have people flit in and out of your life; everyone is important enough to have an interaction with, even if just for the duration of buying a bottle of water.

The Dominican psyche is to always have a song in your head and to sing it out loud no matter who is around. It is to have a sense of humor about their own world and the world outside of the DR. Laughing is a big part of life. At the same time, there is a very strong sense of pride in their culture and nationality. This is evident in Dominican expats in other countries. When they find each other amongst the sea of other Latinos, they are instant *compadres* (friends).

FAMOUS DOMINICANS

Oscar de la Renta – fashion designer
Julia Alvarez – writer
Junot Díaz – writer
Michelle Rodríguez – actress
María Montez – actress
Zoë Saldaña – actress
Ashanti – R&B singer
D.M.C. – rapper
Moisés Alou – baseball player
Robinson Cano – baseball player
Sammy Sosa – baseball player
Juan Marichal – baseball player

Family is a thick bond that goes beyond blood. Loyalty to those they care about is a more accurate statement. It is perhaps the most welcoming sensation, to be invited into a Dominican home and made to feel included with such honest warmth.

But it would be overly romantic to say that there aren't some fissures of discontent or discord running through the cultural fabric. Race relations is just one sore spot and by far the worst. There is a great deal of emphasis put on color and how one fits on that spectrum, and it is strongly tied to class. This is especially obvious when it comes to Haitian/Dominican relations.

While Dominicans are hospitable and loving people, they are for the most part quite conservative. The day-to-day male chauvinism and homophobia can be quite unsettling to an outsider but is incredibly normal there.

THE PEOPLE

It is difficult to talk about race and class separately in the Dominican Republic. Dominicans see skin color as a definite line between upper and lower class. Perhaps this is an inherited outlook from centuries of ingrained thought passed on from Taíno/Spanish and Spanish/Haitian relations.

Most light-skinned Dominicans (about 70 percent of the entire population) refer to themselves as white but are usually of "mixed heritage," showing more European features than African or indigenous ones.

The wide ethnic variety is largely due to the various waves of different immigrants to come through here—Jewish, Middle Eastern, African, Spanish, Japanese, German, Italian, English, as well as other Caribbean islanders, to name just a few. Of course the Haitians have the longest history as immigrants to the Dominican Republic. Thousands of Haitians live and work in the sugarcane fields and live in poverty-stricken conditions despite their great contribution to the Dominican workforce and economy. They are often mistreated and discriminated against.

All you need to do to see the class differen-tial is to take a drive through the country or cities. Luxury cars and shopping malls contrast with dirt roads and poor wages. Look into the faces and you'll see the color distinctions. The whiter the skin, the higher the class. It is a sad fact. The Dominican Republic is a nation fragmented along the color lines of its people. A very small percentage of people (5 percent at best) enjoy wealth, status, and power, whereas 80 percent live in poverty. But living in the pressure of the middle (as all middle children do) is the growing and struggling-to-hang-on middle class (roughly 15 percent).

RELIGION

More than 90 percent of Dominicans practice Roman Catholicism, the official religion of the Dominican Republic. However, it is not as strictly adhered to today as it once was. And few practice a pure form of Catholicism. Instead they often practice the symbolic gestures of it.

Folk religions and beliefs are practiced (as is Vodou), but they often are in more closed circles and private spheres since they are berated as "evil." *Curanderos* are a kind of folk healer that many seek for healing herbs and incantations for the purpose of healing. At many open markets, you will see various herbs and candles being sold for just this purpose.

During World War II, a small population of Jewish families were invited by Trujillo to immigrate to La Costa Ámbar. They were given land to farm and stayed for a short while, but after suffering anti-Semitic ridicule, many left after a few years. Some 20 families still remain and maintain a synagogue in the town of Sosúa.

GENDER ROLES

Like many Latin American countries, the Dominican Republic exhibits a strong, male-oriented culture, much of which was inherited from Spanish colonialists. Latino machismo, an exaggerated sense of masculine power, is very prevalent here. Dominican men carry the hefty reputation of being womanizers. Performing acts that flaunt sexual prowess is central to

LA BANDERA DOMINICANA (THE DOMINICAN FLAG)

This national dish is a culinary symbol of the country, eaten by many Dominicans on a regular basis. The recipe consists of three parts: meat (usually chicken), rice and beans, and fried plantains.

BRAISED CHICKEN

Ingredients:
    1 whole chicken, cut up
    1 onion, chopped
    3-5 garlic cloves, minced
    1 green bell pepper, chopped
    1 tbsp. oregano
    1 dry hot red pepper
    2 tbsp. tomato paste diluted in water
    cilantro to taste
    1 tbsp. capers
    salt and pepper to taste
    few splashes of lemon juice (either fresh or bottled)
    olive oil (enough to coat pan generously)

Combine all of the above ingredients except the olive oil. Cover and refrigerate for one hour. When chicken is done marinating, set aside. Heat oil in large frying pan or Dutch oven. Remove chicken from mixture and add to pan. Brown chicken on all sides. Add the rest of the mixture to pan, gradually adding up to 2 or 3 cups of water. (If the water is added in large amounts, the result is a stew-like consistency, which you don't want.) Continue cooking until chicken is heated all the way through. Set aside.

FRIED RIPE PLANTAINS (PLÁTANO MADURO FRITO)

Ingredients:
    4 very ripe plantains
    oil to coat pan

Peel plaintains. Cut plantains in half across. Slice each half lengthwise into three pieces. Fry in oil (3-4 slices at a time) until brown. Drain on paper towel to remove excess oil.

RICE AND BEANS

Ingredients:
    1 cup dry white rice
    1-1½ cups water
    1 tbsp. olive oil
    1 tsp. salt

Rinse rice under cold water until water runs clear. Combine all ingredients and cook over medium-high to high heat until boiling. Reduce heat to medium and cover, cooking until all the water has been absorbed.

Ingredients:
    1 can red or pinto beans, rinsed, plus ½ can water
    ½ onion, chopped
    ½ green bell pepper, chopped
    2-3 garlic cloves, minced
    ½ tsp. oregano
    1 pinch dry red pepper (hot)
    1 pinch anise seed
    cilantro to taste
    1 tbsp. tomato paste diluted in water

Combine all ingredients and cook over medium heat until mixture thickens. Remove from heat. Add cooked rice and mix together. Serve the chicken, fried plantains, and the beans and rice together.

the macho attitude. Leering, gestures, and the ever-so-infamous hissing noise made toward women of all ages and types that pass by are just some of the ways they choose to flaunt their colors. Simply ignoring them will usually stop the behavior. The more you engage with them, the more they keep at it. It is not so much meant as a direct pass as it is about proving something to themselves and other men.

While women in the Dominican Republic have made gigantic strides toward equality, there is still a really long way to go. Today, women make up a majority of high school and college graduates and are increasing the likelihood of getting equal jobs and equal pay as men. Slaying the machismo dragon is a hard battle, but one that Dominican women are more than ready for.

On the home front, women are usually in charge of organizing and maintaining all family rituals and events. One of the foundations of Dominican culture is their sense of family, and women are what hold that together.

While many Dominican men are worried about proving their sexual prowess, many Dominican women are very concerned with their physical appearance. A great amount of pressure is put on women of all ages to be thin, and women spend hours on their hair,

straightening it to look more "European" or desirable to men.

LANGUAGE

The official language of the Dominican Republic is Spanish, although in the coastal tourist areas, English, French, Italian, and German are all spoken. Dominican Spanish is a far cry from the official Spanish of Spain. Less formal and laced with innuendo and colloquialisms, it is a hard form of Spanish to get hold of, especially when Dominicans drop S's off the ends of words. But Dominicans are usually very happy to know that a foreigner wants to learn their language and are very patient listeners and teachers. Most are willing to walk you through whatever you're trying to say and correct you politely when you make an error. They may even be eager to learn a few words in your language in exchange.

Dominican Spanish is filled with riddles and limericks used to describe even the most mundane of occurrences. It is a sort of oral tradition passed down for generations. If you are faced with an expression and you don't understand it, politely ask for an explanation. Although the translation might not be as funny in your language, it is probably a laugh-riot in Spanish, so try to conjure a giggle.

ESSENTIALS

Getting There

BY AIR

The Dominican Republic is fortunate enough to have nine international airports. The major ones are **Aeropuerto Internacional Las Américas** (SDQ, Santo Domingo, tel. 809/549-0081), **Aeropuerto Internacional Punta Cana** (PUJ, Punta Cana/Bávaro, tel. 809/959-2473), **Aeropuerto Internacional Gregorio Luperón** (POP, Puerto Plata/Playa Dorada, tel. 809/586-1992), **Aeropuerto Internacional Cibao** (STI, Santiago, tel. 809/581-8072), and **Aeropuerto Internacional La Romana** (LRM, La Romana/Casa de Campo, tel. 809/689-1548).

Some airlines that fly to the Dominican Republic include: **American Airlines** (tel. 809/542-5151, www.aa.com), **Air Canada** (tel. 809/541-2929, www.aircanada.ca), **Continental Airlines** (tel. 809/262-1060, www.continental.com), and **Jet Blue** (tel. 809/549-1793, www.jetblue.com).

The Internet is the best place to look for affordable flights to the Dominican Republic. There are often deals depending on what time of the year, what day you fly (for instance not over a weekend), and how long you stay.

If you want to check into all-inclusive resort vacations, check online or with a travel agent

© ANA CHAVIER CAAMAÑO

as they have package deals where you pay one lump sum that includes air, hotel, food, drink, and often transportation from the airport.

BY FERRY

Ferries del Caribe (Santo Domingo port, tel. 809/688-4400; Puerto Rico port, tel. 787/832-4400) is the only ferry company that can get you to the Dominican Republic. It is based in Puerto Rico and offers three-times-a-week service. All are overnight trips. If you can swing the cost, getting a private cabin is the way to go; that way you can sleep for the 12-hour boat ride rather than sit in an airplane-style seat across the ocean (see the *Santo Domingo* chapter for more information).

Getting Around

AIRPLANES

The Dominican Republic is a very small country. Most people either take the bus or drive everywhere. But if you want to wing it, literally, there are a few domestic air charters available. Most flights cost under US$100. Two such companies are: **Aerodomca** (tel. 809/567-1195, www.aerodomca.com) and **Caribair** (tel. 809/542-6688).

BUSES

There are two good bus options in the Dominican Republic, and both are very affordable. The country is so small that most trips are under four hours. The first type of service is a **first-class** bus. Much like Greyhound buses, these are modern and have the big comfortable seats with toilets on board. Some even have movies playing on small TVs. Most tickets cost US$3–10. Some notable bus companies are: **Caribe Tours** (tel. 809/221-4422), perhaps the best one with the most departure times, and **Metro Tours** (tel. 809/566-7126), which has similar service at less frequent intervals. The second option is a *guagua*. *Guaguas* are the true Dominican transportation system (aside from the *motoconcho*). They are minivan-sized buses that can hold up to 30 people. To flag one down (which is the way you do it), just stand on the side of the road for the direction that you want to travel in and wave it down, or wait to find out what the *cobrador* (charger) says. He is the man who hangs out the side of the bus and takes the fares and says the destination of the *guagua*. They rarely display destination signs, so don't feel bad if you have to flag down a couple before getting the right one. As always, most Dominicans are happy to help if you have questions. The typical fare for a ride is US$2.

RENTAL CARS

Renting a car can be a fantastic way to experience and see the real Dominican Republic for yourself. Many international companies have offices in Santo Domingo, at major airports and in high tourist areas like Punta Cana and Puerto Plata. Before renting a car in the Dominican Republic, check with your credit card company to see if you are automatically covered for international rentals. If not, getting the optional car insurance through your chosen rental agency can be expensive but worth it considering the road conditions, lack of rules being obeyed by other drivers, and potential for accidents.

Driving Conditions

Driving here can be downright scary. If you don't have experience driving in fast conditions with quick reflexes, perhaps you should consider the bus. Road conditions can change quickly; there are often pedestrians on the sides of the roads, and even people crossing very busy thoroughfares.

But, if you really want to try it, you're in for a fun experience. Some words of advice: Keep your eyes peeled for potholes and random speed bumps, known as *policía acostada* (sleeping policemen), in the middle of the highway. Always drive defensively. Trucks, *motoconchos*,

© ANA CHAVIER CAAMAÑO

a common way to travel for locals

and other cars do not follow very many rules—you have to be ready for anything. Just because there is a red light does *not* mean they will stop. Try to run with the pack; otherwise, you might cause a pile-up.

PÚBLICOS

These jalopies are found in the bigger cities. They are usually minivans, trucks, or regular cars, and they pick passengers up along main drags. Similar to *guaguas, públicos* can be hailed from anywhere. They will usually slow down enough for you to gesture. If you don't, they'll zoom past you quickly. They don't have signs (although technically they're supposed to), and the fare is usually US$0.30. Often, drivers cram them to the breaking point. Hold your purse here—pick-pocketing can occur when it gets full.

MOTOCONCHOS

These mopeds are a cheap and easy-to-find transportation option. You can find them usually around main town squares or tourist-frequented areas. Flag them down and secure a price before hopping on. Never expect a helmet to be offered up—they won't have them. Beware: The drivers can be downright maniacal. While very dangerous for trips on the highway, they are undeniably cheap and easy to find in small towns. They are more suitable for short distances and you can always request that the driver go slowly. They are used to this request from the tourists. Samaná's multi-person version of the *motoconcho* is considered safer than the more common one-passenger type because it is more like a carriage that is pulled by a motorcycle and is therefore slower-going and more visible to other motorists.

Visas and Officialdom

As of December 2006, all tourists will need a passport to enter the Dominican Republic. You will also be required to purchase a US$10 tourist card to enter the country via one of the airports, so make sure you take exact change and a pen to fill out the card. Check to see if your passport is valid and that you have sufficient room for an entrance and exit stamp prior to departure.

Tourist cards can be purchased in your arrival airport and allow you to stay for 60 days. Once you get off the airplane, you will be led (or just follow the crowd) to the immigration room. Here there will be a window where you need to get in line and purchase a card. Fill it out (make sure to have a pen with you) and then get in the appropriate line in front of the immigration officers. They'll check your passport and approve your visit for however many days you say you'll be there. By the time all of this business is taken care of, your luggage will most likely meet you in customs. Usually it's quite painless, and they don't tear your luggage apart unless you're carrying a lot.

If you decide to stay longer than a 60-day period, you'll need to visit the **Migration Department in Santo Domingo** (Centro de los Heroes, Autopista 30 de Mayo, tel. 809/508-2555, open 8 A.M.–3 P.M. Mon.–Fri.) and request an extension, or you can pay a scaled charge at the airport upon departure from the Dominican Republic.

For those who fly into the Dominican Republic, departure tax is charged upon leaving. The cost is US$20 and must be paid before leaving the airport.

Those who use a visa to enter the country and overstay the legal period will be charged a fee. This fee ranges from RD$60 (an overstay of one day to three months) to at least RD$250 (an overstay of more than two years).

Traveling with Children

Children under the age of 13 who are traveling with a parent or legal guardian are not required to have a passport but should carry a birth certificate. Children traveling with non-parents should have a passport. No special letter of authorization is required for children traveling with non-parents, so long as they return with the same adults with whom they arrived. However, get in touch with the Dominican Republic consulate or embassy to confirm the situation has not changed.

Traveling with Pets

If you are traveling with your cat or dog, you must bring a veterinarian's certificate of vaccination against rabies, which has to have been issued within 30 days of entry into the Dominican Republic. You are also required to bring a veterinarian's certificate of health, issued within 14 days prior to entry. For further details on traveling with a pet check out www.dominicanrepublic.com or www.hispaniola.com under Travel or Tourism.

Conduct and Customs

Dominicans are incredibly fun-loving people. While not stuffy by any means, they do adhere to codes of behavior that are rooted in politeness. It is a very important aspect of Dominican culture. For instance, it is considered impolite to get right down to business with someone, which tends to be the American way. Instead, if you don't speak Spanish, a nice smile with a *"buenos días"* is a good way to start a conversation. If you speak Spanish, you might even venture forth into a small dialogue about something pleasant (like what a nice day it is) before you go into what you are about to ask of them. This is the same for telephone etiquette.

The Spanish words *por favor* (please) and *gracias* (thank you) go a long way to bridging cultures and making new friends. When faced with street or beach vendors, if you're not interested in what they're selling, politely say *no, gracias*. They will try again and again, but just keep a smile and say *no gracias*.

Capturing the Dominican culture can be a lot of fun for photographers, but always keep in mind that taking a photo without permission is not respectful. It is culturally acceptable to ask permission first and then offer a tip if they let you. Most young people will be happy to pose and will be very smiley for your photos, but it's best to ask first.

While Dominican vendors expect you to haggle, already hiking prices up for the challenge, don't take advantage of it. It is tempting to haggle in flea markets and with vendors for the lowest of the low prices. But just keep in mind, that it is their livelihood. Paying a fair price is a respectful thing to do. The same thing goes for the service industries. If you get good service somewhere, let them know you appreciated it and tip well. Ten percent of a bill is considered a generous gratuity.

Dominicans are famous for being very hospitable people. They are excited to show their culture and country to newcomers who want to learn. They don't mind answering questions at all when asked politely. They might even offer to show you around or help you beyond what you had asked.

The Dominican Republic is notorious for fantastic music, great festivals, and all-night dancing. They are also famous for their rum drinks. However, partying to Dominicans doesn't mean excessive drunkenness. In fact, it is highly frowned upon.

Tips for Travelers

ACCESS FOR TRAVELERS WITH DISABILITIES

By law, resorts and hotels on beach properties cannot exceed three floors. This isn't a disability-friendly law, but it does, by default, make navigation over the resort grounds a bit easier since most restaurants and facilities will be on the ground floor. Make sure to request a room on the ground floor, in case there is no elevator. Many of the all-inclusive resorts have rooms for travelers with disabilities. However, outside of the all-inclusives, the Dominican Republic isn't exactly an easy place to get around, so expect some logistical glitches. It's best to check with a travel agent prior to booking. Your agent should make the right reservations at the right hotels.

WOMEN TRAVELING ALONE

It's generally safe for women to travel in the Dominican Republic. Women traveling alone are best off playing it safe and doing any trekking during the day and on public transportation so that they are not alone. Generally, you will be given a great deal of advice and opposition if you tell a Dominican (male or female) that you

WEDDING CELEBRATIONS IN PARADISE: IDEAS AND MUST-DOS FOR YOUR I-DOS

How does a wedding in paradise sound? On the beach? Amidst 15th-century buildings in the colonial city of Santo Domingo? The Dominican Republic offers wildly romantic venues for beginning your life together. Major resorts and hotels throughout the DR have experts on staff to coordinate a flawless wedding that will give you and your guests lifetime memories.

Most wedding packages include the following: judge, license, flowers, music, cake, champagne, and special touches for the bridal accommodations. Here are some more tips for a carefree wedding celebration:

a romantic wedding in the Dominican Republic

© ANA CHAVIER CAAMAÑO

1. Start planning your wedding at least six months in advance. This way you are sure to get better deals than a last-minute booking; vacancies are more likely, and most hotels prefer at least a three-month leeway to make all necessary arrangements. If you choose a wedding on the beach or under the stars, what will you do if it rains? Religious ceremonies take longer to prepare.

2. Research venue options by visiting their websites. Often, venues will provide complimentary wedding services, but they have other wedding packages for additional cost that offer options above and beyond bare essentials for your stay, wedding, and honeymoon (e.g., religious ceremonies, couple's massage, breakfast in bed, pre-wedding day breakfasts, or spa treatments for the wedding party).

3. Ask if the hotel has a photographer on staff. If not, can they recommend one?

4. Do you need a translator? Ask if the hotel has someone who can translate the ceremony if need be.

5. Consider decorations. When arranging for decorations and cake toppers, ask what the staff can do. Tropical flowers are an easy and low-cost choice. Orchids are abundant in the Dominican Republic. How about seashells? If you have a cake in mind, send a photo of your dream cake and see if they can copy it.

6. What will you wear? When choosing attire for your ceremony, keep in mind the Caribbean climate. Sleeveless dresses are great, but consider the fabric. And what will the groom wear? Does he want to be in a full tuxedo under the blazing sun or are there other options? If you plan a wedding right on the beach, remember that a dress with a train will not stay white.

7. Plan on being at the resort or hotel at least three workdays in advance. This is best for any last-minute arrangements. Use the time to ready yourself for any guests that will join you. Perhaps put together a welcome basket with local fare or might-need items like suntan lotion or disposable cameras, for their room upon check-in. Or simply work on getting the perfect tan for your wedding.

What You'll Need for Marriage Paperwork
- Passport
- Original birth certificate
- Single status affidavit in Spanish
- Divorce act in Spanish. Legal transcripts of the single status affidavit and divorce act can be prepared at the Dominican consulate nearest to you.
- Two witnesses. If they are not Dominican, they will need to bring their passports.
- You will receive the wedding certificate from the justice of the peace.

wish to travel throughout the country alone. It is not seen as "right" for women to "have" to travel alone. The major thing you will come face to face with is the machismo of Dominican men in the form of whistling and ogling. They mean no harm. Just be smart about whom you talk to and whom you decide to befriend.

GAY AND LESBIAN TRAVELERS

There have been positive strides made in the gay and lesbian community of the Dominican Republic recently: Gay bars are able to have a longer shelf-life than before without being forced to close their doors; the first all-gay, all-inclusive resort opened up on the Península de Samaná; and the first gay pride parade was held July 1, 2001, in Santo Domingo to little opposition.

Still, homosexuality is relatively taboo, while not intolerable to most, and just isn't something that can be openly shown. If you're traveling with your partner (or you meet someone there), showing affection, even holding hands in public, is not acceptable.

For gay and lesbian nightlife options, Santo Domingo has the best scene. Many of the bars are in the Ciudad Colonial. Check out www.monaga.com/casamonaga.htm and www.santo-domingo-gay-tourism.com/ for some info on where to go. Some venues can be more discreet than others.

Health and Safety

BEFORE YOU GO
Vaccinations and Medications

For those who take prescription medications, it is important to bring enough for the duration of your trip—and perhaps even a little extra—as there is no guarantee specific types will be available. Also, pack medication in carry-on luggage to ensure it does not get lost if there are complications with the airline. If you will be traveling with children who are prone to childhood illnesses such as ear infections, be sure to bring along the appropriate antibiotics.

Vaccinations for typhoid and hepatitis A are important for both adults and children. Check with your doctor at least eight weeks in advance to make sure the timing of the vaccinations is appropriate. Updates of routine immunizations (for children in particular) such as tetanus, polio, diphtheria, measles/mumps, and varicella are highly recommended. Also speak to your doctor about malaria and diarrhea medications.

Internet Information

Consult the **World Health Organization (WHO)** website (www.who.int/ith/) for any information on your destination. Look for its book, called *International Travel and Health.* Also, **MD Travel Health** (www.mdtravelhealth.com) has a Dominican Republic page that is updated regularly.

STAYING HEALTHY
Bottled Water

Drink only bottled water in the Dominican Republic. Even brush your teeth with it. It's better safe than sorry. Fortunately, most restaurants, resorts, and hotels now use bottled water even for their ice cubes, but if you're not certain, ask for no ice in your drinks.

Most all-inclusive resorts (and some smaller hotels) have small refrigerators in the rooms. If they provide water for you, drink it only if the seal isn't broken. If they don't provide it, go buy some at the local *colmado* (corner store); you'll need it, especially for all those hot days spent in the sun. Don't forget to hydrate yourself with pure water. Nothing keeps away the stomach-yuckies like flushing your system with tons of water.

Sunstroke

Many folks who get a form of heatstroke think that they've gotten food poisoning, when really, they are just starved for water. Most vacationers tend to overdo the sun exposure in the first days, drinking alcohol and sweating more body moisture than they're used to. The key, once again, is to drink lots of water. Use sunscreen of at least SPF 30 and take a hat or seek out some shade under a nice palm. Oh, and lots of water. If you do get burned, get some aloe to *gently* rub on your skin and take it easy. Oh, and drink water.

Traveler's Diarrhea

The only way to avoid this is to avoid tap water and to avoid fresh fruits and vegetables (if they're raw). You can tell it is simple "traveler's diarrhea" if there are no other symptoms like fever.

If you get diarrhea just let it pass. Your body is trying to tell you that something is wrong. Taking Imodium should only be for emergency situations, like the plane trip home or salsa dancing. Drink lots of fluids that replace the electrolytes you're losing with fluids. A few loose stools is normal; if it's more than five a day, you should take an antibiotic. If you develop a bloody stool or a fever, see a doctor.

Hepatitis A and B

Hepatitis A is a viral infection that attacks the liver and is passed via contaminated food, water, ice, or another infected person. Symptoms may include fever, jaundice, malaise, nausea, vomiting, and abdominal pain. There is no treatment for hepatitis A, but most cases will resolve themselves. Occasionally, though, it can cause severe liver damage. Ask your doctor for the vaccine against hepatitis A. It is not a safe vaccine for pregnant women or children under two, but it's very safe and effective for everyone else.

Hepatitis B also affects the liver but is transmitted sexually or through infected blood (like via a blood transfusion). Getting vaccinated against it is important for those who will be traveling longer than six months.

Dengue Fever

Dengue fever is a viral infection specific to the Caribbean that is transmitted by a certain type of mosquito. These mosquitoes bite during the daytime and like to hang out wherever humans are, in stagnant water containers like jars or cisterns. Symptoms feel flu-like and include joint pain, muscle aches, headache, nausea, and vomiting and a rash to follow. Most cases will only last a couple of days. There is no treatment. But you can take acetaminophen like Tylenol and drink lots of fluids. There is no vaccine. Protect yourself from mosquito bites for prevention.

Malaria

Malaria is also transmitted by mosquitos; these usually attack around dawn and dusk. Symptoms include a high spiked fever, with chills, sweats, headache, body aches, weakness, vomiting, and diarrhea. Severe cases can lead to complications in the central nervous system, including seizures, confusion, coma, and death. Ask your doctor about malaria pills; they are sometimes recommended for areas in the Dominican Republic (mostly near the Haitian border, but also in Punta Cana). If your doctor prescribes malaria pills for you, continue taking them four weeks after you've returned from your vacation.

Women's Health

The Dominican Republic has all of the women's sanitary products you may need. Although the exact brand might not be available, pads, tampons, and panty liners all are readily available at the big supermarkets, pharmacies, and corner stores.

Small Necessities

Bring a small medical kit with Band-Aids/gauze, rehydration salt packets, duct tape for blisters, tweezers, antiseptic cream, strong sunblock, aloe for sunburns, antibiotics, Imodium (just in case), Tylenol, birth control, condoms, and anti-fungal cream. And by all means, throw in a roll of toilet paper. Traveling through the Dominican Republic, you never know what kind of bathroom you'll get.

HEALTH AND EMERGENCIES

In case of a crime emergency, find your nearest Politur office. This is a specifically appointed outfit of police to serve the tourists. Politur officers are appointed in their jobs because they are able to speak a language other than Spanish. For any other emergency, call 911.

Health Emergencies and Clinics

Foreigners seeking medical attention are advised to go to **Clínica Abreu** (Santo Domingo, Calle Beller 42 at Av. Independencia, tel. 809/688-4411) or **Clínica Gómez Patiño** (701 Independencia, tel. 809/685-9131). These clinics are high cost, but the level of care is good and they have 24-hour emergency rooms.

While this may sound strange, calling a taxi might get you to an emergency room quicker than calling an ambulance. A company like **Techni-Taxi** (Santo Domingo, tel. 809/566-0109) is a good one to call. They will have one at your door in usually 3–5 minutes. That is, call for a taxi, obviously, only if you think you won't be needing medical care on the way to the clinic.

Insurance

Check with your health insurance provider to make sure you are covered while traveling abroad. Don't forget to carry proof of your health insurance with you. Another option is to get traveler's insurance. If you are booking your trip through a travel agent, ask for some suggestions. Policies can get you some short-term coverage for medical, evacuation, flight accident, and life insurance. Do an Internet search for providers in your area.

Information and Services

MONEY

The monetary unit of the Dominican Republic is the Dominican peso. Most banks in the main towns have ATM machines that dispense pesos. Go to the big banks like Banco Popular, BanReservas, ScotiaBank, and Banco León.

Items marked in stores are priced in pesos, but you can always ask if they'll take your currency. Before you do this, you should know the daily exchange rate, which is published in the newspaper every day. Because the exchange rate fluctuates frequently, the prices presented in this book are in U.S. dollars. A recent exmaple of an exchange rate is US$1–RD$32.21. In general, it is best to exchange your money in the large commercial banks as opposed to with the moneychangers who approach you.

Although debit cards are becoming more common, it is still primarily a paper money exchange. Credit cards are widely accepted in bigger venues, especially where tourists go. Traveler's checks are almost obsolete but can be exchanged at almost any bank or exchange booth.

COMMUNICATIONS

Without a doubt, the easiest and most readily accessible way to make a long-distance call is by using a Verizon Comunicard. You can buy them at hotels, gift shops, corner stores, pharmacies—everywhere, it seems. All you do is follow the directions on the back of the card and it is a prepaid long-distance phone call.

If you are going to be staying in the Dominican Republic for an extended amount of time and have an old cell phone to spare, take it with you. You can then take it to any Verizon office and they will activate it for you for a small fee. You can then receive phone calls on it and buy phone cards to use from it. It is a very convenient way to communicate, probably the most cost effective if you're staying for a while. Placing long-distance calls in the Dominican Republic is easy. What looks like the area code (809) is actually the Dominican country code and doesn't need to be dialed before a phone number within the country. If a Dominican phone number is 809/555-0012, then while in the country you only need to dial 555-0012. Calling from the U.S. or Canada, you would dial 1-809/555-0012.

Verizon also happens to be the country's number one Internet access provider. Most bigger towns, especially ones that are frequented by tourists, have a Verizon office. Cybercafés are becoming more and more popular and are in towns such as Santo Domingo, Puerto Plata, Bayahibe, Boca Chica, Cabarete, Bávaro, and Las Terrenas.

For an excellent Internet source for all things Dominican (news, travel information, business and legal concerns, message boards, directories, exchange rate, weather) in English, go to www.dr1.com. It is far superior to all other English-language, Dominican reference websites.

There are two main newspapers—*Listin Diario* (www.listin.com.do) and *El Caribe* (www.elcaribecdn.com). Others include: *Hoy* (www.hoy.com.do), *El Nacional* (www.elnacional.com.do), and *Diario Libre* (www.diariolibre.com)

The **postal** system in the Dominican Republic is a completely useless organization, not to be trusted with any important documents or packages. However, most hotel front desks will mail things for you. For really reliable service pay extra for FedEx (tel. 809/565-3636) or DHL Dominicana (tel. 809/543-7888).

TIPPING AND TAXES

Restaurants: There's a 16 percent sales tax on food and drink items, plus a 10 percent service charge added to checks. It's also a good idea to tip an extra 5-10 percent if you liked the service.

Shopping: Shops add a 16 percent sales tax for products and services.

Hotels: A 23 percent sales tax will be added to the bill. It is customary to tip the bellhop US$1-2 per bag and leave around US$1-2 per day for maid service.

Departure tax: You pay US$20 upon leaving the country.

MAPS AND TOURIST INFORMATION

The national tourist office, **Secretaría de Estado de Turismo** (Oficinas Gubernmentales, Bloque D, tel. 809/221-4660, www.dominicana.com.do), is an administrative office where you will most likely need an appointment to talk to anyone.

Specific tourist offices *(oficinas de turismo)* for each region in the book are in that destination's chapter. Go to those offices if you want information regarding the region you are visiting. They may or may not be of any help. Sometimes they just have brochures to hand you, other times they are very chatty and have a wealth of information.

RESOURCES

Glossary

apagón power failure
avenida avenue
bachata a type of music and dance (like Dominican country music)
bahía bay
balnearios freshwater swimming holes
bandera dominicana rice and beans and meat dish (literally, the Dominican flag)
barca a big boat
bizcocho cake
bohío thatch hut
botánica a shop where religious and Santeria articles are found
bulto luggage
calle street
campesino a country peasant
campo the countryside
Carnaval pre-Lenten celebration
carretera highway
carroza a horse-drawn wagon
caretas masks; like Carnaval masks
casa house
casabe traditional bread made from yucca plant
casa de cambio money exchange business
catedral cathedral
cerveza beer
civiles civilians; traditional Carnaval character
chicharrones deep-fried meat
chichi baby
chivo goat
colmado small grocery store
Colón, Cristóbal Christopher Columbus

comedor a small restaurant serving Dominican-style food
comida criolla Dominican-style food (literally, Creole food)
conuco a traditional Dominican farm
cuba libre rum and Coke
cueva a cave
fiesta patronal patron saint festival
fortaleza fort
freidurías fried food vendors
fucú an item of bad luck
gallera cock-fighting ring
gomero tire repair shop
guagua small public bus
hostal inn
iglesia church
jeepeta an SUV-type vehicle
la frontera the Haitian border
lago lake
lambí conch (type of seafood)
larimar a semiprecious blue stone found only in the southwestern Dominican Republic
lavanderóa Laundromat
lechón piglet; traditional Carnaval character
longaniza sausage
malecón any boulevard that runs along the ocean
Mamajuana a traditional aphrodisiac drink
mantecado made with lard or butter
mercado market
merengue type of music and dance
mofongo a mashed plantain dish
monasterio monastery
motoconcho motorcycle taxi

museo museum
oficina de turismo tourism office
oro gold
paella seafood and rice dish
palacio palace
parada a stop
parque park
parque central central park or town plaza
pastelito meat- or cheese-filled pastry
pensión inn
pepin a duck-like Carnaval character with spiked horns
peso the monetary unit of the Dominican Republic
plata silver

plátano plantain
playa beach
públicos privately owned cars, trucks, or minivans that act as shared taxis, picking up passengers on city streets for a small fee
Presidente a very popular brand of beer
puerta door
puerto port
ruinas ruins
Taíno Amerindian indigenous people
toros bulls; a traditional Carnaval character
vejiga inflated animal bladder; traditional Carnaval prop
yaniqueques johnnycakes; fried bread
yuca yucca plant

Spanish Phrasebook

Your Dominican Republic adventure will be more fun if you use a little Spanish. Dominican folks, although they may smile at your funny accent, will appreciate your halting efforts to break the ice and transform yourself from a foreigner to a potential friend.

Spanish commonly uses 30 letters—the familiar English 26, plus four straightforward additions: ch, ll, ñ, and rr, which are explained under *Consonants.*

PRONUNCIATION

Once you learn them, Spanish pronunciation rules—in contrast to English—don't change. Spanish vowels generally sound softer than in English. (Note: The capitalized syllables below receive stronger accents.)

Vowels

- **a** like ah, as in "hah": *agua* AH-gooah (water), *pan* PAHN (bread), and *casa* CAH-sah (house)
- **e** like ay, as in "may:" *mesa* MAY-sah (table), *tela* TAY-lah (cloth), and *de* DAY (of, from)
- **i** like ee, as in "need": *diez* dee-AYZ (ten), *comida* ko-MEE-dah (meal), and *fin* FEEN (end)
- **o** like oh, as in "go": *peso* PAY-soh (weight),

ocho OH-choh (eight), and *poco* POH-koh (a bit)
- **u** like oo, as in "cool": *uno* OO-noh (one), *cuarto* KOOAHR-toh (room), and *usted* oos-TAYD (you); when it follows a "q" the **u** is silent; when it follows an "h" or has an umlaut (ü), it's pronounced like "w"

Consonants

b, d, f, k, l, m, n, p, q, s, t, v, w, x, y, z, and **ch** pronounced almost as in English; h occurs, but is silent not pronounced at all

- **c** like k as in "keep": *cuarto* KOOAR-toh (room); when it precedes "e" or "i," pronounce **c** like s, as in "sit": *cerveza* sayr-VAY-sah (beer), *encima* ayn-SEE-mah (atop)
- **g** like g as in "gift" when it precedes "a," "o," "u," or a consonant: *gato* GAH-toh (cat), *hago* AH-goh (I do, make); otherwise, pronounce g like h as in "hat": *giro* HEE-roh (money order), *gente* HAYN-tay (people)
- **j** like h, as in "has": *jueves* HOOAY-vays (Thursday), *mejor* may-HOR (better)
- **ll** like y, as in "yes": *toalla* toh-AH-yah (towel), *ellos* AY-yohs (they, them)
- **ñ** like ny, as in "canyon": *año* AH-nyo (year), *señor* SAY-nyor (Mr., sir)

r lightly trilled, with your tongue at the roof of your mouth like a very light English d, as in "ready": *pero* PAY-doh (but), *tres* TRAYS (three), *cuatro* KOOAH-tdoh (four)

rr like a Spanish r, but with much more emphasis and trill. Let your tongue flap. Practice with *burro* (donkey), *carretera* (highway), and *Carrillo* (proper name), then really let go with *ferrocarril* (railroad).

Note: The single small but common exception to all of the above is the pronunciation of Spanish **y** when it's being used as the Spanish word for "and," as in "Ron y Kathy." In such case, pronounce it like the English ee, as in "keep": Ron "ee" Kathy (Ron and Kathy).

Accent

The rule for accent, the relative stress given to syllables within a given word, is straightforward. If a word ends in a vowel, an n, or an s, accent the next-to-last syllable; if not, accent the last syllable.

Pronounce *gracias* GRAH-seeahs (thank you), *orden* OHR-dayn (order), and *carretera* kah-ray-TAY-rah (highway) with stress on the next-to-last syllable.

Otherwise, accent the last syllable: *venir* vay-NEER (to come), *ferrocarril* fay-roh-cah-REEL (railroad), and *edad* ay-DAHD (age).

Exceptions to the accent rule are always marked with an accent sign: (á, é, í, ó, or ú), such as *teléfono* tay-LAY-foh-noh (telephone), *jabón* hah-BON (soap), and *rápido* RAH-pee-doh (rapid).

BASIC AND COURTEOUS EXPRESSIONS

Most Spanish-speaking people consider formalities important. Whenever approaching anyone for information or some other reason, do not forget the appropriate salutation—good morning, good evening, etc. Standing alone, the greeting *hola* (hello) can sound brusque.

Hello. *Hola* or *Saludos.*
Good morning. *Buenos días.*
Good afternoon. *Buenas tardes.*
Good evening. *Buenas noches.*

How are you? *¿Cómo está usted?*
Very well, thank you. *Muy bien, gracias.*
Okay; good. *Bien.*
Not okay; bad. *Mal*
So-so. *Más o menos.*
And you? *¿Y usted?*
Thank you. *Gracias.*
Thank you very much. *Muchas gracias.*
You're very kind. *Muy amable.*
You're welcome. *De nada.*
Goodbye. *Adios.*
See you later. *Hasta luego.*
please *por favor*
yes *sí*
no *no*
I don't know. *No sé.*
Just a moment, please. *Momentito, por favor.*
Excuse me, please (when you're trying to get attention). *Con permiso.*
Pardon me *Perdón*
Excuse me (when you've made a boo-boo). *Lo siento* or *Permiso*
Pleased to meet you. *Mucho gusto.*
What is your name? *¿Cómo se llama usted?*
My name is... *Me llamo...*
Do you speak English? *¿Habla usted inglés?*
Is English spoken here? (Does anyone here speak English?) *¿Se habla inglés?*
I don't speak Spanish well. *No hablo bien el español.*
I don't understand. *No entiendo.*
How do you say... in Spanish? *¿Cómo se dice... en español?*
Would you like... *¿Quisiera usted...*
Let's go to... *Vamos a...*

TERMS OF ADDRESS

When in doubt, use the formal *usted* (you) as a form of address.

I *yo*
you (formal) *usted*
you (familiar) *tu*
he/him *él*
she/her *ella*
we/us *nosotros*
you (plural) *ustedes*

they/them *ellos* (all males or mixed gender); *ellas* (all females)
Mr., sir *señor*
Mrs., madam *señora*
miss, young lady *señorita*
wife *esposa*
husband *esposo*
friend *amigo* (male); *amiga* (female)
sweetheart *novio* (male); *novia* (female)
son; daughter *hijo; hija*
brother; sister *hermano; hermana*
father; mother *padre; madre*
grandfather; grandmother *abuelo; abuela*

TRANSPORTATION

Where is... ? *¿Dónde está... ?*
How far is it to... ? *¿A cuánto está... ?*
from... to... *de... a...*
How many blocks? *¿Cuántas cuadras?*
Where (Which) is the way to... ? *¿Dónde está el camino a... ?*
the bus station *la terminal de autobuses*
the bus stop *la parada de autobuses*
Where is this bus going? *¿Adónde va este autobús?*
the taxi stand *la parada de taxis*
the train station *la estación de ferrocarril*
the boat *el barco*
the airport *el aeropuerto*
I'd like a ticket to... *Quisiera un boleto a...*
first (second) class *primera (segunda) clase*
round-trip *ida y vuelta*
reservation *reservación*
baggage *equipaje*
Stop here, please. *Pare aquí, por favor.*
the entrance *la entrada*
the exit *la salida*
the ticket office *la oficina de boletos*
(very) near; far *(muy) cerca; lejos*
to; toward *a*
by; through *por*
from *de*
the right *la derecha*
the left *la izquierda*
straight ahead *derecho; directo*
in front *en frente*
beside *al lado*
behind *atrás*

the corner *la esquina*
the stoplight *la semáforo*
a turn *una vuelta*
right here *aquí*
somewhere around here *por acá*
right there *allí*
somewhere around there *por allá*
street; boulevard *calle; bulevar*
highway *carretera*
bridge; toll *puente; cuota*
address *dirección*
north; south *norte; sur*
east; west *oriente (este); poniente (oeste)*

ACCOMMODATIONS

hotel *hotel*
Is there a room? *¿Hay cuarto?*
May I (may we) see it? *¿Puedo (podemos) verlo?*
What is the rate? *¿Cuál es el precio?*
Is that your best rate? *¿Es su mejor precio?*
Is there something cheaper? *¿Hay algo más económico?*
a single room *un cuarto sencillo*
a double room *un cuarto doble*
double bed *cama matrimonial*
twin beds *camas gemelas*
with private bath *con baño*
hot water *agua caliente*
shower *ducha*
towels *toallas*
soap *jabón*
toilet paper *papel higiénico*
blanket *frazada; manta*
sheets *sábanas*
air-conditioned *aire acondicionado*
fan *abanico; ventilador*
key *llave*
manager *gerente*

FOOD

I'm hungry *Tengo hambre.*
I'm thirsty. *Tengo sed.*
menu *lista; menú*
order *orden*
glass *vaso*
fork *tenedor*
knife *cuchillo*

spoon *cuchara*
napkin *servilleta*
soft drink *refresco*
coffee *café*
tea *té*
drinking water *agua pura; agua potable*
bottled carbonated water *agua mineral*
bottled uncarbonated water *agua sin gas*
beer *cerveza*
wine *vino*
milk *leche*
juice *jugo*
cream *crema*
sugar *azúcar*
cheese *queso*
snack *antojo; botana*
breakfast *desayuno*
lunch *almuerzo*
daily lunch special *comida corrida* (or *el menú del día* depending on region)
dinner *comida* (often eaten in late afternoon); *cena* (a late-night snack)
the check *la cuenta*
eggs *huevos*
bread *pan*
salad *ensalada*
fruit *fruta*
mango *mango*
watermelon *sandía*
papaya *lechosa*
banana *guineo*
apple *manzana*
orange *naranja*
lime *limón*
fish *pescado*
shellfish *mariscos*
shrimp *camarones*
meat (without) *(sin) carne*
chicken *pollo*
pork *puerco*
beef; steak *res; bistec*
bacon; ham *tocino; jamón*
fried *frito*
roasted *asada*
barbecue; barbecued *barbacoa; al carbón*

SHOPPING
money *dinero*

money-exchange bureau *casa de cambio*
I would like to exchange traveler's checks. *Quisiera cambiar cheques de viajero.*
What is the exchange rate? *¿Cuál es el tipo de cambio?*
How much is the commission? *¿Cuánto cuesta la comisión?*
Do you accept credit cards? *¿Aceptan tarjetas de crédito?*
money order *giro*
How much does it cost? *¿Cuánto cuesta?*
What is your final price? *¿Cuál es su último precio?*
expensive *caro*
cheap *barato; económico*
more *más*
less *menos*
a little *un poco*
too much *demasiado*

HEALTH
Help me please. *Ayúdeme por favor.*
I am ill. *Estoy enfermo.*
Call a doctor. *Llame un doctor.*
Take me to... *Lléveme a...*
hospital *hospital; sanatorio*
drugstore *farmacia*
pain *dolor*
fever *fiebre*
headache *dolor de cabeza*
stomach ache *dolor de estómago*
burn *quemadura*
cramp *calambre*
nausea *náusea*
vomiting *vomitar*
medicine *medicina*
antibiotic *antibiótico*
pill; tablet *pastilla*
aspirin *aspirina*
ointment; cream *pomada; crema*
bandage *venda*
cotton *algodón*
sanitary napkins *use brand name, e.g.,* Kotex
birth control pills *pastillas anticonceptivas*
contraceptive foam *espuma anticonceptiva*
condoms *preservativos; condones*

toothbrush *cepilla dental*
dental floss *hilo dental*
toothpaste *crema dental*
dentist *dentista*
toothache *dolor de muelas*

POST OFFICE AND COMMUNICATIONS

long-distance telephone *teléfono larga distancia*
I would like to call... *Quisiera llamar a...*
collect *por cobrar*
station to station *a quien contesta*
person to person *persona a persona*
credit card *tarjeta de crédito*
post office *correo*
general delivery *lista de correo*
letter *carta*
stamp *estampilla, timbre*
postcard *tarjeta*
aerogram *aerograma*
air mail *correo aereo*
registered *registrado*
money order *giro*
package; box *paquete; caja*
string; tape *cuerda; cinta*

AT THE BORDER

border *frontera*
customs *aduana*
immigration *migración*
tourist card *tarjeta de turista*
inspection *inspección; revisión*
passport *pasaporte*
profession *profesión*
marital status *estado civil*
single *soltero*
married; divorced *casado; divorciado*
widowed *viudado*
insurance *seguros*
title *título*
driver's license *licencia de manejar*

AT THE GAS STATION

gas station *gasolinera*
gasoline *gasolina*
unleaded *sin plomo*
full, please *lleno, por favor*

tire *llanta*
tire repair shop *vulcanizadora*
air *aire*
water *agua*
oil (change) *aceite (cambio)*
grease *grasa*
My... doesn't work. *Mi... no sirve.*
battery *batería*
radiator *radiador*
alternator *alternador*
generator *generador*
tow truck *grúa*
repair shop *taller mecánico*
tune-up *afinación*
auto parts store *refaccionería*

VERBS

Verbs are the key to getting along in Spanish. They employ mostly predictable forms and come in three classes, which end in *ar, er,* and *ir,* respectively:

to buy *comprar*
I buy, you (he, she, it) buy *compro, compra*
we buy, you (they) buy *compramos, compran*
to eat *comer*
I eat, you (he, she, it) eat *como, come*
we eat, you (they) eat *comemos, comen*
to climb *subir*
I climb, you (he, she, it) climb *subo, sube*
we climb, you (they) climb *subimos, suben*

Got the idea? Here are more (with irregularities marked in **bold**).
to do or make *hacer*
I do or make, you (he, she, it) do or make ***hago,*** *hace*
we do or make, you (they) do or make *hacemos, hacen*
to go *ir*
I go, you (he, she, it) go ***voy, va***
we go, you (they) go ***vamos, van***
to go (walk) *andar*
to love *amar*
to work *trabajar*
to want *desear, querer*
to need *necesitar*

to **read** *leer*
to **write** *escribir*
to **repair** *reparar*
to **stop** *parar*
to **get off (the bus)** *bajar*
to **arrive** *llegar*
to **stay (remain)** *quedar*
to **stay (lodge)** *hospedar*
to **leave** *salir (regular except for **salgo,** I leave)*
to **look at** *mirar*
to **look for** *buscar*
to **give** *dar (regular except for **doy,** I give)*
to **carry** *llevar*
to **have** *tener (irregular but important: **tengo, tiene,** tenemos, **tienen**)*
to **come** *venir (similarly irregular: **vengo, viene,** venimos, **vienen**)*

Spanish has two forms of "to be." Use *estar* when speaking of location or a temporary state of being:
"I am at home." *"Estoy en casa."*
"I'm sick." *"Estoy enfermo."*
    Use *ser* for a permanent state of being:
"I am a doctor." *"Soy doctora."*
Estar is regular except for **estoy,** I am. *Ser* is very irregular:
to **be** *ser*
I am, you (he, she, it) are *soy, es*
we are, you (they) are *somos, son*

NUMBERS
0 *cero*
1 *uno*
2 *dos*
3 *tres*
4 *cuatro*
5 *cinco*
6 *seis*
7 *siete*
8 *ocho*
9 *nueve*
10 *diez*
11 *once*
12 *doce*
13 *trece*
14 *catorce*
15 *quince*
16 *dieciseis*
17 *diecisiete*
18 *dieciocho*
19 *diecinueve*
20 *veinte*
21 *veinte y uno or veintiuno*
30 *treinta*
40 *cuarenta*
50 *cincuenta*
60 *sesenta*
70 *setenta*
80 *ochenta*
90 *noventa*
100 *ciento*
101 *ciento y uno or cientiuno*
200 *doscientos*
500 *quinientos*
1,000 *mil*
10,000 *diez mil*
100,000 *cien mil*
1,000,000 *millón*
one-half *medio*
one-third *un tercio*
one-fourth *un cuarto*

TIME
What time is it? *¿Qué hora es?*
It's one o'clock. *Es la una.*
It's three in the afternoon. *Son las tres de la tarde.*
It's 4 A.M. *Son las cuatro de la mañana.*
six-thirty *seis y media*
a quarter till eleven *un cuarto para las once*
a quarter past five *las cinco y cuarto*
an hour *una hora*

DAYS AND MONTHS
Monday *lunes*
Tuesday *martes*
Wednesday *miércoles*
Thursday *jueves*
Friday *viernes*
Saturday *sábado*
Sunday *domingo*
today *hoy*
tomorrow *mañana*
yesterday *ayer*

January *enero*	**September** *septiembre*
February *febrero*	**October** *octubre*
March *marzo*	**November** *noviembre*
April *abril*	**December** *diciembre*
May *mayo*	**a week** *una semana*
June *junio*	**a month** *un mes*
July *julio*	**after** *después*
August *agosto*	**before** *antes*

Courtesy of Bruce Whipperman, author of *Moon Pacific Mexico.*

Suggested Reading

FICTION AND HISTORICAL FICTION

Alvarez, Julia. *A Cafecito Story.* White River Junction, VT: Chelsea Green Publishing Company, 2001. A parable about people participating in sustainability: growing coffee, caring for land, consumerism, and impacting tourism.

Alvarez, Julia. *How the Garcia Girls Lost Their Accents.* Chapel Hill, NC: Algonquin Books, 1994. Alvarez paints a beautiful and honest portrait of a Dominican family and their struggle and desire to Americanize. The details of Dominican society, the immigrant views, and the first-generation rebellion stories are both subtly written and profoundly present.

Alvarez, Julia. *In the Time of the Butterflies.* Chapel Hill, NC: Algonquin Books, 1994. The award-winning, historical-fiction novel about the Mirabal sisters who died for the underground movement to overthrow Trujillo.

Danticat, Edwidge. *The Farming of the Bones.* New York: Soho, 1999. Set in the Dominican Republic of 1937, this is a historical-fiction tale of the Haitian experience in the Dominican Republic under the brutal tyranny of Trujillo.

Díaz, Junot. *Drown.* New York: Penguin Putnam, 2000. A collection of 10 short stories set in the Dominican Republic and in America brimming with sensory accuracy, complex characters, and evocative language.

Vargas Llosa, Mario. *The Feast of the Goat.* New York, NY: Farrar, Straus and Giroux, 2001. A historical-fiction story of the final days and assassination of Trujillo. A Spanish film company made the novel into a film in 2005 with the Spanish name *La Fiesta del Chivo,* starring Isabella Rossellini.

NONFICTION

Bierhorst, John. *Latin American Folktales: Stories from Hispanic and Indian Traditions.* New York, NY: Pantheon Books, 2003. A wonderful collection of Latin-American folktales, including some early colonial tales.

Cambeira, Alan. *Quisqueya LA Bella: The Dominican Republic in Historical and Cultural Perspective (Perspectives on Latin America and the Caribbean).* Armonk, NY: M.E. Sharpe, Inc., 1996. A look at pre-Columbian Hispaniola, the various peoples and cultures that have occupied the island, and modern-day DR.

Klein, Alan. *Sugarball: The American Game, the Dominican Dream.* London, England: Yale University Press, 1993. This book outlines the history, growth, and obsession of baseball in the Dominican Republic and how it has affected the country's relations with the United States.

Ruck, Rob. *The Tropic of Baseball: Baseball in the Dominican Republic.* Lincoln, NE: University of Nebraska Press, 1999. The history and present state of Dominican baseball, its impact on the country's collective dream, and its effect on society as a whole.

HISTORY

Chester, Eric Thomas. *Rag-Tags, Scum, Riff-Raff, and Commies: The U.S. Intervention in the Dominican Republic, 1965–1966.* New York, NY: New York University Press, 2001. A historical look at U.S. and Latin American relations with a focus on the events of the 1965 U.S. invasion of the Dominican Republic using recently declassified intelligence documents.

Diederich, Bernard. *Trujillo: The Death of the Dictator.* Princeton, NJ: Markus Wiener Publishers, 2000. A look at how Trujillo was assassinated and how his politics shaped the country and its people for decades even after his death.

Hall, Michael R. *Sugar and Power in the Dominican Republic: Eisenhower, Kennedy, and the Trujillos.* Westport, CT: Greenwood Press, 2000. An examination of the sugar industry in the Dominican Republic, the effect it had on U.S.–Dominican relations, and how leaders of both countries manipulated one another through the industry.

Kelsey, Harry. *Sir Francis Drake: The Queen's Pirate.* London, England: Yale University Press, 2000. Brave explorer or ruthless pirate? Depends on who you ask. In Sir Francis Drake's exploits through the Caribbean, he repeatedly sacked Spanish ships and ports (like Santo Domingo), yet was awarded by the queen of England and quite admired by his countrymen (but hated by his shipmates). This biography offers the potent opinion that the history books didn't get it right, suggesting that Drake was a very selfish and often cowardly man.

Lowenthal, Abraham F. *The Dominican Intervention.* Baltimore, MD: The Johns Hopkins University Press, 1972. A good resource for data, politics, origins, and understanding of the American "intervention" in the Dominican Republic using over 100 personal interviews and classified documents.

Matibag, Eugenio. *Haitian-Dominican Counterpoint.* New York, NY: Palgrave Macmillan, 2002. The complicated history of the Haitian–Dominican border and relations. Cultural differences and likenesses are also examined.

Wucker, Michele. *Why the Cocks Fight: Dominicans, Haitians, and the Fight for Hispaniola.* New York, NY: Hill and Wang, 2000. This book looks at the over-exaggerated differences between Haitain and Dominican cultures and tries to examine what is truly at the center of so much tumult.

Taíno History

Alegria, Ricardo, and José Arrom. *Taíno: Pre-Columbian Art and Culture from the Caribbean.* New York, NY: Monacelli, 1998. It didn't take even 100 years for Columbus's men to wipe out the Taíno civilization, but some of their art, language, and cultural practices survive in modern societies throughout the Caribbean.

Deagan, Kathleen, and José María Cruxent. *Columbus's Outpost among the Taínos: Spain and America at La Isabela, 1493–1498.* London, England: Yale University Press, 2002. The authors studied the settlement of La Isabela for 10 years along with scores of colonial-era documents. They draw conclusions about the reasons why Columbus failed at La Isabela.

Rouse, Irving. *The Taínos: Rise and Decline of the People Who Greeted Columbus.* New Haven, CT: Yale University Press, 1993.

Thirty-five years of archaeological research went into this author's examination of Taíno society.

CULTURE

Gonzalez, Clara. *Aunt Clara's Dominican Cookbook.* New York, NY: Lunch Club Press, 2005. Learn to make a killer *sancocho* for your next celebration! A must-have cookbook for good, basic Dominican fare.

Pacini Hernandez, Deborah. *Bachata: A Social History of Dominican Popular Music.* Philadelphia, PA: Temple University Press, 1995. Often called the country music or blues of the Dominican Republic, *bachata* emerged in the 1960s and has been enjoying a resurgence since Juan Luis Guerra won a Latin Grammy award in 1992. This book examines the culture and politics of *bachata* as a stand-alone medium and in relationship to merengue.

Sellers, Julie A. *Merengue and Dominican Identity: Music as National Unifier.* Jefferson, NC: McFarland & Company, 2004. Music and dance is the unifying thread that connects all Dominicans, whether at home or abroad. Book and CD edition.

ECOLOGY

Bond, James. *A Field Guide to the Birds of the West Indies.* New York, NY: Houghton Mifflin, 1999. This is a very thorough catalogue of more than 400 birds in the West Indies.

Poinar, George O. and Roberta. *The Amber Forest: A Reconstruction of a Vanished World.* Princeton, NJ: Princeton University Press, 1999. The resin of the algorrobo tree created a sap 15–45 million years ago. The authors of this book use their knowledge of amber today to recreate what the Dominican ecosystem would've been like back when the sap still flowed.

Spalding, Mark. *A Guide to the Coral Reefs of the Caribbean.* Berkeley, CA: University of California Press, 2004. This guide is endorsed by the United Nations Environment Programme (UNEP) and the World Wildlife Fund (WWF) for those who not only want to explore the reefs of the Caribbean, but who also want to protect them.

ADVENTURE

Bory, Marc. *Kitesurfing.* Paris, France: Fitway Publishing, 2005. A guide to help you become a real kitesurfing fanatic.

Boyce, Jeremy. *The Ultimate Book of Power Kiting and Kiteboarding.* Augusta, GA: The Lyons Press, 2004. A good resource for learning how to buy a kite, care for the equipment, and how to use it.

Leubben, Craig. *Rock Climbing: Mastering Basic Skills.* Seattle, WA: Mountaineers Books, 2004. Plenty of how-to tips on the technique, movement, and strength required when learning how to rock climb. Photos and graphics further illustrate the necessary skills for the novice.

Internet Resources

Active Cabarete
www.activecabarete.com

Look here for any information on water sports, accommodations, upcoming events, restaurants, bars, and general services for Cabarete, a water-sports hot spot.

Cabarete Kiteboarding
www.cabaretekiteboarding.com

This site has lots of great info on kiteboarding schools, lodging (hotels and other options), weather, and water conditions.

Caribe Tours
http://caribetours.com.do

While this bus company's site is only in Spanish, navigating through it is simple and you'll find addresses to the bus stations in the country as well as departure times from Santo Domingo to the rest of the towns *(Horarios desde Santo Domingo)* and to Santo Domingo from the other towns *(Horarios desde el interior)*.

DR1
www.dr1.com

DR1 is the best online English-language source for Dominican news, travel information, weather, currency exchange rates, and just about anything you might need to know. There is even a forum to post questions or talk to other English speakers about the country.

DR Pure: Adventure in the Dominican Republic
www.drpure.com

This website gives loads of information on the adventure options in the Dominican Republic, where you can do them, in addition to some handy general information.

Embassy of the Dominican Republic in the United States of America
www.domrep.org

The embassy site has information on tourism, airlines that service the DR, immigration, and even what you'll need to get a quick Dominican divorce.

Golf Dominican Republic
www.punta-cana-golf.com

While the website sounds like it has info only on golfing in Punta Cana, there are links to other regions in the DR, complete with information on greens fees, course designers' names, hours, and even which hole is the most challenging.

Hispaniola.com
www.hispaniola.com

This is another good website for travel and tourism information, including helpful information on where to stay.

Iguana Mamma
www.iguanamamma.com

Iguana Mamma is perhaps the most respected, safest, and most well-organized adventure travel tour company; it's located in Cabarete.

Ministry of Tourism
www.dominicanrepublic.com/Tourism/ or www.dominicana.com.do/

This site offers information not only about the Dominican Republic in general, but also about transportation, shopping, visa regulations, what you'll need to get married, and events calendars.

Samana.net
www.samana.net

Try this site for all information about the Península de Samaná (including the towns of Las Galeras, Las Terrenas, and Samaná)—accommodations, restaurants, and visitor's guides.

Tours, Trips, Treks & Travel
www.4tdomrep.com

This tour company offers treks to lesser-known areas and interesting packages like educational tours or exciting helicopter trips.

Index

Acknowledgments

Thanks to the people of the Dominican Republic, who are the most hospitable people in the Caribbean and perhaps the world.

Mi gran agradecimiento va hacia la Secretaria de Estado de Turismo por su ayuda durante mi estadia en la Republica Dominicana, muy especialmente a Luis Simo, a Doña Tatis de Olmos, Celeste de Leon, a Prudencio Ferdinand por ensenarme el país, y a Arturo, el conductor, por llevarnos rapido.

Gracias mil a Fausto Fontana por su hermosa fotografía y a mi prima, Alicia Caamaño de Selman, por introducirme a Fausto.

Muchas gracias a mi prima Milagros Cartagena Infante (Ito) por introducirme en la Secretaria de Turismo.

Angel Pacheco, thank you for the new friendship, the debate over Chinese food, and for sharing your knowledge about nightlife and the country.

A very special thank you to Rebecca Browning, for encouraging me and helping me in my journey from intern to author. Thank you to my editor, Erin Raber, for good advice, good work, amazing patience, and being good to a newbie. To the staff and interns of Avalon Travel Publishing and their hard work on maps, marketing, publishing, editing, graphics, filing, copying, faxing, and answering phones—you all have my sincere thanks. You are the reason these things work out.

Gracias a mis familias Chavier Frias y Caamaño Sanchez. Los quiero a todos. Su ayuda con mi libro es invalorable. La generosidad, hospitalidad, y amor de todos significa mucho para mi. Gracias desde el fondo de mi corazón.

Mom, thank you for everything: the linen suits, the translation work, the footwork in the homeland, the phone and Internet work, the fact checking, for the Caamaño name, and Dominican blood. Dad, thank you for all the talks about Dominican culture and folklore we had over *tazitas de café.* But I thank you the most for the hug of encouragement, for the Chavier name, and Dominican blood. Thank you to my siblings: John for being the coolest brother ever, Isabel for reminding me about *mantecado* ice cream, Alicia for architecture advice, and Sofia for simply being The Baey—it always helps me. Thank you to my brothers-in-law Sam and Gordon for embracing our Dominican family.

Thanks to my friends—Clay, Colleen, Jess, Angie, Mara, Daniel, Mario, Poppy, Anna, and Shelly—for your support, encouragement, and making me laugh during all the hard work. I am deeply grateful to Marcelle for being a great friend and housemate and for the laughing fits over many glasses of wine—a shout-out to Yellow Tail! To my earthly guardian angel Jodi Paper, it was just like the old days. Thank you for your work, research, encouragement, and friendship. Without you I may have drowned.

To five-year-old Maribel from El Café on the Samaná Peninsula. Thumbs up! And to the little boy in the blue boat from Las Cuevas near Bahía de las Águilas.

Thank you Sally, Tommy, Shala, The Crid, and Moto.

Most importantly, a big thanks to SaBrina. Without you it would have been hell. Your support was everything and unwavering. Thank you for the help with the maps, the encouragement, and for saying, "get 'er done," when I thought I'd lost my mind. Thank you for finding my mind. Traveling isn't so bad when you know where home is.

To everyone else who supported me and that I had the pleasure of meeting and working with during the research and writing of this book, thank you.

www.moon.com

For helpful advice on planning a trip, visit www.moon.com for the **TRAVEL PLANNER** and get access to useful travel strategies and valuable information about great places to visit. When you travel with Moon, expect an experience that is uncommon and truly unique.

HANDBOOKS | METRO | OUTDOORS | LIVING ABROAD

MAP SYMBOLS

▦▦▦ Expressway	**◖** Highlight	✗, Airfield	⚲ Golf Course
— Primary Road	○ City/Town	✗ Airport	**P** Parking Area
▬ Secondary Road	◉ State Capital	▲ Mountain	≜ Archaeological Site
▪▪▪▪ Unpaved Road	⊛ National Capital	✛ Unique Natural Feature	⬟ Church
------- Trail	★ Point of Interest		⬚ Gas Station
·········· Ferry	• Accommodation	⌇ Waterfall	⬭ Glacier
─┼─┼─ Railroad	▼ Restaurant/Bar	▲ Park	▨ Mangrove
▦▦ Pedestrian Walkway	▪ Other Location	⊓ Trailhead	▨ Reef
▥▥▥ Stairs	⋀ Campground	⛷ Skiing Area	▥ Swamp

CONVERSION TABLES

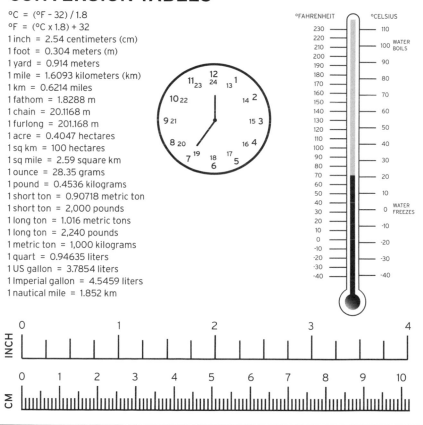

°C = (°F – 32) / 1.8
°F = (°C x 1.8) + 32
1 inch = 2.54 centimeters (cm)
1 foot = 0.304 meters (m)
1 yard = 0.914 meters
1 mile = 1.6093 kilometers (km)
1 km = 0.6214 miles
1 fathom = 1.8288 m
1 chain = 20.1168 m
1 furlong = 201.168 m
1 acre = 0.4047 hectares
1 sq km = 100 hectares
1 sq mile = 2.59 square km
1 ounce = 28.35 grams
1 pound = 0.4536 kilograms
1 short ton = 0.90718 metric ton
1 short ton = 2,000 pounds
1 long ton = 1.016 metric tons
1 long ton = 2,240 pounds
1 metric ton = 1,000 kilograms
1 quart = 0.94635 liters
1 US gallon = 3.7854 liters
1 Imperial gallon = 4.5459 liters
1 nautical mile = 1.852 km

MOON DOMINICAN REPUBLIC

Avalon Travel Publishing
An Imprint of
Avalon Publishing Group, Inc.

AVALON
publishing group incorporated

1400 65th Street, Suite 250
Emeryville, CA 94608, USA
www.moon.com

Editor: Erin Raber
Series Manager: Kathryn Ettinger
Acquisitions Manager: Rebecca K. Browning
Copy Editor & Indexer: Deana Shields
Graphics Coordinator: Stefano Boni
Production Coordinators: Nicole Schultz,
    Jane Musser
Cover & Interior Designer: Gerilyn Attebery
Map Editor: Kat Smith
Cartographer: Kat Bennett
Proofreader: Ellie Behrstock

ISBN-10: 1-56691-609-7
ISBN-13: 978-1-56691-609-7
ISSN: 1092-3349

Printing History
1st Edition – 1997
3rd Edition – October 2006
5 4 3 2 1

Front cover photo: El Limón waterfall, La Península
    de Samaná © Alberto Biscaro/Masterfile
Title page photo: © Fausto Fontana

Printed in United States by Malloy

KEEPING CURRENT

If you have a favorite gem you'd like to see included in the next edition, or see anything
that needs updating, clarification, or correction, please drop us a line. Send your
comments via email to feedback@moon.com, or use the address above.